LUKE:
SLAVE & PHYSICIAN

KATHERYN MADDOX HADDAD

A COMMENTARY IN NARRATIVE FORM

OTHER BOOKS BY THIS AUTHOR

HISTORICAL NOVELS & Storybooks
Series of 8: They Met Jesus
Ongoing Series of 8: Intrepid Men of God
Mysteries of the Empire with Klaudius & Hektor
Christmas: They Rocked the Cradle that Rocked the World
Series of 8: A Child's Life of Christ
Series of 10: A Child's Bible Heroes
Series of 8: A Child's Bible Kids
Series of 10: A Child's Bible Ladies

HISTORICAL RESEARCH BIBLE
for Novel, Screenwriter, Documentary & Thesis Writers

TOPICAL
Applied Christianity: Handbook 500 Good Works
Christianity or Islam? The Contrast
The Holy Spirit: 592 Verses Examined
The Road to Heaven
Inside the Hearts of Bible Women-Reader+Audio+Leader
Revelation: A Love Letter From God
Worship Changes Since 1st Century + Worship 1sr Century Way
Was Jesus God? (Why Evil)
365 Life-Changing Scriptures Day by Date
The Road to Heaven
The Lord's Supper: 52 Readings with Prayers

FUN BOOKS
Bible Puzzles, Bible Song Book, Bible Numbers

TOUCHING GOD SERIES
365 Golden Bible Thoughts: God's Heart to Yours
365 Pearls of Wisdom: God's Soul to Yours
365 Silver-Winged Prayers: Your Spirit to God's

SURVEY SERIES: EASY BIBLE WORKBOOKS
→Old Testament & New Testament Surveys
→Questions You Have Asked-Part I & II

Genealogy: How to Climb Your Family Tree Without Falling Out
Volume I & 2: Beginner-Intermediate & Colonial-Medieval

Copyright © 2016 Katheryn Maddox Haddad
NORTHERN LIGHTS PUBLISHING HOUSE

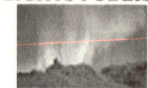

Cover design by Sharon A. Lavy. Images from DepositPhotos.
Scriptures taken from the HOLY BIBLE, NEW INTERNATIONAL VERSION.
Copyright © 1973, 1978, 1984 International Bible Society.
Used by permission of Zondervan Bible Publishers.
ISBN-978-1-948462-22-8
Printed in the United States

TABLE OF CONTENTS

MAP: LUKE'S TRAVELS 3
1 ~ The Promise 4
2 ~ Disappearance 10
3 ~ Making & Breaking 20
4 ~ Accused 30
5 ~ Civilization 41
6 ~ East 53
7 ~ The First Clue 61
8 ~ The Search Begins 70
9 ~ South 79
10 ~ Caught 89
11 ~ Collapse 100
12 ~ Compassion 109
13 ~ Wandering 118
14 ~ The Impossible 127
15 ~ Summits & Valleys 137
16 ~ Escape 146
17 ~ Vagabond 156
18 ~ The Mountain 166
19 ~ The Struggle 175
20 ~ At last 186
21 ~ Dream Revived 196
22 ~ Decisions 207
23 ~ The Challenge 217
24 ~ Ghost from the Past 227
25 ~ New Directions 236
26 ~ Jerusalem 248
27 ~ Back to the Beginning 258
28 ~ Limbo 267
29 ~ Survival 278
30 ~ Doomed 289
31 ~ Visitors 301
32 ~ Goodbye 313
33 ~ New Beginning 325
34 ~ And Beyond 339
35 ~ More Mountains 352
36 ~ A Returning 363

37 ~ The Sacrifice..373
38 ~ Rescues..384
39 ~ Near..393
40 ~ Renewal..404
41 ~ Overcoming 413
42 ~ Home..422

THANK YOU 436
GET ALL 8 BOOKS IN THE HISTORICAL SERIES 437

HISTORICAL BACKGROUND 438
BUY YOUR NEXT BOOK NOW 444

DISCUSSION QUESTIONS......................................445
ABOUT THE AUTHOR...453

CONNECT WITH KATHERYN MADDOX HADDAD 454
GET A FREE BOOK..455
Join My Dream Team 456

MAP: LUKE'S TRAVELS

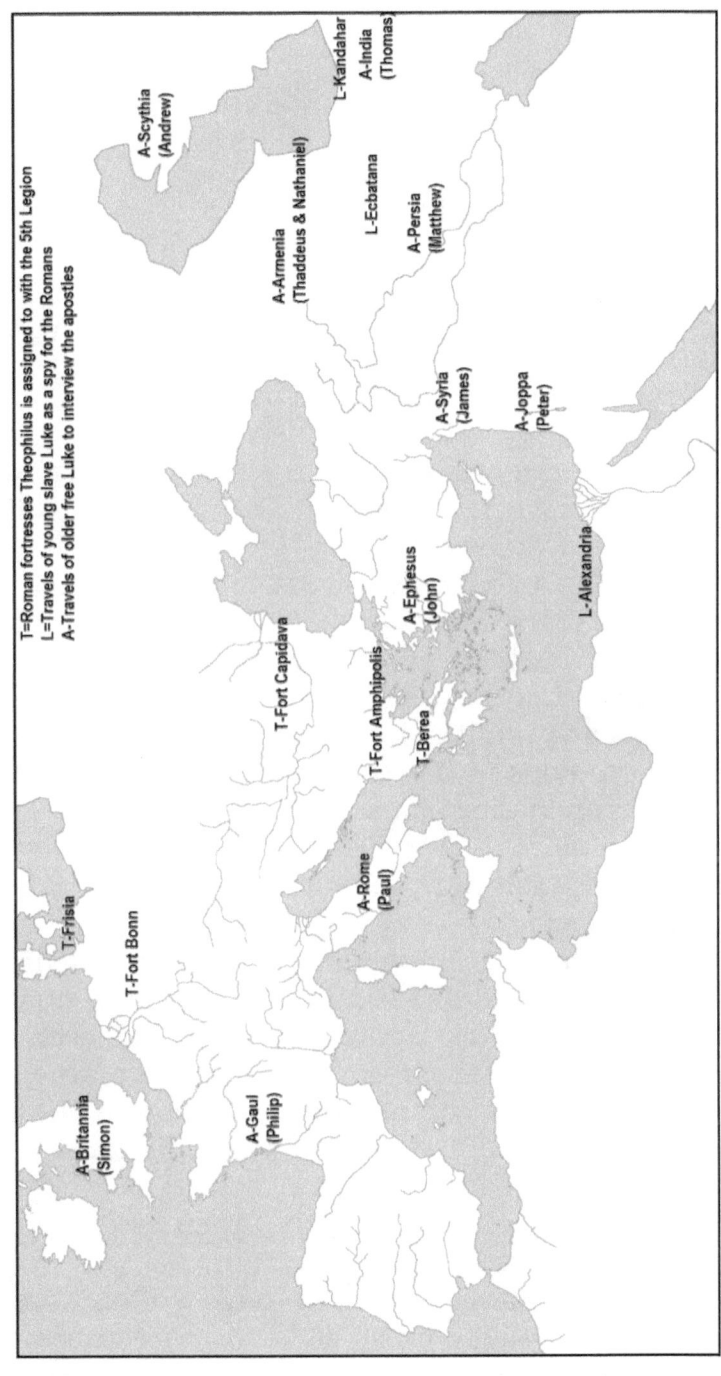

1 ~ THE PROMISE

"Und so, my broders, dhis must stop. Ve can no longer allow da unyust Romans on our lands."

Cruptorix's icy blue eyes flash as he looks over the other men who have arrived from their respective villages.

"It has been vorty years since Legate Claudius Drusus came to us vith promises his people did not keep."

The Frisian tribal chief pivots to face the men sitting where the cows are normally kept in his longhouse. His yellow hair shifts around his bulky shoulders.

"A small tax to keep da Chaucis, Batavis, und Bructeris tribes vrom attacking us vas bearable at virst. He yust vanted da hides uv a vew uv our cattle. I was yust a lad dhen, und hardly noticed da soldiers patrolling our borders. Life vent on as usual."

The veins push out on his rugged neck, and he pulls on his yellow beard.

"But, dhen, he appointed Centurion Olennius to govern us. He declared dhat da hides given him must be da same size as da vild bulls in our vorests. It has been almost impossible, so he punishes us. He could have accepted da hides of da wild bulls themselves und dhat ve could have done. But alvays, he has insisted on da hides uv our domestic bulls. He is destroying us."

He turns back toward the men sitting in the residential area of his longhouse.

"Vor twenty-two years dhey have gotten vorse und vorse. Life vor us has gotten so bad, it is now unbearable."

The muscles in his arms bulge as he pounds his fist

into his other hand.

"I have been gone vrom you vor ten years serving as an auxiliary in da Roman army. I know how dhey tink. Ve can stop dhem. Ve vill stop dhem."

"Dhey took halv my herd of cattle yust last year," Dieuwer shouts from the back of the room. "Called it a tax raise."

"Dhey took all my sheep two years ago," Jeltje says from over in the animal section of the longhouse.

Mienke stands and says nothing for a moment. Everyone knows and waits for him. He whispers, "Dhree months ago, dhey took my beautiful vife." He sits, and a friend on the bench next to him puts his bulky arm over Mienke's shoulder.

Vestel stands, and he, too, says nothing at first. The other men watch as his big freckled hand brushes away a tear. "My daughters, Ane und Ade. dhey took my daughters." He sits, lowers his head into his open hands, and his shoulders shake.

Cruptorix pauses in respect for the sorrows being expressed, then continues. "Legate Lucius Apronius has become a monster, und it is up to us to put un end to him."

"Odelegge!" someone shouts.

"Odelegge!" another bellows.

"Odelegge!"

"Odelegge!"

"Destroy dhem!"

"Destroy dhem!"

The rumble of protests makes its way out to the melting snow of the cold spring, and down to the shores of the Nordic Sea.

"Tomorrow," the Frisian tribal chief continues, "ve vill sacrifice to our goddess uv da battle, Baduhenna, in her oak grove. She vill give us strength to do battle vith da barbarian Romans."

"Vrom now on," Cruptorix continues, "any time da soldiers arrive in your village, you vill dispose of dhem by vhatever method you prefer, dhen put dhem on display as a varning to any other Romans coming to collect their vretched taxes."

Logmarr sits on the floor at his father's feet. He looks up at the giant with a mixture of fear and pride. Cruptorix notices, ruffles his son's hair, smiles, and turns his attention back to the war council.

"Den vhat?" one of the men shouts out with his husky voice.

"Den ve vait. Eventually, Governor Apronius vill send us Cethegus Labeo und his legion. Spend da summer in extra veapons training. Ve vill be ready vor dem. Dhen comes da slaughter und our independence."

The leaders of each village rise. The door to the cooking area is flung wide, and Cruptorix's wife and daughters enter with trays of clay mugs filled with ale.

Immediately, Lukvert leaves his father's side and joins his best friend, Logmarr.

"I can't vait vor summer to come," Logmarr says.

"Me too," Lukvert replies. "I'm pretty good vith da javelin."

"My vather is having a special sword made vor me vhen I get old enough to use it," Logmarr replies.

"I'm eight," Lukvert announces.

"Vell, I'm older dhan you. I'm ten und going to get a real sword in two years, my vather says."

Sigmundrr brings a long woolen cape and leather hat to his son and stoops to hook the top of the cape together. He straightens, steps over to his tribal chief, clasps hands and forearms with him, then opens the outside door to face the strong wind.

The big man grabs his son's hand, they duck to ward off the icy wind from the Nordic Sea, make their way down a path lined with stones, and arrive at their own longhouse.

"Lukvert, go to da back und bring some more virewood," Sigmundrr says, stoking the embers of an earlier fire on the floor pit.

"Iv your mother vere still alive, she vould have a hot drink vaiting for us. Vell, fill dhese two mugs vid milk vrom our cow. It vill be warm enough."

Moments later, Lukvert returns with the mugs.

"Come. Sit wid me, Son. I need to tell you more uv our tribe's history. You must remember all dhese stories."

"Yes, sir."

Though he misses his mother, Elke, with her gentle touch and lyrical voice, Lukvert also likes that his father is now spending more time with him.

"You know how da Romans make marks on da inside of skins vith blackener, dhen go back und say vords dhat dose marks mean?"

"Yes, sir. It's called vriting, und dheir black marks are vords."

"This is vhat I vant you to do someday. I vant you to vigure out a vay to put our language in black marks dhat mean vords. dhen I vant you to put our history down wid dose black marks, so no one vill ever forget vhere the great people of Frisia came vrom und how brave ve are."

"Yes, sir. Someday when I am grown."

"Now, Son, dhis is da story about..."

"No, Vather," Lukvert objects, setting down his mug of warm milk and putting both tiny hands on his father's cheeks.

"Vhat do you mean, no?"

"Your song, Vather. Sing your song again so I can alvays know it."

Sigmundrr smiles in approval. "Okay, my song it is."

> *Tho I vander long avay*
> *Over all da mounts und seas*
> *To da end uv da verld,*
> *I vill alvays dhink uv home*
> *Und keep you in my heart*
> *Til I hold you once again.*

Lukvert sings with his father. Over and over, they sing it while Lukvert swings in circles in the middle of the floor. "One more time, Vather. One more time."

Sigmundrr grabs his son's hand. "Come sit on my lap a moment, Son."

Lukvert does so and looks up in his father's deep blue

eyes.

"Son, alvays remember dhis song. If da Romans ever take you avay vrom me und sell you as a slave, alvays sing dhis song. Dhen I vill find you."

The big man embraces his son, then sets him on the wooden bench next to him.

"Vould you like to hear about, King Volevald?" Without waiting for approval by his son, Sigmundrr begins.

"A very long time ago vhen our tribe vas very young, King Volevald brought our people to dhis land und settled. But da virst spring vhen da snows began to melt, all da longhouses patiently built by da vathers und sons vere flooded by da melted snow und vashed avay by da Nordic Sea."

Lukvert closes his eyes and imagines bowing down to the king.

"Other dhan the flooding, King Volewald saw dhat it vas good land. So, one morning, he made a large bag vrom the hide of an elk, took it to da seashore, filled it vith sand, put it on his back, took it to da spot vhere dheir new village used to be, und emptied his bag.

"Dhen he valked back to da seashore und did it again. All day long, he valked back and vorth, dumping his load uv sand on da same spot."

Lukvert leans his head onto his father's strong arm.

"By da time it vas dark, he vas very tired and vell vast asleep under a nearby sacred oak tree. In da morning, he rose, stretched, und looked around vor his bag. He found it, dhen another, und another, und another. Dhey vere everywhere! Dhen he looked up, und guess vhat he saw?"

Lukvert groans out an "uh-huh" and his father goes on.

"He saw a hill large enough to put da entire village on, safe vrom vloods. The elves. Dousands of elves. Dhey had come togeder during da night und built up da hill vor our people."

"Veah?" Lukvert mutters.

"So da very virst village among our people vas built, and it is dhere to dhis day. Guess vhat da name of dhat village is."

Sigmundrr looks down at his son. Lukvert's head falls over in his father's lap.

"It's been a long day, Son," he says, lifting little Lukvert up in his arms and taking him to his cot on a leather hinge coming out from the wall.

"Just remember our history so you can vrite it in vords someday. Und so everyone vill know vor hundreds uv years vrom now."

He lays his son on the straw mattress and covers him with a deer hide.

"Und my song, Lukvert. Remember my song."

He kisses his son good night.

"Vather," Lukvert whispers, his eyes still closed. "Vould you hug me?"

Sigmundrr kneels, slips an arm under his son's shoulders, and gently embraces him.

"Vather, is dhere going to be a var?"

"Yes, Son. Dhere is going to be a var."

"Vill you be a warrior in it?"

"Yes, Son," he whispers. "I vill do my part to protect you und all our people."

"Vill you be killed?" Lukvert asks, opening his blue eyes.

"I vill try not to be."

"Iv you are, I vill be un orphan. Please don't die, Vather," the boy says, tears now in his eyes. "Promise me, Vather."

"I vill try very hard, my son," he says, pulling back and watching his son, both now with tears in their eyes. "Yust remember our song. Alvays remember our song."

The next day, the big men of the village tie their long hair up into buns on the side of their head, grab their swords, knives, and javelins, and begin preparing to defend their land. They prepare for war.

2 ~ DISAPPEARANCE

"Sir, the legionnaire veterans along with the auxiliary infantry and cavalry, have arrived from Upper Germanicus, as ordered," Tribune Theophilus says, his square jaw jutting forward.

"This time, we will do it right and gain full control of those rebels." Legate Lucius Apronius looks up at his sizeable tribune, the legate having been appointed because of his family's prominence in Rome rather than his physical prowess.

"Where is Centurion Olennius?" he asks his aide. "Summon him."

"That bumbling idiot," Legate Apronius growls. "Coward. Whenever the Frisians attack our tax collectors, he runs and hides in Fortress Flevum on the Nordic coast." He paces while Tribune Theophilus waits to one side.

Centurion Olennius enters the headquarters tent and salutes. He is immaculately dressed, the fingernails on his hands clean, and every black hair on his head neatly in place.

"Olennius, I am going to give you a chance to redeem your reputation," the legate says, looking up at the tall, thin centurion.

"Yes, sir," Olennius replies in a squeaky voice.

"You are to take the fresh troops from Upper Germanicus and attack Fortress Flevum, which you let fall into the hands of the Frisians. How that happened, only the gods know. Dismissed."

The senior centurion salutes and leaves. The rounded

circular horn is heard at intervals calling for assembly and attack readiness.

The rest of the week, Legate Apronius spends with his tribunes as their spies report back the activities of the Frisians in various villages.

"They not only outsize us, but they also outweigh us," one tribune reports.

"But we have numbers on our side," the legate says.

"They are experts with the javelin and knife, preferring close combat," another tribune explains. "Their archers are few but good."

"That's fine," the legate says. "We have many more archers than they do, and will dispose of their bowmen from the beginning."

"They do not use cavalry much but do have one. Our horses are no match for their black horses, which are huge in bulk and weight, just like their masters."

"We will flank them, attack in waves, and destroy them before they know what happened to them," the legate assures his tribunes.

"The cowards will run away, and we will catch them and turn them into our slaves," Legate Apronius says. "From henceforth, there will be no free Frisians."

At the end of the week, Centurion Olennius returns with his troops and shouts of victory.

"The fortress is ours again," the centurion announces two hours after returning, washing, combing his hair, and putting on a clean uniform.

"How many infantrymen are left?" the legate asks.

"Well, uh, sir, about half of them. But we did get the fortress back."

"And our cavalry?"

"Their black horses are so much larger than ours..."

"Never mind. Go to your victory celebration, get drunk, then crawl into a hole somewhere."

Three weeks later, Tribune Theophilus returns to the legate's large leather tent.

"Sir, the roads into Frisia have been completed and are ready for our troops to invade and destroy the rebels."

"Good. Now have you contacted Tribune Cethegus Labeo of the Fifth Legion?"

"Yes, sir. They should be here any day."

Two days later, the horn of the Fifth Legion is sounded. Legate Apronius mounts his horse and goes out to meet them where they are already setting up camp.

"One day is all they get to rest," the legate announces.

"Yes, sir. We will be ready," Tribune Labeo replies.

Within the week, all of the Fifth Legion with its six thousand trained Roman legionnaires, along with the auxiliary infantry and cavalry of upper Germanicus are on the edge of Baduhenna Wood.

"No time to waste," Legate Apronius announces from his horse. "We will attack in the morning just before daylight."

He dismisses his ten tribunes, dismounts, and sits under a tree to wait for the raising of his tent by infantrymen.

Out of nowhere, sounds of screaming and whizzing. An arrow is shot into the tree. By the time he jumps up, an otherworldly sound is coming out of the shadowy woods.

Apronius remounts his horse and motions for the hornblower to sound the alarm.

Yellow-haired giants shouting in a shrill and haunting flutter appear from Baduhenna Wood, scatter among the nearest troops, strike down with their daggers every Roman soldier still unarmed, then just as quickly disappear back into the woods.

"What just happened?" Legate Apronius bellows.

Tribune Theophilus is nearest him and heads his horse over to his superior.

"Sir, my company is completely intact. It was the companies nearest the woods that sustained the casualties."

Tribune Nerius reports in. "My cavalry is untouched. So is my infantry."

"All right, Tribune Nerius. You will take your cavalry and infantry and march tonight over along the coast until you can get on the back side of the woods. You will attack at dawn."

"Yes, sir."

Within the hour, Tribune Nerius' cavalry and all the infantry are gone from the main camp. He allows his men to stop and rest once they are close to their destination.

At dawn, they charge at the Frisians from behind them. But the Frisians are ready for them. Those mounted on their giant black horses charge.

The Roman cavalry tries to fight back with their long javelins, but the giant blacks circle around behind them and ram the Roman horses. The cavalry switches to sabers, but they are no match for the Frisians. The cavalry survives only by taking the defensive and staying out of the Frisians' way.

Men in the infantry raise their shields over their lowered heads to defend themselves. Whenever they come out of hiding, they are mowed down. Seeing the cavalry retreat and leaving them with no support, what is left of the Roman infantry retreats also.

Still, they are followed by the ferocious yellow-haired Frisian warriors, and many are stricken down.

Tribune Nerius sends his aide to report to the commander in charge of the army of Lower Germanicus. Legate Apronius orders three companies of twelve hundred men to support Tribune Nerius' distressed men and force them back into the battle.

He paces and waits.

"Tribune Theophilus, send one of your centurions to find out what is going on."

The legate paces and waits longer. Finally, the centurion returns. "They are being defeated, sir," he reports.

"Send in the remaining infantry," Apronius roars. "We outnumber them. How can we be losing? Send them all in."

His pacing resumes as his remaining tribunes wait with him. He hears nothing.

"Tribune Labeo, I want the remainder of your Fifth Legion to attack from this side of the woods," Legate Apronius roars. "Go around them or through them. But do whatever is necessary to contain the barbarian Frisians."

Tribune Cethegus Labeo is of medium build, but muscular. He salutes the legate, dons his brass helmet, turns, mounts his horse, and bellows commands to half of his centurions.

Within an hour, they are marching into Baduhenna Wood. Shouts from the crazed Frisian warriors echo out of the oak trees, across the plain to the Roman camp, and to the legate's remaining troops.

A horse is seen galloping out of the woods and back toward Legate Apronius.

Blood smears the messenger's uniform, his arms and his legs. "Sir," he says upon arrival, "Tribune Labeo begs you to send the rest of his troops in."

"Tribune Theophilus, you will lead this charge. May the gods help you. May Mars be superior to their Oden or Baduhenna or whoever they depend on for their strength. Go, Theophilus. Prove the Mars of Rome to be the only real god of war. May his blessings fall upon you."

By the time Theophilus arrives in the woods, the Roman legionnaires and Frisian warriors are entangled, crashing into each other, stabbing, strangling, and devouring.

Theophilus recognizes many cavalrymen who have abandoned their horses in order to manipulate through the trees. Each side brandishes their weapons to defend their own cause.

Romans with their metal coats of arms and helmets. Frisians with their leather tunics, ornate capes flowing behind them, and their long yellow hair tied up in knots out of their way.

Though at first, Theophilus sees Romans ducking behind their raised shields, now they take courage and lower them to fight the giant warriors once again.

The fury of the giant Frisians grows. The remaining legionnaires of the Fifth Legion spring forward. There are too many. The Frisians are on the run.

Gradually the roar dies down. Baduhenna Wood is still. The only sounds now are groans of the wounded and dying.

The sun goes down. Sentry during the night at the Roman camp is quadrupled.

The Roman legion is awakened at dawn, ready for

another surprise attack out of the woods. It does not come.

"We are not finished here," Legate Apronius announces to his tribunes. "There is a deserter in their village. He served with our army for ten years, then deserted."

"I think I know who you mean," one of the tribunes says. "He served with me. Giant of a man. Bigger than any of the other Frisian warriors I have ever seen. His name is Cruptorix."

"I have sent spies out this morning and have located his house," Legate Apronius continues. "Tribune Nerius, I want you to take four companies with you and attack Cruptorix's house."

"Will he have family inside, sir?"

"It is the Frisian command post. It will be full of their bravest warriors. Go now."

Once more, the wait. Mid-day comes and still no word. Apronius sends two spies to find out what is going on. An hour later they are back.

"Complete slaughter," they report. "All of theirs and all of ours. All dead."

"Do not go back and pick up our dead," Tribune Labeo, leader of the Fifth Legion, orders

"Out! All of you out!" the legate bellows. From outside his tent they hear, "How am I going to face Caesar? Twelve hundred legionnaires of the finest military in the world destroyed."

Knowing the commander of the Frisian army is now dead, and hoping his warriors have given up the fight until they select a new commander, the tribunes go to what is left of their respective companies and disappear in their tents to get drunk.

All but Tribune Theophilus. He orders his men to check among the bodies to find those still alive and help them back to the Roman camp. He stays with them.

The process is slow. He leads his horse through the woods, looking as he goes at the bodies strewn everywhere. Some in bronze armor with protective helmets still intact, some bare-skinned with the knots of yellow hair coming loose from their heads and blowing in the wind.

"Vather! Vather!" he hears. "Vather, vhere are you?"

Though Theophilus does not understand the Frisian tongue, he recognizes it is the voice of a child. He turns his horse one way and the other in an effort to find the voice. When he does, he dismounts and walks slowly toward the boy.

The yellow-haired child does not notice.

As he draws closer, Theophilus realizes the boy is covered with blood. Alarmed, he rushes toward the child and takes hold of his arm. "Are you all right?"

The boy screams and backs away from the big enemy soldier.

Immediately Theophilus raises his hands to show he is not armed. "Are you all right?" he repeats. "Are you hurt anywhere?"

The boy sits on the ground, brings his little fists up to his eyes, and resumes his crying.

"Are you looking for your father?" he asks the boy. "Is that where all the blood is from?"

The boy looks up, looks all around them at the bodies, and cries once again.

Theophilus goes to one of the Frisian bodies, rolls it over so the boy can see the face, and the boy shakes his head no. He goes to others, and the boy continues to shake his head no.

Theophilus holds out his hand and the boy takes it. They continue through the woods. Whenever they come to the body of a yellow-haired warrior, Theophilus turns it over so the boy can see the face, the boy shakes his head, and they resume their search. They make their way out of the woods and follow the stream of bodies down to the seashore where the original attack had occurred that morning.

One by one. "Is this your father? How about this one?"

They move to the village where the slaughter of the last of the Frisian warriors had taken place. He lets the boy look among the bodies for his father while he quickly goes to the bodies of women and children, and turns them over so their faces do not show, or drags them behind a nearby bush.

The sun is now low in the sky. Realizing his horse has been following them all afternoon, Theophilus whistles and the horse comes trotting up to them. Theophilus picks up the boy in his arms, the boy immediately lays his head on Theophilus' shoulder and falls asleep.

Slowly they make their way back to the camp and what is left of the Roman legion of Lower Germanicus.

"Theophilus," Legate Apronius says when he sees them, "are you saving the monsters now?"

"He is my slave, sir. He is my slave."

"Get him out of my sight. I never want to see another Frisian again."

Theophilus looks for the standard of the Fifth Legion and guides his horse over to Tribune Cethegus Labeo, his superior.

"At last the Frisians are under control, or at least temporarily so" he says.

"Yes, but at the humiliation of Rome."

"How many did we lose, sir?" Theophilus says, still sitting on his horse.

"Nine hundred yesterday, four hundred today. We have trained cowards. That is going to change. So, I see you've picked up a slave. Rather young, isn't he?"

"He'll be more trainable. Now, I need to go to my tent if you will excuse me, Tribune."

They salute. Theophilus turns his mount in the direction of his leather tent.

An aide takes the reins. The tribune dismounts, still holding the boy.

"Sir," Centurion Blasius says, waddling over, looking up at his tall superior in the moonlight, and saluting. "Will there be anything you require before I retire?"

"Tell the cook to bring me food for two. And be sure to include milk."

Theophilus enters his tent and lays the boy on his own cot.

I wonder if I killed the boy's father. Still, we never found his body. Maybe he was taken as a slave by someone.

Morning comes. Lukvert opens his eyes and screams.

"Shhh, boy. You are safe," Theophilus says, confident the boy does not understand his Latin, but hopeful he will his tone of voice.

"Here is some warm milk for you," he says, handing the boy milk from the evening before. The big officer drops to his knees to be eye level with the boy. "And here is some fresh bread."

Lukvert looks at the milk and bread, curls up his fists and puts them on his teary eyes.

Theophilus takes the boy's fists down, and the boy punches the tribune in his eye. The Roman officer falls back, puts his hands up defensively and calls out, "Oh, please, don't hurt me, don't hurt me."

Lukvert stares a moment at the tribune and giggles.

The tribune stands, walks to the far side of his tent, and picks up a small white linen tunic. "I ordered this for you last night. Try it on. See if it will fit."

Lukvert faces the tribune and shakes his head no.

"Ah-ha!," the tribune says. "You do know Latin after all. You can't fool me. Probably learned it from those greedy legionnaires of the greedier Centurion Olennius. Well, you certainly cannot go outside like that."

Lukvert looks down toward his toes and sees that he is naked. He sits again and resumes crying.

Legate Theophilus kneels again. "I don't blame you, boy. But I want you to know that I am going to take care of you until we can find your father. We did not find his body anywhere, so that means he is either alive or crawled away and... Well, anyway, you and I are going to spend the day walking among the soldier tents and asking if your father is here."

Lukvert stops crying and stands. He slips into the white tunic provided for him and takes Theophilus' big hand as they go outside. As they walk, the boy begins to sing.

Tho I vander long avay
Over all da mounts und seas
To the end uv da verld,
I vill alvays dhink uv home

*Und keep you in my heart
Till I hold you once again.*

3 ~ MAKING & BREAKING

*T*heophilus looks up from the writing-table in his tribunal tent.

"After you are through polishing my helmet, Luke, I need you to take my sandal to the shoemaker and see if he will put a new strap on it."

"Yes, sir," the boy replies in Latin. "When I am done with those two things, will you look at what I have been writing in your Latin language?" the twelve-year-old asks. "And, sir, why don't you call me by my real name, Lukvert?"

"Yes, you can show me what you have been writing. And I call you Luke because Lukvert is not a name common to my people, plus Luke is a name given to slaves, which is what you are, though sometimes you tend to forget that fact."

"Do you think I will ever find my father so I will not have to be a slave anymore?"

"I don't know. It is a big world. If he was taken as someone's slave, his master must have transferred to another legion as soon as we were through fighting the Frisians."

"Is this shiny enough for your helmet?" Luke asks, holding it up.

"Yes, now take my sandal to the shoemaker." He turns to his bursar, Centurion Blasius, at a nearby table. "Do you need anything at that end of the fortress?"

Blasius looks up from his work. "A helmet as shiny as yours, sir," he says with a wink. "No, I do not need anything."

As Luke walks among the rows of military tents, he

hears the usual taunts.

"Hey, barbarian, come clean my fingernails."

"Hey, barbarian, come chew my food for me."

"Hey, barbarian, you are a nothing."

After four years, he has learned to pay no attention to the insults. Instead, he whistles as Theophilus has told him to do.

His errand completed, the boy is back at the tribune's tent.

"Luke, it is time for your lesson. It is still a little too cold in the Rhine to be swimming yet. I think you need to mature a little more before learning about sword fighting. So, you will practice your javelin throwing."

Theophilus grabs a javelin, one of several he keeps on hand, and they walk out to the parade grounds.

"There are several ways to throw it, depending on battle conditions. If you are in close quarters, thrust it underhand to jab your enemy. With a little more room, you can thrust it overhand into your enemy. You can use it to best advantage out in the open where you can send it flying through the air to your enemy.

"I want you to practice the running thrust into that bale of straw over there. Do it fifty times. When done, I will come inspect the target, or I will send Centurion Blasius out to do it."

Alone now, Luke takes the javelin in his hand, turns his fingers the way he had been shown, runs, and thrusts. His weapon misses the target completely.

He walks forward to retrieve his javelin, walks back to his starting point, and goes through the thrusting procedure again. Once again, he misses, and once again, he retrieves it, walks back to his starting point, and does it once more.

He twists around his mouth, rolls his eyes upward, then looks around to see if anyone is watching. No one is. He grasps the javelin with both hands over his head and thrusts it at the target. He hits the bottom edge.

With a smirk, he walks up, takes the javelin, walks back to his starting point, holds the weapon between his legs with his hands behind them, and thrusts it forward. It skims across the dirt and lands in front of the target.

He wags his head back and forth, looks up at the sky, creeps up to the javelin, turns with his back to the target while looking elsewhere, picks it up, and saunters back to his starting point.

He opens his eyes wide, puts his tongue in his cheek, looks up at the sky, turns his back on the target, raises the javelin above his head with both hands, and thrusts it behind him.

He does not hear it land. He turns around to face the target and sees Centurion Blasius holding it in one of his big hands.

"Uh, oh," Luke says under his breath.

"Is this what your master told you to be doing?" the centurion demands.

"Uh, no, sir."

"Come with me," the officer says. "You need to be put in your place and punished soundly. Three days without food would be good to start with."

Luke obeys and follows Centurion Blasius to his master's tent. He stands at the tent flap and stops. The centurion waddles up to Theophilus' writing table, notices Luke is not with him, curls his forefinger at him, and jerks his head back.

Luke comes forward and stands next to Centurion Blasius, being careful to lower his head and eyes, and to slump his shoulders in the manner he had learned long ago. Inside he is glad he is as tall as the centurion. Or is it that the centurion is as short as him? Luke fights back a slight smile.

"Sir, your slave boy is not obeying orders," Centurion Blasius announces. "He is not thrusting the javelin properly. If we ever have to depend on him, his actions will cause us to lose the battle. Why do you put up with him?"

Theophilus looks up at the two standing before him and raises his hand to his mouth, though his eyes still glint.

"Is that true, Luke?"

"Well, yes, sir. But what will happen if there are men above us, and the only way we can get the enemy is from below?"

Theophilus puts a hand back up to his mouth and clears his throat. He says nothing.

"And, what if the enemy gets the best of us, and we begin to retreat, then get a shot at them behind us?"

"I see I'm going to have to discipline you," Luke's master says. "Come with me. And you, Blasius, may go back to work with my thanks."

Theophilus leaves his tent, followed by Luke walking several steps behind him. They come to a corral.

"Okay, let's see what you can do on my Frisian horse."

"Really, sir? I'm not in trouble, sir?"

"I keep forgetting, since you have grown physically so much, that you are still only twelve years old," Theophilus says. "I cannot expect you to perform like an adult."

Luke's brows furrow. "Well, I'm big enough to be a grown-up," he objects.

"If you want me to think of you as an adult, you may as well see if you can handle Odin. Get on it without my help, and you can ride him for a while."

Luke looks around, sees a pail, turns it over, steps on it, and mounts Theophilus' big black Frisian horse.

"Walk him around the camp so he can get used to you," Theophilus says.

Grinning, Luke takes the reins and guides the horse around the parade grounds.

He waves, and Theophilus walks back into his tent. Luke pulls on the reins, so the horse stops. He stares at his master's tent a moment, then whips Thor into a gallop.

As it charges through the stone gate of Fortress Nova-Esium, it knocks over anything in its way. Luke and Thor reach the outer grounds, and Thor stretches his legs farther.

The wind blows through Luke's yellow hair as he lowers his head and becomes one with the horse. Faster. Faster. Jump that stream. Jump that log. Jump that barricade.

Odin moves forward, but Luke does not. Luke clings to the reins, but they twist out of his hand. The world becomes sideways, then upside down, then sideways again.

He hears the horse run off without him as he lands on the ground. Then he hears nothing.

"Luke?"

"Luke? Wake up. You've had a fall."

He opens his eyes, looks up, and sees the sentry hovered over him.

"Do you hurt anywhere?" the sentry asks.

"No. Yes. No. Well, my head hurts," he says as he sits up. "Ohhh." He grabs his leg, then rocks back and forth.

"Looks like you may have broken it. Wait here while I bring up that cart so I can take you to the hospitium tent. You're just lucky this is a legion fortress."

The sentry stands between the braces of the small cart and pulls it over to Luke. He helps the boy onto it, goes back between the braces, and pulls the cart back into the fortress and over to the medical tent.

"Is the *medicus* here?" he asks, going in through the tent flap. He sees the *medicus* on a stool treating a sore spot on a dairy cow.

"Tell him I'll be out in a moment," the *medicus* calls over his shoulder.

An aide goes out with the sentry and carries Luke inside and onto a table of rough-cut wood.

Luke does not know when the *medicus* arrives. The first thing he recalls is screaming when the doctor pulls on his leg while the aide and guard hold on to his shoulders.

"That should fix you," *Medicus* Alekto says. "You must be a slave. I think I've seen you around here. Do you belong to Tribune Theophilus?"

Luke nods amidst unwanted tears and while clinging with both hands to his reset leg.

"I'll notify him on my way back to my post," the guard says.

"Give him some chamomile to make him sleep and forget his pain," the *medicus* orders his aide.

Luke does not waken until the following day. When he does, the pain wakens with him. Luke clenches his teeth, remembering that his father told him a good Frisian never shows strong emotions because it is a sign of weakness.

When the emotion of the pain surpasses Luke's determination, he calls out, "Oh, my leg!" and then is ashamed.

Medicus Alekto goes over to his patient, who is now on a mat on the floor, and examines Luke's leg. "It seems to still be in place. I will have my aide give you some willow-bark tea. Drink as much as you want; it's not like opium. I will tell him to leave some by your mat so you can drink it whenever the pain starts to come back."

A week goes by, and gradually Luke's need for the willow-bark tea diminishes. One morning when no one is in the tent but other patients, Luke looks around and sees a stick. He leans over, crawls on his side, and touches it. He works his way up the stick until he is standing.

"Hey, what are you doing?" the aide says.

"I thought I'd try walking now that I'm nearly healed," Luke replies. "But my leg is throbbing now. I guess it's not healed yet."

"That's right, it's not," the aide replies. "But it's not a bad idea to at least try to walk sometimes. So I'm going to leave the crutch near you so you can do what you can when you can."

Another week passes. Luke is now up and on his crutch more. He visits with the other patients, both men and beasts. He talks with the men and pets the beasts.

"What are you here for," he asks each man.

"An old wound is festering again. I can't seem to get it to heal completely."

"I was hit on the head with the back end of a javelin when we fought that last Germanic skirmish and now have headaches."

"The scars on my back from the lashing my centurion gave me are acting up."

Luke begins following Alekto around. "Can I bandage him up now?" he asks after the *medicus* finishes with each man.

"I think you are wanting to be a *medicus* yourself someday," Alekto says in one of his rare moments of small talk.

"Well, yes, sir," Luke says, his eyes shining. "I think that is what I would like to be when I grow up. If my master will allow it, I would like to be a *medicus*."

Luke and the aide become good friends. Now, when a new patient comes in, the aide sits back and lets Luke tell him which table to lie down on for his initial examination by *Medicus* Alekto.

"He is a very good *medicus*, and I am going to be just like him when I grow up," Luke is often heard to say.

"I am going to be gone two or three days, Luke," Alekto tells him one day. "We have been having good weather. So my aide and I are going out into the woods and look for herbal cures to restock my supply. If we do not find much, we will be back by tonight. If we are in luck, we will stay gone longer."

"Yes, sir," Luke responds, teasing an ant on the floor with the end of his crutch.

"I have no other patients right now, but you. Do you think you can man the medical tent until I return?"

"Yes, sir."

"Now, if someone comes into the with a serious cut or anything that is too hard or you to handle while I am gone, we are going straight across the Rhine. Send someone to get me. We'll be on foot, so will not be too far away for them to find me."

Luke grins. "Yes, sir," he says, his chest inflated, his grin broad, and his excitement barely contained.

Shortly the *medicus* and his aide leave. Luke walks around the hospitium tent with his one good leg and his crutch. He would strut if he could.

How proud my father would be of me. My mother, too, though I hardly remember her anymore.

Luke walks around a small table and sits on the bench the *medicus* uses when mixing his herbs. He puts both hands together on the bench and looks around at the vials of mixtures on the shelves nearby. He stands, hobbles over to the nearest shelf, and reads the labels etched into the clay of each vial.

He looks at another table and notices bittersweet

branches laying on it.

The medicus has too much to do. I think I'll crush up the leaves and mix them with oil so it will be ready next time he needs to treat the men's wounds.

Luke takes down an empty bowl and plucks the leaves off the stem. That done, he stares at the thin stems a moment, then decides to break them up, crushes them, and adds them to the leaves. Finally, he is left with the berries.

These berries are probably the best part of the plant. If I add this to the leaves and branches, healing will be twice a fast.

Luke crushes the berries, adds olive oil to everything, stirs the mixture until only small bits are seen in it, and pours it from the bowl into a vial. He takes the stylus kept nearby and labels the vial properly: BITTERSWEET.

That done, Luke moves over to one of the examination tables, sits on it, and stares with satisfaction at the shelves of medications.

Night comes. It has been quiet. An aide from the cooking area comes in to see if he would like an evening meal brought to him. Luke indicates that a meal would be fine.

Once the meal is consumed, he lies down on his mat and falls asleep.

"*Medicus! Medicus!*"

Luke raises his head and looks around through the darkness. Light comes from the tent entrance, and he sees two silhouettes in it.

"Over here," he says, rising and grabbing an oil lamp. He lights it with the visitor's torch and waits while the patient is placed on the table.

"He was digging a trench that the legate requires be done by tomorrow morning. One of the other men got too close and jabbed the shovel into Dov's foot. It's cut real bad. Can you stop the bleeding? Where is the *medicus*?"

"He is not here," Luke responds. "He left me in charge. I can help you."

"If you are all that is here, I guess we'll have to trust you."

Luke leans over, holds the oil lamp close, and

examines the gash on the infantryman's foot.

"I have just the thing for you," he tells Dov. "Stay still while I get it."

Luke hobbles with his crutch over to the medicine shelves, reads the labels etched in the vials, and takes the vial he had just filled a few hours earlier.

He hobbles back over to the injured man, pours the oil over the cut, then wraps it with strips of linen. He makes his way back to the shelves, takes down a large vial marked chamomile, grabs a cup, mixes it with water, and takes them to his patient.

"Drink all of this you want," he tells Dov. "It will ease the pain and help you sleep tonight."

Luke turns to the other soldier. "Can you help Dov down off the table? Here is a mat where he can sleep."

They get Dov over to his mat and cover him with a deer hide.

"You are no longer needed," Luke says authoritatively but not without compassion. "Go on back to your tent. You can come back tomorrow to visit your friend."

"I will be out on patrol tomorrow morning, but will be able to come by the next day."

"Fine. He is in good hands. Good night."

Luke checks over his new patient one last time. He goes over to his own mat, lies down, and closes his eyes, satisfied his patient has already begun healing, and he himself will be a good *medicus* someday.

Morning comes, and Luke sees that his patient is sleeping well. *I certainly do not need to give him something to make him sleep.*

He wanders around the hospitium tent a while and finally settles at a table near a medical book he sometimes sees Alekto read, and opens the scroll. He looks through it a while, decides the words are too big for him, closes it back, and goes outside to get a little fresh air.

A few hours later, he sees *Medicus* Alekto and his aide heading toward the hospitium tent. They are smiling.

"How did things go for you? Did you find many medical herbs over there?" Luke asks.

"Indeed we did," Alekto replies. "How have things been here?"

"Oh, fine. I had a patient come in during the night with a bad cut on his foot, but I put the proper medical oil on him, and he has been sleeping and healing well since then," Luke says with a wide grin.

The *medicus* frowns and enters the hospitium tent. He goes over to the patient, puts his hand on the patient's forehead, and opens his eyelids.

He looks back over at Luke.

He stares.

"What have you done?" he roars.

"Your patient is dead."

4 ~ ACCUSED

"Luke, how long have we been at Fort Bonn?"

"Two weeks, Master."

"That's right. And it is time you get over what happened with that man."

"But, Master, I killed him."

"It was an accident. You did not know the berries were poison."

Luke sets the new parchments in a basket near Tribune Theophilus' writing table, then goes over to his corner, sits, puts his elbows on his crossed knees, his hands under his chin, and closes his eyes.

"That is exactly what I am talking about. If I catch you moping like that again, I will have to punish you, and you will not like the punishment."

"But, Master."

"Stop it. I do not ever want you to bring it up again. Now, I want you to go to the blacksmith and see if he has my new shield made yet. When you get back, I expect to see the old Luke back. Is that understood?"

"Yes, Master."

Luke leaves, and out through a small window, Theophilus can hear the boy's song of courage:

> *Tho I vander long avay*
> *Over all da mounts und seas*
> *To da end uv da verld,*
> *I vill alvays tink uv home*
> *Und keep you in my heart*

Till I hold you once again.

Theophilus looks at the supply orders given him by various centurions in the legion. He then looks over at his assisting centurion. "That boy could make a good physician someday. Too bad, he put up his tent as far from the hospitium as he could get it."

"Fortress Bonn is certainly more advanced than the one we came from," Centurion Blassius says, looking through the writing supplies that have just been delivered. "No more tent living for the officers, at least."

Theophilus glares at Blassius, but says nothing more about the boy.

Two weeks go by. It is now early evening. Centurion Blasius has just left. Luke sitting in his corner, practicing with his abacus so he can help count supplies.

There is a loud bang on his door. Without waiting for a response, the door is opened.

"Tribune Theophilus?"

Theophilus looks up from his work. He sees four legionnaires led by a centurion he does not recognize. The officer's sword is drawn, and the four men behind him have spears.

The centurion unrolls a small parchment and reads:

TRIBUNE THEOPHILUS: YOU ARE HEREBY ARRESTED ON THE CHARGE OF GRAND THEFT. YOU WILL BE HELD IN CONFINEMENT UNTIL A TRIBUNAL IS HELD. YOUR PUNISHMENT WILL BE ONE HUNDRED STRIPES AND DEMOTION.

"Theft of what?" Theophilus demands, standing.

"Supplies. That is all I know."

"It would take a lot of missing supplies to result in such punishment."

"Yes, sir. Please turn around so I can chain your hands and feet."

"Luke," the tribune calls out. "Find out what is missing, then find out who the real thief is."

"Yes, sir," Luke says, standing in place.

"Investigate," Theophilus says as he is led away. "Investigate. And get Blasius to do the same."

Luke spends the night in his master's *officium*, so is on hand when Centurion Blasius arrives the next morning.

"You are to do the investigating," the centurion says after Luke explains what had happened the previous night. "Report to me whenever you discover anything new. Is that clear?"

"Yes, sir," Luke says, looking down on the short centurion. He leaves and walks down the corridor to the *officium* of Legate Lucius Apronius.

"Sir, I am the slave of Titus Pontus Theophilus," Luke tells the clerk. "He was arrested last night for theft. May I have a list of the missing items?"

Luke uses his most manly voice and stands straight and tall.

"Yes, I learned about it this morning. You must go next door to the *officium* of Tribune Cethegus Labeo, who is in command of the Fifth Legion."

Luke walks to the next office and repeats his request.

"I have been expecting you. Well, not a slave, but someone," the clerk says. "Here is the list of missing items."

Luke looks at the list etched on a clay tablet, then back at the clerk. "Are you sure this is correct?"

"Yes, we are sure. No one realized there was so much missing until we moved to this fortress. You may have the tablet."

Luke takes it, excuses himself, and walks over to the prison. He requests to see his master.

The guard takes him to an empty room. "You'll have to talk to him from up here." Thereupon, the guard raises a door in the floor and stands to one side.

"Luke, is that you?"

Luke looks down into the hole and sees the tribune shading his eyes and looking up at him. The stench rises up and Luke gags a moment.

"Master! What have they done to you?"

"Luke, we do not have much time. Have you learned what I am accused of taking?"

"You are accused of taking 120 pack animals, one full suit of armor for a legate, two Frisian horses, 48 wagons, and 39 barrels of wine."

Theophilus' jaw drops. "That cannot be," he says, turning and running his big fingers through his dark hair.

"Investigate, Luke. Find the person who really did this. Look for people who have more of or better than others of their rank. And what about Blasius?"

"He says he has the work of two now, so to report to him anything I find."

"That is true. Do what he tells you."

"Time's up," the guard declares. He slams the round door in the floor shut with a bang.

Luke leaves the prison and walks up and down the side streets where the legionnaires' tents are set up. He looks for clues.

After a while, he sees a man who could be the real thief of fortress supplies, and stops in front of his tent.

"Uh, sir," he says to the archer. "I couldn't help but notice your fancy bow. Could I look at it?"

The man twitches his nose. "Sure. Here. Isn't it a masterpiece?"

Luke examines the inlaid mother of pearl. "Where did you get your bow?"

"Who wants to know?" the archer asks.

"Oh, I was just wondering. That's all. By the way, My name is Luke. I am from Frisia."

"My name is Erebus from Syria," the archer replies, still seated.

"Well, I guess I'll be going."

Luke tries not to run as he heads back to the fortress headquarters and the *officium* of his master.

"Centurion Blasius," he says when entering, "I think I found the man who stole all those things from the legion. He is Erebus from Syria, an archer. He has a bow full of mother-of-pearl, and I know he wouldn't be able to afford it."

The centurion lays down the parchment he has been making tally marks on to record the amount of grain in storage.

"Fine," the officer responds, standing. "Come with me. We are going to get Theophilus out of jail today."

Luke follows the centurion down the corridor to Tribune Labeo's *officium* and is escorted into the tribune's office.

"Sir, we have found the culprit who stole all those things from our legion. I would like to select four of my men to accompany me for the arrest."

"Are you sure?"

"Yes, sir."

"All right. Go ahead and make the arrest. But this does not mean Tribune Theophilus is free. He does not go free until we know for sure someone else stole the supplies."

"Uh, sir, Tribune Labeo."

"You are dismissed. I'm busy," he says as he picks up a scroll on his writing-table.

"But what is my master doing in a hole in the ground?"

Labeo jerks his head up. "What did you say?"

Luke wipes away a tear. "He's in a hole in the ground, and it's dark and cold and…"

"Who ordered him put there? Centurion Blasius, did you? Get him out of there. He's a tribune. He deserves respect no matter what he may or may not have done. Confine him in the *hospitium*. Send one guard with him and chain his feet but not his hands."

"Yes, sir," the centurion says. "What about the new suspect?"

"If he's just a legionnaire, put him in the hole. But not a tribune. Blasius, where is your head?"

Blassius salutes and leaves, Luke behind him.

Now confined to the hospitium, Theophilus waits. Luke is not allowed to visit him more than once again and not for very long. For three days the tribune waits, in chains and guarded. Four. Five.

A week later escorts Erebus into the hearing room of Legate Lucius Apronius. He salutes.

Legate Lucius is seated in a chair arranged on a high platform. Standing to one side are Centurion Blasius, the accuser, and Cethegus Labeo, Tribune of the Fifth Legion, and Legate Lucius Apronius. A strange woman and Luke are also present.

"Erebus of Syria," the legate begins. "you have been accused of taking 120 pack animals, one full suit of armor for a legate, two Frisian horses, 48 wagons, and 39 barrels of wine. What say you?"

"I am not guilty of stealing anything," Erebus replies, his nose twitching and one foot involuntarily tapping.

Centurion Blasius walks forward. "This ornate mother-of-pearl-inlaid bow was found in the defendant's possession. He could not have afforded this without income from somewhere else."

"Are there any witnesses?" the legate asks.

"Yes, sir," Blasius replies. "My aide, Luke of Frisia, is a witness."

Luke steps forward.

"Well?"

"Yes, I saw that very bow in the possession of the accused. He even admitted it was his."

"You're a slave, aren't you?"

"Yes, sir."

"I will decide later whether I accept your testimony. Are there any more witnesses?"

"Yes, sir," a small voice says from the sidelines.

"Step forward and state your name and any connection you have with the defendant."

The young lady walks forward. She has dark skin and black eyes. "My name is Dacia of Syria. I am a close friend of Erebus, also of Syria. I follow the legion around so we can be close. I got the bow from my brother. He was killed in the Battle of Baduhenna Wood six years ago. I saved it for a while, but gave it to my, uh, friend when your legion moved to this fortress."

"Hand me the bow," the legate orders.

"Hmmm. Nice bow. But it hardly requires all the missing supplies to purchase it. Are there any other witnesses? No? Then, young man, you may go. I find you not guilty."

The legate stands and leaves the room.

"You're going to have to do better than this, Luke. If the tribune is not freed, it will be your fault. Now get out there and see who you can find to blame."

Luke resumes walking up and down the aisles between legionnaires' tents, looking for someone who looks suspicious.

Seventeen days later, he finds another suspect. The culprit is held in the hole until court day.

Legate Lucius Apronius and Tribune Cethegus Labeo both walk in through a back door and are seated in front of the people, the legate on a high platform.

"The proceedings may begin," Legate Apronius says.

Tribune Labeo reads the charges. "Silenus of Crete, you are accused of taking 120 pack animals, one full suit of armor for a legate, two Frisian horses, 48 wagons, and 39 barrels of wine. What say you?"

"Not guilty," Silenus says, saluting, then wiping his big mouth and forehead with a handkerchief.

"Sir," Blasius announces, "I have found the man guilty of taking all the supplies. I have a witness."

Luke steps forward. "Sirs, I saw this man with a brass helmet, the kind that was with the full suit of armor that is missing."

"This is the very helmet," Centurion Blasius says, taking it from one of his infantrymen. "I expect we will find the rest of the armor upon permission to search the suspect's tent."

"You haven't searched it yet?" Tribune Labeo asks, shaking his head. "Now, are there any other witnesses?"

Another soldier steps forward.

"Sir, I am Dachas of Cyprus. I traded the helmet for a Frisian horse Silenus captured after the Battle of Baduhenna Wood. The helmet came from my uncle, a tribune in Britannia. It was a gift to him from his legate. I have a letter with me signed by my uncle explaining all this."

"Hand it to the clerk," the legate orders.

The clerk takes it to the legate who reads it, then hands it to the tribune who reads it.

"Not guilty," Legate Apronius states, glaring at Blasius.

A month passes. Luke resumes his search for a

suspect. He no longer entertains Theophilus with stories of his people.

"Master, how can I tell you of happy things when you are here and you didn't do anything wrong?"

"Be strong, Luke. You must be strong. I am doing fine. I am learning all kinds of new things about medicines. You cannot help me if you are moping. Stand up and be strong."

"But why doesn't Centurion Blasius help me?"

"He is too busy, You know that."

Two weeks pass. Luke finally finds another suspect and Blasius prosecutes him in court.

Two days later there is a hearing. Once again Legate Lucius Apronius, Governor of Lower Germanicus, enters the hearing room, followed by Tribune Cethegus Labeo, commander of the Fifth Roman Legion.

"This had better be good," the legate says, looking down from his elevated chair at Centurion Blasius. "Read the charges, Tribune."

"Iduma of Parthia, you are accused of taking 120 pack animals, one full suit of armor for a legate, two Frisian horses, 48 wagons, and 39 barrels of wine. What say you?"

"I am not guilty," the soldier says.

"Sir, this is the silver statue of our esteemed god, Mars, that was found in his possession. No one with his pay could afford such an elegant statue." Blassius holds it up in front of him for the judges to see.

"And I suppose you have the same witness that you did the other times."

"Yes, sir," Luke responds.

"Are there any other witnesses?" Legate Apronius asks.

"Yes, sir," seven men say in unison, stepping forward in full uniform.

"What have we here? One of you speak for the others," the legate responds.

"Sir, I am Dawud of Parthia. The eight of us were on patrol on the other side of the Rhine and came upon a deserted village. We went through the things that were left behind and found this statue. We all agreed we would take it back for our own personal worship of Mars. We already feel his presence in our tent and in using our skills as lancers on behalf of Caesar."

Legate Apronius rises. "Not guilty. All of you not guilty. And if I see you here again, Centurion Blasius, I will have you jailed instead of them."

The two officials leave, then the rest of the men at the hearing do so.

"Luke, you must do something to free your master. It's your fault you have failed so far. Do you want to spend the rest of your life a failure?" With that, Centurion Blasius returns to Tribune Theophilus' *officium* and slams the door.

"Oh, master. What am I going to do? You should have me put down in that hole in the ground and bury me forever. I'm worthless. I have no brains, just like Centurion Blasius tells me."

"I have no answers for you, Luke. But you are smart and good and do not let anyone tell you any different. Just make sure you prove everything. Do not go to court without proof. Now stop your crying and go pray to the gods."

"But which ones, Master?"

Three weeks go by. Some days Luke does not go to the hospitium to visit with Tribune Theophilus.

"Master, I am ashamed and scared. They need to kill me dead, not you."

"No one is going to be killed," Theophilus intervenes."

"Centurion Blasius says the thief should be beaten and then killed."

Theophilus bristles, then smiles at the boy. "Don't let him frighten you. Now, you must be strong."

Nineteen days later, Luke finds a young legionnaire with a gold-handled sword that he could never have been able to pay for. The court day is set up and Blassius appears to prosecute.

Phorcys of Gaul pleads not guilty. Centurion Blasius presents the gold-handled sword to the legate and tribune. He is proud. He can now put an end to it.

"Are there any other witnesses besides this slave?" Legate Apronius asks. He pauses. "I didn't think so." Then rises to leave.

"Sir."

"Yes, Tribune Gavius," Tribune Labeo replies, sitting back down in his chair. The legate reseats himself also.

"I am appearing on behalf of my cavalryman. His father was my friend while we were camped together in Gaul. His father was Tribune Zeno, and he used the gold-handled sword in many battles alongside me. When Tribune Zeno died, he left the sword to his son, Phorcys, and I personally delivered it to him."

The legate's face turns red, he pounds the arm of his judge's seat, and points at Centurion Blasius and Luke.

"Throw them in the hole. Charges are conspiracy. I do not know conspiracy of what yet, but I will think of something."

Immediately, the chains are taken off the accused man's wrists and put on Centurion Blasius' wrists, and the chains on the accused man's ankles are put on Luke's ankles. They are delivered to the hole.

The next day, Legate Labeo orders Theophilus' *officium* searched. Centurion Pyrrus Accius Sopater is put in charge. After reading through the records for two days, he finds a scroll of tallies on supplies and animals that he takes to the tribune who is senior to Tribune Theophilus.

"These figures do not make sense," Tribune Labeo says upon reading them.

"Go to Centurion Blasius' room. Search it. Be thorough. Then search anything else he owns—horses, chariots, anything—that is stored elsewhere.

Three hours later, Sopater reports to Tribune Labeo's *officium*. Behind him are two men carrying a saddle.

"This saddle has Blasius' brand on it. This is what we found inside." Sopater nods to his men who set the saddle on the floor and reach into the leather bags on each side. They slowly set the contents on the floor next to the saddle.

"Sir, there is one talent of gold in each of these bricks. They are worth one million denari each."

"Wait here," Tribune Labeo says. Shortly he returns with Legate Apronius.

"Centurion Sopater," the tribune says, "go to the *hospitium* and set Tribune Theophilus free. Then go to the prison and get his slave, Luke of Frisia, out of there."

"Yes, sir."

"Then take Centurion Blasius to the parade ground. On your way out, order that the call to assemble be sounded throughout the fortress.

An hour later, Tribune Labeo goes out to the parade grounds. Centurion Blasius is still chained to a stake.

"You are hereby demoted to infantryman. Should you try to escape, you will be executed where ever you are found by whichever means those who find you determine."

He turns and shouts loud enough that every man in the legion can hear. "One hundred lashes!" And marches away.

5 ~ CIVILIZATION

"What is our next military assignment like, Master? Do you know?"

Slave Luke, Tribune Theophilus, and Centurion Sopater are on the new Roman-built Via Egnatia headed south toward the Aegean Sea. They are already in Macedonia.

Tribune Theophilus is on his black Frisian named Odin. Centurion Sopater is on his chestnut Mecklenburger, and Luke is riding behind his saddle.

"Yes, I have heard a lot about it," Tribune Theophilus says. "We are lucky I had an understanding legate and he let me transfer to another legion after that unfortunate misunderstanding."

"Thank you, sir, for having me reassigned to continue serving with you," the tall, black-haired centurion says.

"Sopater, you were my lifesaver. If it hadn't been for you discovering and deciphering all the transactions made to sell the fortress's equipment and supplies for Blasius' own profit, I fear I would have not survived the one hundred lashes."

"Did you know I was born and raised near our new assignment?" Sopater asks.

"Where was that?" Theophilus says, twisting in his saddle and putting his hand on the small of his back.

"Berea. When I retire, I plan to go back there. My father, Pyrrus, is there. You may have heard of him. We descend from an old royal family."

"What's that over on the other side of the river?" Luke asks.

"That's the tomb of the royal family of Philip and Alexander the Great," Sopater says. "Everyone in Macedonia knows about it."

They ride along in silence until they come to the bridge crossing the Stymon River. On the other side, they go through an unguarded old city gate. They see only a few homes and public buildings located among rubble.

"Amphipolis must have been a great city at one time," Theophilus says. "Not much of it left."

"Everyone says Alexander pretty much killed the city when he took most of its men to war with him," Sopater says.

They ease up on the reins of their horses to give them a chance to go around or jump over low obstacles, mostly fallen columns of the old market place and forum.

"I see another wall ahead," Luke announces.

"Sir," Sopater calls up to the guards at the city gate, "Can you tell us where the fortress is?"

"Just keep going, exit through the south gate, and you will see the acropolis—highest point around. Actually, you will be able to see it before you leave the city."

"Thank you, sir," Theophilus says, leading the way. "And let's stop at the market and get something to eat,"

"I'm starved," Luke says.

They stop, pick out some figs and cheese, and watch the people passing by, some with civilized tunics of linen and nearly all with dark brown hair. Others—mostly the yellowheads and redheads—wear leather tunics and colored capes worn by the Thracians, distant cousins of the Frisians.

"That man over there is my father!" Luke announces. "Praise Baduhenna."

He runs after the man. "Vather! Vather!"

The man turns.

Luke stares at the stranger a moment, his brow wrinkled, his lips pressed together, and fights back unmanly tears.

He returns to the fruit stand, and says nothing.

"Someday you will find him, Luke. If it is the will of Baduhenna and Mars, someday you will."

Having finished off their mid-day meal, the three remount and go out the south gate where they see a well. They stop, brush down their horses, and give them a drink and some oats to eat while they clean themselves up. Theophilus and Sopater don the rest of their uniforms including their shining brass helmets. Luke is given a clean tunic to put on.

Once at the gate into the fortress, they pause and hand their orders to the guard on duty. The guard promptly salutes Tribune Theophilus.

"Welcome to the fortress of the Tenth Legion, sir. Go straight ahead and you will see the headquarters. They will tell you where your *officium* and your quarters will be. Can you verify this is your slave?"

"No, I cannot," Theophilus says. "You will have to accept my word."

They arrive at the headquarters *officium*, enter, and identify themselves.

The clerk on duty salutes. "You are in luck, Tribune Theophilus," he says with a wide grin. "Our governor is here. Arrived from Corinth just yesterday."

"So ole Publius Memmius Regulus is here. It will be good to see him again," Tribune Theophilus says.

"He is in his *officium*. Would you like...."

"Well, if it isn't Titus Pontus Theophilus," they hear behind the clerk. The senator and governor has a wide jaw, high cheekbones, wavy dark hair, and furrows in his forehead. The two men walk toward each other and clasp hands and forearms.

"I was just on my way out," Regulus says. "I did not know you were stationed at this fortress."

"I am just checking in. I've spent most of my career in Germanicus, but am not too many years from retirement now."

"Well, come to the banquet tonight. It is in honor of me," the senator says with a wink. "And bring the centurion with you."

"Yes, sir. We will see you then. Thank you."

The rest of the day is a whirlwind of settling in, meeting new people, and reviving old friendships of long ago.

The next morning Theophilus is the first to arrive at his *officium*. Luke follows him in.

"What are we going to be doing today, Master?" he asks. Luke is now fifteen years old and the same height as Theophilus.

"You may not remember, but today is the seventh anniversary of your coming to me. I have a little present for you."

Theophilus strides over to a corner of his spacious new *officium* where he has stored new parchments ready to be used for correspondence and legion-wide supply requests.

"Come here, boy," he tells Luke. "You have learned the Latin well."

"Yes, sir. Thank you, sir."

"Didn't your father tell you to write the history of your people so it would not be forgotten? Pick out four parchments. Today you will begin keeping your promise."

"Really?" Luke says, beaming.

"Choose four. And here is a pen and some blackener."

Luke chooses four parchments and lays them in a corner of his master's *officium*. He sits cross-legged on the floor and sets one of the parchments on a piece of wood in his lap.

"What will you write about first?" Theophilus asks.

Luke wrinkles his brow, squints his eyes, looks up at the ceiling, then back at his master. "I think I will tell how one of our ancestors long ago in a village near ours actually killed a draugr."

"What is a draugr?" Theophilus asks.

"Well, when someone dies, he lives on underground in his grave. None of the draugrs do anything unless they want to come up here where they used to live. But it has do be dark when they do. They are always in their body, but sometimes they make it swell, so they look like giants or small like elves. Usually, they don't come back up unless they are jealous of people who are still alive."

"They do not go to where the gods live?"

"Oh, no. There is no good place for them to go, so they like to come back to earth and roam at night so they can feel home again. But they are so jealous of those of us who are living, they sometimes attack us. A strong man can overpower them and drive a wooden stake into their heart so that they die a second time and never come back to earth again."

"Is that so?" Theophilus says, picking up his pen to begin his work.

"You don't believe me, but it is true. One of our forefathers, Fenrer the Great, wrestled one. He got the stake into the dragur, and he never came back again. My people are very brave."

"Luke," Theophilus begins, putting down his pen, "have you investigated this story?"

"What do you mean?"

"Have you checked to see if people live on in their coffins?"

"Well, no, but that's what everyone says."

"Go ahead and write your story, Luke, but someday you must investigate it."

"Yes, sir."

Luke sits in his corner all day, writing as much as he can remember about his people. *Oh, goddess Baduhenna. Please help me remember. It's been so long. Help me remember.*

He stops writing. He stands and walks around the *officium*. An hours goes by. He leaves. Without a word, he leaves.

Centurion Sopater enters the *officium*. "What's wrong with Luke?"

"Why? What is he doing?" the tribune asks.

"He running up and down the side streets where the legionnaire tents are."

"Running, huh? He does that when he's confused and trying to make up his mind about something. He'll be back when he wears himself out."

The centurion picks up a list of supplies and leaves.

On his way out, Luke returns.

"Okay, what is bothering you, Luke?" Theophilus asks. "I cannot have you disrupting the fortress."

"I can't remember," he says, throwing his hands up in the air, then landing them on top of his yellow-haired head. "I have only filled half of a parchment all day. I need help."

Luke sits in his corner, stares at his three and one half blank parchments, and stands again.

"Do you know any gods I could pray to for help? I really need it."

"Well, my God is Mars. He is the son of Zeus and watches over our safety in war and peace. Part of what he does is give us wisdom. Do you think he could help you?"

"He sounds like Odin of my people."

"Yes, they could be related. Now, let me see. A half brother of Mars is Apollo, who watches out for our safety and gives us wisdom. So now you have three gods to pray to."

Luke looks over at his master and presses his lips together, then takes a deep breath. "Do you think it will really help?" He moves to a kneeling position, puts his hands on his knees, and looks up at the ceiling. "Do you think, if I pray to three gods, my prayers will be stronger?"

"I would think so."

He stands, turns in circles, still looking at the ceiling.

"I can't forget. I just can't. I have to keep my promise to my father. Vather! Come und help me!" he cries out, reverting to his Frisian tongue.

Luke leaves the *officium* the rest of the day. Theophilus does not send for him. But, out in the street, he hears the haunting song:

> *Tho I vander long avay*
> *Over all da mounts und seas*
> *To da end uv da verld,*
> *I vill alvays dhink uv home*
> *Und keep you in my heart*
> *Till I hold you once again.*

The next morning, Luke bounds into the *officium*

whistling.

"I remembered another one," he announces on his way to his corner.

"Tell me about it," Centurion Sopater says, smiling. "That is, if it will not disturb the tribune."

"Tell it fast," Theophilus says.

"Well," Luke begins, "a million years ago, thousands and thousands and thousands of good fairies left the sun and came to earth. But they didn't stop there. They dove down inside the earth. There, they changed their shape into roots, then shot up and became trees. They were everywhere on earth.

"In my homeland, the fairy elves became pine trees, birch trees, ash trees, and oak trees. See there? I even remember the kinds of trees that became Frisia."

Luke beams. "And, you know what? The fairies that did this have a name—Moss Maidens. And the most special fairies are in the oak trees. That's why we always set aside oak groves to worship."

Luke spends most of the rest of the day carefully writing the story of his people onto his parchment.

Sometimes Luke stands, stretches his arms, and touches his toes. "Praying to all those gods really helped." He takes his place in his corner of the *officium* and writes again.

It is quiet for a while. Theophilus leaves his writing-table moves over to a bench near the young man. "Uh, Luke," he says, "there is something else you need to be doing."

"Yeah, I know. I haven't swept the floor yet today, and I haven't gone to the legate's office to see if he has any messages for you, and I haven't washed any of your clothes."

"That is true. But I have been thinking. You are an intelligent young man. I could use you better as a personal scribe and even my personal physician."

"No!" Luke responds. "No! Please, Master. Not that. I cannot be a physician. I refuse to kill you. I can be a scribe, but never a physician."

The tribune watches his slave.

"Okay. We will put off your being my physician

temporarily, and concentrate on skills needed to be my scribe. Now, one of the things you need to do is learn another language: Greek. Some of my correspondence is in Greek."

"I like languages," Luke replies. "I can speak Frisian and Latin both. I already know a few Greek words."

"That's not all," Theophilus says. "Now that we are back in the civilized world away from barbaric Germanicus, you have opportunities you did not have before. If I am sent to Britannia or Gaul or Parthia next, you will not have the opportunity you have in Greece. Let's take advantage of educating you while I am at Fortress Amphipolis.

"Will it help me remember and write my country's history?"

"Yes, I believe so. You need to also learn geography, literature, and philosophy."

"Will I find more gods to help me?" Luke asks.

"Yes, you will. You will learn about more gods than you ever thought possible."

"Will I learn about any gods of travel to help me find my father?"

"I'm sure you will."

"Do all the gods answer everyone's prayers? If I pray to a thousand gods, will I get a thousand answers?"

"I never thought of it, Luke. I think I know someone who will help you. Proconsul Regulus is here for a few days.

"Governor Regulus is a priest for our deified Augustus Caesar and arrange festivals to the gods at games along with the annual sacrifices to the lares and gods. I will ask him if he can explain things to you better than I."

"What's a proconsul?"

"A proconsul is a senator who has taken over governing one of the Roman provinces."

"What are lares," Luke asks.

"They're pretty much household gods. He can answer your questions. Now I need you to brush down my horse."

"And he'll talk to me, a slave?"

"The governor and senator is a personal friend. I am sure he will."

The following day, a message is handed to Theophilus. "Luke, come with me."

Luke stops polishing his master's shield and follows him to the governor's *officium*. Theophilus salutes. "I have brought Luke who covets your knowledge and wisdom."

"Well, young man, sit on that cushion, and I will try to answer your questions," the governor says, winking at Theophilus. "And you may sit over here by me."

"Uh, sir," Luke begins, you know hundreds of gods."

"I suppose I do," the governor replies, smiling.

"Do you pray to all of them?"

"All at once? Oh, no. I pray to the god of whatever I need. There are enough of them that they rule different parts of the earth and different events."

"What if I pray to the wrong god?"

"I suppose he'll send a message to the correct god and ask him to listen to you."

"Don't you know, sir? I mean…"

"No one has ever asked me that before."

Theophilus puts a hand up over his mouth to hide his grin.

"Well, what if I prayed to hundreds of gods—thousands even—and they all answered my prayers at once. Will they send so much power to earth that the whole world explodes?"

The governor turns to his friend. "Where did you find this young man? I would like to surround myself with such inquisitive advisors." Both men grin.

"Luke. Is that your name? Luke? What plans does your master have for you?"

"He wants me to be a physician, but I cannot do it, so I am going to be his scribe."

"You're smart enough to be a healer. Why not?"

Luke turns to Theophilus. "Do I have to tell him?"

"There was an unfortunate incident a few years ago, sir," Theophilus replies. "Well, Luke, I think we have taken up enough of the senator's time."

―――

Two years have gone by, and Luke's curiosity over the gods has not waned. While the sixteen-year-old is having his lesson on philosophy, he asks his tutor another question. "What do they do all day between listening to people's prayers?"

"Some say they play games, some say they play with the weather down here and keep us guessing what tomorrow will bring, and some say they do bad things with each other."

Romulus, having been named after one of the founders of Rome and proud of it, has black hair, a hooked nose, and is rotund in his middle. He sits on a bench in Luke's corner of the *officium*.

"But, if they are gods, they shouldn't be doing bad things," Luke says, hitting the back of his head against the wall, but not enough to hurt.

"That is exactly what Zollus thought. He was a great philosopher who lived in this city three centuries ago when it was still thriving. You have been reading Homer. He criticized Homer for depicting the gods as just being overgrown humans."

"He criticized the great Homer?" Luke asks, fidgeting with the hem of his tunic.

"Indeed, he did. He was not very popular around here. Everyone says the gods can do whatever they want simply because they are bigger and stronger than us."

"Then how do we know they are gods?" Luke asks, leaning his chin on his knees. "Maybe they are demons that look like gods."

"I have a copy of what Zollus wrote about Homer's portrayals of the gods. I brought it, knowing your curiosity about them. Read it when you get a chance and tell me what you think.

"Now, the rest of the day, you may work on your book about your countrymen."

Luke's eyes brighten. "I have been praying to Baduhenna, Odin, Apollo, and Mars, who all give wisdom. I have remembered another story. Then I will have five parchments sewn together. My scroll is now nine hand-spans long. The history of my people will never die."

Luke writes the rest of the day in his corner. It is a hot day, and often he interrupts his writing to make trips to the fortress well and fill a pitcher with cool water for his master and the centurion.

Darkness approaches. "I think I'll take my scroll back with me to my tent. I may think of something later. Oh well, I probably shouldn't. I'll leave it here where it will be safe."

Luke, Sopater, and Theophilus leave together.

"It's so hot, I'm going swimming in the Strymon," Luke says.

Look at that sky," Sopater says. "It looks almost green. I've got to get out of this uniform."

Misty clouds stir overhead. The air is still.

"I've seen skies like this before," Theophilus says, bringing a handkerchief across his perspiring brow. "I don't like it."

He stops and stares at the sky a little longer. "Luke, don't go swimming. Go to my quarters with me. You will be safer."

"Safer from what?" Luke asks.

"Hurry," Theophilus demands, breaking into a run. "Get to your quarters, Sopater. And fast."

A roar is heard just as they enter Theophilus' quarters. The door blows open, they rush in, and Luke bars it closed.

Theophilus shoves his bed next to a wall for added protection, grabs the mattress off of it, and throws it at Luke. "Get under this next to a wall," he shouts, diving under his bed.

The roar grows louder. They hear tree branches cracking and loose gear and pottery hitting against the building. Now the banging. The rattling. Knocking. Pounding.

The roof beams overhead straining and shaking.

A crash.

A small hole in the roof.

Shingles flying.

Roof trusses straining.

Then the quiet.

As fast as it had arrived, it leaves.

"Are you okay, Luke?"

"Yes. Are you, sir?"

The two crawl out from their hiding place and stand. They look around. "Well, not much damage inside."

Theophilus looks up. "The carpenters will be busy all over the fortress. Luke, you're going to have to take a quick lesson from one of them and go up there to fix my roof. Now, unbolt the door, and let's see what else is left of the fortress."

Scores of legionnaires are marching toward what is left of the fortress walls to stand guard. Others not on duty wander through the street.

"I wonder if my tent is still there," Luke asks.

"Probably not. Let's check out my *officium*."

They draw close to it, then stop in the middle of the street. The *officium* is gone.

"My scroll. My people. My history. No!"

6 ~ EAST

"Let's stop here and give our horses a rest," Tribune Theophilus says, now on his way to his new assignment.

They dismount at the *mille* marker and pull out their traveling cups for a drink, and a larger bowl for their horses to drink from.

"Four more days, and we should be there," Centurion Sopater says.

Luke slides off the back of the centurion's horse and wanders in the opposite direction of the public well.

"Come get a drink," Sopater tells him.

Luke does not respond. Sopater pours water from the well's pail into his extra cup and takes it over to the young man. Luke does not take it.

"We have time, Luke," Theophilus says from the other side of the road, "if you would like to go for one of your runs."

Luke turns and looks at his master. Dark shadows encircle his eyes, his shoulders are bent, his arms are crossed as though embracing himself.

"We'll wait for you."

Luke turns and looks into the woods on his side of the road. Then he runs. Over bushes and fallen branches and logs. Fallen like the fulfillment of a dream now crumbled and lost forever. He ducks low-hanging branches but sometimes runs into an unseen one, unseen like the story of his people.

His breathing grows stronger and deeper, deep into his being that is gasping for life. His heart races as though desperately racing back in time to when the story of his people was still alive.

He beats back unwanted tears, and finally stumbles onto the ground. In his isolation, he trembles and sobs. He looks up into the sky. "Why?" he shouts. "Why?" And sobs some more.

A hand touches his shoulder. He looks up.

"Luke, it's time to go."

Sopater helps him to his feet and brushes the leaves off his tunic.

"You are a real mess. You know that?" Sopater says with a smile while Luke returns to reality and the now.

"Here is my handkerchief and a skin of water. Wipe your face and take a drink. That's good. Now let's get back to the road. We don't want to keep our master waiting any longer."

Sopater leads and Luke follows, taking a deep breath now and then, twisting his face now and then, and brushing the hair out of his eyes to see better.

Refreshed, the three men remount their horses.

"Ah, the smell of these woods," Theophilus says. "I love that smell, don't you, Luke?"

He looks over and sees Luke nod and force a small smile.

"I certainly do," Sopater agrees.

They ride along in silence a while.

"Tribune, you have been with the Roman legions a long time," Sopater finally says. "How old were you when you enlisted?"

"I was seventeen and sent immediately to Germanicus. Did you ever hear of the infamous Battle of Teutoburg Forest? It was a disaster for Rome. We lost two entire legions—twenty-thousand men dead, plus others captured and enslaved."

"Yes, everyone has heard about it," Sopater says. "How could it have possibly happened against the strongest legions in the world?"

Luke shifts in his seat. Sopater looks back at him and pats him on his leg.

"The rebellious Germans were led by Arminius, who

had been educated and trained in Rome and even fought with us in our legions. He was a big man, bigger even than most other Germans. Then he deserted and went back to his own people. He knew how we fight, so knew how to defeat us."

"Wasn't it Governor Varus who led our troops?"

"Yes. He had exacted too many taxes on the Germanic people, and they rebelled.

"Anyway, he caught us in a ravine between a mountain on one side and marsh on the other. We couldn't get into formation. At first, they were up on the ridges and too far for our swords or even our javelins to reach. The only thing that could get to them were arrows, and we were packed so tightly in that ravine, the archers couldn't get their bows out to shoot at them.

"There was something else against us: The rain. It rained day and night. The men were up to our knees in mud and sliding around. The supply wagons were getting hopelessly stuck in the mire. The rain kept coming. Hard. We could barely move. For some reason, the gods were against us."

"How did you get out alive, sir?" Sopater asks.

"I was just an ordinary legionnaire then, but I did have a horse, so was in the cavalry. We were bringing up the rear. It was the infantry that took most of the beating. Legions Seven and Eight were wiped out. All that was left was Legion Nine, the one I was in."

Theophilus becomes quiet. Sopater respects the silence. Luke does not understand what the men are thinking and feeling. They go around a bend in the road.

"Master," Luke says. "What's that up there?"

The two horses are guided off the road, and the men dismount. Tribune Theophilus quickly dons his helmet, and Centurion Sopater does the same. They stand at attention as the legionnaires file by, heading west, ten in a row.

As the legionnaires pass, they turn their heads to the left and salute the tribune.

They wait while forty columns pass them by, headed west.

"I wonder where they are going," Luke says after they return to the road.

"Probably back to Amphipolis to replace the ones who were killed in the cyclone," Theophilus answers.

He looks at Luke, and a slight smile appears on his lips. "Welcome back, young man. You will survive this."

"Yes, sir."

"So, what happened after Teutoburg Forest?" Sopater asks.

"We were recalled to Rome to reorganize our legion, then sent back to Germanicus. This time we were led by Legate Germanicus, Tiberius' adopted son. I served under him for seven years. Then the Battle of Weser River happened."

"Arminius again?"

"Yes, Arminius again. But this time, we defeated him, destroying nearly twenty thousand Germans. I directed the other cavalrymen near me during the battle. The men actually listened to me, even though they were my peers, and I guess the officers noticed. I was promoted to centurion at the age of twenty-four.

"We had avenged our loss at Teutoburg Forest but withdrew from Upper Germanicus after that. The Rhine River became our border. Someday we will return and add Upper Germanicus to our empire."

"Luke, how are you doing back there?" Sopater asks.

"Well, could I walk?"

"We cannot slow down for you. We have to cover twenty-five *milles* a day."

"I'm seventeen and strong. I know how to trot along beside you and keep up."

Sopater reins in his horse, and Luke slides off the back. He moves over beside the tribune and into his promised trot.

"Well, we were transferred to North Africa under Quintus Junius Blasius. A rebel tribesman and deserter of the Roman legions already in place there started harassing our legion. They weren't very destructive, but they were like mosquitoes. This had been going on for years.

"The Ninth arrived in the winter when the skirmishes did not normally occur. So I went up into the mountains to try to figure out where their summer camps were.

"Summer returned, and so did the attacks by the rebel. I decided to take my men back up into the mountains to find the leader. We went at night. I thought I knew where he was camped. At daylight, we thought we captured the leader. However, the one we captured turned out to be his brother."

The horses neigh when a deer runs across the road.

"Wow! Did you see that?" Luke says, looking up at the tribune, but maintaining his pace.

Theophilus smiles down at his slave, then back to the road.

"When we took our captive back to our fortress," he continues, "you should have heard the cheers. Blastus said this was the beginning of the end for the rebel leader. His men started deserting him, and eventually, he committed suicide when surrounded by our men."

"What then, Luke asks?"

"When we returned to Rome, I was knighted by Tiberius himself and made a tribune. I was thirty. Then the Ninth was sent back up into Germanicus."

"Sir, there is an inn up ahead."

"That is fine, Sopater. That is where we will spend the night."

They settle in, splash water on their head and arms, then go to the room where the food is served. They seat themselves, a maid comes in with a large bowl of water, and she washes the two men's feet.

Luke sits on the floor over by the kitchen area and falls asleep. He is awakened by a foot in his rib.

"Come on now. You have work to do before going to sleep."

The next morning they rise at daylight, eat some bread, and are given enough dried fruit and cheese to get them through the day, courtesy of the Roman government.

Well rested, the two officers mount their horses and continue their journey east. Luke resumes trotting between them.

The air is cool, and there is a slight breeze. Leaves on the trees on both sides of the Roman road rustle.

"Master, when did you find me?" Luke looks up and asks.

"I have been waiting for that question, young man. Well, they had a big celebration in Rome just for capturing the rebel leader's brother. Then our Ninth Legion was sent back to Germanicus, this time Lower Germanicus.

"We were there six years, and everything went along smoothly. But when I was thirty-six, the new governor of your territory—Lucius Apronius—started raising your taxes. If they couldn't pay in animal skins, he took their wives and children to be his servants. The governor gradually turned from a benefactor of your people to a bully.

"Everyone knew what would happen once your people were pushed too far. I tried to reason with him, but he refused to listen to any of his advisors."

Luke stops and looks up at Theophilus.

"It's time we had a talk," he says, reining in his horse and dismounts. They walk over to the bench next to the *mille* marker and Theophilus motions to Luke that he is allowed to sit beside him. Sopater dismounts, takes the reins of the tribune's horse, and walks over to the well out of hearing distance.

"I just barely remember sitting on my father's lap the day before the battle," Luke says, almost in a whisper. "He was a big man. He promised me he would try very hard not to die."

Silence.

"The last thing he ever said to me was to remember his song.

Silence.

"I woke up the morning of the battle listening to the footsteps of my father. He had a dagger in his waist, sword in one hand, shield in the other, and walked out the door."

Silence.

"I never saw him again. But, you know what? I know he is still alive. I know it. So, I must keep looking for him."

"Well, I have had you nearly ten years now.," Theophilus says. "He would be proud of how smart and honest and tall you are."

Luke laughs. "Yeah, I'm as tall as you now. Almost."

Sopater returns with the horses, Theophilus stands and remounts his, and the two men guide their mounts back onto the road. Luke trots alongside.

"Have you ever been to the Capidava Fortress, sir?" Sopater asks his senior.

"No. It is run by the Eleventh Legion. I do know that being on the Black Sea, it is both a naval port and guardian against the barbarians to the north. The Danube River, dividing us from Germanicus, ends at the fortress. They have supply ships that come up from the Aegean through the straits and into the Black Sea. They need an experienced man to direct the supply operation there, and that man is me."

"Do you think we can make it by tomorrow night?" Luke asks.

"We have made good time," Theophilus replies. "There is a possibility we can make it before they close the gates for the night."

Three wagons the same size and each being pulled by a single oxen pass them headed west.

"I'll bet there is wine in those barrels," Sopater says.

"Or perhaps olive oil," Theophilus responds.

"We are passing more wagons now. We are closer to our destination," Sopater says. "There is another *mille* marker up ahead. Do you think our horses need a rest?"

"Let's keep going. The inn should not be much farther," Theophilus says.

As the sun dips low in the horizon, they reach the inn. They leave Luke to take the horses around to the stable and go inside.

That taken care of, Luke goes inside, sees that his master is already seated with Sopater at one of the tables, and finds a corner to hunker down in.

He looks around, watches food and drink being taken to his master's table, and waits his turn at the leftovers.

He watches travelers come inside and disappear to their assigned rooms, and others appear from their rooms to sit at a table and be served an evening meal.

He can hear low talking among the guests. But a single word jumps out at him as though it had been shouted.

Luke stands and rushes over to the table from whence the word had come.

"Did you say Sigmundrr?"

The travelers look up at the slave.

"Excuse me, but I do not talk to slaves. Where is your master?"

Sopater approaches the strangers. "He is the slave of Tribune Theophilus at the table in that corner," he says, putting his hand on Luke's shoulder. "Now, I believe this young man asked you a valid question."

"Well," one of the traveler's says, "He was the slave of a centurion. That's all we know. The centurion seemed to beat on his slave a lot."

"What did the slave look like?" Sopater asks.

"He was a big man. Almost a giant. And he had long yellow hair."

"Vather," Luke says aloud.

The centurion squeezes Luke's shoulder. "Who was the centurion?"

"We don't know. We just remember he repeated his slave's name a lot, telling him how rebellious he was."

"Where did you see them?" Sopater asks.

"Seems like they were coming from either Parthia or Scythia. That's all we know."

"Thank you for your trouble," Sopater says, handing each man a drachma.

Luke runs over to Theophilus. "He's alive, Master. He's alive!"

7 ~ THE FIRST CLUE

"Sir, your slave is at it again," The aide of Legate Septimius Alvinius Nereus enters Theophilus' spacious *officium* and salutes.

"Sir, your slave is at it again," he repeats. "He is bothering the men in the fortress."

Theophilus sets his stylus down and looks up at the messenger from his ornate writing table. "He is harmless. Let him sing."

"No, sir. I am sorry, sir, but the legate says he must stop. Uh, sir, if I may say so, a lot of us like the song, but, well, you know."

"Yes, I understand. I will take care of it. You are dismissed."

Centurion Sopater, sitting at his own writing table, smiles when the aide leaves. "I'm surprised the old man has lasted these two years. I heard he doesn't even like music."

"He definitely is ill-tempered and sometimes downright grouchy."

"Shall I go out and find Luke? I need to check on my men to see if any need tent repairs anyway."

"Fine."

Centurion Sopater goes out to the main street of the fortress, which runs parallel to the shore of the Black Sea. He heads toward the tents of his men and hears him.

Tho I vander long avay
Over all da mounts und seas
To da end uv da verld,

I vill alvays dhink uv home
Und keep you in my heart
Till I hold you once again.

He approaches Luke. "Come with me," he says.

"Am I in trouble?" nineteen-year-old Luke asks.

"You could say that."

Luke follows behind the centurion. "I did all my work."

"How do you manage to remember the Frisian language after all these years?" Sopater asks as they approach the *officium*.

"That I will never forget. To forget my native tongue is to forget the song and my father. That I will never do."

They enter the *officium*. "Yes, Master?"

"You have had two years to determine that your father and no one your father ever knew is in our fortress. It is time to stop singing his song."

"Master, could I sing it in the village, and maybe go up the road along the Danube in case a traveler recognizes it?"

"I suppose that would work. Now, Luke, you seem to have too much time on your hands. From now on, you are to go down to the dock and inventory all the supplies being brought onshore."

"Master, some of the legionnaires already do that."

"Then you are to do it a second time. You have a better mind than all of them put together. You are good with numbers."

"Yes, Master."

A month goes by.

"Master, I am through with the inventory of wine casks brought in by the last ship."

"Fine," Theophilus says.

"Sir, I heard something odd among the sailors."

"Oh? Was it serious?"

"They were talking about the Parthians sending a lot of iron to a smelter in their country."

Theophilus stands. "What did you say? What smelter? Where?"

"A city named Batan or Banan or something like that.

That's all I know."

"Do you realize what they make with iron?" the tribune asks.

"Weapons, Master?"

"I believe Centurion Sopater has some work for you," he says, calling back over his shoulder. "I have to go see Legate Nereus immediately. Better yet, come with me. You are the witness."

Luke follows behind the tribune, and they go down the corridor to the legate's *officium*.

"I have an urgent message for Legate Nereus," Theophilus tells the clerk.

Having heard from the other side of the room, the legate calls out.

"Come," he tells his tribune. "But what is that damnable singing slave doing with you?"

Legate Nereus is a head shorter than Theophilus and broader in girth. He has high cheekbones, a straight nose, curly black hair, and carries himself with the bearing of a Roman patrician.

"He is the witness."

"You cannot take the word of a slave," the legate growls. "You know that. It is not admissible anywhere."

"He is honest. I have had him since he was eight years old and have made sure he always told the truth.

"Slaves do not tell the truth."

"This one does. You can believe whatever he tells you. Now Luke, tell Legate Nereus what you heard."

"Sir," Luke says, holding his arms straight by his side and trying to control shaking legs, "the sailors from the last corn ship to come in were talking about the Parthians sending a lot of iron down to some smelter in Parthia."

"You're not Roman. You can tell just by looking at you and that yellow hair. You are not one of us and never will be. You would like for us to be attacked and destroyed so you can go free. Admit it."

"Sir, I think he is talking about the Parthian city of Ecbatana that has a summer palace."

"Oh. Well, uh, you may be right. And your slave had

better not repeat this. Now go over and sit in that corner."

Luke obeys.

"I will make sure he does not repeat anything. May I ask where exactly the smelter is?"

"Ecbatana is not too far from the southern Scythian border and the Caucus Mountains," Legate Nereus says. "Then Ecbatana is sitting in a pass up in some Parthian mountains. The smelter could be anywhere in them."

The legate turns his back on Theophilus, then faces him again. "They already have iron mines down there. What do they need more for? This must be something big they are planning."

"Sir, may I make a suggestion? Do you think it would be advantageous for us to send a spy to find out exactly what is going on down there?"

"A spy, you say?" The legate stands and looks out a window toward the Danube River, where it empties into the sea. After some time, he turns.

"The spy could not look Roman. We have a few in our infantry that do not, but I doubt they'd be smart enough to carry it off."

"I know the exact person for us."

"You do? Name him."

"Luke, my slave."

"No! Absolutely not. Never. Cannot trust slaves."

Luke looks up from his seat on the floor, his eyes wide, takes a deep breath, and struggles not to smile.

"Sir, he brought you this information. He could have sneaked on board the ship and left with the sailors. In fact, he could have sneaked on board any of the ships that dock here, but in our two years here, he has never done so."

"Well, is he as ignorant as he looks?"

"He is highly intelligent. I have had him tutored in philosophy, science, mathematics, and physical prowess. He is an expert with the javelin, and can handle a sword almost as well."

Now is my chance. I can search for my father.

"Does he know their language?"

"No. But he knows one of the Germanic languages—

Frisian—as well as Latin and Greek. He is fast with languages, and I believe could pick it up enough to at least understand what other people are saying. If he does not speak it, they won't know he understands them and may reveal their secrets in his presence."

"Well, he certainly does not look like one of us," the legate says. "He could go around singing that dratted song of his and make everyone think he is a lunatic."

"Then you agree, sir?" Theophilus asks.

"Yes, I agree. But only under the condition that you guarantee his return."

"Sir, I am willing to put up nine hundred sesterces, a full year's wage for me. If he does not return within two years, the money is yours."

For the first time, Legate Nereus smiles. "In that case, make the arrangements."

The tribune and slave return to Theophilus' *officium*. They close the door. Theophilus turns toward Sopater.

"What you are about to hear will go no further than this room. Is that understood?"

"Yes, sir."

"Come over here."

The three men step toward three marble benches placed in one corner of the *officium*. The two officers sit on the benches. Luke sits on the floor.

"No, Luke. You are no longer to act like a slave. Sit on the bench with us."

Luke grins, stands, reseats himself on the marble bench, and puts his hands on each side as though making sure the bench is real.

"Now, Luke," Theophilus begins, "I have never given you a choice before, but I am now. What you will be doing is dangerous. You will have to pretend you are someone you are not. You will have to be on your guard at all times. If discovered, you will be tortured to death."

"Sir, I could dress like someone I am. I can dress like a Frisian."

"I am always amazed by you, Luke. Does that brilliant mind of yours ever slow down?"

"I don't know how to slow it down, Master."

"And you have to stop calling people master. Now, if you are going to dress like a Frisian, we will have to come up with high-topped leather boots and a leather tunic."

"The fort butcher and shoemaker should be able to take care of that," Sopater says.

"Good. Now we also need a cape for Luke. It must have many colors in it."

"We are so close to the southern border of Germanicus, there will probably be some men in the village out here with such a cape," Sopater says. "I can go there tomorrow and find out."

"No, you cannot do that. It would be suspicious for a Roman to be looking for Germanic clothing. Luke can do it. He can pretend he is traveling, and his was stolen from him while he was swimming in the Danube."

"Just think. I'll be my old self again," Luke jests.

"Well, I suppose so," Theophilus says. "Now, this is all for tonight. Luke, do you think you can remember enough of the Frisian language to speak it again?"

"Well, while I'm in the village tomorrow, I will listen to people as I walk through the market," Luke says. "If I recognize anyone speaking the Frisian tongue, I will make an excuse to sit nearby and listen to them. After a few days, I should be able to remember most of it."

"Fine. So, both of you have your assignments for tomorrow. While you are doing that, I will look over my ship-arrival schedule to see if I can find a ship headed south."

"I get to go on a ship?" Luke says.

"Indeed, you will. It is at least 600 *milles* to the south end of the Black Sea. That will be the easy part. Then you will have to walk through Scythia between the Pontic Mountain range on your right and the Caucus Mountain range on your left."

"Sir, he may need a horse in case he has to outrun highwaymen in those mountains or enemy soldiers."

"A horse for me?" Luke asks, still trying to digest everything that is happening.

"You are right, centurion. Tomorrow, after going to the

butcher and shoemaker, check out our supply of horses and select one that is surefooted and experienced in mountains."

"Yes, sir."

Centurion Sopater salutes and leaves. Right behind him are Tribune Theophilus and slave Luke who shut the door and head toward their respective quarters.

The next day arrives, and Luke is sitting on the floor by the door to his master's *officium* when Theophilus arrives.

"Couldn't sleep last night?" he says.

"How did you guess, Master?"

"Well, when you get tired enough, you will. You need to go on into the village now and find some Frisians to spy on. Once you have remembered your language well enough, you can use it to ask around for a cape."

Four days later, Luke reports in with a multi-colored cape. "It's just like the one my father used to wear."

"Let me hear you say something in Frisian," Theophilus says.

"Þórr heitir áss, ok er sterkr mjök ok oft reiðr. Hann á hamar góðan. Þórr ferr oft til Jötunheima ok vegr þar marga jötna með hamrinum. Þórr á ok vagn er flýgr. Hann ekr vagninum um himininn. Þar er Þórr ekr, er stormr."

"And what does it mean?"

"A god is named Thor. He is very strong and often angry. He has a good hammer. Thor often goes to Gianthome and slays many giants there with the hammer. Thor also has a carriage that flies. He drives the carriage through the sky. Where Thor drives, there is storm."

"Well done, Luke. I knew you could do it. Now there is a ship leaving for the south coast of the sea tomorrow. You will be on it."

"Are my boots and tunic ready?"

"They're right here," Centurion Sopater says from the other writing table in the room. He sets them on his table.

Luke walks over and checks them out. He pulls his tunic over his head.

"What are you doing, Luke? Put your clothes back on."

"But I want to try on the kind of clothes my father wore."

"No, you cannot take a chance of being caught," Theophilus says. "You will take them on board the ship with you. You will not change into these clothes until you get in the mountains, and no one is around."

"But we do have something for you right now," Sopater says. "Come outside with us."

Out on the street is a tan horse with long flowing mane. He is thick and stands the same height as Luke.

"He is a Nordic Voorde horse, and I was lucky to find one this tall," Sopater explains. "He is sure on his feet, agile, and can stand cold weather. He will get you through the mountains with no problem."

"May I ride him now, Master?"

"Yes, ride him all you want so you will get used to each other," Theophilus says. "Go outside the fortress and see what he will do for you. I will see you tomorrow morning."

Morning comes, and Luke reports to his master's *officium*.

"Here is a map of where you will be going," Theophilus explains. "You will go southeast through Scythian territory on the Anatolian Plateau until you reach the headwaters of the Tigris River. Follow the river almost to its south end. You will be on the Royal Highway; it is well marked. Head south to where the Tigris almost joins the Euphrates River at Opis—or maybe they call it Cunaxa now.

"Then you will go east on the High Road across the Zagros Mountains. They are high and usually have snow in them, so be prepared. Your leather tunic and high boots will help considerably. Just before entering the mountains, buy an extra cloak or two with a hood to help keep the wind off you. Follow this pass through the mountains until you reach Ecbatana.

"Be on the watch for wagons carrying ore and follow them. Also, go into the city and see what you can find out."

"The ship is ready, sir," Sopater says.

Theophilus walks Luke to the other end of the corridor and requests to see Legate Nereus briefly.

"You had better bring back something useful for us or don't come back at all," The legate says.

"Yes, sir," Luke replies.

Theophilus assures his superior Luke will do a fine job.

They walk out of the *officium* building together. Sopater is waiting for them out front with Luke's Nordic horse.

"Here are the reins, Luke. Your clothes are in the saddle pouch on this side, and most of your money has been sewn into the hem of your cape. There is a pack of enough food in the other saddle pouch to take care of you for about ten days. On the back of your horse is enough barley to keep him fed and content. Also on his back is a tent and a leather pouch with a blanket inside for you. When you take it out, you can use the pouch to water your horse."

"Here is a small pouch of money to carry with you," Theophilus says, "that should cover your needs for a couple weeks."

The three walk slowly down to the docks. There is only one ship—the *Armata*. Sopater looks at Luke and embraces him. "You will do fine, young man. You will do fine."

Luke looks over at Theophilus. "May the gods go with you," the tribune says.

"Which ones?"

"All of them?"

"All thousand?"

"Yes, all thousand. I will see you in a year or so. Make me proud."

"I will, Master. I will."

Luke walks up the heavy and wide gangplank of the *Armata*, leading his horse behind him. Sopater and Theophilus stand on the dock watching.

"He's only nineteen years old," Theophilus says. "What have we done?"

8 ~ THE SEARCH BEGINS

"Over here, sir," the crewman calls to Luke. "We have two stalls on each side of the ship. Choose one to put your horse in. You alone will be responsible for it, so I would recommend you never be very far from it. If you need to exercise your horse, get the captain's permission first, and only take it around the deck, led by its reins, not riding it. If we hit a storm, you will be responsible for keeping your horse calm. If he causes trouble, we will throw him and you overboard. Is everything clear?"

"Yes, sir. Vhat about vater?" Luke asks in Greek but with a heavy Frisian accent.

"The water of the Black Sea is drinkable," he replies. "Help yourself," he says, walking away.

"Und about how long to get to da shore?"

The sailor looks back over his shoulder and shouts, "Maybe six days."

Luke walks his horse toward the nearest stall. He does so very slowly with pauses to give him a chance to get use to the ship rolling on the waves. The stall is wide enough that Luke can stand in it next to the horse. He pats the animal on its nose and lets him nuzzle Luke under his chin. He takes a hand full of barley and feeds it.

"Dhere ve go," Luke says, practicing his Frisian accent.

Once he is satisfied the animal is at ease, Luke sits on the deck nearby.

"Let's see. We need to give you a name. What about Varsang—father's song? Yes, Varsang is now your name."

Luke watches the crewmen unwind ropes from the pilings and weigh anchor. The red sails are unfurled and snap in the wind. The captain is at the helm.

Before long, Luke realizes they have pulled away from land. He stands and takes one last look at the coast and realizes Tribune Theophilus and Centurion Sopater are still standing on the dock. He waves at them. They wave back.

A few passengers stroll past him, and he stands to introduce himself, just as Sopater had told him gentlemen do. "I am Lukvert from Germanicus," he says. He reseats himself before conversation, and inquiries into his business can begin.

Luke leans back against the front of the horse stall, closes his eyes, and dreams he is on his horse racing through the barley grass on top of a high cliff overlooking the Nordic Sea. He sees his father racing his black Frisian horse, much larger than his own. Then the two horses merge, so they are still two horses, but the same size, with black bodies and tan heads and tails.

"Oh, Vather," he says, waking himself by the sound of his own voice. He takes a deep breath of the sea air and sighs. "I vill vind you someday, Vather. I promise I vill."

The sun dips in the west, and Luke brings out a few more hands full of barley for Varsang and some grapes, which he knows will be the last fresh fruit he will have for the next week. His meal over, he pulls out the blanket, puts it on the deck, rolls himself up in it, and falls asleep for the night.

The next morning he wakens to crewmen shouting to each other in what he assumes is their morning routine.

He brings out a little more food for himself and Varsang. Then he takes the leather pouch off the back of Varsang to dip in the sea and give himself and Varsang a drink. But, noticing it is heavier than it should be, he looks closer inside and sees a large scroll.

Smiling and forgetting the water, he takes the scroll out and sits in his place on the deck. He unrolls some of it, reads the first few words, and throws it against the side of the stall.

"No. I vill not. Never. He cannot make me."

He squats, raises his knees, and puts his forehead on them, then raises his head back up.

"No!" he shouts at the sky. "I vill never do it. You cannot make me."

One of the crewmen walks by, trips on the scroll, and picks it up. Just before the sailor throws it into the sea, Luke grabs his hand and rescues the book.

"Keep it out of the way," the sailor warns.

Luke dips the now-empty leather pouch into the sea, takes a few gulps for himself, and gives the rest to Varsang. He then calls up to the captain at the helm asking for permission to walk his horse. Permission is granted, and he walks it around the deck three trips.

As he walks, he sings his father's song.

> *Tho I vander long avay*
> *Over all da mounts und seas*
> *To da end uv da verld,*
> *I vill alvays dhink uv home*
> *Und keep you in my heart*
> *Till I hold you once again.*

He looks hard among the crewmen. None are yellow-haired. None are giants. None are Luke's father.

Varsang back in his stall, Luke sits at his feet and toys with the scroll. He opens it. He reads that it was written by Aulus Cornelius Celeus. He sets it on the deck in front of him and rolls through it: A history of medicine, general pathology, diseases, parts of the body, pharmacology, surgery, orthopedics.

He grits his teeth, twists his mouth around, rolls the scroll back up, sets it on his folded blanket, stands, and pets Varsang.

He lays his head on the horse's neck. "Do you like to run?" he whispers. "I promise you we vill run. Run like da wind. But virst, we must go dhrough some mountains. It won't be bad, though, because we vill be between two mountain ranges. I dhink you'll like da mountains."

He sits back down and stares at the scroll on his blanket. He kicks it aside, walks over to the helm and asks the captain for permission to walk his horse. He returns, opens the stall door, and leads Varsang out. Together they walk, slowly, around the deck of the ship. Three times as before.

With Varsang now back in his stall, Luke squats next to his blanket and the scroll, closes his eyes, and dreams the man he killed at the hospitium is chasing him with the horn of a bull. Just as the horn begins to dig into his back, Varsang neighs and wakes him up.

He stands, gives Varsang a couple more hands full of barley, and watches him eat.

"I guess you vant me to give it anoder try too," Luke says to the horse. "I yust can't. I killed him because of my idiotic ignorance. How could I know da leaves vere good but da berries poison? I should have known better. Known. Knowledge. I lacked knowledge."

He stands at the railing nearby and looks out over the Black Sea. *The wind is in our favor. The ship seems to be making good progress. But how should I know? I've never been trained in seamanship?*

He watches the crew at their work. He notices two men argue, then pat each on the back, and resume their work together. He watches the captain give a tongue lashing to one of his officers, the officer salute in return, then they look at a chart together. *Forgiveness? Is dhat forgiveness?*

He looks at the scroll again, unrolls the first part, glances at it, then rolls it back up. He lays it back on the blanket, lays his head on the scroll and dreams. This time the man he killed is sitting on a cloud smiling. There is a woman at his side who seems to be his. There are children on his lap. He stands and salutes Luke. Then calls down to him, "Hey, there. Hey, there."

Suddenly Luke jerks and realizes he is back on the deck, and a sailor is calling down to him. "Hey, there. We need to swab the deck where you are. You need to move."

Luke sits up, grabs the scroll and blanket, and steps aside. He watches as the sailor throws water on the deck to clean it.

Then, without warning, he slips and cuts his ankle on a metal strip at the bottom of one of the horse stalls. The blood spurts out. Luke calls for help. Other sailors come to his aid and stretch him out on the deck.

Luke tears off one end of his blanket and puts it around the man's ankle. It is immediately soaked with blood. He tears off another piece, wraps it around the ankle, but it too is soaked with blood almost immediately.

The other sailors stand around him and watch. The captain comes over and watches. Luke watches. A short time later, the man stops wincing in pain, closes his eyes, and dies.

The sailors tie his arms close to his body, the captain says a few words to his god, and they throw the sailor's remains overboard.

In his helplessness, Luke watches the water

Not again. The first time because I was ignorant of what not to do. This time because I was ignorant of what to do. Ignorance. Ignorance.

Luke shakes his head back and forth, looking down at the deck, over at the sea waters, and up at the sky. He clenches his teeth. His brows turn down. He puts his hands on his elbows as though hugging himself. He presses his lips together, then looks back up at the sky.

"Varsang, vhat vould you do?" he asks, walking toward his horse and putting one arm over his big neck. The horse neighs and Luke laughs.

"Is dhat so? You vould, vould you?"

Giving into what he knows he must do, Luke sits down next to his blanket and the scroll. He opens the scroll and rolls through it until he finds what he is looking for: Surgery.

He narrows down his search to caring for gashes in the skin. It requires flax or linen thread and a needle. It also requires a small supply of wine, oil, or vinegar to soak bandages in. Luke knows what he must do.

From his seat, he looks around. Where can he get linen thread? No one is wearing linen. Then he looks down and smiles. *Of course, the hem of my tunic.* He works at the hem carefully so as to not break the thread. He ends up with three strands of linen thread. But what to use as a needle?

"Pardon me, sir," he says to one of the crewmen passing by. "Do you happen to know what cargo ve are carrying?"

"Well, there are barrels of amber down there. And entire compartments of oats and barley. And, well, I think there is a stall full of whale bones. Then maybe…"

"Perfect," Luke says, interrupting. "I vould like to buy a vhale bone."

"Mister, they are big."

"Vhat did you call me?" Luke asks, shocked.

"Mister."

"Oh. I thought you said someting else. Well, I yust need a small bone about da size of a finger or even smaller. I can pay you vor it."

"No need. There are splinters of bone laying around down there. Maybe tomorrow I can get some time to go down and get one for you."

"I vould like to pay you vor your trouble," Luke says.

"In that case, I guess I can go now."

Luke squats on the deck and waits.

Soon the sailor is back with several splinters of whalebone, and Luke gives him a copper coin. With the smallest bone, he creates a needle.

Hmmm. This one is large enough to provide something else I need. With the dagger at his side provided him by Sopater, he carves on the largest piece of bone and forms a hook. He carefully pulls several threads off his wool blanket, ties them end to end, then ties the last end to his hook. He steps over to the edge of the ship and lets his hook drop down in the water.

He waits.

Then comes the tug. Luke happily pulls up his thread, and on the end is a fish large enough for his dinner and to supply his other needs. He stops a sailor. "Do you know vhat kind of fish dhis is?"

"It's a mackerel. Good for eating and rubbing on whatever hurts."

"Tank you, sir," he says, handing the sailor a small copper coin.

Luke sits on the deck and splits open the fish. He looks around and realizes the stomach area is full of oil. He reaches into the pack with his leather tunic and boots and cuts a section out. He threads the wool from his fishing line through the needle he had made earlier and sews the edges together so that he has a small pouch. Carefully, he pours the fish oil in that.

He looks through the fish again. *Hmmm. I vonder if I can use da spine bone vor anyting? I dhink I'll save dhat. Und da skin. If I let it dry, maybe I can make anoder pouch out ov it.*

He looks back in his food pouch and finds a small bow drill. He pulls out some dried dung in the horse stall, sets it in front of him, puts his bow drill between his feet, spins it until it catches the dung on fire, and dangles the fish over it.

After eating his dinner and making sure Varsang has eaten and been watered, Luke reads a little more in the scroll about surgery. Darkness closes in, he puts his whalebone, fish hook, needle, and small pouch of oil in the larger pouch to take up the space where his grapes had been.

Morning comes. Luke eats, feeds and waters Varsang, takes him for a walk three times around the deck, resettles him in his stall, and pulls out his scroll.

"Listen to dis, Varsang. Celeus says to use a strip uv leather as a tourniquet to stop da flow uv blood in an arm or leg until da vound can be sewn up. I vonder if doing dhis vould have saved dhat man."

Luke recalls the day before—his day of decision--then returns to his book. "Hmm, dhis section is on medicinal roots, leaves, and berries," he tells his horse. "I vish I had known dhis dhat day. He vould be alive today if I had known.

"Celeus says in here dhat some patients vill die. Da physician has to know he did all he could, and go on to the next patient. I vill try to do dat, Varsang."

Each day is the same. Eating, exercising Varsang, reading, trying to remember, and collecting what he can of medicinal value to store in his food pouch, which is gradually becoming his medical pouch.

Then he hears it.

"Land ho."

The ship docks. The captain comes to Luke as the ship is anchored and secured.

"I have never seen anyone so absorbed in reading as you have been these six days. Well, whatever your destination, young man, good luck."

"Dank you, sir," Luke says, putting the rest of his belongings on the horse and preparing to lead him off the ship.

The ship captain holds out his hand. Embarrassed, Luke holds his out, and they grasp hands and forearms. The captain leaves, and Luke watches him.

No one has ever shook hands with me before in all my life. Is that what it feels like to be free?

Finally, the gangplank is put in place, and Luke leads his horse onto the shore. They stand in place a moment, getting used to not swaying with the waves. They take a few more steps and stop again.

Luke looks around. Toward the east, he sees the snowcapped Caucus Mountains, and to the west, he sees the Pontic Mountains, also with snow on the higher elevations. He decides to follow a Roman road going south across the high plateau between the two mountain ranges.

"Okay, dhis is it, Varsang. Ve vill look vor da iron mines und ve vill look vor my vather. May da gods watch over us. All tousand of dhem."

With the barley now used up, there is room for Luke on the back of his horse. He slides up on his back, and they head south.

Once out away from villages, Luke looks around to see if anyone is nearby. He leads his horse up into the trees, takes off his linen tunic, puts on the leather one, ties on his high leather shoes, and attaches his cape to his shoulders.

With the linen tunic and sandals tucked out of sight, Luke slides back up onto Varsang.

He goes back out onto the Roman road heading into a

strange world he has only heard about. A world of Scythians and Parthians. A world of iron and copper. A world of silver and gold. A world of free and slave.

"Vather, I am coming. Vait vor me, Vather. Vait vor me."

And as he makes his way into a future of the unknown, Luke sings.

Tho I vander long avay
Over all da mounts und seas
To da end uv da verld,
I vill alvays dhink uv home
Und keep you in my heart
Till I hold you once again.

9 ~ SOUTH

"Vell, Varsang, ve're almost dhere. Danks to your sure-footedness, you got us dhrough dhose mountains. Your long hair kept you varm; I'll bet you have been missing da cold air up in Frisia.

"I'm sure glad I had you to practice my Frisian accent on. Und I'm more glad we made it dhrough da cold und snow.

"Now ve are thirsty, aren't ve? Dhere's a well up ahead. Let's stop."

Varsang neighs, shakes his head, perks his ears, and goes into a high-stepping trot.

"Varsang, vhat has gotten into you? Oh, I see now. Isn't she a beauty? No vonder, you're in a hurry. Look at dhat shimmery golden coat on dhat filly."

As they draw closer to the well outside of Ecbatana, Luke sees a dark-haired beauty of the human sort. The moment she sees Luke, she slides up onto her golden horse, grins broadly, and takes off toward the foothills nearby.

"Ve cannot let such beauties get avay vrom us, Varsang. Get going!"

As Luke's horse draws closer to that of the lady, she looks back, then spurs her golden into a sprint. He chases her until she is in the higher hills.

When the climb becomes too steep for speed, she dismounts, turns her horse around, and leads it back down to flatter ground.

"Voo Voo, Varsang! Look at dat! One vor you and one vor me."

Luke waits for her return. He dismounts, then walks to her.

"Vhat is dhis beautiful horse uv yours named?"

"Wouldn't you like to know?" she answers, tipping her head to one side, grinning and looking up at the tall, yellow-haired stranger.

The young lady has black hair and black eyes with long eyelashes. Her hair is parted in the middle, and she wears a band around her head to keep her veil in place. She has long sleeves on her many-folded blouse and loose-fitting billowy trousers. Her face and clothes are full of dust.

"Shall I beg? Okay, I shall beg." Luke drops to his knees and pulls on Varsang's reins until he does his version of the same thing.

"You certainly have your horse trained," she laughs. What kind is he? He has such long hair."

"He is a Nordic Voorde."

"That explains your yellow hair, height, and funny accent."

"So I am funny, am I?" Luke responds. "I'll have you know dhat my horse, und I have yust arrived on serious business vrom my homeland."

"And yust vhat homeland is that?"

"You mock my accent. Vell, I'll have you know I have recently arrived vrom Frisia by the Nordic Sea. Have you ever been dhere?"

"Makes me cold, just thinking about it," she says. "It's cold and snowy enough here in the winter."

"So, are you going to make your subjects stay kneeling like dhis forever?"

The young lady in the white, dusty tunic positions herself directly in front of Luke, clears her throat, and slowly pronounces, "You may rise."

"By da vay, my name is, is um Lukvert. Und my horse is Varsang. Now, your turn."

"If you insist, I am Rashah, and my horse is Meira."

"Vhat kind of horse is yours?"

"She is an Akhal-Teke. We are famous here for our golden Akhal-Teke horses."

The two laugh as Luke's Varsang takes a few steps forward and nudges Rashah's Meira with his nose.

"Are you thirsty?"

"Oh, dhat is right. Ve Vere stopping to get a drink."

"I will go with you to make sure no one from around here harasses you."

"Vhy vould dhey harass me?"

"You look different from them and talk different from them. Actually, my people do not trust anyone but themselves."

"Hey, vhere did you get that beautivul golden bracelet? It is gold, isn't it?"

"Yes, it is. All my jewelry is gold. My father is the great Jotapa, overseer of a gold mine up in the hills north of here."

"Great, huh?"

"In his eyes, he is great. Would you like to come home with me? You can freshen up and meet him. He might even deign to let you eat with us."

"Da men und da vomen eat at da same table here?" Luke asks.

"We're not supposed to, but my mother died, and our servants don't tell. I give him someone to talk to while he consumes his favorite morsels."

"Vell, if you insist. But virst let me draw some vater vor you and your horse."

"How did you get to be so big?" Rashah asks Luke, watching the muscles on his arms flex as he pulls the bucket up from the water below.

"I don't know. I guess I got it vrom my vather. He vas a giant. At least he vas da last time I saw him."

"How long ago was that?"

"Eleven years ago. But I still remember him. His name vas, his name is Sigmundrr."

"Hmmm. Seems like I have heard that name somewhere," she responds.

Luke jerks around. "You have?" His eyes brighten, and a broad grin lightens his face.

"Oh, I'm not sure. And it was only once. I don't even remember when or where."

"Vell, I vill help you remember."

"How can you help me member? You don't know anything that is going on around here. You're a stranger."

"Dis is how."

Luke takes the bucket of water over to Rashah's horse, then stands, arms to his side, and looking up into the hills.

Tho I vander long avay
Over all da mounts und seas
To da end uv da verld,
I vill alvays dhink uv home
Und keep you in my heart
Till I hold you once again.

"That's so beautiful," Rashah says. "Where did you learn it? Is it a Frisian song?"

"Yes, und no," Luke says, bringing his attention back to the present. "It is my vather's song. He taught it to me und said dhat, if either of us vas ever kidnapped, ve should keep singing his song until ve are togeder again."

"So, this is why you are here in Parthia?"

"Mostly, yes."

"Well, our horses are good and watered," she says. "Hop on and follow me."

As they ride toward the city, Luke calls up to Rashah. "Aren't you going in da wrong direction?" He asks. "Da city is over dhere." He points to his right.

Rashah slows and lets Luke catch up with her.

"Well, yes, I guess you could call it a city. It's nearly a *mille* across. Inside those walls is the summer palace built centuries ago by Emperor Darius. They say the palace itself, the treasury building, the royal mint, and national archives are in there. King Vardanes may be in there right now. Or his brother, Gotarzes."

"Vat is dhat shiny silver on dhat roof?"

"You may not believe this, but Darius was so rich, he had silver tiles put on his palace roof."

"No vonder da vall looks so thick."

"It isn't just one wall. It has six walls around it. And I

mean literally around. They form a giant circle."

"A round city? Vell, no use trying to get in dhere. Let us go on into the commoner's city."

The two ride side by side the rest of the way to Ecbatana. Shortly, they arrive at the city gate. Rashah calls over to the guard. "It's all right. He is my guest."

"Are you sure? He's not Parthian."

"I'm sure."

"Do you guarantee he is not a spy?"

"Does he look like a spy?" Rashah says, tipping her head and twisting her mouth.

"Okay. He may pass. Just don't let your father get me fired."

Once inside the city, Luke sees a large stone lion. "Is dhat a cemetery he's guarding?" he asks.

"Yes, it is. Let's cross the river here to get on the residential side," she says.

They cross on a bridge and go past a market place. They reach a neighborhood of smaller houses, and Rashah turns to her left. When they arrive near the north gate of the city, Rashah takes them to a street going up a hill. At the top is a house with columns.

"Here we are," she says. "Home."

They dismount, and a stable hand comes out to take the reins of their horses. At the same time, Luke lets out a yelp, and Rashah smiles. They step toward the massive front gate. "Is dhat gold on your gate?" Luke asks, his eyes wide.

"Of course. The gate is covered with gold."

Having heard the stable hand's signal, a doorman opens the gate and bows as Rashah walks in.

"Where is Father? Is he here yet?"

"Yes, and he has someone with him."

Rashah walks into the solarium and finds her father talking with a man about Luke's age.

Jotapa rises and holds out his hands to his daughter, both of which don several gold rings. He is a big man with black-and-gray hair, a bulbous nose, and a gray pallor to his skin.

"It's about time you got here," he growls with a low

gravelly voice. "What are you doing wearing men's clothes again? Go change them."

He hears a cough behind him. "But first, you remember Pouritus, my assistant at the mine."

Pouritus stands in place. "Rashah, do I dare say it in front of your father that you are more beautiful than ever?"

The young man grins and bows deeply. He is wearing a gold pendant with the Zoroaster symbol of the winged guardian angel, which is now hitting his nose. He is of medium build, and his hair shines with olive oil, some of it dripping down his forehead.

Luke raises his hand to his mouth to conceal a snicker.

Rashah smiles. "Nice to see you again, Pouritus."

"I have a surprise for you, Rash," he continues. "Your father has granted me permission to give you lessons in shooting arrows like our warriors do—guiding your horse with your knees, and looking behind you to shoot your arrows at the enemy. No other warriors in the world can master it."

Jotapa clears his throat. "Since you, my daughter insists on acting and dressing like a man, you may as well learn to act like a warrior."

"You're the one, Father, who always wished your only child had been a boy," she says, pulling off the veil from her head and throwing it on a nearby bench. "So, I am just helping you fulfill your wish."

Luke clears his throat.

"Oh, forgive me for being rude. Father, I would like to introduce Lukvert to you."

"Hullo, kind sir," Luke says, bowing, unsure what else to do. *Centurion Sopater would bow. Maybe even my master would.*

"State your business in my city," the old man says with his gravelly voice. "And what are you doing with my daughter?"

"He is just traveling through," Rashah says, interceding.

"Where are you from? And I repeat, what are you doing

in my city?"

"I am vrom Frisia by the Nordic Sea, kind sir."

"Stop calling me kind," Jotapa barks. "And for the third and last time, what are you doing in my city?"

"Uh, well..."

"Speak up, or you will be imprisoned as a spy."

"I am looking vor my vather. I have not seen him since I vas a boy. He vas an expert svord maker."

Pouritus glances at his superior with dark eyes, and Jotapa returns his glance.

Luke notices. "He vas a singer vith no one his equal." He grins and shakes his head. "Vhy, no one could bellow out da old Norse songs like he could. All da other villages vere always vanting him to come sing at dheir festivities. Finally Caligula Caesar heard about him and recruited him to entertain at his palace in Rome."

"Then why aren't you in Rome?"

"Uh, I vent dhere last year, but dhey said he had been sold to da high priest of Mafdet in Egypt. I am on my vay dhere now."

"Makes no sense," Pouritus says, lifting his eyes up to the ceiling.

Realizing he has just raised yet more suspicion, Luke continues before he can be interrupted.

"I have relatives in da Black Vorest and vent to see dhem virst. By dhen I vas near da Black Sea so decided to go straight south bevore heading vest."

The old man approaches Luke, and the young man's yellow-haired head jerks back. Jotapa takes hold of Luke's shoulders, and the young man trembles inside.

Oh, no. I'm doomed even before I begin.

Rashah's father kisses Luke on one cheek and then the other. Rashah smiles.

"Any son as dedicated to his father as you are is to be admired and encouraged. Welcome to my home, young sir. And what did you say your name is?"

"Lukvert, sir. Lukvert."

"Now, about the arrow-shooting lessons..."

"Not now, Pouritus. We're hungry."

Jotapa puts his hand on Luke's shoulder and leads him to a side room where a servant waits with jars of water.

"As soon as they get all that dust off of you, and Rashah changes into proper dress, we shall dine. Then you shall spend the night here before you go on your way."

Rashah glances at Luke and winks.

"When you are done with their feet," Jotapa says to the servant, "go out to Lukvert's horse and bring his belongings to him."

"Oh, no need vor dhat," Luke says. "I vill do dhat so I can say goodnight to my horse. Ve have been through a lot togeder."

The next morning, Luke is escorted to the courtyard where maids are standing next to trays of grapes, cheese, whey, and bread.

"Ah, there you are," Jotapa says, already indulging. "Rashah will be here soon, and you can say goodbye to her."

Rashah descends steep stairs into the courtyard wearing a many-folded white silk dress. "Uh, father, Lukvert has never seen a gold mine. Do you think you could show him around? Then he can leave after that."

Luke looks over at her and smiles.

"I could go along so that, afterward, I can direct him back off the mountain and on his way."

"I suppose you already have a harness on your horse and are ready to go up there," Jotapa says to his daughter.

She grins.

"She has been talking about being my assistant at the mine someday, Lukvert," Jotapa says. "That will never happen. I would never get any work out of my men." He looks over at his daughter. "Well, I suppose. But you have to stay in my *officium*. I don't want you down in the mine where those naked men are."

"Naked?" Luke asks, his eyes wide.

"Oh, you won't have to take off your clothes. But by the time you get that far underground, you will wish you had. It's hot down there."

"I thought it vould be cold."

"Only at first," Jotapa says. "Then it gets hotter and

hotter the farther down you go."

"Vhy?"

"No one knows. Well, some priests say it is because we are digging down closer to the underworld fires."

After their morning breaking of the fast, the three head to the stables.

"Luke, can your horse handle the mountains?"

"He vas born in da mountains around the Nordic Sea. I dhink he is happiest in mountains."

Rashah hikes her many-folded dress up, and Luke notices she has trousers on under it. She grins at him.

After leaving the city, they stay on the main road for a brief time before veering off onto a wide path.

"Do vagons go up und down dhis path?" Luke asks the mine overseer.

"Yes, they do. We have very sure-footed oxen. However, we usually don't send the gold down at all. We take it over to the smelter, which is between this mine and another one."

"Two gold mines!" Luke says.

"No, they're not both gold. One is..."

Jotapa stops. "Well, you do not want to know all that. It must be boring to you."

They arrive at the mine and go into the *officium*.

"Rashah, if you want to be of benefit to me while we're here," her father says, "put those parchments on the floor over there in a decent pile and set them on my writing table. Then shake out the rugs; they're full of sand. Oh, and would you trim the candles?"

Jotapa looks over at Luke. "Down in the mine, some of the miners wear small oil lamps on their forehead, and others prefer candles with a small drip catcher, so they don't get burned. Follow me."

"Yes, mast...uh, sir," Luke replies.

The men leave, and Pouritus enters, his hair freshly greased. He smiles at Rashah.

"So, what do you think, dear?" he says, taking Rashah's hand. "I would make a perfect husband for you. Your father has known me most of my life, and I am sure he would give his permission. It's only natural."

"I like you a lot," Rashah replies. "We played together as children." She looks up into his dark eyes. "Perhaps, Pouritus. But there are still things I want to do before I start having babies for you."

"Like what? What is more important than marrying me and bearing children fit to be emperor of Parthia?"

She walks over to the basket of candles and begins to trim them.

"Well, I love to go riding every day, and that alone you would stop."

"Not right away, my dear. But eventually. I will build you such a magnificent house, you will never want to leave it. We will have servants to watch over you and..."

"You mean servants to keep watch and report..."

"No, nothing like that. You will be my queen. You will be pampered and given your every desire."

They hear footsteps and the door into the *officium* squeaks. Pouritus steps away from his intended.

"Well, what did you think?" Jotapa asks as he walks in with Luke behind him.

"It vas very interesting, mas...uh, sir."

"What was that song you were humming?"

"Oh, nothing. Yust a song my vather und I used to sing togeder."

"You took this stranger down into our mine?" Pouritus shouts. "What were you thinking? He could be a spy."

Jotapa smiles. "Now, does he look like a spy? I doubt he is more than perhaps eighteen years old. Nineteen at the most."

Luke smiles. "Tventy."

"I don't like it," Pouritus says. "You will regret this someday."

"Pouritus, do not forget who you are talking to," Jotapa warns. "Now, get to the mine and do your job."

As he leaves, Pouritus steps near Luke. "You will regret this," he whispers.

10 ~ CAUGHT

Rashah leads Luke down the mountain and through the city of Ecbatana. They leave out the south gate and head to the mountain pass he had used to get there. They stop at the well.

"I guess this is as far as I will be going with you," Rashah says.

They dismount.

"Are dhose tears I see?" Luke asks.

"Oh, Lukvert, I am torn. Pouritus wants to marry me. We have known each other all our lives. I have been thinking seriously of asking Father's permission. But now that I have met you and..."

Luke puts a finger up to her lips. "Hush, my little von. You should not be tinking such thoughts about someone you hardly know."

"Will I ever see you again?" she asks, looking up into his blue eyes.

"I do not know. I cannot know. My life is more complicated dhan you realize."

"It cannot be that complicated if you love someone," she responds.

"You love Pouritus. Dhat is enough,"

"Is it possible to love two men at the same time?"

"You love him. You do not love me. You have not known me long enough. Dhere are tings you do not know about me."

"I know enough."

Luke wipes a tear from her eye.

"You are young."

"I'll have you know I am fifteen years old," she counters.

Luke smiles. "Vell, you are still young. Vait to... Vhat vas dat?"

Luke swings around. "Oh, yust a lot uv horses."

"Run, Lukvert. Run!" Rashah shouts.

Stunned, Luke looks back at Rashah, then the approaching horses, then his own horse.

"Halt!" they hear. "Do not move, or there will be an arrow in your heart."

The horseman in front stops but stays mounted. Four armed men behind him dismount and approach Luke. As they attach chains to his wrists behind his back and around his ankles, the man in front makes the pronouncement.

"Lukvert, you are under arrest for spying."

"What?" Rashah says. "You have it all wrong."

"No, we don't. I have known all along, my dear, that he was a spy."

Rashah looks over at a sixth horseman who has just arrived.

"Pouritus, how could you?"

"It is for the best, my dear," he says with a sneer.

"I hate you, Pouritus," she says. "I have always hated you."

"Whatever. It does not matter. Your father has given his consent for us to marry."

Pouritus turns his mount back toward the city and gallops away, leaving behind dust, and fog, and a black mist that grows still darker.

A rope is snagged around Luke's neck and one of the soldiers ties the other end around his own waist. The armed men turn back toward the city.

"Where are you taking him?" Rashah screams. "You've got it all wrong," she calls out, running after them but falling farther behind.

"He doesn't deserve this," she groans as she stops where she is.

Rashah crumples to the ground and puts her hands

up to her face. "You've got it all wrong," she whispers.

"I vill be all right," she hears from a distance.

Luke breaks into a trot in order to keep up with the horse, and not trip. They go through the city to the north gate. They move off the road and veer onto a trail going in a different direction than the gold-mine trail.

"How far did he say to take this Norseman?" one of the thugs asks their leader.

"All the way to the iron mine. We will be paid when he is delivered."

They continue through the trees and arrive at a clearing. Though nearly dark by now, Luke sees a mud-brick *officium* and skinny men with long beards walk or lie around.

"We've got him delivered," the leader of the armed men says. "We want our money now."

"Not here. We don't want him. Take him to the gold mine."

"That will take half the night," the leader says.

"So be it. We don't want him here."

Luke panics. *What if my father is here. I must try.* As he is pushed away from the smelter and back into the woods, he bellows as loud as he can.

> *Tho I vander long avay*
> *Over all da mounts und seas*
> *To da end uv da verld,*
> *I vill alvays dhink uv home*
> *Und keep you in my heart*
> *Till I hold you once again.*

"Shut up!" One of the thugs shouts at Luke. "Just shut up."

Stumbling on the path with only the moon for light, they finally arrive at the iron mine.

"Welcome home," the leader says. He pushes Luke to the ground, takes the rope off his neck, and unchains him.

"If you run away, you'll be hunted down, brought back, and executed," another thug tells him.

Luke hears voices that seem nearby, but aren't. Voices

that snarl and growl like wolves. Voices that haunt the air, then die.

"Friend," Luke hears near his elbow. "Welcome to hell."

Morning comes. A tall but thin man calls out. "Okay, you rebels. Up. Here is your breakfast." He throws small loaves of bread in different directions, and men scramble to get theirs. Some take two, and those nearest him beat up the greedy ones.

"Better grab one," the voice next to him says. "That will be it until dark."

Having distributed all the bread, the tall, thin man cracks a whip. "All right, men. Down the hole."

One by one, the men are given a candle with a band around it. Each put his on his head, the candle to one side, and starts down the hole. It is dark. Luke feels a basket under his feet.

"Okay, it's full. Take it down."

The basket teeters. "Be still," one of the men barks, then coughs. "You want to dump us? It's a long way down there."

"Shut up, Haifa," someone else growls.

Quiet. Dark. Down. Slowly down. Swaying. A rope on a pulley above squeaking. The earth shifting and moaning on all sides.

"She's restless this morning," someone whispers.

"She doesn't like what we're doing to her. Gutting her. She's going to get us someday."

Luke feels the basket touch the floor of the mine. The men climb out. Someone shouts, and the basket is pulled up.

The sound of drip, drip, dripping. Voices hollow in the hollow earth. Smells of clay and rock and metal. Coughing.

They ease toward a small light. Luke is moved along by the men around him. He thinks they are taking off their clothes, but is not sure in the darkness.

"Take it easy, you dregs of the earth," he hears coming out of the blackness. "You'll get your chance soon enough."

It is Luke's turn. A man with an oil lamp looks up at

the tall young man. "New here, I see. Well, you have the candle on your head wrong. Move it over to the side. Now, lean over so I can light it. When the candle burns down, your shift will be over."

"Am I in da gold mine?" Luke asks.

"I'm afraid so, young man. This is where you will be spending the rest of your life. Wait here until I'm through lighting the other men."

Luke steps to one side and watches as each man—thin with a long beard and no clothes except his loin cloth—gets his candle lit and moves on.

"You may as well take your clothes off. It grows hot down here. The farther from the surface you go, the hotter it grows."

"But vhy?" Luke asks.

"Well, you're in the underworld. The underworld is where bad people go after they die. You're dead while you're alive, so get to go to the underworld ahead of time. Here, give me your candle while you undress."

The man busies himself pouring more oil in his lamp while Luke strips. He coughs as he does.

"You've got a leather tunic and boots," he says, turning back toward Luke. "Well, put them inside your cape and tie them around your waist the best you can. You'll need them tonight when it turns cold. And it definitely turns cold at night up there on the surface. Especially in the winter."

"Now here's a pick and hammer. Take these. Now walk behind me until you come to a wall. Look for yellow and hammer around it until it loosens. Slave boys will be by after a while to gather up what you've dug out of the wall and take them away."

"Tank you."

Luke walks carefully through the blackness with only his small candle lighting the way. He heads toward a point between two small lights, which he assumes are the candles of two men.

When he reaches the wall, he moves his head around to see if there is any gold in his spot.

"What are you waiting for?" a voice says several paces

from him. "Get to work."

"But I don't see any gold."

"Hammer anyway. There will be some back there somewhere."

"How long have you been here?" Luke asks.

"If it's any of your business, ten winters."

"When do ve get paid?"

"You idiot! You don't get paid. You're a slave now. We're all slaves. To the day we die, we will be slaves."

Luke falls to his knees, bows his head, and chuckles.

"What's so funny?" the voice asks. "You don't know how bad life can get until you are a slave. You are about to learn that lesson."

Luke leans his head back and breaks out into laughter that echoes around the chamber.

"Ha, ha, ha! Ha, ha, ha! Ha, ha, ha!"

"Okay, now that you got that out of your system, be quiet and get to work."

Luke controls himself, decides on a spot on the wall, and the sound of his hammer joins the sounds of countless other hammers chipping, chipping, chipping away at Mother Earth.

Twice a slave. They have enslaved a slave. What Homer could do with that in one of his epoch tales.

"Watch out below!" he hears from above and over his right shoulder, followed by rock crashing to the floor of the mine.

The voice next to Luke speaks again. "It's his job to climb the pillars we leave behind and check the ceiling with a long rod."

"Vhat pillars?" Luke asks.

"We don't mine everything. The superintendent or overseer comes down now and then and marks off an area on a wall about two or three man-lengths wide. We are not to touch it. We go around it. When we get two or three man-lengths deep on both sides, we can start breaking the wall behind it. That leaves a column."

"Vhat if dhere is gold in da column?"

"Doesn't matter. We'll go back and get it when they

collapse the column."

"How does da man get up to da ceiling?"

"Why all the questions? He makes notches in the column and climbs up. A really dangerous job. He jabs the ceiling all around to break off loose rock and calls down a warning so we can get out of the way."

"Vhat if a man doesn't get out uv da vay?"

"What do you think?"

"Hey, shut up over there," someone says, then coughs.

The rest of the day is spent hammering and chiseling, hammering and chiseling. Gradually men's candles flicker and begin to go out. A large light from an oil lamp appears. "All right men. Turn in your tools and get outa here so the night shift can come in."

Luke walks in the darkness toward the brighter light.

"I see you made it through your first day," the day-shift supervisor says. "Well, don't worry. Tomorrow will be the same."

Luke is pushed along by other men crowding around him. Men with the scent of sweat and urine and vomit. Men whose lives no longer have meaning. Living only to get another morsel of bread so they can do it all again the next day and the next. Men doomed to a nothing existence until the day they die. The welcomed day they die.

"All right, we have room for one more man in the basket," a miner growls out and coughs. Someone shoves Luke, and he climbs into the basket.

"Okay, pull us up" a booming voice bellows. Someone rings a bell five times. The basket moves.

When they reach the surface, it is dark, though not as dark as the hole they just climbed out of.

Luke sees men drop to the ground and put their clothes back on. Luke chooses a spot and squats.

"Hey, that's my spot."

Luke moves several paces.

"Hey, get outa there. That's my spot."

Luke steps aside and waits until he thinks everyone has gone to his spot, then chooses one for himself. No one bothers him. He squats and puts on his clothes. More tired than he ever remembers being, he wraps his multi-colored cape around him, turns over on his side, and falls asleep.

"Hey, you'd better eat that chunk of bread before someone else gets it, namely me."

Another voice.

Luke wakens with a start, sits up, and feels around the ground until his hand touches the small loaf of bread. He eats it, then falls back to sleep.

He dreams he is running across the silver roof of the palace, but a mountain lion is after him. He finally leaps over to one of the walls and goes round and round and round in circles. The mountain lion catches up with him and opens its mouth wide, his teeth threatening.

The lion's head changes, and now it is Pouritus. Luke turns to face his enemy, but now the lion is laughing at him. Luke lunges at the lion and suddenly feels cold. He awakens and finds that someone has stolen his cape. He hugs himself to keep warm, and once again falls asleep.

Morning. Luke rises, eats his morsel of bread, and follows the other men to the shaft.

"Hey, you. You with the leather on."

Luke turns to see Pouritus. "Follow me. I have a special job for you."

Luke follows him around to one side of the mountain where there is a small tunnel.

"We need another air adit. You're going to dig it. Well, you're going to chisel it. We estimate it is twenty man lengths from here to the inside of the mine.

"If you haven't chipped away two man-lengths by tonight, you will stay here until you do. Tomorrow you will do the same thing—two more man lengths in. It is up to you how you get the chips out."

"May da tousand gods punish you," Luke pronounces.

"Ha! The one and only god has blessed me. Rashah will be my wife by the next full moon. And you will be down in the mountain, scampering around like a rat."

"I vill vind a vay out."

"Ha! Rashah will bear my children, and you will still be down there."

"You dhink I am stupid. I am not. You vill pay."

"Ha! I will build my empire and rule not only the city, but all of Parthia, and you will still be down there rotting."

"No!"

Pouritus throws his arm back and then forward. The whip lands on Luke's face. Luke puts his head down into his hands.

"Now, get to work, or the next one will be my sword."

Luke falls to the rocky ground, sees a small hammer and chisel, and begins to work his way to the inside of the mountain.

Another man approaches.

"Make sure he stops for nothing, Pouritus tells the guard. "If he tries to escape, kill him."

At first, Luke kneels to get the hole for the air adit started. When he can no longer see what he is doing, he turns over onto his back and eases into the beginnings of the narrow tunnel.

He chisels beside his shoulders, then chisels overhead. The granite chips fall on his chest and face. When he can no longer breathe because of the dust, he works his way out of the horizontal hole, bringing the chips with him.

He stands, shakes off the chips, takes a deep breath, returns to his back, and scoots once again into the beginnings of the tunneled air adit.

As he works his way in deeper, it becomes almost impossible to breathe. Luke comes back out and looks around.

"What are you looking for?" his guard asks him. "If it's food, you are out of luck. If it is a weapon, you are out of luck."

"I vas hoping to see a piece uv cloth to wrap around my head in dhere."

"Well, I've got a big handkerchief I don't want. Take it, but do not tell anyone, especially my boss. You saw how mean he can get."

"You talk mean, but you are not," Luke responds, taking the handkerchief from the guard. He wraps it around his head and re-enters the tunnel just wide enough he can work his way into it.

The sun sinks low in the horizon. Luke feels a tug on his foot. He works his way out of the air adit.

"I told you what you had to accomplish today, and you have not done it," Pouritus declares. "You will not get any supper until you have gone in two man-lengths. If you have to work all night to get it done, you will work all night. Then tomorrow morning, you will start all over again. Now get back into your hole."

Pouritus turns to the guard. "You will be relieved shortly."

Days and nights merge for Luke. He finds himself falling asleep in the narrow tunnel. To keep himself awake, he sings.

> *Tho I vander long avay*
> *Over all da mounts und seas*
> *To da end uv da verld,*
> *I vill alvays dhink uv home*
> *Und keep you in my heart*
> *Till I hold you once again.*

"Vather," he calls out each time the song ends. "Help me, Vather. I need you, Vather."

"Sir," the guard tells Pouritus the third day as the sun dips below the horizon. "He has to get some sleep."

"Whose side are you on?" Pouritus snaps.

"I am on your side. That is why he must get sleep. No human can go without sleep and survive. He is the strongest man you have. He will get the adit chiseled out in time if he is allowed to sleep sometimes."

"Well, maybe you're right. Even rats sleep sometimes, I suppose. Okay, the next time he comes out to dump the chips, let him sleep. But chain his leg to your leg in case he tries to escape. Am I clear?"

"Yes, sir."

"And he is not to sleep every night. Let him sleep every other night."

"Yes, sir."

"And when he is done here, I want him back down in the mine. This time he will be the one climbing the columns to get loose rock down. And if he falls to his death, he falls to his death."

11 ~ COLLAPSE

Two years pass. The men are coming up out of the mine. Luke does not settle in his regular spot right away.

"Have you seen Pouritus?" he asks the guards in the local Aramaic language but still with his Frisian accent.

"Not me."

"I haven't."

"You'd be better off not talking to him."

"Yes, I have. He is in the *officium*. But I wouldn't go in there. Wait until he comes out."

Luke squats on the ground and watches the *officium*. Finally, he sees the door open and hears laughter.

"That'll show them," Pouritus says to someone still inside. He closes the door behind him and walks toward his horse.

"Sir. Pouritus, sir," Luke says, catching up with him. "I need to tell you someting important."

"So, it is Lukvert. There is nothing you could possibly know that is important.

"But, sir, da noises inside da mountain grow louder. Ve have all noticed dhem."

"That's normal. Now leave me alone," he says, calling over his shoulder.

"Sir, dhere is more vater coming dhrough cracks, und the cracks are getting larger."

"Patch them."

"Da supervisor has had dhem patched, but dhey grow larger anyvay."

Pouritus stops walking. "Go crawl back into your hole.

Now leave me alone."

"But, sir."

"Why don't you jump down the shaft and see how far you can go before you hit bottom."

Pouritus mounts his horse and heads down the mountain.

The next day the miners do not rush to enter the basket.

"The mountain. She is moaning too much."

"We have invaded her too many times."

"She is fuming and crying through the walls."

"She is bleeding from all those rocks falling from the ceiling."

"She is shaking with fever."

"She is about to turn on herself and die."

"And us with her."

"Lukvert, what do you think?"

"I climb to da ceiling every day. I hear and feel tings. Da mountain is svaying. Da mountain is becoming dizzy. Da mountain vill fall down vrom its dizziness."

Nothing more is said. The men ride the rest of the way down to the stope they are working in. Silently their candles are lit. They pick up the tools they will need that day. They strip, tie their clothes around their waist, then begin the routine.

No talking. No laughing. No yelling. Nothing. Quiet. An eerie quiet.

Clang. Clang. Clang.

"What was that?"

Everyone stops.

"Listen."

"Oh, it's nothing."

Back to work.

Clang. Clang. Clang

"Vatch out below," Luke calls out. The men scramble.

"It got me! My arm! I can't lift it!"

The voice heads in the direction of their supervisor. The supervisor wraps something around the injured miner's arm.

"Stay here the rest of the shift. If you leave early, you will be hung."

Back to work.

Clang. Clang. Clang.

An hour passes. Another hour. Another. But what is time?

Pounding. Listening. Pounding. Listening.

"It's flooding!"

A man comes running through the drift from the stope deeper in the mountain.

"Quick, everyone," the shift supervisor calls out. "Grab as big a rock as you can and block the drift into that stope."

Each man fumbles around in his darkness near his feet, looking for the largest slab of rock he has taken from the mountain, and runs with it in the direction of their supervisor's larger light.

The drift is narrow, and only two men can get into it at a time. As each man runs into it toward the fast-flooding inner stope, a previous man runs out to get another rock.

Sweating. Breathing hard. Straining muscles. Trying to stay alive.

Finally, they hear the words. "The drift is completely blocked off. Go back to work."

Once again, the pounding and listening, pounding, and listening.

Time for the next shift to take over.

The men climb into the basket and take themselves out of the earth like moles.

"Has anyvon seen Jotapa?" Luke asks. "Have you seen Jotapa?"

"You are not allowed to talk to him."

"Has anyvon seen Jotapa?"

"I'd avoid Pouritus if I were you."

"Has anyvon seen Jotapa?"

Luke walks up to the *officium* door and knocks. Jotapa himself answers and stands in the doorway.

"Lukvert. What's going on? What are you doing here? I thought you left to find your father years ago."

"Sir, da mine is getting ready to vall in on itself. Da

mine is groaning, and creaking. Da mine is moaning, and crying."

"I do not believe it is that serious. This mine has been going for twenty years. It has never collapsed."

"But, sir."

"What are you doing here, anyway? You've got dust all over you. I thought you were in Egypt by now."

"No, sir."

Jotapa pauses. "Ohhh, I get it. You both wanted my daughter. That rascal Pouritus."

"Sir, da men do not vant to return into da mine."

"Well, I tell you what, Lukvert. Since it is you and I always liked you—though I never completely trusted you—I will check it in a couple days.

"Too late. We vill all be dead dhen."

"Nonsense, Lukvert. I have been overseer of this mine since gold was discovered in it twenty years ago. Never any serious problems. Now go back to where ever you came from."

Jotapa backs a few steps and closes the door.

Luke returns to his spot, puts his clothes back on, eats his bit of bread, turns over on his side, puts his arms around himself, and falls asleep. He does not dream.

Morning. Time to return to the belly of the mountain—and their grave. Will it happen this time?

The basket sways more than usual.

"Who's moving around?"

"No one. It's the mountain. She is nervous."

Once again, they get their candles lit, take their tools, and go over to their part of the wall they will begin anew to assault.

Mountain, it is nothing personal. Mountain, won't you share with us? Mountain, we are trying to be gentle. Mountain, don't be angry.

Luke grabs his long rod, ties it to his back, and climbs the footholds up one of the columns to check the ceiling for loose rocks.

More than usual he hears the creaking and groaning of the mountain. More than usual, he hears rocks falling and bouncing somewhere that cannot be seen.

Months earlier, he had been able to attach metal nets to parts of the roof. This morning he sees they have been torn through. It has been a hard night for the mountain. A sad night of weeping and unending tears falling down.

Does he dare poke and prod the mountain until it can take no more? Do the men below dare chisel one more hand span away from the mountain's face? How much more can the mountain take?

A rumble. The mountain shaking. Men stop their work. Hang on to the mountain that no longer wants to be friends. The whole stope quivers. Then stops.

Silence for a while.

"Get back to work," they hear their shift supervisor call out.

"But, sir."

"If the mountain doesn't kill you, our boss will. Now, get back to work."

Pounding.
Listening.
Pounding.
Listening.

Luke works his long rod around the ceiling, poking and prodding loose rocks to fall so the men below will at least get a warning before it happens.

He climbs down and goes to his supervisor.

"Dhere are too many loose rocks. I am making tings vorse."

"Well, there is more water coming up in that crack over your left shoulder. Go over there and see if you can patch it."

Luke finds the leak. A pool of water has formed in a low place below it. The water in the pool is vibrating.

Another rumble.
Silence.
The mountain screams in pain.
A loud crack.
Then the blast.
The air blows up like a cyclone.

Luke and the other men are plastered to the nearest wall. Their breath is taken away. Their ears explode.

Blinded. Deafened. Choked. Covered with dust a hand-span thick.

Miners now on their knees. Crawling. Over rocks. Over each other. Over the final tears of the mountain. Not knowing where to go. Just crawling to feel still alive.

Chaos. The mountain continues to groan and scream to feel still alive. But now a monster out to destroy her destroyers.

More water coming in from the walls. The mountain crying in pain.

The supervisor calls out in the darkness. "I need a count. Call out your name."

The miners comply. But not enough. Only eight left alive.

"Look for air coming in," the supervisor orders.

"I dhink I see light," one of the survivors shouts.

"Keep talking so we can find you," the supervisor says.

Instead, he sings. In the dusty cloud, he sings and chokes. It is a graveling sound. But he sings.

> *Tho I vander long avay*
> *Over all da mounts und seas*
> *To da end uv da verld,*
> *I vill alvays dhink uv home*
> *Und keep you in my heart*
> *Till I hold you once again.*

Once all eight have arrived, Luke, the tallest, reaches up toward the small light. He takes one stone near it and carefully moves it out of its place. The other stones around it shift and fall toward the men. They move out of the way.

The light is gone.

"What did you have to go and do that for, Lukvert?"

"Now, we're doomed for sure."

"We're going to die of suffocation."

"If the rising water doesn't drown us first."

"Vait. I vill try again."

"What's the use?"

"He can't make things worse," someone chokes out. "We're doomed if we don't get out of here."

Luke reaches up to a rock above where he had seen the light. It does not move. He feels around to each rock until he finds one that is already loose. He loosens it a little more. The other rocks around it do not move. He nudges it even more. Having completely brought it out of its place without disturbing the other rocks, he hands it down to the man nearest him and begins a relay.

He feels around and finds another rock already loose and repeats the procedure. One by one, Luke removes rocks until the light is back.

"But will it last?" a miner says, his throat assaulted by the clinging thick cloud of dust.

"It could disappear again," another man chokes out.

"Hullo, up dhere!" Luke calls out.

Nothing.

"Hulo, up dhere!"

"Hullo. Can anyvon hear us?"

"Wait," someone says. "I think I feel your poking rod by my foot."

Several of the miners move toward the voice, still on their knees, and help pull rocks off it.

"Oh, no. We broke part of it off."

"Hand up vhat you have."

By the little bit of light shining through the small opening, Luke finds it and pushes it through the hole.

For the next hour, Luke moves the pole around to help it be seen from the surface, and calls up, "Hello. Anyvon hear me?"

His voice finally gives in to the unrelenting cloud of dust now assaulting both his lungs and his throat.

"Lukvert, we'll take turns."

After all eight have had a turn with swinging the rod around above the hole and calling up into the outside world, they give up. Their voices are ruined. They settle at the bottom of the sparse opening of light and air and try to sleep.

"The light is gone," someone finally croaks.

"Maybe it's night," another says.

They fall silent again.

Somehow, light returns to the little opening. With the thick dust still clinging to the air, the miners still can no longer speak. They take turns holding the rod through the hole and moving it around.

The light disappears again, they stop and rest, and wait once more for another day to come.

When the light is back, one of the miners hands a multi-colored cape up to whoever is working the rod. He understands and ties it to the top. It is Luke's turn, and he recognizes his cape.

Well, that's one way to get my cape back.

9All day they take turns waving their rod with the red and blue flag now on it. By now, their voices are back, though weak.

"Hello! Hello! Can anyone hear us?"

They hear voices from above.

"Over there! I think I hear something."

"Hello! Yes! Hello up there! Can anyone hear me?"

They hear a voice from the outside world. "There it is! See the flag? It's moving. It's coming up from below."

A few rocks are moved aside from above to make the opening larger.

"Vait," Luke calls up. "Da rocks down here are shifting too much."

"Okay. Try to move the shifting ones," a rescuer calls back down, "then we'll move a few more up here."

First, bread and water are sent down the hole. Then a routine is set in motion, and the opening made larger.

"Demeter, you are the smallest among us," the supervisor croaks with his scratchy voice. "See if you can get through."

The others help Demeter climb up to the opening without shifting too many rocks out of place. He raises his arms, hands from above reach down, and he is pulled through the opening.

Cheers from outside.

"No von else is dhat small. Ve need to make it larger."

The routine is set up again. For the first time since the collapse, the miners hope.

Night.

"We cannot see."

Someone hands down candle holders with straps for the men to put around their heads then lit candles.

The trapped miners resume their work of moving rocks a finger-span at a time.

"Now, let's try it," the supervisor finally says.

A second miner works his way up to the opening, and those below help push him up. He raises his arms, hands from above take hold of him, and he is brought to the outside surface.

Cheering from above ground, but not below. Each prays to his god to live again. Luke prays to his dhousand gods.

More moving and clearing out of the way. More testing and switching and finding and moving and making the opening into the real world large enough for them all.

One by one, the miners are helped by their peers to reach the opening and escape. Finally, two are left—the supervisor and Luke.

"Let me go last. I am da tallest. I can do it alone."

"Are you sure?"

"I vill escape wit da rest uv you. I vill trust all my gods und dhey vill help."

12 ~ COMPASSION

Now outside, Luke looks around through the ash from the mountain that is still falling like snow and sees the damage the mountain has caused above ground. Gray ash everywhere, even in the tops of the trees. Quick graves for the dead. Injured workers lying helpless.

He sees a dust-covered injured man in the lap of someone who appears to have come up from the city. Luke walks over to them.

"He has a broken leg. No one knows how to fix it. He will be lame the rest of his life."

"I dhink I can help," Luke says with a low, hoarse voice.

He squats in the hand-span-deep ash from the mountain and notices a broken bone protruding from the side of the injured worker's leg.

"Dhis is going to hurt a lot," he warns. "Can you handle it?"

"The man from town moves aside and slams his fist into the injured man."

"Vhat did you do dhat for?"

"He is unconscious now. If you can help him, do it now while he doesn't know it."

Luke pushes the broken bone back into position. "Are dhere bandages anyvhere?"

"Hey," the man from the city calls out. "We need bandages over here. This man can fix wounds."

Someone arrives with a basket of white linen strips.

"Are you a physician?"

"Not exactly. Don't you have a physician anyvhere in da city?"

"There is one at the palace, but he is not allowed to tend anyone but the royal family. One of the rich families owns a physician, but he has gone out to the Salt Desert east of here to gather some medicinal plants."

"Virst, vater. Und vine so the wound doesn't get vorse. Und a strong stick."

The man with the basket pulls a vial of wine out while another nearby fetches a stick.

Luke pours the wine over the wound and stick, holds the splintered bone in place, and places the stick beside it while the other man wraps it with strips of white linen.

"Attention, everyone, the man with the baskets says, standing. "We have a physician among us."

"I am not," Luke protests. No one hears his gravely voice.

"Over here! This man's arm is broken."

"Over here! This man's head is bleeding bad."

"Over here! The blast made this man blind."

"Over here! This man lost his foot."

The rest of the day, Luke moves from man to man, doing what he can.

Oh, tousand gods. Do not let anyone die because of me.

Night comes. He lies flat on the ground and dreams. He is back in his childhood home and piling up wood from the far end of the longhouse for the fire pit. His father is putting together his favorite stew.

"Lukvert. Da stew is ready. Come, Lukvert. Lukvert. Lukvert."

Luke opens his eyes and sees above him Rashah. "Follow me. Quickly," she whispers.

She grabs Luke's hand. He stands and follows her as she makes her way through the ash and shadows, dodging sleepers and rocks and fallen trees.

She continues on into the woods. They make their way down an unseen path. Sometimes in the darkness, they stumble over an uprooted tree, then stand back up. On through the forest they stumble and walk, stumble and walk.

As daylight edges its way up a new gray sky and the blood-red sun shows its face through the ash-filled air, they stop.

Rashah turns and looks up at Luke.

"We're here. You're safe."

She moves some bushes aside and exposes the low mouth of a cave. Near the entrance is a torch she had set in a pottery stand just before leaving to rescue Luke. She rescues it before it finishes burning out and uses it to light a fresh torch.

Now inside, Luke no longer has to bend his head. The ceiling is so high, he cannot see it. They walk a little farther back in the cave, and Luke sees a bed set up, several baskets of food, a pile of clothing, and some jars of water.

"You will stay hidden here until I come back to let you know they have stopped searching for you. And, oh my darling, I have missed you. What Pouritus did to you is unthinkable. It took me a while to find out where he took you. When I did, I told my father I never wanted to see him again."

"He told me you married."

"He lied."

"Dhank you, Rashah. Dhank you. Dhank you."

They look into each other's eyes, then Rashah draws back.

"Here are a couple of benches, so we don't have to sit on the cold ground."

"Dhat is good," Luke responds, not knowing how to thank her and wanting to.

"The clothes I brought you are Parthian, of course. Now, to make you better disguised, I brought some blackener from my father's scribe. Put it all over your hair so you will look like us. Nothing we can do about your blue eyes.

"To dye your hair, put some blackener in a jar of water, lean way over, and pour it over your head. Do not touch it with your hands unless you want them to be as black as your hair.

"We can decide later where you can escape to. I have a black goat-hair tent for you. In the hem of the tent is enough silver to take care of your expenses for a year.

"Oh, Rashah, how can I dhank you?"

They hear a noise from deeper in the cave. Luke's eyes dart toward the blackness.

"Oh, and there is one more thing," she says with a giggle.

"Vhat vas dat?" Luke says, straining to hear it again. "Ve have been found out."

Rashah whistles, and Luke hears clomping of hooves.

"Varsang, is dhat you?" Luke's eyes widen, he forms a broad grin and rushes toward his horse.

"Well, you wouldn't get far on foot," Rashah says, her eyes laughing.

Luke lays his hands on Varsang's nose and pats him. Varsang neighs and nods his head up and down.

"Ha, ha," Luke responds. "I am glad to see you, too, my old vriend."

He moves around to the horse's side, lays his head on Varsang's neck, and pats his back.

"Oh Varsang, I dhought I vould never see you again. Vould you like some vater?"

Luke looks at Rashah. She hands a large bowl to him and points to a jug of water. Luke set the bowl on the floor of the cave and fills it.

"Come here, my Varsang. Come und get it."

Rashah lets out a whistle. "Ah, here is my Meira. She will want a drink too."

"Ah. You have her here, ready to take you back down to da city,"

"Yes," Rashah says, sitting back down. "Now, sit and tell me what has been going on in the mine."

"Not much to tell. I tried varning your vather und Pouritus both, but dhey did not listen. Ve knew it vas coming. Now, tell me about you."

"I have been praying for you."

"To da tousand gods?"

"No, of course not. There is only one god."

"Von? Dhat cannot be. How is he going to know vhat to do vhen I need help traveling or getting my next meal or escaping an enemy, or even making it rain?"

"He can do all that because he made the world in the first place.

"Vhat is his name, so I can get to know him?"

His name is Ahura Mazda. He is order, truth, and justice. He sees all things, hears all things, and does all things.

"I do not understand," Luke says, his brows scrunched together.

"Ahura means Lord Creator, and Mazda means Supreme Wise One."

"How do you know dhis?"

"In the mystic hymns of Zoroaster called the *Gathas*. I memorized them. There are two hundred stanzas, but I know them all. Would you like to hear them? They are beautiful."

"Ov course, I vould. Anyting you vant to recite out ov your beautivul lips, I vill listen to, even if it takes hours."

Rashah stands, puts her hands behind her back, and begins. Her voice is lyrical.

"I approach you with good thought, O Mazda Ahura, so that you may grant me two existences—that of the material and that of thought—the blessing emanating from Truth...."

Luke watches her lips as they move to make their different sounds. He watches her nose as it sometimes wrinkles. He watches her eyes as they sparkle.

"Let good rulers assume rule with actions of Good Insight, O right-mindedness. Let not bad rulers assume rule over us...."

Rashah paces from one side of the cave to the other. When she turns, her many-folded silk dress swooshes.

"Truth is the best good. As desired, what is being desired is...."

Now Rashah stands in the center of the cave right in front of Luke, holds her arms out to her side, and spins in place, her eyes looking to the ceiling and beyond.

Luke drinks it all in.

"Brilliant things instead of weeping will be for the person who comes to the truthful one. But a long period of darkness, foul food, and the word 'woe'—to such an existence your religious view will lead you, O deceitful ones."

Rashah stops in front of Luke and puts her arms behind her back. "Well, how did you like them?"

"Vell, I did not understand everyting. I shall have to dhink about it."

"I'm getting hungry. Do you want something to eat, Lukvert?"

Rashah moves over to a basket, takes the lid off, and places grapes and figs on the lid. "We need to eat the fresh food first," she says.

"You are too good for me, Rashah."

"I love how you say my name. Say it again."

"Rashah, the sun is getting low. Maybe you should go back down into da city bevore your vather starts to vorry."

"You are right, of course, Lukvert. But I do not want to leave you."

"You must, or you vill arouse suspicions."

"I will come back tomorrow. I promise." She leaves.

Alone now, Luke looks around the cold cave for a blanket. He finds two. He hears the mountain wind blow through the trees outside and is grateful for his shelter and fire. And for Rashah.

Morning comes. Luke hears neighing outside the cave's entrance. Suspicious, he takes Varsang with him to the dark back of the cave.

"Lukvert. Are you here?" It is his beloved Rashah.

He walks forward, holds out his hands to her, and they touch. How he wishes he could hold all of her close to him. But he fears, if he squeezes too hard, the image of his dreams will disappear.

"Come in, my little von," he says.

"Rashah," Luke says. "Vould you mind iv I asked your vather to let me marry you? I vould be good to you. I promise."

"Oh, Luke. Yes. Yes. Yes. I want to be your wife. After they are through looking for you, perhaps we could go back to your homeland."

"No, I cannot."

"Why?"

"Is it true, Rashah, dhat your people are bringing iron ore to your smelter on dhis mountain from countries to da north? Do you not have enough iron in your own mine?"

"Well, I guess they are. I have noticed a lot of wagons filled with swords going out to the palace. But, I thought they just wanted to protect themselves more. And what does that have to do with going to your homeland after we marry?"

"Vell, I dhink dhay are planning a var with da Scythians or Romans. Rashah, I need to go back to my master und report vhat I found out about it."

"Your master? Lukvert, what are you talking about?"

"I must be truthful vith you, Rashah. I am a slave. I belong to Tribune Titus Pontus Theophilus of the Ninth Legion of Rome. The Romans do not vant war with Parthia. They are too busy keeping Germanicus and Espanola under control, and taking over Britannia."

Rashah stands and backs up.

"Lukvert, where is your accent? Who are you?"

"I am what Pouritus said I was—a spy. My master sent me to find out if the Parthians are smelting their imported iron into swords and spears. I must return and tell them what I found out. They do not want to attack, but must be ready if Parthia attacks them."

Rashah walks toward the cave entrance and returns. "No, you can't be a spy."

"They just want to protect the Roman Empire. That's all."

"But, if you go back, you will be a slave again."

"I was rescued by Theophilus when I was eight years old. Although I am his slave, he treats me like a son. He trusts me. I must return."

"No! I will help you escape. You can go the opposite direction. You can go down to Qom, then through the desert to Ysatip or Dozdaab. No one will look for you in the desert. It is so hot there, people not used to it die.

"If that is your will, then I will go there. I love you,

Rashah. I will send a message to my master about the swords, and promise to buy my freedom from him as soon as possible."

The sun is low again.

"I will return tomorrow with fresh fruit."

For the next three months, Luke stays in hiding in the cave. Each day Rashah returns. They talk and plan Luke's escape, and where they will settle someday, and how many children they will have.

"Well, I have to go. Father has been asking where I disappear to every day. I'd better go home early."

"Yes, that would be wise."

Rashah holds out her arms to Luke, and Luke draws her close. He looks down at her, and their eyes meet.

"Tomorrow, then."

The next day Luke waits for Rashah's return, but it does not happen. He leaves the cave and walks around to see if he can hear her horse tramping on undergrowth on their way up to the cave. Nothing.

He returns to the cave and waits. All day he alternates between pacing outside and pacing in the cave. Night comes. He has trouble sleeping.

Morning. Luke waits for Rashah, but still, she does not come.

Maybe her father found out she is coming up here and made her stop.

Maybe a bear got her on the way down.

Maybe she drowned in the river.

Once more, all day, he waits. Once more, it is night.

Morning comes. He knows what he must do. He pours the blackener over his hair and dabs some with a leaf onto his beard, and waits for them to dry. He dons the many folded shirt, billowy trousers, and turban she had brought him for his escape. He gathers as many supplies as he can in the pouches, loads them on his horse, and starts down the mountain.

He arrives in Ecbatana and sees two upright poles by the river. On the two poles are two bodies. He recognizes them—Jotapa and Pouritus.

Two guards stand nearby. Luke approaches them.

"Sir, what happened?" he says in Greek with no accent. "I am new to the city. I certainly do not want to anger anyone as much as these two apparently did."

"They were the overseer and his assistant to a gold mine up in the mountain. It collapsed a few weeks ago so completely, it will be years before gold can be taken out again."

"Oh, I see," Luke responds. "Does either of them leave behind a home? Perhaps I would like to buy it. Can you tell me the name of a wife or son or daughter I can talk to?"

"The overseer had a fine home, but it has been taken over by the king. He had one daughter, I think, and she was sold as a slave to a Prince Vima down in the desert somewhere."

Luke struggles to hide his shock. He turns his horse, rides slowly to the south gate of the city, and to the south well. He fills his water skin and a water skin for Varsang. He remounts his horse, heads south, and when he is far enough away, he allows his emotions to rush to the surface like the mountain that had been abused far too long.

"NO!" It echoes from the mountains to his right and across the desert valley to his left.

"NO!" he repeats. It reverberates through his mind, his heart, his very being.

"WHY?"

13 ~ WANDERING

As Luke descends out of the Alvand Mountains on his trusted Varsang, his heart descends into an abyss he cannot climb out of.

What if I cannot find her?
What if the guard heard wrong?
What if the guard was lying?
Did they kill her? Kill my beloved?

Gradually the forest thins, and he is in a mixture of trees and bushes and an occasional meadow. On he goes.

Oh, thousand gods. Or the one god of my beloved. Help me find my Rashah.

As the sun descends behind the mountains he has finally left, Luke arrives at the city of Qom. Rather than enter the city so late, he goes over to the side of the road and dismounts. He sets up the black goat-hair tent his beloved had provided for him and crawls inside.

If only he could crawl out of this blackness and the sun be shining again. If only he could crawl out of this nightmare and have Rashah at his side once more. He does not sleep. Or perhaps he dreams he does not sleep.

Morning finally comes. As Luke picks up his tent, he notices one side heavier than the other sides and remembers Rashah had hidden money for him there.

Oh, my little one. I will find you.

He goes on into the city and finds a bazaar. He buys some cheese and figs and walks around among the other booths as he eats. He sees a stable and buys water and barley for Varsang.

Leading Varsang by the reins, Luke sees a booth selling maps. He speaks in his best Greek. "Do you have any maps of the desert?"

"North or south," the map seller asks.

"I am not sure. The man I talked to told me to go down in the desert, so I guess south."

"Sorry, I do not have any such maps. There are only two settlements in the south desert—Ysatis and Dozdaab. After that, you are in India. Or you could head east from Dozdaab and still be in the south desert, but there is hardly anything there either. There is one city named Kandahar."

"Doesn't the desert have any oases?"

"Oh, plenty of them. But it is so hot in the south desert, you couldn't survive. It's the hottest place in the world. But, if you are fool enough to go south, there is only one road going that direction. You can't miss it."

"How far am I to the next settlement?"

"Ysatis? Well, you'd still be in the middle desert. So, you might be able to make it in three days. Take plenty of water."

"Yes, sir," Luke responds, handing the merchant ten copper coins for his information. "Oh, and which street takes me to the south gate?" he asks.

"That one."

"Oh, and one more question: Is there some way I can get a message to a port on the Black Sea? I need to request something be delivered to me at the Parthian Gulf."

"Go on out of the city, and you will see camels gathering to form the next caravan. Ask around there to see if any are going down to the gulf. If so, you can pay them to get your message put on a ship headed for the Indian Ocean, then up into Egypt. Maybe it can be put on a ship across the Great Sea, and eventually to the Black Sea. It's quicker overland, but that's what is available right now. Take it or leave it."

Luke purchases a small scroll and writes.

SWORDS. I'M TRYING TO GET OUT.

He hands it to a merchant headed for the Parthian Gulf. *It has been four years. I hope it is in time to help.*

Luke remounts his Nordic Voorde horse, and they head down to the next settlement.

"I hope it stays cool enough for you," he tells his horse. "Your long hair is going to be a problem, I fear. Perhaps I can shear some of it off when we get to Ysatis."

All day Luke makes his way down the road heading south deeper into the desert. The first night after setting up his tent, he notices the North Star and realizes he has been going southeast, not straight south.

Well, this is the only road out here, so I must be going right. Rashah, am I getting closer to you? Oh, my little one. Hang on until I come. I will rescue you, and we will be together again.

For three days, Luke travels on the south road. On the third day, Luke arrives in Ysatis. Once inside the city, he sees many representations of the Zoroaster religion.

My little one loved this religion. Maybe they took her here to be a priestess or something.

Luke goes to the bazaar, buys some cheese and grapes for himself and hay for Varsang.

"By the way," he asks the stable owner, "do you have Zoroaster temples here?"

"Yes, we do have one, but it is not for the public. It is called a firehouse because it houses the eternal fire. It is watched over only by the magi of Ahura Mazda. They keep the eternal flame of goodness lit."

"Can you tell me how to get to it?"

"Yes. Just keep going the way you are."

Luke leads his horse down the street until he reaches the Fire House. A magus meets him outside.

"I am looking for someone who believes as you do. The lady's name is Rashah. She was sold as a slave from Ecbatana. Is she here?"

"We do not have priestesses. I have not heard of any young ladies newly enslaved coming to our town. Are you sure she came this way?"

"All I know is that they went south in the desert."

Luke and Varsang walk slowly up and down each street in the settlement, and Luke sings.

Tho I vander long avay
Over all da mounts und seas
To da end uv da verld,
I vill alvays tink uv home
Und keep you in my heart
Till I hold you once again.

His father's song is slow and haunting. His father's song is now for his beloved. Will she remember his song? If she hears it, will she recognize his song?

"Sir. Oh, sir," Luke hears. He turns in the direction of the voice.

A man is calling from his pottery booth. Luke walks over to him.

"That song you are singing," the potter says. "I've heard it before. Haunting song in that strange language, but beautiful."

Luke's mouth drops open, and his head jerks forward. "Are you sure? When was it? How long ago? Was it a man or a woman singing it? Do you remember their names?"

It is all Luke can to do keep from holding his breath while waiting for the answer.

"I think I heard it about five years ago. I was visiting a relative down in Dozdaab. But I don't think I'll ever forget it. It was being sung by a big man with a deep voice."

"A man?" Luke asks, aware that his heartbeat is speeding out of control, and his knees are growing weak. "Are you sure? What color was the man's hair?"

"I'm pretty sure it was yellow. He had a yellow beard too. Big man. Strong. Like a giant."

Luke takes a step back, then lunges at the man. He takes hold of the man's shoulders and pulls him up to him.

"Are you sure? Would you swear to it by all the gods? And it was a man, not a woman?"

"Well, I would swear to it by the god Ahura Mazda. Is that good enough for you? And let go of my shirt."

Luke backs up until he is in the middle of the street. People, animals, wagons, and chariots all go around him. Some yell for him to get out of the way. He does not hear.

He turns in circles, his head tilted up to the sky. "Vather? Vather?" he says, still turning. "Are you alive? Vather! Can you hear me?"

Luke spends the night in Ysatis. The next morning at dawn, he is back at the bazaar singing his song. Singing with hope. And remembering that day so long ago when he was only eight years old. *Could it be? Have I at last found my father?*

Not hearing anything else favorable, Luke finally packs up and rides out of the south gate of the town, heading toward Dozdaab.

The heat bears down on them.

"Oh, Varsang. I forgot to shear you. I shall dismount and walk beside you. There is no hurry. Well, for you, there is no hurry; for me, there is. I shall go slow for you. You have been faithful to me through a lot. I owe this to you."

They walk slowly along.

"Oh, I see water ahead. You take your time. I shall run get some and be right back.

Luke rushes to the pool.

It is full of mud, but I will put his water skin under the scum on top.

Luke steps into the water to get what is cleaner away from the edge. He lifts his foot and realizes it will not come up. He lifts his other foot, but it will not come up either.

"Oh, no! Quicksand."

He whistles and Varsang ambles up to his master. Dragging the reins on the ground. Luke cannot reach them.

"Turn around," Luke says, hoping the horse knows what he is telling it.

Varsang looks at his master a moment.

"Hurry, Varsang. I'm in trouble."

So far, he is stuck only up to his calves. He must escape before he sinks deeper.

The horse turns around. His long tail nearly touches the ground. "Just a little closer now," Luke says in as gentle a voice as he can. "But not too close."

Varsang backs up another step.

"Okay, Varsang. This is where we part forever or are friends forever."

Luke looks up in the sky. "Oh, thousand gods, and Rashah's god, help me!" He holds out his arms and lunges forward. He stretches his long frame and grabs hold of the bottom of Varsang's tail.

"Forward, Varsang," He shouts. "Go forward."

Little by little, Varsang walks forward, Luke still hanging on to the horse's tail.

Little by little, Luke is dragged to solid ground. He lies on his front a while and turns over. His arms and legs are both outstretched.

"Thank you, thousand gods. And Mazda too."

Luke stands and puts his muddy arm around Varsang's neck. "Mostly, I thank you, my friend. Mostly I thank you."

Luke looks around. There are a few boulders grouped together amidst the sand dunes. He walks over to them. "Stay here in the shade, Varsang. I shall do the same. It is a three-day trip to Zahedon. If we make it a four-day trip so we can go slower, that will be fine too." He falls asleep.

When Luke wakens, it is dark. He stands It is cooler now. *Perhaps we will travel at night the rest of the time we are in this desert.*

He takes out his horse's large waterskin, pours some in a bowl, sets it on the ground, and takes a swig of his own water.

Luke stares at the pack on Varsang's back, takes it off, and puts it on his own back. "I'm as tall as you, friend," he says to his horse. "It's my turn."

They travel the rest of the night. When the sun comes up, they stop.

"No tent last night, and I slept better. So no tent from now on," he says to the horse.

On the fourth day, they reach the settlement of Zahedon. Luke ties up his horse at the well where he gives him and himself a long draw of water.

He holds out a copper coin. "Would you like this?" he asks a boy not much older than he was when his father had disappeared so long ago.

"If you will watch my horse while I go into town, I will give you another coin just like this when I return."

The boy smiles and takes the reins from Luke.

Not long after, Luke is back with a stableman from town and gives the boy his other copper coin.

"Can you help my horse?" he asks the stableman. "He is not used to the heat. He is a Nordic horse used to snow and mountains, not heat and sand dunes."

"Well, first, we need to get some wet cloths and put over his back to cool him off. I brought a supply with me."

That done, the men sit and wait. Finally, the stableman stands.

"I think we can take those off him now. The sun has dried them out anyway. I brought along some sheep shears. Steady him, now, while I cut all that hair off him."

Luke walks around to face Varsang and pats him on the nose. "We're going to do something else to help you now. Just stand still, and it will be over before you know it. Steady now, Varsang. That's right. Don't move. He is being gentle with you. He will not cut you. He will help you. You will be glad he did."

"There. I've got it all," the stableman says. "This is some beautiful hair I got off him. Do you have any use for it? It is very valuable. All other horses around here are short-haired."

"No, I have no use for it. You may have it."

"Wonderful. I shall consider you paid in full. Now let your horse rest some more before you bring him into town."

Alone again, Luke pats his horse on the nose. "Varsang, your eyes are not bright anymore. You are hanging your head so low. You are so tired. What can I do for you?"

Luke looks through their supplies, spreading them out on the ground.

"Why not?" he tells himself. "It could work."

Luke picks up his black goat-hair tent, takes the binding off, reattaches the ropes to the corners, and lowers it into the well.

"This is heavy," he grunts.

Once out of the well, he hefts it onto Varsang's back. "Goat hair keeps water from seeping through. So, the water touching your skin should stay there a while."

Luke repeats the process three more times before the sun begins to set.

"Well, friend, let's go into the city and find the two people in the world I love more than you and Theophilus."

Luke finds a hostel that allows owners to sleep in cubicles with their animals and falls asleep.

Morning comes. "You look better today, Varsang. But I am not going to push you. You just stay here in the shade today. I will be back."

Luke walks over to the bazaar. As he does, he sings his song. No one shows any indication of recognizing it.

He notices a shop selling gold jewelry.

"Excuse me, sir. Do you happen to know where a Prince Vima lives?"

The shop keeper jerks his head up. "You have business with him?"

"Well, I might. Someone told me up in Ecbatana that a friend of mine might be with the prince. Does he live here?"

"No, but, if you have traveled that far, I would say you are nearly there."

"Really? Where is he?"

"You must head east from here. If you have a horse, you might be able to make it in one day, or two. You will, of course, have to go slow in this heat. You're traveling at night, aren't you?"

"Yes."

"If you do not have a horse, it may take you four or five days of walking. You're tall. I think you could make it in five days. Other people would take a week."

Luke leaves and begins walking up and down the street, singing his song. The desert town is small, and it does not take him long to cover it all.

With no one recognizing the song, he returns to the stall where he had left Varsang, gives him a good drink, and takes an afternoon nap.

Dark comes, and just before the gates are closed, Luke leads Varsang out the east gate and on the road once more.

"Just think, Varsang. We are close to my father. After all these years. And maybe also to my Rashah. Oh, Varsang. I am so happy."

The night air gives a little relief from the heat, and they walk steadily toward the fulfillment of Luke's dream.

Daylight comes. They stop for their time of sleep, but a wind stirs up. It grows stronger until it is whining and growling both at the same time.

The sky turns brown in the west. Then he sees it. The wall of sand higher than many cities on top of each other. He looks all around and finds some boulders.

"Hurry, Varsang." He pulls the reins hard and reaches the boulders just as the sand engulfs them. He makes the horse lie down, and he lies on top of its back, his face hidden in the back of Varsang's neck.

He does not know how long the blast of sand lasts, but finally, it ends, and Luke sees it move on toward the east.

Luke slides off Varsang's back and the two stand.

"Whew. How do people stand to live in the desert? Let's go a little farther to see if we can find an oasis."

They do, but there is no water ahead.

"Well, we shall drink what we have, friend." Luke takes a draw of his own water and fills Varsang's bowl.

They stop and sleep the rest of the day. That night Luke rises, ready to continue their journey. But Varsang is dead.

14 ~ THE IMPOSSIBLE

*L*uke walks on alone. He leaves behind Varsang covered with the black goat-hair tent, hoping to keep the vultures away.

Luke's natural yellow is beginning to show at the roots of his blackened hair. He does not care. Or he thinks he does not.

Three more nights of walking, walking, walking. Sometimes he detects a slight breeze coming from the south where he is told the Indian Ocean is. Mostly the heat remains stifling both day and night.

When he stumbles, he stops. He prays to his thousand gods, and Rashah's one god that he will keep his right mind in the sun.

Not many oases down here in the south. Varsang's waterskin is large and heavy, but it will see me through.

After three more nights of trodding through a maelstrom of sand, Luke sees it. "The city of my dreams," he whispers to himself, "Kandahar."

Would it be asking too much, oh holy gods, for me to find both my father and my wife here? Well, she is not my wife yet, but I will make her so as soon as I find and free her.

Luke enters through the west gate of Kandahar and walks over to one of the guards.

"Sir," he says in Greek, "could you tell me where the palace is?"

"We have no palace here. But, if you are asking about Prince Vima, he has an estate here."

"Yes, that is what I mean," Luke responds. "Could you

point me in that direction?"

"First, he is not there now. Second, even if he were, you would not be allowed even close to it without an invitation. It is surrounded by the prince's personal guards."

"Oh. Well, is there something I could do to get an invitation?"

The guard guffaws and calls over to another guard. "This man wants an invitation to visit Prince Vima. Ha. Ha. Ha."

Luke twists his mouth, looks down, grits his teeth, and walks on through the gate into the city.

As always, he heads to the bazaar nearby and buys something to eat. Without thinking, he walks on down the narrow street eating his bread and looking for a resting place for Varsang, then remembers.

He looks around and finds a seller of parchment.

"Kind sir," he says. "Could you tell me where Prince Vima's estate is?"

"Yes, I can tell you. I go there sometimes to make deliveries. But, if you think you're going to get an audience with the prince, the sun has sunk into your brains and cooked them."

"Please. Is there any way a stranger could get in to see him?"

"Of course not. Well, I suppose if you saved his life, you could get in to see him. Other than that, I see absolutely no way. Most of the people who have lived in Kandahar their whole lives have never been inside his estate, so why should you?"

"Could you tell me where it is so I can at least walk by it?"

"Certainly. Keep going down this street. Turn left at the statue of his father, King Kujala Kadphises, and follow it until you see the estate. But you'll never get in. Never in a thousand years."

Luke thanks the man for his information and heads toward the royal estate. As he walks, he sings.

Tho I vander long avay

Over all da mounts und seas
To da end uv da verld,
I vill alvays dhink uv home
Und keep you in my heart
Till I hold you once again.

When he sees the statue of the king of the tribes of Kushan Afgan-Archostan, he stops and stares up at it. *Could you help me get in to see your son, the prince? I heard you might even be a god. If you are, help me free Rashah.*

He turns and walks on. Ahead, he sees the walls of the royal estate rise high above the narrow street. The front double gate is tall and wide and adorned with gold, silver, and copper.

On each side is a guard with wide, curved sword on one side, a dagger on the other, and holding an upright spear. His helmet is conical with spikes on top.

At the apex of the wall are archers with their long arched bows at the ready.

He stares at the scene a moment, then goes to the opposite side of the street, squats, and begins his vigil.

Oh, my beloved. I am here. I will get inside and rescue you. As you walk the halls, know that I am here. As you rise in the morning and go to sleep at night, know that I am here. Rescue is near my little one. Be brave. Be brave.

The sun beats down with an unrelenting severity. His heart races. His breathing becomes uneven and shallow and rapid. His head throbs. He becomes nauseated. He sometimes thinks he is back in Frisia and sometimes on a ship, and sometimes where he actually is.

"Hey," someone shouts, passing by. "You'd better get inside for a while."

Luke looks around and realizes he and the guards are the only ones left on the street. He stands, steadies himself, and finds a hostel. The walls are eight hand spans thick, and it is cool inside.

He sleeps. He dreams. He is a giant looking down on a palace. He lifts the roof off and sees Rashah. She is screaming. He gently lifts her out, sets her on his hand, and suddenly she is a giant with him. But the palace grows too, and now there are horsemen after them. Their hooves pound the ground. They shout, "Sir. Sir. Sir."

Luke wakens with a start. Someone is pounding on his door. He opens it.

"It is nearly dark. A meal is ready in the inn if you are hungry."

Luke buys a meal, eats it heartily, then leaves. Arriving back at the royal estate, once again he squats on the side of the street across from the golden gates, and watches.

When daylight arrives, he walks up to the gate.

"I am here to see Rashah. I believe she is on the prince's staff. I need to see her a moment."

Neither guard answers.

Luke repeats himself. Still nothing.

Not giving up, he says it again.

After the third time, the guards cross spears between Luke and the double gates.

"It won't take me long," Luke responds.

"You must leave," one of the guards says

"If you do not, you will be considered a spy, put in the dungeon, then beheaded."

Luke leaves but does not go far. He steps back to his spot on the other side of the street. Again, squatting and watching and thinking.

Oh, my love, Rashah. Do not give up. I will not. I will stay here until you are free and are my wife.

A week goes by. A month. Still the same response. Luke is nearly out of money.

One day he returns to the bazaar and locates the man selling parchments.

"Sir, I talked to you about a month ago, and..."

"Oh, yes. You are the one who thought you could get in to see Prince Vima. Never got in, did you?" he chuckles.

"No, sir. But I intend to keep trying."

"Ohhh. It isn't the prince you want to see at all," he says with a grin. "There is a lady involved. Perhaps she is in his harem?"

"Oh, no. I hadn't thought of that. I just thought she... I must try harder."

The parchment merchant shakes his head.

"Sir, I need a job."

"I do not need any help."

"Sir, I can write the Greek language clearly and am fairly fast."

"So?" the merchant says, picking up two pieces of parchments to sew together for a new scroll.

"Perhaps you have customers needing legal documents drawn up. They can tell me what they want in the document, and I will word it for them."

Farnad looks up from his work and stares at the young man before him.

"Hmmm. But of course. I have people asking me all the time for scribes, and I send them down the street to someone. Why not keep the money for myself? Brilliant, young man, brilliant."

"Does that mean I'm hired?"

"Indeed it does, young man." He stands and holds out his hand. Luke takes it.

"So, my name is Farnad. What is yours?"

Luke notices the man has many rings on his long fingers, his many-folded shirt is green, his green billowy trousers are blue, and his turban is both green and blue. Farnad is short and has a beard that is both black and gray. Some of his teeth are missing.

"Luke is my name."

"Do you want money or a place to stay?"

"I'll take the place to stay. And if you ever need help sewing the parchments together, I have some experience with that and would appreciate money."

"Good. When can you start?"

"Well, sir, could I begin when the sun is high in the sky? I could work in the cool of your shop."

"Then, you will start right now."

More months pass. Luke continues to go to Prince Vima's estate every morning, return to the shop to work in the heat of the day, return to the estate in the evening, and sleep at night. He becomes the center of conversation all over the city.

"That man with a half black and half yellow beard is there every day, no matter what the weather." Some take bets as to when he will give up and go away.

I am no longer that naïve nineteen-year-old who boarded the ship on the Black Sea that morning and being waved off by my master. I wonder if he is still there. Did my message get through? If I return to the fortress someday, will I be praised or executed?

One morning while squatting in position, Luke notices several men hanging around the front gates he hasn't seen before. Sometimes they talk to each other, and sometimes they seem to purposely avoid each other. Their billowy trousers are shorter than usual. Their skin a little darker. Their black eyes somehow different.

Why are they wearing those cloaks in this heat? Are they waiting to be admitted? Why haven't they said anything to the guards?

He notices heads appearing at the top of the high wall between the archers, then disappearing. The gates are opened, two more guards come out, and the gates are closed again.

Still, the strange men wander around in front of the royal estate. More heads at the top of the wall. More guards coming out.

Then it happens. One of the strange men throws off his cloak and raises a dagger in his hand. He lunges at a guard and draws blood.

Now all the cloaks are off. Daggers and swords flash. The guards thrust spears and pull out their swords.

Shouting. Charging and counter charging. Scuffling, wrestling. Muscles bulging. Teeth gritting. Growling.

The royal archers from atop the wall shoot their arrows straight down, and more of the strangers fall.

A wind comes up off the desert. A brown wind. The fighting continues.

Luke stands, his eyes darting around the action. *Do something!*

He runs forward, grabs one of the spears on the ground with both hands, and pushes his way toward the strangers. An enemy sword cuts it in two. He grabs a sword from a fallen guard. An attack comes, and he darts out of the way. Another parry and he leaps the other way.

Next to Luke, the helmet of one of the guards is pushed off by a sword missing its mark.

Between warding off attacks, Luke looks over and sees that the missing helmet has revealed what he has been searching for most of his life. *Can it be?*

He hears the voice of the big yellow-haired guard. "Take dhat und dat, you devil. You vill not vin."

Luke parries another blow and calls out, "Vather? Vather?"

The big guard next to him thrusts his sword and gets another enemy in the hand holding his dagger. He glances in the direction of the voice calling amid the shouting, the dying, and the blowing wind.

"Vhat? Vhat did you say?" the guard growls.

"Vather. It's me. *Tho I vander long avay*," Luke shouts.

The guard next to him grabs a spear off a dead soldier and jabs at the enemy. "*Over all da mounts und seas*" bellows the big guard.

Luke hears a "Watch out" and turns in time to grab the arm of an attacker, twist the dagger out of his hand, and beat him over the head with his bare fist.

"*To da end uv da verld*," Luke shouts back.

Now the two fight back to back, one covering half of a circle and the other covering the other half. No matter which way the enemy comes, they are covered.

"*I vill alvays dhink uv home*," the guard bellows.

Slowly they turn in place. Fighting off the enemy, one with a spear, the other with a sword.

"*Und keep you in my heart*," Luke shouts.

The few strangers that remain alive look around, realize they cannot win, and race down the street.

"*Till I hold you once again*," both men say in unison, turning to face each other.

They drop their weapons.

They stare.

"Vather?" Luke whispers.

"My son," Sigmundrr rumbles, grabbing Luke by the shoulders.

They embrace. In the middle of the street among bodies of both the living and the dead. Other royal guards stop and stare at the two big men.

"What's going on?" one asks.

"Why is Sigmundrr hugging that civilian?" another asks.

"Has he lost his mind?"

They wait.

At last, the two big yellow-haired men step back from each other, turn to face the other guards, their arms on each other's shoulders. Sigmundrr raises his other arm.

"My son! My son! I have vound my son!"

While servants from inside the royal estate rush out with wagons and throw bodies on them, and fresh guards are put in place on either side of the gates, the bloodied royal guards walk into the grand courtyard of the Prince of Kushan Afgan-Archostan.

Luke holds back. "No, I cannot go in," he says, reverting to his native Frisian tongue. "Dey vill not allow me."

"As long as you are vith me, my son, you vill be allowed in. Let us go to da barracks. Ve vill clean up und talk."

The men enter the barracks. "This way," Sigmundrr says, leading his son to a low-lipped bath. They stand while water is poured over their heads and laugh in celebration. Then they advance to a pool where they wash off the rest of the dirt and blood and still hardly take their eyes off each other lest the other vanishes again.

Sigmundrr brags to a servant that his son is one of the men who helped save the life of the prince. Shortly, Luke is given a clean shirt, billowy pants, and turban, all made of silk.

"Ah, dhat is a good sign," Sigmundrr says, hardly taking his big arms off his son's shoulders long enough for him to dress. "Only da prince vould order a stranger to be so dressed. But now, tell me vhat happened to you after da battle?" he says, leading his son to a nearby bench.

Luke tells his father every major thing that has happened to him since he was eight years old, and what has brought him so far from home to the desert of Kandahar.

"But, vather, I lost it. I learned to write like you told me to. I wrote down everyding I could remember about our homeland and da people who made it so. Dhen I lost it. It vas destroyed in a storm. It took me years to put it togeder in a scroll. Dhen it vas all destroyed. All gone. I couldn't remember any of it after."

Tears escape Luke's blue eyes. "I am sorry, Vather. I am so sorry."

"Dhat's okay, Son. I remember. We are togeder at last, und you vill vrite it down again."

The other guards watch the father and son from a distance. Some wonder if their father is still alive.

"Vather, vhy couldn't I find you after da battle?"

"Dhere vas a centurion in da Roman army named Olennius. He pointed his sword at me, took avay my veapons, and hid me in his tent. Somehow, after da battle, he transferred to anoter legion und vas sent to Espanola. Knowing I was too var avay to try to escape, he made me one uv his bodyguards."

The two men rise and walk around inside the barracks, their heads together in non-stop speech, which the other guards do not understand.

"I vas in Espanola about den years. Dhen one day, Prince Vima vent dhere to buy iron. His vather vas alvays expanding his kingdom—the number of tribes he ruled. He needed more swords. Dhat is vhat da prince vas doing in Espanola. He saw me and bought me vrom the centurion, but not vitout paying much gold vor me. I have been here vor eight years now."

Mealtime comes and goes. Still, they talk. And sometimes laugh. Sometimes cry. Night comes. Sigmundrr takes the blankets of one of the deceased guards and give it to Luke. They sleep that night. It is a fitful sleep.

Sometimes Sigmundrr dreams that old dream of finding his son, and suddenly his son turns into a cloud.

Sometimes Luke dreams he is with his father, but his father turns into a ship and floats away.

Morning comes. This time they eat the usual bread and yogurt.

They resume their non-stop talking. Some of the other guards look over at them sometimes and grin. Others complain. "Why can't they speak Greek like everyone else?"

The headmaster of the household appears in the doorway. Everyone stops what they are doing. He walks over to Sigmundrr and the civilian.

"The prince requires your attendance."

"Vhen?"

"Now."

15 ~ SUMMITS & VALLEYS

Sigmundrr grabs his military turban and puts his ceremonial dagger in his wide belt.

They follow the headmaster. As they walk through the front courtyard. Luke notices for the first time that it has a pool in the middle with trees of every kind surrounding it.

"It's a little like being home again," Sigmundrr whispers, "und valking through the vorest."

They are escorted down a long corridor, up a long flight of stairs along one wall, and down another corridor. The floor is multi-colored tile, and the walls are intricately carved cedar from Parthia's mountains. They stop at double doors.

"When you walk in," the headmaster says, "you must bow to your knees. If he were king, you would bow prostrate completely to the floor. You do not raise your head until the prince acknowledges you and grants you permission to approach him. There will be a narrow table in front of his princely throne, and you will not walk any closer than that."

As the headmaster talks, Luke notices the ceiling is as high as five man-lengths and wonders if the reception hall ceiling is the same or higher. He is not disappointed.

Guards open the double doors. The headmaster walks in first, followed by Luke and Sigmundrr. They bow, are invited to walk forward, and stop at the narrow carved table.

"Your highness, may I present to you Sigmundrr and Lukvert, both of the north country around the Nordic Sea.

Prince Vimi smiles. "It is always cold up there from what I have heard. Is that true?"

"Yes, sir," Sigmundrr rumbles.

Prince Vima has a large head with a long broad nose and trim black beard. He is considerable in the shoulders and belly and smiles easily.

"How long have you been with me, Sigmundrr?"

"Eight years, sir."

"I hope they have been good years. I try to make them so, even for my slaves."

"You have been more dhan fair, your highness."

"Now, who is this young man beside you?"

Sigmundrr begins to raise an arm up to his son's shoulder, catches the warning nod of the headmaster, and puts his arm back down to his side.

"Dhis, your highness, is my son. We have been separated vor vivteen long years. But now I have found him und ve are togeder again."

"That is wonderful. How did you get separated? Was he with you in Espanola?"

"No, ve got separated during a battle in our homeland."

"I looked for my vather many days, but could not vind him. I was only eight years old." Luke notices the headmaster's frown and realizes too late he had not been addressed by the prince.

"So, how did you find each other?" Prince Vima asks.

"A song my vather taught me. He said, if ve ever got separated, ve could vind each other by singing da song vhere ever ve vent. I have been singing it ever since." Luke speaks in Greek as does his father now, but with the Frisian accent in respect of his father.

"Und ve found each other doing battle togeder," Sigmundrr says, a wide grin on his face and a twinkle in his eyes.

"Well, I think I will make you my slave, Lukvert. That way, you can remain with your father. I will give you a responsible position."

"Sir. I already belong to someone else. I belong to Tribune Titus Pontus Theophilus."

"He sounds like a Roman officer. What are you doing

so far away from Rome?"

"I vas sent here by him."

"To do what?" the prince demands, his smile gone, pressing hard on the arms of his throne and turning his knuckles white.

"Uh, to see if Rome could import some uv your famous lapis lazuli," Luke responds, glad he discovered the beautiful blue mineral two weeks earlier in the bazaar.

"I see. And where did you learn to fight so well?"

"Part of it vas my doing," Sigmundrr responds. "We Norsemen began teaching our sons da art uv var as soon as dhey could valk. He was vairly good at the javelin by da time he vas eight."

"And the rest of what you learned?" the prince asks, looking back to Luke.

"My master educated me. I learned about vriting und mathematics, but also all forms of combat. But, as alvays, I vas best at using da spear."

"I went up on the roof and could see you swinging that thing everywhere. Everyone was afraid of you. Did you realize that?"

Neither man replies.

I vish dhis interview vas over so I could be vith my son again.

"Well, I want to reward you, Lukvert. What can I give you?"

Luke's mouth falls open, and he jerks his head back. His eyes widen, and he forces back a grin.

"Sir, may I be bold?"

"Go ahead, but not too bold," the prince replies.

"I believe you have a young lady in your service who you bought while in Ecbatana about three years ago. Her name is Rashah. She is not very tall, but has beautiful black hair that shines and eyes that sparkle."

The prince, about the same age as Luke, leans to one side, puts his elbow on the arm of his throne, and rests his chin in his hand. He says nothing, but grins.

Luke waits. *Oh, thousand gods, give me my Rashah.*

"And I suppose you love her," the prince finally says.

"Oh, yes, sir. Ve vere going to be married."

"I think I know who you are talking about. She is a lady in waiting for one of my wives, and goes horseback riding with her in the winter when the weather cools off."

"Dhat's her," Luke blurts out. The headmaster clears his throat, and Luke takes a deep breath in an effort to control himself. "She vas good vith horses."

Prince Vima motions for his headmaster to approach his throne. He whispers to the headmaster, who then leaves. Prince Vima says no more.

What is happening? Have I gone too far? Is he sending for guards to arrest me, then kill me?

They continue to wait.

Sigmundrr stands straight and tall and at attention, looking straight ahead with no expression. His son tries to do the same, but his heartbeat refuses to slow, and he shifts from one foot to the other.

Silence.

Is he lying to me? Has he taken Rashah to be one of his wives?

They hear a side door open. The headmaster walks in. Behind him is Rashah. She looks frightened.

Oh, my darling. My little one.

"Rashah, is that your name?" the prince asks. "Rashah, come closer."

She walks to a half wall between the side door and throne and stops.

"Do you see anyone in this room you recognize?"

Rashah looks around, and immediately her eyes fall on her Luke. She gasps and raises a hand to her heart.

Luke watches the love of his life with eyes that refuse to even blink, for fear she will disappear.

The prince sits back in his throne and watches them both. He grins. "Hmmm... What have we here? True love?"

He turns back to Luke.

"I tell you what I will do for you for saving my life. You shall have the life of my servant girl."

"Yes, sir. Thank..."

"You are interrupting."

"And, since I am in the mood for a party and haven't had an excuse to throw one lately, I am going to throw a betrothal party. Of course, since you are not my equals, you cannot attend. But I now declare you betrothed to each other, so it is legal. How's that? Is that enough reward for you?"

"Oh, sir, your highness. How can I dhank you?" Luke says, his face beaming.

"You have already thanked me. You saved my life. Now, I have other things to do today."

The prince stands to leave. "Oh, and sign the parchment on your way out," he says, now halfway to a private back door.

Once Prince Vima is gone, Luke rushes over to her. The headmaster stops him, and Rashah disappears through the same door she had come in through.

"Come, my son," Sigmundrr says. "Dhere are proper vays to do dhings."

They leave through the double doors. A high table has been placed in the corridor, and a clay tablet set on it for Luke to etch his name.

"Vhat is dhis?"

"It is your betrothal agreement," the headmaster says. "You agree to build a house before you wed, and have it supplied with appropriate furnishings."

"Then, our marriage is final?" Luke asks.

"Then it is final. Here is your stylus. Sign the document."

That done, Luke and Sigmundrr follow the headmaster back down to the front courtyard.

"Vather," Luke says once they are alone in the barracks again, "I need money to buy land to put da house on."

"You vill have to get a yob then."

"I have a yob, Vather, but it is just vor a place to sleep. I vill go see him and promise to vork all day for him instead of halv days."

"Und I vill ask to change duty, und patrol da streets instead of da palace," Luke's father says. "Dhat vay I vill be able to see you sometimes."

For the first time since their reunion the day before, father and son part.

It takes Luke four months to save up enough money to buy a small piece of land on which to build a house for him and his bride, Rashah. Another ten months go by making bricks and building a small house in his spare time.

Every day Sigmundrr stops by the parchment shop on his city rounds and says hello to his son.

"Vather, I am getting so excited. Soon I can bring my little Rashah home vith me."

"I am happy vor you, Son. It is vonderful. It is good to have a good vife. Your mother vas good to me. I still miss her. But, vhen I look at you, I see a bit of her."

Sometimes Sigmundrr manages to slip out of the bazaar where most of his guard work is carried out, and go see Luke's house.

"Do you dhink she vill like the pottery I bought her for to do da cooking vith, Vather?"

"Yes, it all looks very good, Son."

"I vill be ready vor my bride in only a vew days now. Und I am so happy, Vather. Now I have both you and her. I now have a family."

"Und you vill make me a grandvather too. Then it vill be like having you all over again to sit on my knee."

"Oh, I am so happy, Vather."

The following week Luke goes over to the royal estate and requests entrance.

The guards cross spears in front of him. "You are not allowed entrance," one of them says.

Undeterred, Luke smiles and says, "Vell, vill you get a message to my Rashah for me?" he says. "Our house is almost done, so get ready. I vill be back here in a vew days to take her home vith me to be my bride and my vife."

"One moment. Stay here," the other guard says. He knocks on the gate, and it is opened. He slips in, and the gate is closed behind him.

Luke waits. He paces. *Oh, my darling Rashah. We will be together at last.*

The gate opens and the guard returns.

"I am sorry, but Rashah is dead."

Luke sucks in his breath, it stops midway in his throat, and he lets out the sound of a dying dove. His eyes tear.

"Vhat? Vhat did you say?"

"She is dead."

"No. You have it all vrong. She is not dead. She is healthy and is getting ready to move to our house und be my vife."

"She has been dead for a month. That is all we know."

Luke brings the ball of his hand up to his forehead, raises his eyes to the blinding sun, and turns in circles.

"No. You are vrong. My Rashah is not dead. She is alive."

"Sir, you are going to have to leave."

"But..."

The guards resume their position on each side of the ornate double gates. They look straight ahead. They do not speak.

Luke turns toward the street but sees an abyss. He takes a step, but his foot sets down on nothingness. He looks, and sees barrenness. All around him laughing heads of monsters. Laughing and scorning and mocking. Ha. Ha. Ha.

He takes another step, and reality returns like a mountain tipping over and landing on him. He sees ahead of him his beautiful Rashah, reaches out to touch her, and she disappears.

He stumbles over to a wall along the street and leans on it. He tries to push it over, but it will not move. It stays, blank and staring and stark and barren, just like his dream.

He slides down the wall and puts his head on the hard clay of the street. He pounds the ground and cries out, "No. No. No." And his tears drown him.

A hand. A hand on his shoulder.

"Come, my son. Let me help you up. We vill go somevhere togeder."

"Not da house, Vather," Luke says, now on his knees.

"Not da house."

"Okay, Son. Ve vill go to da parchment shop."

Sigmundrr gets his son onto his feet, brings Luke's arm over his big shoulder, and holds him up.

"Come now, Son."

They turn in the direction of King Kadphises' statue. Luke takes a step.

"Dhat's right, my son. Now, take anoder step. You can do it."

Luke obeys and takes another step, and another.

He stops. Turns. Grabs hold of his father and buries his face in the old man's chest. His sobs echo through his mind, his heart, his very being. He trembles, his knees grow weak, he begins to slide down.

Sigmundrr takes a firm hold under Luke's arms, and lifts him again. "Be a man, Son. I know dhis is hard. I lost my own vife, you remember. Be a man."

The big father turns so he is beside Luke once again and once again guides him up the street toward the statue.

"Dhat's right. Take anoder step now. Good. Und another von."

Somehow they reach the statue. Luke looks into his father's eyes, though he does not see them.

"Oh, vather. Dhis cannot be. Dhis cannot happen. Oh, vather."

"I know, Son. I know. Now let's turn here. Ve have to go to da bazaar."

Like a lifeless statue, Luke makes his legs do the impossible and move. One step at a time. Then another. And another. Farther and farther from his dream. From his beautiful Rashah.

"Ve are here, Son." Sigmundrr says.

Shocked upon seeing Luke, Farnad rushes out a side door, joins them on the street, moves to Luke's other side, and helps Sigmundrr get him into the shop.

"Take him in here where he used to sleep," Farnad says.

They guide Luke to his mat, Luke turns over on his side, and he sobs.

"What happened?" Farnad asks.

"His promised vife has died."

"Oh, no. What is he going to do?"

"I do not know. He does not know. Dhis is impossible. She vas young und healthy," Sigmundrr says. "Vhat possibly could have happened unless she vas killed in some kind of accident."

"Didn't you say she rode horses?"

"Yes. Maybe dhat vas it. Maybe she vell off her horse und vas killed."

"Well, he still has a job if he wants to stay here in Kandahar. With you here, he will not want to leave. You have no choice where to live. He will stay here. I know it."

"Dhat is very kind uv you to let him keep his yob," Sigmundrr says.

"He is a good man and honest and smart. He has brought in a lot of business for me."

"Ve have not asked him, but he vas happy vith you. I am sure he vill want to stay vith you."

"I wonder if he would like something to eat," Farnad says.

"I do not dhink so. He has begun to mourn. It vill take a long time to mourn."

"Of course, you are right."

"I vould stay vith him tonight, but must return to da barracks. Da other men are covering for me, but I must get back now. I vill return tomorrow."

Sigmundrr steps over to his son, now half sobbing and half engulfed in shock. The big man kneels, leans low, and kisses his son on the cheek.

"Oh, my son," he whispers. "My son."

16 ~ ESCAPE

"Vather, go vith me."

"You know I cannot do dhat, Son."

"But I can no longer stay here. Every time I turn around, I dhink I see Rashah. Everyting reminds me of her. I must leave. Ve can go back to our homeland. Dhen ve vill alvays be togeder."

"You know it is impossible vor me to leave. I am a slave."

"I am a slave too. But it is too late vor me to return to my master. I have been gone too long. He vould never forgive me."

"No. It is too hard to escape. I have seen people try, and they yust find dhem, bring dhem back und put dhem to death."

"It von't happen dhis time. I know where I am going. Ve can outsmart dhem. I cannot lose you both—my wife and my vather. I need you, Vather."

"Lukvert, I have only lived three places in my entire life—up in Frisia, over in Espanola, and now in Parthia. I don't even know where I am. All I know is dhat it vas alvays cold in my homeland, it is alvays hot here, und it vas in between in Espanola."

"Vather, I know where we are. I know where Espanola is und Rome und Greece und Anatolia und Scythia und China. I know where everyting in the vorld is."

"But vhere do you plan to go?"

"Back to da homeland. Back to Frisia. Back home. Go home vith me, Vather. Go home vith me. Please."

Silence.

"It vill take me a vew days," Sigmunder says. "I'll have to bring you a few clothes und some blankets to save for me. Und I'll have to vait until a day vhen dhey expect me to be gone a long time."

"Don't be frightened, Vather. I vill take care of us. I know what I am doing."

The following day, Luke is helping Farnad sew together some parchments to make a large scroll.

"Sir, I need a horse. Do you have enough money to buy a horse?"

Farnad stares at Luke, his brow furrowed together and his eyebrows lowered. "You want me to buy you a what? Never."

"Sir, if you vill buy a horse vor me, I vill give you my house."

Farnad puts down his work.

"Your house is worth two horses."

"Then vill you buy me two horses?"

"One I can see. But two?"

"I am dhinking of going back to Ecbatana. I could use an extra horse to carry vater, a tent, and other supplies."

"What you need are a couple of camels."

"No, dhey must be horses."

"Well, okay. I'll start checking around."

"Und, sir, can you not tell dhem dhey vill be vor me?"

"Okay. I will think of something."

Farnad goes over and checks his supply of blackener. "Hmmm, looks like we're almost out. Oh, I forgot. You're leaving. When will that be?"

"I do not know. I vill know when it happens."

A week later, Farnad has two horses for Luke, and Luke hands him the keys to his house.

"This will give me a chance to get away from the shop at night. And I will be able to have a feast for my friends," Farnad says. "I'm glad you thought of it, Luke, though I think I got the better deal."

Over the next month, Sigmundrr stops by as usual, but he and Luke speak longer with each other, and often out of the hearing of Farnad.

No, it couldn't be, the shop owner sometimes thinks to himself.

One morning, Farnad returns to the shop from his new house to resume work from the day before. He walks into the back section calling out, "Luke. Luke, time to wake up. Time to open up the shop. Luke."

He walks into the small room where Luke normally sleeps and he is gone. So are his blankets.

"So, he finally did it." He shakes his head. "I'll bet Sigmundrr doesn't show up today either."

―――

"Hurry, Vather. We must get as var away as possible before dhey discover you are gone."

"I must stop and rest, Son. Remember, I am dwenty years older dhan you."

Luke pulls on the reins of his Arabian horse, and slows it down.

Sigmundrr slides off his horse, sits by the side of the road, and takes a long draw of water. He takes off his turban, wipes perspiration off his face, and rewraps the turban around his head.

Luke follows suit.

"It has been so long since I have been on a horse. I am beginning to ache."

"It is only a two-day ride to da Indian Ocean. Dhen ve can board a ship and be safe."

"You have planned dhis trip well," Sigmundrr says. "I am proud of you, Son. Okay, I am ready to go again."

He reaches over, puts his big hand on the back of Luke's neck, and shakes it playfully.

Luke laughs. "Let's go."

Back on their horses, they bring them to a comfortable pace.

"Do you know vhat da virst ting is dhat I am going to do when ve get home, Vather?"

"Vhat's that, Son?"

"I am going to get me one of dhose big black Frisian

horses."

"You vill have to get a yob."

"I can do lots of tings. I can open up a school or be a scribe or teach weaponry."

"Vhat if our village is no longer dhere?"

"Oh. I hadn't thought of dhat. Vell, if it isn't, ve'll start it again. Won't ve, Vather?"

Sigmundrr does not reply.

"Vhat do you tink, Vather?"

"Shhh. I'm listening. Do you hear anyting?"

They ride the rest of the day in near silence, stopping to water their horses often, and give themselves a drink.

"I don't dhink we need our tent yet," Luke says when they stop for the night. "It vill come in handy vhen ve go varther north."

"I do not dhink we should stop now. Let us travel tonight, and rest tomorrow during da day."

"Whatever you say, Vather. It is a good idea."

They remount their horses and work their way by a half-moon on the road south to the Indian Ocean, freedom and an old life renewed.

Sometimes during the night as they ride, Sigmundrr dozes. Luke moves his horse close, reaches over, hangs on to his father's arm, and lets him sleep.

The sky turns light gray with slight purple and pink.

"Time to stop und rest," Luke says.

Sigmundrr jerks his head and opens his eyes. "How did it get to be daylight so vast?"

"It yust did. There is some brush. Let's go over dhere.

"How close do you dhink we are, Son?"

"I vould say another half day's or half night's ride."

The father and son lay their blankets on the ground, roll up in them and fall asleep. A spear is near the hands of them both. Sleep is fitful.

"Vather, da sun is going down. Ve can go now."

The two men shake out their blankets, put them back on their horses, and give them a large drink and a few hands full of barley. They shake out their clothes and splash a little precious water on their heads, then take a swig.

"Yust tink," Sigmundrr says smiling. "Me a vree man. Vhat is it like, Son? Being vree? I have forgotten."

"Vell, you can make your own decisions like vhere to live, but you also have to have a yob. Vell, I guess if you vere a farmer, you could eat your own food and sell the rest. Is that vhat you're going to do vhen ve get home, Vather?"

"Yes. I vill go back to my own home vhere I buried your mother. It vill have to be fixed up, of course, after so many vinters vith no one taking care of it."

"Do you dhink it is still dhere, Vather?"

"I hope so. If it is not, we shall build anoter one."

"Vhat about our village? Do you dhink it vill be dhere?"

"Yes, I dhink so. Even though dhose barbarian Romans von da battle in dhose woods, I don't dhink it ended dhere. I dhink dhey left us alone after dhat. Vhat do you dhink, Son?"

"My master did not stay dhere, but vent to other fortresses along da river. I did not hear anyting about going back. I dhink they yust vanted revenge for a battle they lost in Teutonia."

Sigmundrr pulls on his horse's reins until it stops. Luke turns his horse around and joins him.

"Vhat is it, Vather?"

"Do you hear anyone behind us?"

They both become quiet and listen.

"Vell, I guess it vas nothing. How much varther do you tink it is now?"

"If we don't stop vhen it becomes daylight, I dhink we can be dhere before da sun is very high."

"Dhen ve shall rest aboard the ship. Oh, Son, it has been so long. So very long. Home again. Home again vith my son und never to be parted again."

When the sun is pink in the sky, the two men stop to water their horses and give them some barley to eat. They take a draw of their own water and share a large chunk of cheese.

"Ve vill have to buy more food at da docks. It vill be a long voyage home."

"I have never been to Egypt. At least I don't dhink I

have. Maybe ve vent there on our vay from Espanola to Parthia."

"It is hot in Egypt too, from vhat I hear," Luke says, "but not as hot as Parthia. Nothing in da vorld is as hot as Parthia."

They ride along in silence.

"Look. Seagulls. We're close, Vather."

"Vree at last. It has been so long. Vree at last."

"I smell da saltwater from the ocean," Luke says farther down the road. "Do you hear dhat?"

"Vhat?" Sigmundrr asks, startled and pulling back on his horse's reins.

"Da bells," Luke says with a reassuring smile. "Dhey ring bells as signals on ships. Sometimes it signals fog. I hope dhere is no fog down at the docks dhis morning."

"Ah, I see it. Do you see it, Vather? Look down da hill. Da water."

The men put their horses into a trot and begin the last lap of their long journey.

"Okay, Vather, stay here vhile I find a ship going up to Egypt, and pay vor our passage. I vill be right back."

Sigmundrr dismounts and looks around. He sees rich people in litters and on fine horses, poor people on wagons and riding donkeys. He sees camels being loaded and unloaded, people milling around the dock, and people running back and forth giving orders. He looks up and watches the seagulls, breathes in the fresh ocean air, and feels the breeze against his cheeks.

So dhis is what vreedom is like. I had almost forgot.

"Okay, Vather. I found us a ship und it is leaving soon. Ve are yust in time."

"Ve are going so far, Son, vhy don't ve sell our horses? Surely dhere are people just arriving who need transportation."

"You are right, Vather. Da money can be used vor da next ship to take us north across da Great Sea."

The two men walk their horses down toward the docks.

"Horses vor sale. Horses vor sale."

"Hey, you."

Sigmundrr jerks around, his eyes dark and his brows lowered.

"Do you have two horses for sale?" they hear. "Can they travel in the desert?"

"Indeed, yes," Luke replies.

"How much?"

"Five hundred denarii vor each."

"I'll give you two hundred."

"No. No. Ve cannot part vith them dhat cheap. Ve vill take four hundred denarii."

"I don't have that much money on me. I'll give you three hundred denarii."

"Take it, Son."

"Okay. You have the horses vor three hundred denarii each."

"Wait here while I go back to my partner who has the money. I will be back shortly."

"It isn't as much money as I had hoped vor, but I guess I can get a yob if we need more."

Sigmundrr is not listening. He looks around. Down the row of docks. On board the ships. Up the hill.

The man returns with the money and takes the horses.

"Dhere is da bell, Vather. Let us go on board und be vree."

Father and son step on the wide gangplank and walk up to the deck of the ship side by side, their emotions barely in check.

Once on board, they turn, walk over to the stern of the ship, and look down at the waters of the Indian Ocean.

Sigmundrr looks at his son. "I am really vree, aren't I? After all dhese years—nearly twenty of dhem—I am vree."

"Sir, you are going to have to come with us."

Sigmundrr tries to turn, but his hands are being pulled behind his back and chained. Then his ankles.

"Vhat is da meaning of dhis?" Luke declares. "Stop. You have no right."

They turn and see the captain of the ship. "I had no

choice. They are soldiers of Prince Vima. His father, King Kadphises, is very powerful."

"No!" Luke shouts.

"Stand back sir," one of the soldiers says.

"Son, go on vithout me. I vill yoin you someday."

"I wouldn't be so sure about that," another soldier says.

"No, Vather!"

"Go on home und get ready vor me."

"That'll be a long wait, old man. When we deliver you back to Kandahar, you will be executed."

"No! You cannot do dhis! No!"

"Stay here, Son. I am still your vather, und I am ordering you to stay here."

"No!" Luke says from deep in his throat.

"Do vhat I say, Son. Obey me."

"If I were you," the first soldier says, "I would do what he says. That, or be executed with him for aiding in his escape."

"Goodbye vor now, Son," Sigmundrr shouts over his shoulder. "Remember our song. Alvays remember our song."

Luke follows his father to the gangplank, hangs on to the railing with white knuckles, and with unmanly tears, watches through a mist as his father disappears from his life once again.

As soon as they are off the ship, a bell is rung, the ropes are unwrapped from the pilings, the anchors are hoisted on board, and the sails are unfurled.

Luke is still there when the ship is out of the harbor. He is still there when the coast grows smaller and smaller. He is still there when it all disappears. All his hopes and dreams. All alone again.

No more father.

No more wife.

No more of anything.

Free for what reason? Free to gain, then lose it all again?

When night comes, he slumps to the deck, takes off the pack on his back, leans over, lays his head on it, and dreams. He is riding on a ship, but it is not a ship. It is a monster. The monster flies through the air, then dives down into the ocean. Luke holds his breath. Can't breathe. Can't breathe. Oh, to breathe again. But for what? So he can live and die again? He gasps for air.

"Sir, are you okay?" one of the passengers asks in Greek.

Luke sits up. It is nearly daylight. He pushes the hair out of his eyes. He looks at the passenger. "What did you say?" Luke answers.

"Are you all right? You seem to have been having a nightmare. But it is morning and I do not have anyone to talk to. Plus I hate eating alone. May I introduce myself? My name is Obasi."

"Oh," Luke says standing. "My name is Luke." *Can I trust him? Why is he talking to me?*

"I see you are Parthian by your dress," Obasi says. "But you do not look Parthian. May I ask what nationality you are?"

"Sir, I do not wish to be rude," Luke says in his best Greek voice, "but I prefer to be alone. I am sure someone else on board will be happy to talk and eat with you."

"My apologies," Obasi says, dipping his head. And he leaves.

Luke turns back to take hold of the railing and watch the sea once again. As he does, his memories come rushing in and invade his soul. He weeps once more.

Alone. All alone. Again. What am I going to do? I cannot face life like this. Oh, thousand gods, what am I going to do?

The day passes like a fog. In the distance he hears sailors barking orders to each other, passengers telling jokes to each other, seagulls overhead squawking to each other.

All in a far distance. Like his dreams. Like his Rashah. His father. And going home again.

He welcomes night. Now he can sleep and forget. Now he can transport his mind to a faraway place of dreams that do not exist.

He does not dream. He does not sleep. Once it is too dark he cannot see the water, Luke walks around. Round

and round the ship. In circles always ending up back where he began.
    Alone.
    All alone.
    Nothing.
    Nowhere.
    No one.

17 ~ VAGABOND

Luke walks down the gangplank onto Egyptian soil at the north end of the Red Sea. He looks around, but does not see what he needs. He taps the shoulder of one of the other newly arrived passenger and Obasi turns around.

"It seems we meet again," Obasi says. "Did you have a nice rest?"

"I was just wondering where I can buy a decent tunic and shoes, and perhaps get a haircut."

"You are in luck. I know exactly where those shops are. I was headed there myself."

After Luke changes out of his Parthian clothes and is refreshed, he walks back out onto the street and looks around. He takes out one of his last coins and buys some bread.

"Where is the road to Alexandria?" he asks the baker.

"You can go on up to the coast of the Great Sea, which is a two- or three-day journey, then go west along the delta until you hit Alexandria. Or you can go west now until you hit the Nile River about a two-day journey, then north through the delta to Alexandria. Your choice."

"I know the way," someone behind Luke says.

Luke looks over his shoulder. "Obasi, why can't you leave me alone?"

"Because you need me, my friend."

"I am not your friend."

"Well, you will be. Besides, you need a friend. No, no arguing. We are taking the west route to the Nile, then north. Come, my friend. I bought two new water skins—one for you and one for me."

He hands one to Luke, and Luke takes it.

The two men head out of the city and into the desert.

"If you've been in Parthia, you know our Egyptian deserts aren't nearly as hot as those Parthian ones. For one thing, we get a breeze off the Red Sea to our East, the Nile River in the middle, and the Great Sea to the north."

"Shut up, Obasi."

Their trip to the Nile is uneventful. Obasi alternately tells stories and sings. Luke tunes him out.

Both men have long legs and make it to the Nile in less than two days.

"Here is where we get on a passenger boat the rest of the way," Obasi says. "I bought passage for both of us because my guess is that you have run out of money. Perhaps you were robbed in Parthia. Who knows?"

Luke follows him to the riverboat. Within a day, they are in Alexandria. They leave the boat and walk a way toward the city itself. Luke stops and sits on a bench. Obasi sits next to him.

"Now what?" Obasi asks. "I've gotten you this far."

"You didn't have to," Luke says, still living in a world of unfeeling.

"Sir, you have been through something heavy. I don't know what it was. I heard some other passengers talk about some soldiers taking your companion away. I guess that was part of it, but I think it was more. Am I right?"

Luke does not answer.

"All I know is that you needed someone to take over your life, while you sorted through whatever was consuming you. I've been there a few times myself. Don't think I didn't care, just because I was jabbering and singing around you. I was just giving you a little dose of reality to help you stay anchored."

For the first time since meeting that first day on the ship, Luke looks directly at Obasi.

The man is as tall as Luke, but portly in the middle. He has a mixture of black and gray hair, part of which shows at the edges of the short shawl over his head. He has a square jaw, long thick nose, and thick lips.

"Sir," Luke says, "don't think I am ungrateful. It's just that..."

"Don't worry about it. Now, since you obviously do not have any money left, you are going to have to make some so you can either settle here or go on to some other place. You speak Greek well. Can you write?"

"Not Egyptian. But I can Greek. And I know Latin. Also Nordic. Also a little Parthian."

"That's what I thought. Well, how would you like to work for me?"

"Doing what?"

"Tutoring my children. I will provide you with a room in my house and a small stipend. Oh, you may be wondering how I can afford a tutor. I am an importer of Lapis Lazuli from eastern Parthia. It's very popular here. The noble ladies especially love it to decorate their eyes."

Luke twists his mouth.

"Never tutored before? You'll catch on. The children will help you. Anyway, I have two sons—Irsu who is seven, and Hotep who is nine."

"Sir," Luke says. "I want to thank you for all you have done. I was not ungrateful."

"I know," Obasi says, punching Luke in his muscular arm and smiling. "Now, I need to rent a chariot and horse, so we can get home before sundown. My wife and her cook can come up with some of the best meals."

The children are in bed by the time Obasi and Luke arrive. Luke is given a room and settles in. The next day he meets the children, finds out what they already know, and takes them toward the next level.

Two weeks go by. Luke's tutoring for the day is over.

It's time I do what I need to do, Luke tells himself. He goes into Alexandria, purchases several parchments, prepared to sew them together into a scroll in the event he writes more than he intends.

Back home, he goes up the steps from the courtyard and enters his small room. It is hot inside, but he must do this in private.

He sits on a cushion on the floor as he had done so many years before while learning to write, then later while writing a history of his people.

> MOST HUMBLE GREETINGS FROM YOUR ETERNAL SLAVE, LUKE OF FRISIA, AND NOW OF ALEXANDRIA, EGYPT, IN THE EMPLOY OF PANASI OBASI.
>
> MY MOST EXCELLENT THEOPHILUS, I HAVE NOT EVER FORGOTTEN YOU. DO NOT THINK I HAVE RUN AWAY FROM YOU. CIRCUMSTANCES KEPT GETTING OUT OF CONTROL OR REQUIRED MY MOST URGENT ATTENTION.
>
> FIRST OF ALL, I ARRIVED IN ECBATANA AS PLANNED, THE PLACE OF THE WINTER PALACE OF PARTHIA'S EMPEROR. IT TOOK ME NEARLY A YEAR BECAUSE OF THE BLIZZARD CONDITIONS IN THE MOUNTAINS TO ARRIVE THERE. ECBATANA HAS BOTH GOLD AND IRON MINES. BEFORE I COULD LEARN MORE ABOUT THE POSSIBILITY OF THEM IMPORTING MORE IRON THAN THEIR OWN MINE COULD OUTPUT, I WAS FALSELY ACCUSED AND FORCED TO WORK IN THEIR GOLD MINE.
>
> I SLAVED IN THE MINE TWO YEARS BEFORE IT COLLAPSED. YOU WILL BE PLEASED TO KNOW I TREATED THE INJURED. BUT AFTER THAT, A MAIDEN WHOM I ADMIRE HELPED ME ESCAPE. I LIVED IN A CAVE FOR MANY MONTHS. WHEN THE MAIDEN DID NOT RETURN WITH MY DAILY FOOD, I LEARNED SHE HAD BEEN TAKEN AS A SLAVE INTO EASTERN PARTHIA ACROSS A BLAZING DESERT.
>
> I COULD NOT FORSAKE HER, SO CROSSED THE DESERT UNDER MANY DIFFICULTIES, AND BY THE TIME I ARRIVED, ANOTHER YEAR HAD PASSED. THEN I SPENT STILL ANOTHER YEAR TRYING TO GET HER FREED AS SHE HAD DONE FOR ME. HER FREEDOM WAS FINALLY GRANTED BECAUSE I SAVED HER MASTER'S LIFE, AND THE PRINCE BETROTHED US. BUT I HAD TO BUILD HER A HOUSE FIRST. AT THE END OF THAT YEAR, I WAS TOLD SHE HAD DIED.
>
> WHILE I WAS TRYING TO FIND AND RESCUE THIS MAIDEN, I HAPPENED TO DISCOVER MY FATHER'S WHEREABOUTS—IN THE VERY SAME ESTATE WHERE THE MAIDEN WAS LIVING, AND BOTH AS SLAVES. AFTER I LEARNED SHE HAD DIED, I FOUND A JOB LASTING ANOTHER YEAR TO EARN ENOUGH FOR TWO PASSAGES ABOARD A SHIP, THEN HELPED MY FATHER ESCAPE.
>
> MY FATHER WAS CAUGHT BEFORE WE LEFT PORT, AND SENT BACK TO BE EXECUTED. AND SO I BECAME ALONE AGAIN. I AM NOW IN ALEXANDRIA TRYING TO EARN MONEY TO LEAVE HERE AND GO HOME.
>
> MOST EXCELLENT THEOPHILUS, I KNOW MOST OF THESE NINE YEARS YOU THOUGHT I HAD RUN AWAY FROM YOU. MAYBE I DID, BUT IT WAS EITHER BECAUSE I WAS FORCED TO STAY AWAY, OR I WAS DUTY-BOUND TO SAVE TWO PEOPLE I LOVED. AND SO, I REPENT WITH TEARS.
>
> CAN YOU FORGIVE ME? I BEG OF YOU, MASTER, PROSTRATE UPON MY FACE, PLEASE TAKE ME BACK. PUNISH ME AS YOU SEE FIT, BUT PLEASE LET ME COME HOME.

There is a knock on Luke's door. When he opens it, he sees that it is morning.

"Master," seven-year-old Irsu says, "are you ready to teach me?" The boy pauses. "Have you been crying, Master?"

Luke smiles and ruffles the boy's black hair. "I will be

down in a few moments. Go down and count to one hundred. Then I will be there."

"Hotep too?"

"Hotep must count to one hundred also."

The lessons end just before the heat of the day, as usual. Luke goes up to his room, brings out some silver coins, ties and seals his scroll, and leaves. Within an hour, he is at the docks.

"Sir, is your ship going to the Black Sea?"

"Captain, sir, is your ship going to the Black Sea?"

"By any chance, sir, might your ship be going to the Black Sea?"

"If the weather is in our favor, yes, we will be trying for the Black Sea. Do you have any cargo for us to deliver?"

"No, I just have this letter. Could you see to it that it is delivered to Tribune Titus Pontus Theophilus at Fortress Capidava on the north shore at the mouth of the Danube River?"

"Well..."

"I have ten silver coins for you. Is that enough?"

"I will not be responsible if it is accidentally destroyed in a storm or any other way."

"Yes, sir. I understand, sir."

"How long do you think it will take you to get there?"

"With all the stops we have to make along the coasts going up, it will take at least three months, maybe four."

"That is fine," Luke says. "Here is my letter and the silver."

The captain takes both and Luke returns to Obasi's estate.

He waits. Four months go by and he decides Theophilus has his letter. Four more months go by and Luke begins looking for a reply.

Each afternoon, regardless how hot it is, Luke walks the hour to the docks to see if any of the ships have a letter for him. An hour before dark, he returns to Obasi's house.

One season merges into another, and still no word.

Was Tribune Theophilus killed in a battle? Did my master die of a disease? Was he transferred to another fortress? Was he sent to Rome to serve Caesar? Did he retire? If so, where to?

"Sir," he says one evening after spending the day at the docks, "I have been thinking of settling here and starting a school."

"That is a wonderful idea," Obasi says.

"I have been saving up my stipend money, and..."

"Yes, I have noticed you never seem to spend any money on yourself."

"...and there is a scribe school in the city that I heard has an extra room. Perhaps the owner would allow me to rent that room. I could teach children in it by day, and sleep in it by night.

"I have enough money to rent it for the first month, and tuition from the children should provide enough for the future. And I do not think it would be too far away for a servant to bring your children into the city each morning for lessons."

"He could make contacts for me down at the docks and among the merchants in the market," Obasi says, "and be ready to take my sons home when they are through with their lessons. Brilliant. I think that would work for everyone all around."

Luke smiles. It is a genuine smile. The first one in a very long time.

The school is established. No one questions Luke's status, assuming he is at least a freedman, even though he is not a Roman citizen. Not many men in the world have the privilege of being Roman citizens.

Another year goes by. It is early afternoon. Obasi's servant arrives to take the boys home.

"Oh, by the way, Luke, I have a letter for you."

Luke looks at the servant and takes a quick gulp of air. "A what?"

"A letter. A captain on a ship that originated in Greece asked me if I was a servant of Obasi. When I told him I was, he handed me a letter to be delivered to Luke in the care of Panasi Obasi, an importer of Alexandria."

Luke stands.

"Oh, here it is," the servant says, handing it to Luke. "Come along boys. You do not want to be late."

Luke holds the letter close, then sets it on a small table nearby. As the other students leave by ones, twos and threes with their parents' servants, Luke looks over at the scroll to make sure it is still there.

The last student leaves, Luke locks the door, then sits by a high window, and breaks the seal.

> TRIBUNE TITUS PONTUS THEOPHILUS OF THE CITY OF BEREA, PROVINCE OF MACEDONIA, NATION OF GREECE, AND EMPIRE OF ROME. GREETINGS TO MY BELOVED LUKE.
>
> HOW MY HEART WAS GRATIFIED UPON RECEIPT OF YOUR MOST WELCOMED AND UNEXPECTED LETTER. I MUST SAY IT WAS MIRACULOUS THAT I RECEIVED IT AT ALL. I FINALLY RETIRED AT FORTRESS CAPIDAVA AFTER THIRTY YEARS IN SERVICE TO THE CAESARS. MY LOYAL CENTURION, SOPATER, RETIRED AT THE SAME TIME AND URGED ME TO GO WITH HIM TO BEREA WHERE HIS FATHER LIVES. I DID SO, AND HAVE MADE GOOD FRIENDS WITH HIS FATHER WHO IS NEAR MY SAME AGE.
>
> AS FOR YOU, MY BELOVED LUKE, I NEVER THOUGHT YOU HAD RUN AWAY. RATHER, I DECIDED YOU HAD BEEN KILLED SOMEWHERE ALONG THE WAY. I NEVER DOUBTED YOUR LOYALTY.
>
> I REGRET THAT YOU WENT THROUGH ALL YOU DID TO OBTAIN THE INFORMATION ROME NEEDED. YES, WE RECEIVED YOUR BELATED MESSAGE, APPARENTLY SENT AFTER YOU ESCAPED ALL YOUR TROUBLES IN ECBATANA. IT WAS A LITTLE LATE IN HELPING US MAKE DECISIONS ABOUT PARTHIA, BUT NOT COMPLETELY WITHOUT USEFULNESS. I WILL TELL YOU MORE WHEN YOU COME.
>
> YES, MY BELOVED LUKE, COME HOME. I ONLY REGRET THAT YOU WERE UNABLE TO BE PERMANENTLY REJOINED WITH YOUR FATHER, BUT PERHAPS THE YEAR OR TWO YOU DID HAVE WITH HIM WILL SERVE TO COMFORT YOUR HEART.
>
> NOW, COME TO ME. I NEVER DID TELL YOU THIS, BUT I CONSIDERED YOU JUST AS MUCH MY SON AS MY SLAVE. WHOEVER TREATED THEIR SLAVE BETTER THAN I TREATED YOU? I WANTED TO SPOIL YOU.
>
> AND SO, IT IS WITH LOVE IN MY HEART FOR YOU THAT I SAY, YES, COME HOME. I HAVE PAID FOR PASSAGE FOR YOUR TRIP FROM ALEXANDRIA TO BEREA TO THE SAME SHIP CAPTAIN WHO BROUGHT YOU MY LETTER.
>
> MAY THE THOUSAND GODS PROTECT YOU.

Luke sets down the scroll, closes his eyes, and weeps.

He wants me. When I was all alone after the battle, he took me to be with him. Now he is doing it again. How blessed I am.

Luke opens his eyes and re-read the letter. Over and over he reads it until it is memorized. Then he reads it again.

It is late afternoon. Luke makes the walk to Obasi's

house, only this time he breaks into a run.

"Welcome, friend. What can I do for you?" Obasi says, walking into his courtyard from his *officium*.

"Where is your servant who always picks up your children at school?" Luke asks.

"He is helping me inventory. Do you need him?"

"Yes. It is important."

Obasi disappears a few moments and returns with his servant.

"I need to know the name of the ship that delivered my letter."

"It was the *Thalassa*."

"Thank you," Luke says with a large grin. Soon he is out of the house and in a run again.

Down at the docks just before sunset, Luke rushes past each ship, reading the name on the side.

"There it is," he says aloud. He runs up the gangplank and addresses the officer in charge.

"When are you returning to Greece?"

"Well, in about two weeks. Did you want to go with us?"

"Yes, sir. I believe my passage has already been paid for. Tribune Titus Pontus Theophilus took care of it in Berea."

The officer calls a sailor over to cover for him. "I will check with the bursar."

Moments later he is back. "Are you Luke of Frisia?" he asks.

"Yes, sir."

"Then your passage is covered. We do not normally stop near Berea because of the swamps. There are larger ports at Athens, Thessalonica and Neapolis. You must know someone very important. Well, wait about ten days, and then we should know which day we will be setting out to sea."

"Thank you, sir."

Luke bounds off the gangplank, and runs through the streets to his rented room, his hands outstretched and reaching for the sky. "I'm going home, everyone. I'm going home."

Luke sends word to all the parents that he is closing up the school in ten days. At the end of the last day, he accompanies Obasi's sons home.

"I just want to thank you, Obasi, for rescuing me that day on the ship."

"Yes, I guess I did rescue you. Were you thinking of jumping overboard?"

"No, I'm not like that. But I would have gradually strangled myself with grief. And so, thank you again. The gods must have sent you to me."

"Which gods?"

"All thousand of them."

"You've counted them?" Obasi says, half teasing.

"Well, you know what I mean."

Luke grows serious and holds out his hands to his friend. The men embrace and say goodbye.

Three days later, Luke is on board the *Thalassa*.

A month passes. Luke has brought along some parchments to keep him busy. Sometimes he writes a letter to his beloved Rashah. The next day he scrapes the ink off and writes a letter to his father.

Sometimes he tries to remember the stories his father told him when they were together in Frisia, trying again to write the history of his people. His memories are fuzzy. He begins to write, then is unable to remember who did what.

Vather, if I had only asked you to repeat dhem to me vhile ve vere togeder in Kandahar.

He looks up at the sky. *I thought ve had da rest of our lives togeder to do dhat.*

Sometimes he walks around the ship singing his father's song. He tries not to be melancholy when he does. *Dhis song is for you, Vather, vherever you are.*

Tho I vander long avay
Over all da mounts und seas
To da end uv da verld,
I vill alvays tink uv home
Und keep you in my heart
Til I hold you once again.

He decides to make a list of all thousand gods. *This is confusing. How does anyone keep track? Maybe I should just choose one god. That's what my master did. He chose Mars. I could choose Thor, but I do not like him. Maybe I'll choose Hermes. I do not know. There are so many of them.* Then he returns to listing more gods.

Another month goes by. While in port, he goes ashore and buys a scroll with the writings of Plato on it. It keeps him busy, though by now he has made friends with the sailors and sometimes talks with them when they are not working. They exchange tales of their travels.

The final month. Closer to Greece. Closer to Berea. Closer to home. He sits, he stands, he walks.

Home. I never appreciated it until now. My master had given me a home. Not just a place to live and eat and serve, but a home. My master loved me. He really loved me. I loved him too. Vather, vould you mind if I love Master Theophilus too?

It is morning. The captain calls Luke up to his cabin. "We have a man with a broken leg. Happened during the night. No one here knows how to help him. Do you have any knowledge of things like that?"

"Yes, sir. I used to help a *medicus* in the Roman army. Then I helped when a mine collapsed. Where is he?"

"Go with my first mate. He will show you."

After that, both the sailors and officers come to Luke about their injuries large and small, their illnesses major and minor, and how they feel overall whether real or imagined.

"Land, ho!"

After forever, and waiting for high tide, the ship eases into the small, swampy port, drops anchors, and lowers a rowboat for Luke's transport the rest of the way in.

Luke steps onto the shore, looks around, and sees a man in a Roman tribune's uniform marching toward him. Luke runs in his direction and falls into the arms of his master.

"Welcome home, my son. Welcome home."

18 ~ THE MOUNTAIN

"This way," Tribune Theophilus says with a large grin he cannot hold back. It is some twenty-five *milles* to Berea. This is just a port. It is too swampy for much of a city.

Luke steps behind his master and Theophilus stops. "What are you doing? Come walk beside me."

"I cannot, Master. This is my place and I am contented."

They walk toward a chariot. As they draw closer, Luke recognizes the driver.

"Sopater?" Luke says. "Is that you?"

Theophilus boards the chariot and Luke with him. Sopater turns and holds out his hands to Luke in greeting.

"It is so good to see you after all this time," the centurion says.

"Let us be on our way," Theophilus urges. "I am sure Luke is anxious to see his new home and freshen up."

The chariot works its way onto higher ground, then follows the Haliacmon River south.

Luke feels the breeze from the sea on his face and in his hair. Looking up at the tops of the tall trees on either side of the road and the mountains, he is reminded of the northland where he had grown up.

"What is that tall mountain up there?" he asks.

"It is Mount Olympus, home of the gods," Theophilus answers over the noise of the wheels on the stone Via Ignatia.

"Really? That is where the gods live?"

"That's what the priests tell me, and who am I to question them? They're the experts and know these things."

Luke stares at the snow-capped mountain and tries to envision Zeus and his family up there, and what they may be doing at this very moment.

The chariot comes to the Tripotamos River, and turns west, following its course.

"This river runs right down the middle of Berea," Sopater says, calling over his shoulder. "And that mountain on our left is Mount Bermius."

"Do any gods live there?" Luke asks.

"We do not know."

They ride through the gate into the city. They pass the market on their right, and temples to Zeus, Artemis, Hercules and Dionysius on their left.

"See that fortress up on the ridge at the other end of the city? I am the commander," Theophilus says.

"I thought you retired," Luke responds.

"I did, but when we came here, they were in need of a commander and offered it to me. So I was recommissioned."

The chariot works its way west, then turns left just before the city forum and baths. They cross the Tripotamos River, then continue on west along the higher hills of the city.

"Here we are," Theophilus says.

Sopater slows the horses and stops in front of Theophilus' front gate. The passengers get off, and he continues on to the stable.

The tribune's double gate is copper with a gold image of an elephant attached to the middle of each door.

"Do you remember our Fifth Legion emblem?" Theophilus asks, touching the elephant and knocking on his gate.

"Indeed, I do," Luke responds, just as the gate is opened by Egidius.

"I do not believe you met Egidius. He was a cavalryman who retired about the same time I did. I hired him to come with me to Berea and watch over things in my house."

Egidius is of medium height, has gray hair, and a slim build. Though retired, he wears his old infantry uniform.

"I am pleased to meet you, Master Luke."

Embarrassed, Luke looks over at Theophilus, then back at the doorman. "Oh, no. You have it wrong. I am a slave like you."

Egidius, now is embarrassed also, and turns to Theophilus. "Forgive me, Master. I did not understand."

"Luke has been with me since he was eight years old. I was just a little older than Luke is now. He has been with me longer than anyone else, including Centurion Sopater."

"Did someone say my name?" Sopater asks, coming into the courtyard from the stable. Yes, I have been with Theophilus some fifteen years or more."

Turning to Luke, "Again, welcome back," Sopater says. "We have all missed you. Let me show you to your room. It is down here next to my *officium*."

"You have an *officium* here?" Luke asks.

"Yes, Sopater takes care of my financial and legal affairs," Theophilus says. "Now go on and get cleaned up. I have placed a new tunic and sandals in your room. I did not know what condition you would arrive in," he says with a grin.

Luke shakes his head, smiles, and goes to his room. He closes the door, looks around, and kneels on the mat on the floor. He folds his hands together and bows his head.

"Oh thousand gods. Thank you for all this. Thank you for bringing me home."

Half an hour later, Luke opens his door to the courtyard just as a maid sets out trays of grapes, figs, olives, and cheese.

"Help yourself," Theophilus says.

Luke smiles, takes what he can in his hands, then sits on a silk cushion on the floor near his master's marble bench.

"Now, we've got to set up some duties for you. First, although I have guards outside my house at night, you will guard the inside. That is why your room is where it is."

"Yes, Master. I have been able to keep up my strength

during all my travels. I will be most pleased to guard your house."

"Second, I am building a personal library. I will arrange for you to visit the libraries of some of my friends, and make copies of the books I want. Of course, you will do so at their home to avoid arousing suspicions of borrowing and not returning.

"Third, I want you to investigate the gods. I am not sure Mars should be my god any longer."

"Yes, sir. I look forward to doing these things for you, my master."

"I have made arrangements for you to go to the home of Pyrrus, Sopater's father, first. Today, you will go to the market and purchase a supply of scrolls and blackener. Are you still sewing squares of parchment together to form your scrolls? There is a new glue out which works better. You will pick up a jar of that."

"While you are in the city, walk around and acquaint yourself with it. Stop in at the temples to the four gods and goddesses of our city and introduce yourself to their high priests and priestesses. I want to learn more about them someday."

"Yes, my master."

"Down in the city of Dion at the foot of Mt. Olympus, are sanctuaries dedicated to Zeus and his children. Many people make pilgrimages to Dion. You should go there to copy their holy books. I want to read them for myself. But it will probably be next year after you copy the local books."

"Yes, my master."

"There is a medical academy down in Athens. But it may be two or three years before you get down there."

"No wonder you wanted me back." Luke looks over at his master and notices he is serious. "It is my honor to serve you in this way, Master."

The following day upon his arrival, Sopater tells Luke how to get to his father's house. Being an exporter of silver, his front gate is easily identified, being plated with silver and adorned with a bronze ship.

"Welcome, Luke," Pyrrus says the next day when Luke

arrives. "My son has spoken of you often through the years."

"I am honored to be invited into your home," Luke responds.

Pyrrus is tall with an oval face, long wide nose, high cheekbones, and flared lips.

"My library is this way. I think the most interesting thing you will find are some of the annuls of my famous ancestor who was king of the region northwest of here—Epirus—when Greece was the shining empire of the world. He was considered one of the greatest warriors of all time. I am sure that is why your master is interested in my library."

"Yes, sir. Where would you like me to work?"

"I have a lap table all set up for you."

Luke takes out his writing supplies, looks through Pyrrus' ancestral annals, chooses one, and settles down to copy it.

Each day Luke returns to do his copy work. The days grow into weeks and months. After a year, Luke has copied all the annals of King Pyrrus in his namesake's library, and they have become friends.

"So, where are you going next?"

"I believe my master wants me to go down to Dion and see what books I can find in the sanctuaries of the gods there."

"That should be interesting. Have you chosen one to be your patron god?" Pyrrus asks, scratching his prominent nose.

"No, I have not. There are so many of them that I am confused. However, I do pray to the thousand gods every morning and every evening and sometimes at noon," Luke says, gathering up the last of his writing supplies.

"Thousand gods, you say? I never heard they could be counted."

"Well, I have not actually counted them. It just seems to me there must be that many. So, in order to not leave anyone out and hurt their feelings, I just pray to them all at once."

Pyrrus grins as he walks Luke to the front gate. "Well, someday you must count them all for me. Sometimes they get confusing to me also."

"You are going to Dion next," Theophilus tells Luke the following day. "It is good to know about past kings, and you did well with that. But what about the eternal gods? I must investigate them. I will give you until tomorrow to prepare. That will also give my maid a day to make a supply of bread for you."

Two days later, Luke is on the road to Dion. He crosses the Haliacmon River and works his way to the coast of the Aegean Sea. He arrives at the city, and asks directions to the various sanctuaries.

"Out in the foothills of Olympus," he is told, "you will find sanctuaries of Dionysus, Demeter, Asklepios, Zeus, and Isis. Many pilgrims come here to worship."

"Do you have a sacred library?" he asks.

"Yes, but it is small. It carries all the sacred writings of the gods we know of. We must rely on the priests and our most ancient ancestors for everything else."

Luke finds a hostel to stay in and has an evening meal. The next morning he puts a collection of parchments in his pack. He stops at a produce market to pick up some apples and grapes to eat on the way.

He arrives at the library, and is directed to the Homeric Hymns. Luke faithfully copies the *Hymn to Demeter*, goddess of harvest. A week later he is ready to copy the *Hymn to Apollo*, the god of light, music, and prophecy. Next is the *Hymn to Hermes*, messenger god between Olympus and humans, and protector of travelers and thieves. Finally he comes to the *Hymn to Aphrodite,* goddess of love and beauty and copies it. It takes Luke a month to copy all four of these epic Homeric Hymns. He is more confused than ever.

That evening, he puts his parchments away in his rented room and goes out through the city gates. He walks toward the shore of the Aegean, picks up stones, and throws them in the water as far as he can.

"No!" he shouts over and over.

"It does not make sense," he declares to the sky. These gods are just like us. The only thing different is their holy books who they are stronger and bigger than us. They lie. They cheat. They steal. They have drunken parties. They have illegitimate children," he shouts across the water. "They're just bigger humans."

There are twenty-nine other hymns to other gods, but they are so short, Luke completes copying them all in a week.

After finishing them, Luke takes his evening walk. This time, he faces great Mount Olympus, and shakes his fist.

"What good are you?" he bellows. "We have to keep you happy so you don't punish us. Is that it? Are we just pawns in your game?"

The Homeric hymns completely copied, the librarian tells him another sacred writing is the *Theogony,* an epic poem by Hesiod. The librarian explains that Hesiod expounds on the births and genealogies of the gods, so will be necessary for his understanding of the gods.

Luke takes his seat and realizes the scroll is only about one third as long as Homer's accounts of the gods. He finds the hymn beautiful, but it basically declares Zeus the god of gods, and magnifies his daughters, the muses.

He goes to the librarian and asks about the muses. "Where do they live?"

The librarian takes him outside and points. "See that plateau? That is where the muses live. They sing praises to Zeus all day.

"All nine of them?"

"Yes. All nine."

Luke has now been in Dior two months. He is told the third and final holy writing is *The Golden Verses of Pythagoras.*

The very first three proverbs tell him to worship, revere and honor the gods, national heroes, and demons. He throws his pen down, stands, and goes outside, forgetting he is responsible for the library's copies if they are stolen.

"How?" His arms are raised and he shouts at the sky. People on the street stare at him a moment, then go on their way, grinning and shaking their head at the lunatic stranger.

"How can we make them all happy?" he bellows. He stares at the sky, then down at his feet. He kicks a piece of broken pottery and wishes he hadn't.

They don't even get along with each other, so how are we supposed to? All they do is keep us frightened. If we don't do this right, thunderbolts are thrown down on us. If we don't do that right, we're riddled with disease. If we neglect this god, we drown in a rainstorm or at sea. If we neglect that demon, an earthquake is sent to swallow us. They don't even like us.

Luke walks back inside and resumes his reading and copying of *The Golden Verses*. The proverbs urge people to do right. He sets his pen down and looks up at the ceiling. *But what is right? Right for a god is not right for a demon.*

The last two lines baffle Luke even more. "After you divested yourself of your mortal body and arrive at the most pure Ether, you shall be a god—immortal, incorruptible, eternal."

There. They've admitted it. Gods are just good humans after they die.

It has taken one day to copy *The Golden Verses*. Just before dark, he takes the scroll up to the librarian. "I won't be back," he says.

He walks over to his hostel and packs all is parchments. He lies down on his mat, but cannot sleep. *Why would I want to be one of those gods? That is no reward. They do not like each other, do not like us, and probably do not even like themselves.*

He turns over in bed one way, then the other. *Life. What is it all for? Only wretchedness.*

The next day, Luke goes to the market, and with the last of his money given him by Theophilus, he buys high leather shoes, a leather tunic, and a heavy wool cape, reminiscent of Thracians who lived there in earlier years and of his own boyhood.

He heads for Mount Olympus. Higher into the foothills. "Okay, Hera, Poseidon, Athena, and Apollo. You are surely not all gone to play games somewhere. Surely at least one of you is home today. You claim this is where you live. Prove it. I want to see you."

He reaches the winding trails. He calls out and his voice echoes. "Hey Artemis, Hesta, Hermes. How about you, Aphrodite? Come out and show yourself. That is, if you are really here."

Now the steep inclines. "Where are you, Zeus? Isn't this your throne? Afraid of me? Is that why you hide all the time? Instead of being god of all gods, are you really coward of all cowards?"

Luke spots the plateau the muses are supposed to live on. He climbs over to it.

Out of breath, he shouts, "Hey, daughters of Zeus!" His voice echoes. "You know who you are—muses of poetry and singing and art and all those other decent things in life you take credit for. Bashful are you? Or are you even real?"

Back to the summit where Zeus is supposed to have his throne, Luke stands and stretches his arms upward, the wind blowing through his yellow hair. "Zeus...Zeus...Zeus..." His words echo back to him in their hollowness. "How I hate you...you...you. So, if you dare, strike me dead...dead...dead... Or do you even exist...exist...exist?"

He waits. He sits on the summit of the rock. He waits longer. The sun lowers itself and turns blood red. Still he waits. And falls asleep.

"Luke!"

He wakes with a start. "Huh?" He sees no one, and goes back to sleep.

"Luke!"

He opens his eyes again. He sees the image of a man with dark hair, closely shaven beard, a crooked nose, and one bad eye. "Come to Troas," the man says. "I will show you the one and only real God. The God of Truth. He loves you. Come to Troas."

19 ~ THE STRUGGLE

*T*wo days later, Luke walks into the home of Theophilus with a large basket on his back full of scrolls. He hangs the basket on a peg near the front gate, takes the scrolls out, and walks toward his master's *officium*. He opens the door and sets the scrolls on his writing-table.

Theophilus looks up. "Oh, you're back. Got a lot of copying done, I see."

Luke says nothing.

"But you do not look very happy. What is wrong? Are you sick?"

Luke sits on a bench near the writing table and puts his head in his hands.

"What's wrong?" Theophilus repeats. "Tell me."

"Master, they're all lies. Everything they tell us about the gods are lies. I copied their sacred writings. Read them for yourself. I checked them out. All those gods are not, well, they're not good. You are better than they are. And besides, they are not where they claim to be."

"How do you know?"

"I went to find them and talk to them, but they aren't there. None of them are on Mount Olympus. They are fakes, frauds, charlatans."

"You went looking for them, Luke?" Theophilus says, rising from his writing-table.

"You always said to check things out. I did."

"Luke, you continually amaze me. It seems you have read my mind." He walks out from behind the table and stares at the wall. "Since moving here, I have often looked over at Mount Olympus and wondered if anyone ever questioned whether the gods were really there. Where is people's sanity? But, if we don't believe in the Olympic gods, we are without any gods at all? Then what? We are all alone."

He looks over at Luke. "Well, rest tomorrow, then I want you to go to another friend's house and copy the works of Livy."

"I have heard of him."

"He wrote over a hundred books on the history of Rome. It will take you at least a year to copy them all."

Luke does not have far to walk to get to Brictius' home among the other finer houses up in the foothills of the mountain.

Brictius is of medium build, has gray hair around a half-bald head, and a ready smile.

Luke settles in at Brictius' house. He finishes twenty-three of the books.

"Master ,," Luke says, that afternoon, "I am low on supplies. I need to go into town to buy more parchments."

"That's fine, Luke Do you have money? Of course, you don't. Here is some."

Luke heads toward town, walking east. He loves that the streets are lined with trees and always have a soft breeze flowing through them.

He turns north to cross the river, where it flows in a ravine some distance below the bridge. He looks over at the vacant lot where the Jewish synagogue had been before the fire three months earlier.

Stopping, he looks over the now cold chard remains. *I guess they went through everything to make sure they retrieved what could be salvaged.*

Although the site is now sooty black with a few new weeds popping through, Luke spots something small and reddish-brown. He picks up a small branch fallen from a nearby tree, and carefully steps a little way into the remains of the synagogue.

With the branch, he pushes aside some old charred wood, which he thinks may have been part of the podium. He sees more of the reddish-brown thing.

Luke: Slave & Physician

His curiosity piqued, he continues to push charred wood and ashes aside until he uncovers what seems to be a pottery jar. He scoots it toward him, stoops, and lifts it out of the ashes. It is cracked but still intact, and the lid still in place.

He sets the jar upright and lifts the lid. Inside, he sees a scroll. He replaced the lid, picks up the jar, steps back onto the street, and takes a detour to his home.

"Luke, what have you been in?" Egidius says at the front gate.

Luke smiles. "Would you watch this a few moments?" he asks while setting the jar down. He takes off his sooty sandals and goes to his room. He emerges a little time later, washed up, and wearing a clean tunic.

"Thank you for cleaning it up for me, Egidius. I have to go back to work now. I am anxious to see what is inside tonight."

Luke leaves, retraces his steps and rushes into the market. He purchases the parchments, then hurries back to Brictius' house. The master of the house is no longer there, and no one questions the time Luke had taken to make his simple purchase.

That evening, he hurries to his home, pulls the scroll out of the jar, and lays it on a writing table provided for him by Theophilus. It is in Greek.

THIS TREATISE IS A FAITHFUL TRANSLATION OF THE WRITINGS OF THE JEHOVAH GOD'S PROPHET DANIEL, ORIGINALLY WRITTEN IN ARAMAIC AND HEBREW BETWEEN THE TIME OF NEBUCHADNEZZAR OF BABYLON AND DARIUS OF MEDIA AND PERSIA. MAY JEHOVAH GOD BLESS THIS TRANSLATION TO HIS GLORY.

Luke does not read far before he sees the beginning of an account of Nebuchadnezzar, king of Babylon, now part of the Parthian kingdom. He remembers passing near Babylon as he had followed the Tigris River south from the Black Sea.

He reads on about some young Hebrew captives, one of which claims to be able to interpret dreams.

Well, I'm wasting my time. The priests of our gods pretend all the time they can tell the future and interpret dreams.

Discouraged, Luke puts away the scroll. "Just another one of those fakes," he tells himself.

Three days go by, and Luke finds his thoughts still dwelling on the strange scroll. On the evening of the third day, he opens it and reads more.

This time as he reads, his pulse quickens. He wrinkles his brow and squints his eyes as though doing so will help him read faster.

On he reads. And reads. Nothing else matters. Nothing else exists except the scroll.

"Luke! Luke! What are you doing?"

Luke puts his finger on the line he is reading and forces himself to look up.

"Oh, Master, forgive me." He stands but leans over the scroll in order to keep his finger in place.

"I have been calling you. I need you to look over the list of officers I have appointed at the fortress and make sure I do not have any duplicates."

"Oh, uh, yes sir," Luke responds, but without moving.

"What is so important? What are you reading?" Theophilus asks.

"This was written five hundred years ago," Luke says, his brow still wrinkled.

"It doesn't look that old to me," Theophilus says.

"No, this is a translation into Greek. But listen to this: The writer starts with the Babylonian kingdom, the time in which he lived. Then he says the Persian kingdom will be the next world power. I know this happened because I was there and heard people brag about their former greatness."

"He could have guessed the Persians would be the next great kingdom just by the wars going on at the time," Theophilus replies

"But, he went on to predict Greece would be the next world power, and it happened. And, Master, he predicted Rome would be the great world power after Greece. He predicted us hundreds of years ago."

"Let me see that," Theophilus says, stepping around to stand next to Luke. Luke rolls the scroll backward two turns and shows where the predictions begin.

"That is amazing," Theophilus says after reading.

"I think he is about to predict the next world kingdom.

That's where I stopped reading," Luke responds. "May I read that part, and then go in to read through your list?"

"Luke, you have my curiosity piqued. Read the next part."

Luke reads aloud, and as he does, he holds the scroll closer to his eyes. He reads a little, then checks back over what he has just read. He looks up at his master, then back to the scroll. His breath grows shallow. His heart races. When done, he looks up at his master, his eyes wide and his mouth open.

"It says that during the days of Rome, the God of heaven—not a hundred gods or a thousand gods, but The God—will set up a kingdom that will never be destroyed."

Luke sets the scroll down on his table and stares at his master. His master stares at his slave.

"Could it be true?" Theophilus asks.

"I have not heard of such a kingdom starting anywhere I have been," Luke says.

"I have not either," Tribune Theophilus says. "Surely, our spies would have discovered and destroyed it by now."

"Unless it has not been set up yet," Luke surmises.

Silence.

"Well, come look at my list. You have other things to do now. You can look at it again tomorrow evening."

Luke cannot sleep that night. He rolls over and over on his mat. When morning arrives, he puts the words of the scroll in the back of his mind and makes his way up the street to the home of his master's friend. Brictius is in his library and looks up.

"You look terrible, Luke. Are you ill?"

"No, sir."

Luke sits and resumes his work copying the great historian, Livy. He writes, but his mind is elsewhere. His hand does what it is supposed to do, but his thoughts are on the rescued scroll at home.

How he makes it through the day, he does not know. The time arrives he had thought would never arrive. Luke returns home and settles down once again to read his scroll.

He reads how the king made a statue of himself, but

Daniel's three friends refused to bow to it, so were punished in a furnace. After being in the fire a while, they step out without their clothes even being singed.

"I should have known better. This is just a fake," he tells Theophilus later in the evening. Theophilus is through with his dinner, and Luke is eating his leftovers.

"But the scroll predicted things that happened hundreds of years after Daniel lived. What do you think of that?"

"I do not know. It is very confusing," Luke says.

Though not as enthusiastic as he had been before, Luke still cannot get his mind off the strange scroll. Each evening after work, he reads and studies it.

"In this section of the scroll, Darius of Media and Persia is now king," Luke tells Theophilus one evening. "People are told to only worship Darius, but Daniel continues to worship his Jehovah God. So he is thrown to hungry lions, but the lions do not eat him."

"Is that so?" Theophilus responds.

"Do you think it is true? How can it be? No one can escape hungry lions, especially when locked up in a den with them. I think I have just wasted my time."

"But what about predicting all the world empires?" Theophilus asks.

"Yes, I know. That is what is bothering me. If those predictions came true, everything else this man wrote is true. Still…"

In the following days, Luke brings out the book written by Daniel on occasion and reads a little, becomes confused, then puts it away again.

"No. This cannot be!" Luke calls out, leaving his table and walking around the marble-tiled courtyard of his master. He puts both hands over his yellow-haired head and looks up. He shakes his head and looks down at the marble tile. He runs his hand through his hair and walks in circles.

Theophilus looks up from examining his ceremonial sword. "What is wrong with you, Luke? Confused again?"

Luke looks over at his master, stares in silence, and resumes his pacing.

"Sit down," Theophilus orders. "Now, what is it? That scroll again?"

"I have been looking at some of your scrolls on ancient history of the south countries."

Luke goes into the growing library, pulls out a scroll, unrolls it as he walks, and shows his master one short sentence. "This tells the year King Cyrus ordered Jerusalem to be rebuilt."

"Now, look at this." Luke lays Daniel's book in Theophilus' lap and leans over it, pointing.

"Look. It says that in seventy weeks, the sin of mankind will be forgiven. If weeks is symbolic for years, seventy times seven days in a week could be four hundred ninety years. Then there was another half week, which would take it to 493 years. It has been thirty-three years since that year arrived.

Luke stands straight and watches Theophilus as he reads and rereads. Then he kneels and looks up at his master.

"What happened thirty-three years ago? What did Jerusalem have to do with it? What happened in Jerusalem?"

"I do not know, Luke," Theophilus says. "Why don't you go ask the Jewish rabbi? I think his house is next door to where the synagogue used to be. Besides, it is time we return the book of Daniel to its rightful owner. Have you copied it?"

"Not all of it, but maybe I can borrow it back." Luke rolls it up, places it back in the jar, and picks up the jar and its contents.

"I will go right now," Luke says.

"It is dark."

"The moon is full."

Luke heads out through the gate and down the hill. The rabbi's house is on the same side of the river, but still next to the synagogue. He knocks on the gate. The gate is plain, with no images on it.

Natanel answers. "May I help you?"

The rabbi is short, thin, and has a long black beard."

"My name is Luke. I belong to Tribune Theophilus. I found this jar in the remains of your synagogue," he explains, handing it to Rabbi Natanel.

"I am sorry I did not return it to you right away, but I began reading it, and it had some startling prophecies in it. There is one that confuses me. If the four hundred ninety years Daniel writes about began when Darius ordered the rebuilding of Jerusalem's walls, the final year would have been thirty-three years ago. Did something special happen in Jerusalem that year?"

"First, thank you for returning it. We thought the jar had cracked open, and the scroll burned. Thank you very much."

"But what about thirty-three years ago? Did anything spectacular happen in Jerusalem? Was a new king appointed? Anything?"

"Well, Caesar won't let us have a king right now."

He pauses.

"Hmmm. Let me see. That was the year my youngest son was born. He is now thirty-three. The only thing I can think of having to do with a king that happened around then is that they crucified a man who claimed he was the new king. Crucified for treason against Rome and the Jewish people. I do not remember his name. That's all I know."

Luke watches the rabbi a while, hoping he will remember more, but there is no more.

"Well, thank you, sir."

That night, Luke dreams.

"Luke. Come to Troas."

The man in his dream is the same man he had seen in his dream on the summit of Mount Olympus—short black beard, one good eye, and a crooked nose.

"Come to Troas. I want to help you." The man says. "Come to Troas. Come to Troas..."

Luke opens his eyes and stays awake the rest of the night. *Troas? That is in Anatolia, south of Germanicus. Troas? I do not know anyone in Troas.*

Morning comes, and Luke intercepts the tribune before he leaves for the fortress.

"Master, I had a dream about the scroll. This is the second time I have had the dream. A man keeps telling me to go to Troas so he can help us."

"That's a long way away," Theophilus says. "I cannot spare you that long."

"Master, I heard there is a medical academy in Troas. You always wanted me to be a physician. If I could go and check it out, maybe the man in my dream will appear while I'm there. If he does not, I'll forget the scroll."

Theophilus walks to his gate and puts on the helmet handed to him by Egidius.

"I believe Centurion Sopater is waiting for you out in the street, sir," Egidius says, opening the gate.

Theophilus walks through the gate, then turns back.

"Okay, you can go. You are right. I always wanted you to be a physician. You would be good at it, and I am getting more aches and pains as I grow older."

"Yes, sir," Luke says. "Thank you, sir."

"Stop by the fortress on your way out of the city. Sopater will give you enough money for ship passage there and back and other expenses. Oh, and enough money to bring back the man in your vision."

By the time he hears the chariot head down the street, Luke has reached his room. He takes out a two-man leather tent and puts it on his back. He takes two clean tunics down from a peg and puts them in a leather bag, then takes it to a small storeroom where he has small jars of oil and small pouches of healing herbs. He takes what he might need on his trip across the sea and adds them to his bag. He puts the bag's strap over his shoulder, stops by the kitchen area where he picks up some cheese, bread, and dried apricots in a cloth, adds that to his bag, then goes to the front gate.

"Have a safe trip," Egidius says.

Luke grins broadly and surprises himself when he blurts out, "I think my life is about to change," and leaves.

Knowing few ships dock where the dirty Haliacmon River empties into the Aegean Sea, Luke reaches the Via Egnatia and heads northeast on the broad Roman road toward Thessalonica. With his long legs, he reaches the port there on the evening of the second day.

He sets up his tent on the dock and tries to sleep. Eventually, he hears men shouting and bells ringing and knows it is morning.

He walks along the dock, trying to find a ship going to Troas. One by one, he approaches each ship's first mate on duty at the top of the gangplank to learn its destination. Discouraged, he asks at the last ship and hears the words he had been hoping for.

"Yes, we are going to Troas. We will be leaving this afternoon."

Luke spends the rest of the day alternately looking across the Gulf at Mount Olympus, and recalling Daniel's writings.

Daniel makes more sense than all those gods on Mount Olympus that aren't really there.

That afternoon, Luke boards the ship. The winds are cooperative, and Luke is in Troas within two days. He steps off the gangplank onto the dock and walks straight into the city.

Now what? I didn't have the dream again. Well, I may as well look for a teacher of medicine.

He walks up the street to the market. "Are there any physicians in the city?" he asks.

"None that I know of. But then only rich people have physicians. So, maybe there are."

Luke moves on.

"Is there an academy of medicine here in Troas?" he asks a man at another booth.

"Don't know. Ask someone who is rich."

Luke looks around. "Is there an apothecary shop anywhere in the market?" he asks another merchant.

"Yes, there is one up the street. Just keep going. You will see it on your left."

"Thank you, sir!" Luke says, excitement building.

He continues on and finally sees the apothecary shop. He walks in. "Might there be a medical academy here in Troas?" he asks.

"I don't know. The apothecary is gone for a couple

weeks or more, and I am just filling in for him."

"Thank you," Luke says. He walks back out onto the street and hears the words, "Stop here and be blessed," but does not know where the voice could have come from. *Maybe I imagined it. Or could it have been...could it have been...Daniel's God?*

There is a bench outside the shop. Luke decides to sit and wait, as the voice had told him to.

A few moments later, he senses someone staring at him. He looks up, and there stands the man with the short black beard, the bad eye, and crooked nose of his dreams.

The man walks directly up to Luke and says, "Excuse me, sir."

Luke looks up at the man, smiles, and knows. "I have been expecting you," he says. "I saw you in a dream. Are you prepared to go back with me to Berea?"

"Where is Berea?"

"The province of Macedonia."

The stranger smiles. "Yes, I will go with you. You are the man I saw in my own dream. My name is Paul."

20 ~ AT LAST

"I have to sell my tent first so we can buy passage on the ship," Paul says.

"No need for that. I told my master about you. We have been seeking the same God. He gave me money to bring you back."

"You are a slave?"

"I am afraid so," Luke says with a smile. "You said you have friends you want to bring along. Are they necessary?"

"They are my assistants," Paul explains. "Oh, and I have a donkey. It is carrying my means of supporting myself."

"In that case, we will go to Neapolis, which is closer," Luke says. "I have enough money for everyone to sail that far. We will walk the rest of the way."

"Fine," Paul says. "I like walking. We have to pick up our things at the hostel. We will meet you at the docks."

"By then, I should have found a ship headed for Neapolis," Luke replies.

Two hours later, everyone is on board, the gangplank is pulled up, and the ship slips out of the harbor.

"I have secured a place for us near the bridge," Luke says.

"The donkey too?"

"The donkey too."

"It will probably take us two days if the winds are good," Luke says.

The next day, the men and their donkey are seated in their spot and talking quietly among each other.

"You seem to be very intelligent," Paul says. "How did you end up being a slave?"

"I was eight years old and living by the Nordic Sea. The Roman army came and killed my father in a battle, or so I thought. My mother had already died before that. A tribune found me wandering through the woods where they had fought, looking for my father. With no parents, I was an orphan and alone, but alive."

"Then, God was watching out for you."

"Yes. I just need to find out which God it was. Anyway, I was taken as a slave by the tribune. That was twenty-three years ago. He took me to other forts as he was transferred around Germanicus. He now lives in Berea, where I continue to serve him."

"So you have been searching for God?" Silas asks.

"Yes. A Jewish synagogue burned down near my master's home. One day some time afterward, I noticed a jar mostly buried by rubble. When I investigated, I saw inside a scroll of the writings of a Daniel."

"That was indeed a find," Timothy says.

"You know about it? I took it back to my master and read it."

"You can read?"

"I know five languages. I pick up languages easily. Besides, I was given a good education. My master has been very good to me."

The donkey brays and Paul stands to pat it on the nose and calm it.

"Anyway, Daniel predicted a divine king coming, and it gave a certain year. When I delivered it to the rabbi, I asked him about the year in it. He said his people did not normally become priests or kings until they were thirty years old, so whoever the king was supposed to be, he would have taken over on the four hundred and ninetieth year. He did recall a man being crucified three years later for claiming he was their king."

"You are very astute, Luke," Paul says, sitting back down on the deck and facing his new friend. "That year fits exactly Jesus of Nazareth, who began teaching at age thirty.

He it was who sent your vision to you."

The next morning, they disembark at Neapolis, located on a steep hill rising out of the banks of the sea.

As they walk along the dock, Luke explains they will be walking through Philippi, and Thessalonica before arriving at his home in Berea.

"What is your master's name, by the way?" Silas asks.

"Theophilus."

Once ashore, they head to the Via Egnatia that borders the Aegean Sea. Neapolis is on their right, buildings built on the side of a steep embankment leading up into the mountains with all their gold and silver mines.

By the end of the day, they approach the Roman colony of Philippi.

"The Sabbath is in two days. Let us stay here," Paul says. "Is that agreeable with you, Luke?"

Everyone agrees, and they walk through the gates just before they are closed for the night.

They rent a room at a hostel large enough for four men and stable their donkey.

"What is that on your back?" Luke asks. He steps over to Paul, who has just pulled off his tunic with Timothy's help, and touches his back.

"Oh, that. It's nothing."

Luke looks over at Silas. "Nothing?"

"Luke, Paul will not tell you. I will," Silas says. He looks over at Paul. "And no interference from you.

"If there is any teacher in the world you can believe, it is Paul," Silas begins. "He has risked his life over and over to get the word out about Jesus to as many people as possible."

"How many times has he been lashed? I see old scars there."

"Twice—once in Celicia and once in Phrygia—both by Jewish rabbis. He has also been beaten with rods twice—once by mountain men and once by a pagan priest. He has been shipwrecked off the coast of Egypt, and once off the coast of Cyprus. And he has been thrown overboard by a rogue wave and lost for a night and day in the Great Sea."

Luke shakes his head and stares at Paul, who is now sitting on the side of the bed, staring at the floor. "That's enough, Silas," he growls.

"All of them happened either on his way to tell people about Jesus, or after he told people that Jesus was the Son of the only real God," Silas concludes. "He is unstoppable. He never thinks he has done enough."

"Paul," Luke says, "could I look closer at your back? It is not quite healed. Perhaps I have something to hurry the healing along."

Luke looks in his shoulder pouch and brings out a smaller one. "I have shavings from the turmeric root. I will go to the hostel owner and see if his cook has any honey."

Shortly Luke comes back with the honey and a small bowl. He crumbles up the turmeric shavings and mixes it in with the honey.

"Paul, if you can sleep on your front tonight, this medicine will do a lot of healing while you sleep."

"How did you know about that?" Timothy asks.

"I want to be a physician someday."

"Would you teach me what you know? I have tried to treat Paul, but do not know a lot about the herbs."

"Certainly."

The next morning the four walk around town. "Paul. How does your back feel?" Luke asks.

"Much better. You will make a good physician someday."

"Who are those yellow-haired men dressed in high leather shoes, leather tunics, and wearing those colored capes?" Silas asks.

"They are Thracians," Luke replies. "Philippi was once a Thracian city before Alexander the Great took over and renamed the city after his father. My own people by the Nordic Sea dress the same way."

"What kind of work do they do?"

"Being so big and muscular, they have often hired themselves out as mercenaries. But there are many silver and gold workers among them. They make beautiful statues. And some are even poets. The Thracians around here consider farming demeaning."

As usual, Paul and his friends walk around the city looking for a synagogue. Being in a Roman colony, they do not find any.

"I want you to tell me more about the Jewish religion," Luke tells Paul.

"I will, indeed," Paul replies. "In fact, you will learn even about the Son of God."

"The Son of God? Like the sons of Zeus?"

"No. The Son of the only real God. I have so much to tell you," Paul says. "Tonight, we will talk. But first, I must find out who the Philippians worship."

The four men remember passing the agora and library upon arrival the day before, across from the massive theater. They decide to look around there for signs of the city's deities. What they find are statues of all the deified Caesars for the Roman citizens and statues of Dionysus for the Thracians.

"It is late. We will walk up the acropolis after the Sabbath is over the day after tomorrow. Perhaps we can do some good there," Paul says.

"After we find some Jews tomorrow—if we do—I want to get my beard shaved close so that I look a little bit Roman and a little bit Jew—both of which I am by birth," he adds.

That evening, Luke applies more of the solution on Paul's back. "Another week, and you should be healed," he says. "Well, maybe two weeks."

The rest of the evening is spent with Paul explaining the Jewish religion to Luke along with the prophecies of a divine king. "The remainder I will explain tomorrow. Surely there are Jews somewhere in this big city."

The next morning is the Sabbath. Paul and Silas, Timothy, and Luke check a little way outside the north gate, the west one, and the east one, hoping to find some Jews worshipping. They are unsuccessful.

"Well, there is one more gate," says Silas. "Maybe they are out there—if, indeed, there are any."

The four walk out the southeast gate, then south toward the Ganges River.

"Do you hear that?" Timothy asks as they walk.

"I do," Luke says. "It is beautiful."

"Hey. I recognize it," Silas says. "It is our ancestor David's second Psalm. Listen."

But as for me,
I have installed my king
upon holy Mount Zion.
He said to me,
'you are my Son.
Today I have begotten you.

Shortly, they see a middle-aged woman who is surrounded by ten younger women.

"May we join you?" Paul asks.

"Of course," she says, standing.

"My name is Paul. These are my friends, Silas, Timothy, and Luke."

"Peace be to you. My name is Lydia," she says, her large doe eyes shining. "I will let my servant girls introduce themselves."

Lydia is tall with a straight and delicate nose. She flips back with her slim fingers, the brown tress that has escaped the prayer shawl on her head.

Introductions done, everyone is seated.

"I noticed you were singing a psalm predicting the coming of a divine anointed king, the Son of God. Did you know it has finally happened?"

The next two hours are spent with Paul and Silas explaining how Jesus of Nazareth in Palestine had fulfilled this and all other predictions.

"But don't Jehovah and Jesus argue sometimes?" Luke asks.

"Never."

"What about stealing?" Luke continues. "If Jesus went to Jerusalem to start a new kingdom and be its king, that would be stealing the nation from Rome."

"Not at all. His is a spiritual kingdom. In fact, it is not only over Jerusalem but over the whole world. Lydia here can be a citizen of Philippi as well as a citizen of Jesus' kingdom."

"Even though you are a slave," Timothy says, "and not allowed to be a citizen of any country, you can be a citizen in the kingdom of God."

"Me, a citizen?" Luke asks, smiling.

"Well, how many mistresses and children did this Jesus have?"

"None."

Luke stands and walks over to the nearest tree and leans on it. Paul continues talking with Lydia and the others while Luke thinks.

When he returns, he hears Lydia say, "I want to be baptized."

"Why would you want to be immersed?" Luke asks.

"It's a rebirth," Paul explains. "You are buried in a watery womb, and when you come out, your soul is born all over again, completely innocent of sin."

"That's what Daniel's prediction said," Timothy says. "The divine eternal king would take people's sins away."

"This is a whole new world for me," Luke says. "And I like it."

He looks over at Silas. What are the believers called?"

"Christians."

"Will you accept me as a Christian? I am not a Jew. Are people who are not Jews allowed to be Christians?"

Silas smiles broadly. "Indeed, they are,"

"Were you baptized?" Luke asks.

"All of us were," Paul answers.

"Then, baptize me now."

Luke's body, heart, and soul unite with God's.

The rest of the day is spent at Lydia's home.

"Uh, I have got to go back to Troas in a few days," Luke announces. "Can you find Berea on your own?"

"Yes. But why the change of plans?"

"I promised my master I would look for an academy of medicine there. I got sidetracked when I found you and forgot part of my mission. Besides, I want to go back there and spread the word about Jesus."

Timothy looks at Paul, then at Luke. "If you would like help, I would be happy to go with you. Besides, you can teach me more medical techniques."

Luke looks at Timothy, then at Paul.

"I think that would be a fine idea. Luke knows the people and their habits better than Timothy does, and Timothy knows the scriptures better than Luke does. You will make a good team."

The next morning, Timothy and Luke rise early, and by the time everyone else has risen, they are in deep discussion about the Jewish scriptures. Paul and Silas rise and go into the city.

Late that afternoon, Paul and Silas return, their faces drawn.

Paul sits and stares at the floor a moment. He looks over at Timothy and Luke.

"You must leave," he says in almost a whisper. "It is becoming dangerous. You must live to tell the people what happened here. This afternoon you must leave."

"But, Paul," Timothy says. "If it is too dangerous for us, it is too dangerous for you. Go with us."

"No. We must face the enemies of Jesus. You were both planning to go back to Troas. Now is the time to do it. Go down to Neapolis immediately and get a ship out of there, no matter what direction it is headed."

Luke and Timothy look at each other and know what they will do.

"We will be back," Luke tells Paul and Silas. "I will tell the people in Troas about the good news. And I will look for an academy of medicine. Then I will be back."

"What about your master? Won't he send someone after you if you do not return home on time?" Silas asks.

"He trusts me. I have been away from him for much longer than this, and I returned to him. Theophilus trusts me."

Within the hour, Timothy and Luke are ready. They bid farewell to Paul and Silas.

"Come with us," Timothy says in one last appeal, turning back from the gate and looking at Paul and Silas.

"Come to safety."

"I ran from a fight once, over in Iconium," Paul responds. "I will never run from another."

"Paul and I have been friends nearly our whole life. I will not forsake him now." It is Silas.

"We will meet you in Berea," Luke says as he and Timothy leave.

Both men are tall and make it to Neapolis by dark. They go down to the dock and search for a ship headed for Troas. They find one, but it is not leaving until the next day. Luke and Timothy combine what money they have left, buy passage, and are allowed on board to spend the night.

The winds are strong from the west, and the ship arrives in Troas the next evening at sundown.

Out of money, they spread Luke's two-man tent on the dock.

"I'm hungry," Timothy says the next morning.

"I guess the first thing we need to do is find temporary jobs," Luke says.

"You are good with healing people, and I know a little. Perhaps we can work for an apothecary shop or for a physician," Timothy says.

"Well, since civilian physicians are always slaves of rich families, we can't be hired by one."

Luke pauses. "But there are the *medicus* of the military. There is no fortress right here, but it does have an apothecary shop. Maybe they know where there is a *medicus* we could hire out to."

They return to the apothecary shop where Luke and Paul had first met and go in.

"Do you know of any *medicus* in Troas?" Luke asks.

"Luke? That couldn't be you. You're all grown up."

Luke stares at the apothecary as he searches his memory.

"Did you ever fully recover from that fall off that big Frisian horse? He was a wild one. And so were you, as I recall."

Luke stares at a man he estimates to be in his sixties. He is short, nearly bald, wears a dirty apron, and is dressed in a shabby, stained tunic.

"Alekto?" he finally says. "Are you Alekto?"

The man behind the counter raises his arms in welcome, walks around to the customer side, and puts his hands on Luke's shoulders.

"Yes, I am your old teacher. How have you been, Luke? And how is ole Theophilus? Is he still alive?"

21 ~ DREAM REVIVED

"Alekto," Luke says with a large grin. "I would like you to meet my friend, Timothy."

"Well, you two could almost pass for twins," the old man says. "Both tall and skinny. Red and yellow hair, which are far from the normal black hair around here. It is my pleasure to meet a friend of Luke. So, has Luke been behaving himself?"

Timothy smiles. "I don't know. We haven't known each other very long."

"Well, get ready for a real ride. Luke never sits still. Do you?" he says, turning back to Luke. "By the way, you do not live here, or I would have run into you. So, which hostel are you in?"

"Uh, well, we haven't lined up a hostel yet."

"Broke, are you? What did you spend all your money on? Well, come home with me. The army doesn't allow its men to marry, and I still do not have a wife, but I have a couple of maids who are good cooks."

Alekto hangs up his dirty apron and closes his shop. "I am not always here. Sometimes I have patients to take care of. I've hired myself out to some of the rich families in the city."

They walk up the street through the market, past the many crowded family insulae in the city, past small houses, and up a hill.

"Here is my home," Alekto says.

His gate is copper with a silver snake curling around a rod of the same material in the middle of it.

He knocks on his gate, and a servant opens it.

"Tell Chara we are having company for a few days."

Alekto shows the men to a small room off the courtyard with a large mat on the floor.

"You can stay in here." He calls to his servant. "Bring two bowls and two pitchers of water to this room," he says.

Luke sets down his tent and other supplies. Timothy sets down his small pack containing a fresh tunic and some oil to be used for dry skin and wounds.

Momentarily, they return to the courtyard and are directed to two benches near Alekto.

"So, you never did tell me if Tribune Theophilus is still alive," he says to Luke.

"Yes, he is. We were sent to serve at a few more fortresses along the Rhine, then over to Amphipolis in northern Macedonia, and finally to a fort on the Black Sea. He retired there. Do you remember Centurion Sopater? My master went with the centurion to his father's home at Berea in southern Macedonia. He was pulled out of retirement to command the fortress there."

"Well, well."

"Now, what about you?" Luke asks. "You never did tell me how you became a physician."

"Well, I was born in Pergamum, just south of here. We were poor, my father having died when I was young. We had a pet dog that I loved, and when I was about twelve years old, a passing wagon broke its leg. I reset the dog's leg and saved it. A neighbor heard about it and brought her little girl over. She had a large cut on her arm from broken pottery she had fallen on. My mother had some linen thread, so I sewed the girl's arm up with it. Let's go into the solarium and talk," Alekto says.

He shows them to a reflecting pool with benches on all four sides.

"You were young," Luke says, resuming their conversation. "Didn't you know how painful putting needles in people would be?"

"I guess I didn't care. All I knew is that she was bleeding and weak, and I thought I could save her life by doing it. I know now that she was not near death, but in my young mind, I thought she was."

A maid walks in with a tray of bread, yogurt, and sliced apples.

"Take all you want," Alekto says. "You're young and full of energy and need big meals."

"So, how did you learn so much about medicine after that?" Luke asks.

"Pergamum is where the temple is of Apollo's healing son, Ascilipius. I took Ascilipius as my god. His symbol is the rod with the snake crawling up it. So, anyway, more and more, I visited the temple, and the priests let me help them treat people."

"I helped you," Luke recalls," but it didn't teach me much." He pauses. "I will never forget the mistake I made with that man. I killed him."

"You did the best you could, Luke."

"What happened?" Timothy asks.

"Maybe I will tell you someday," Luke responds. "So, how did you end up in Troas?" Luke asks, turning back to his host.

"I don't know. I served my thirty years in the army. When I retired, I just headed my horse south out of Germanicus toward Pergamum, where I was born. I stopped in Troas on the way, helped out in an epidemic, was hired by a wealthy family, and ended up staying here."

Luke grows serious. "Sir, I am wanting to attend a medical academy. I heard there was one here."

"Well, there isn't one yet, but there is about to be. I have rented a building where I can teach medicine. So, are you going to be my first student?"

"There is your chance," Timothy interjects, reaching over and pounding Luke on the back.

"I told my master I was coming here to look for a medical academy, but he did not give me permission to stay. However, I believe he would not mind me taking a few lessons from you."

"If that is the best you can do, Luke, then I shall settle for that."

"Besides," Luke adds, "I was allowed to come here for another reason. Alekto, sir, I have found God."

"Which one?"

"The only one."

"That is impossible."

Luke moves on. "His name is *The I Am*. He is also called Jehovah. And, best of all, he never sins, and he loves us."

Alekto stands and puts one foot up on the ledge of his reflecting pool.

"Gods don't love us. They are just immortal humans who reign over us like kings and queens. Kings and queens do not love their subjects unless they know them by name."

Luke looks over at Timothy, unsure what to say next.

"Jehovah knows us by name," Timothy interjects.

"Well, of course, some of us. But not everyone." Alekto responds. "That would be impossible. There are millions of us."

"Jehovah knows everyone by name. He knows everything we do and think."

"Look," Alekto retorts. "Our job is just to keep from angering the gods. Then they won't send thunderbolts down on us."

"Oh, no," Timothy adds. "Jehovah God's job is to love us. He IS love."

"Well, believe what you want. I have chosen Ascilipius as my patron god. He is the healer, and his symbol is on my front gate. He has protected me all these years. Otherwise, why am I still alive?"

His maid appears.

She has three plates on a tray, each with bread, more yogurt, figs, and cheese.

"May I thank Jehovah God for blessing us with bountiful crops?" Timothy asks the host.

"Do what you want," Alekto replies, dipping his bread in the yogurt and filling his mouth.

"Isn't she a good cook? I should marry her someday, but I don't think I would be a very good man to live with. I served in the army too long and have long ago forgotten what to do with the gentler sex."

The rest of the evening is filled with talk about the military and Timothy's travels. Luke does not talk about his own.

The following morning when Luke and Timothy come out of their room off the courtyard, they see Alekto descending the steps from his second-floor bedroom.

"Good, you're up," he tells them. "Luke, are you ready for your first class?"

"Yes, sir," Luke replies.

They sit in the courtyard and eat fresh bread to give them energy for the day. Luke is given his first medical lesson. It is now mid-morning.

"Uh, sir," Luke says, "could you use another clerk at your shop? Like maybe me?"

"You really are broke," Alekto says. "Yes, you can be my assistant, and I will tutor you there between customers. But what about Timothy? I am not tutoring him free. I'm tutoring you because I plan to send a bill to Theophilus."

"Sir, there are things I can do in the city," Timothy explains. "If I can find a butcher or leather tent maker, I know how to tan the hides and cut them into squares."

"That's fine. I can show you where a couple of butchers have set up. They are a little past my apothecary shop."

"That's great," Timothy says. "That way, I can pay my share where ever we stay while here."

"You're not planning to stay with me?" Alekto asks with a frown.

"Uh, that would be very fine. But if you have other plans," Luke says, "we can go on over to a hostel."

Alekto smiles and shakes his head. "No, no. I want you to stay with me."

Luke stands. "Uh, sir, Timothy and I do have other business to take care of while we're in Troas. So, if we can have afternoons free, I will spend my evenings mixing some of the medicines together for you."

Alekto glares at Luke. "You're not going to learn enough in half days."

"I'm sorry, sir. But we came for another reason, and I

was not expecting to meet you and have this wonderful opportunity," Luke explains.

"That new God of yours, I'll bet," Alekto answers.

"Yes, sir. If that is objectionable to you..."

"No, go ahead. You have your beliefs, and I have mine. But I'll expect you to keep your promise to mix medications for me every evening."

"Yes, sir."

Alekto stands and takes a coat off a peg near his front gate. "Are you ready to go to my apothecary shop now?"

Luke and Timothy retreat to their room to grab their own coats.

The hours go by fast. The *medicus* and Luke spend it filling orders that come streaming in all morning. Timothy finds a tentmaker who lets him tan the hides.

When the sun is high in the sky, Timothy walks over to the apothecary shop.

"Ready, Luke?"

Luke stares at Alekto a moment, but the older man does not look up. Finally, Luke takes off his apron and lays it on the work table.

"I will see you this evening, sir," he says.

Alekto grunts.

"So, how do we do this?" Luke asks as they walk away.

"First, we need to see if there are any Jewish synagogues in the city."

"Why?"

"Because they already believe in Jehovah and the prophets. So, all we have to do is prove to them that Jesus was the prophesied divine king."

"How do we convince them about Jesus?"

"Same way we did Lydia. You'll learn. Let's just go back to the market and ask around. Look for men with beards."

"I have a beard," Luke says.

"But you're different."

Luke laughs. "Different, am I?"

"You have yellow hair. Men with yellow hair usually are not Jews."

"What about you? Didn't you say you were Jewish? You're red-headed."

"Well, I'm kind of a half breed. Now look especially for men with black beards. That's the best way to narrow down who in this crowd may know about a Jewish synagogue. Otherwise, ask anyone who will talk to you."

The men divide up and ask at booths and shops.

"Is there a synagogue here in Troas?"

"Not that I know of."

"Do you know of any Jews living here?"

"Doubt I'd recognize them if I did see any."

"Are there any synagogues here?"

"What's a synagogue?"

The men meet at an intersection.

"No luck with me," Luke says.

"Me neither. So, next, we find the temples of the local patron gods."

"Won't we get a lot of opposition there?"

"Sometimes. But we also find the sincere people there who are worshipping the local god but are not sure about it."

"Like I was," Luke says.

They walk toward the higher parts of the city to find the temples. They find one to Apollo, one to Poseidon, one to Hermes, and one to Xanthos. They watch worshippers go in and out but say nothing to them.

"We will return tomorrow and begin our work," Timothy says. "Now, on our way back to Alekto' home, I want to explain to you some of the prophecies made about Jesus hundreds of years before he was even born...."

"It's about time you get here," Alekto says upon their arrival. "I have all kinds of medications for you to mix tonight, Luke."

Luke smiles. "I count it my honor and privilege to be working for the great *Medicus* Alekto."

Alekto does not respond.

"Well, we shall eat first. Then you can get to work. Timothy, if you would like to be useful, you could crush those leaves and pour them into separate pouches. Be sure not to mix them with each other." With that, he heads up to his second-floor bedroom.

"Yes, sir," Timothy calls up to him. "I appreciate the confidence you have placed in me," he says.

As the two young men work, Luke explains the use of different herbs to Timothy.

"What about for pain? What is best for pain?"

Just as they finish up the last batch of medications, Timothy notices the moon is high above the city.

"It must be midnight," Luke says. "Today was a good beginning for everything we came to accomplish."

The next morning, the men disburse to their respective places of employment. At noon, Luke and Timothy meet at the temple of Apollo.

"Follow my lead," Timothy says over his shoulder, walking up the grand steps to the temple itself.

"Apollo cannot bring you light," he tells worshippers entering the temple. "Only Jesus Christ can. He is the light of the entire world."

Luke decides to catch the worshippers coming back down the steps. "Apollo cannot tell the future. Only the God who created all things can do that."

After an hour with no positive responses, they move on to the temple of Hermes.

At the top of the steps leading into the temple, Luke tells each worshipper, "If you believe in Jesus, angels will take you to heaven, not the underworld."

At the bottom of the steps, Luke tells worshippers on their return to the street, "Hermes cannot protect travelers. Only the God of heaven who created and loves you can."

Another hour. Still no positive responses from worshippers.

They go to a cliff overlooking the Aegean Sea, where the temple of Poseidon is and have the same results.

"It's not working," Luke laments.

"Never say that. You do not know their hearts," Timothy says. "The temple of Xanthos, god of Troas' rivers, is our last stop. It is closer to the beach."

Though not as grand as the other temples, as always, Timothy goes to the top of the wide steps into the temple.

"Worship Jesus. He has the water of eternal life that can flow through your soul," Timothy says.

"Jesus is the water of life," Luke says at the bottom of the steps.

A worshipper stops and stares at Luke. "What did you say?" The inquirer is a sailor and smells of fish. The hem of his tunic is dirty.

Luke's heart races. "I said Jesus is the water of life. He not only gives life to the fish, but he gives life to you and me—eternal life."

"Who is this Jesus, so I may worship him also?" the man says.

Noticing Luke in conversation, Timothy joins them. "Would you like to know more about Jesus?"

"Yes. I get so tired of praying to gods who don't seem to care what happens to us. By the way, my name is Oceanus."

The man is tall, thin, and has a long and crooked nose.

The three men walk together toward the city square nearby and squat in a circle.

"Jesus is the way, truth, and life. We are all sinful, but he wants to make you pure," Timothy says.

"Will you come home with me and tell my wife and son about this Jesus?"

"Of course, we will."

Oceanus leads Luke and Timothy toward the waterfront down a street with insulae lining both sides. He stops at one of them. "My family lives on the third floor."

When they arrive on the top floor of the insulae, Oceanus opens his apartment door and calls to his wife.

"Cardea, come here. These men have wonderful news for us. Cardea? Are you here?"

As he speaks his last words, a petite woman with an almost child-like voice enters the room.

"Yes, I'm here."

"Is Eutychus here? He needs to hear this."

"He is not quite ready for work," she says. "Eutychus, come here. We have company."

A young man comes out to them. He is husky and tall,

though not as tall as his father.

They sit on old cushions on the floor. Timothy explains the proofs that Jesus really is the Son of God.

Luke explains how Jesus died on a cross down in Jerusalem, and paid the death penalty to Satan so believers can go to heaven instead.

"We can actually live with the God?" Cardea asks.

"Yes. God loves you. He wants to share his home with you."

"What do they call people who worship Jesus?" Oceanus asks.

"Christians. We are called Christians," Luke says. "Why don't you become a Christian, too?" he adds.

The three look at each other and smile. Oceanus speaks for them.

"My family wants to be baptized. Can we do it at the seashore?"

"Indeed, since you believe in Jesus, you may," Timothy says.

They grab three towels and solemnly walk down to the seashore. Timothy baptizes them.

It is dark by the time they arrive back to the insulae.

"I must go to work now," Eutychus says. "I am part of the city fire team. Most fires happen at night. I cannot wait to tell the other men what you told us."

Oceanus and Cardea offer to feed Luke and Timothy.

"We are not very hungry," Luke says, realizing they are relatively poor, "but we will take a few bites of bread."

"I plan to tell all the men who work with me down at the boats," Oceanus says. "Can you men come back tomorrow and tell us more?"

"Yes, of course," Timothy says. "Is mid-afternoon too soon?"

"The fish don't bite in the heat of the day. That time is good."

The following night, there are seven people in Oceanus' third-floor apartment. The night after that, there are ten. Each succeeding afternoon, the group grows until finally there are twenty-three.

"You have started your first congregation," Timothy tells Luke two weeks later in Alekto' home.

"Well, I guess we have accomplished all we set out to do," Luke says. "It is time to return to Berea."

"Wait," Alekto says. "What about your medical education?"

"I will be back. The next time I come, you will have your academy of medicine well established, and I will become a full-time student."

Alekto forms a broad grin. "Yes, yes. You shall come back, and you will be my star pupil."

The following day, Luke and Timothy walk down to the docks and board a ship bound for Neapolis.

"Let's visit Philippi and Thessalonica on our way to Berea," Timothy says. "We told Paul and Silas we would meet them in Berea. I wonder if they made it."

"Luke's smile quickly disappears. "Do you think they are still alive?"

22 ~ DECISIONS

*T*he ship docks in Neapolis. Luke and Timothy walk up through the mountain to Philippi.

"Do you remember where Lydia's house is?" Luke asks.

"Yes, I'm sure I can find it," Timothy replies.

"I can't wait to see her. And while I'm here, I want to go down to the river where I was baptized," Luke says. "I will never forget that day for as long as I live."

Timothy smiles. "It's that way with everyone."

"Here it is," Timothy says, stopping to knock on Lydia's gate.

A doorman answers. As they walk in, they hear Lydia's melodic voice. "Might I be hearing some very good friends at my gate?" she says, gliding into the courtyard.

The friends are reunited, and Lydia tells a maid to bring some refreshments to them.

"So, how did things go after we left town?" Timothy asks.

"Paul was worried. Should he have been?" Luke adds.

"It was worse than we feared," Lydia says. "They were tied down in public and both beaten by two of our pagan priests. If one of the magistrates had not put a stop to it, they probably would have been killed."

Timothy leans forward. His eyes are squinting, and he is clenching his fists. "Do you have any idea where they escaped to?"

"I do not know for sure. They were imprisoned after their beaten. After their release, they may have gone up into the mountains somewhere to wait for their backs to heal."

"Or maybe they stopped to spread the news in Thessalonica, then went on to Berea," Timothy says.

"But, they wouldn't be in any condition to stop in Thessalonica," Luke says. "Maybe they went on to Berea as soon as possible."

"Spend the night here," Lydia says. "Then you can be on your way at dawn."

The next morning before daylight, Timothy and Luke are already on the Via Egnatia. Though most would walk as far as Thessalonica in four days or more, both men are tall with long legs and make the trip in three.

"Shall we go into Thessalonica and see if they are there?" Timothy asks.

"No, I need to get on home. I stayed gone longer than expected, and my master will be worried about me."

"Then, we keep going."

Another two days of walking and they arrive in Berea.

"Whew. Walking with you is like keeping up with a horse," Timothy tells Luke as they go through the south gate into the city.

"You did well," Luke says, grinning broadly while absorbing the familiar sights of home.

Turning left and crossing the river flowing through the middle of the city, they then turn right and pass the temples of Dionysius, Hercules, Artemis, and Zeus, and arrive at Theophilus' home.

They knock on the gate, and Sopater answers it.

"Since when did you become doorman?" Luke asks in greeting.

"Since the tribune sent me here to pick up some parchments he needs at the fortress," the centurion answers. "So, welcome back."

He opens the gate and lets the men in. "By the way," Sopoter says, "I have been meaning to ask you whatever happened to the Nordic Voorde horse I got you for your trip to Parthia."

"You've been to Parthia?" Timothy asks.

"He was very loyal, but he died in the desert," Luke

replies. "He just wasn't used to the heat."

"I'm sorry," Sopater says, going through the gateway into the street and closing it behind him.

"You've been to Parthia?" Timothy repeats.

"Master!" Luke calls. "Master? Are you here?"

Egidius walks into the courtyard. "No, he is at the fortress. They are having inspection, and he expected to be gone all day. So, welcome home, Luke."

"Thank you, Egidius. Did anyone take the room next to mine while I was gone?"

"No. It is still empty."

"Good," he says, turning to Timothy. "You may have that room."

"Egidius, have two men by the name of Paul and Silas been here at all?"

"Not that I know of."

Luke shows Timothy his room, they set down their belongings and clean up.

Back out in the courtyard, they see Egidius has brought them a pitcher of apple juice.

"Is there a synagogue here in Berea?" Timothy asks.

"Yes, we passed close to it on our way through the city. However, it burned down just before I left."

"You've been gone close to a year. Do you think they may have rebuilt?" Timothy asks.

"Why are you curious about it?" Luke asks.

"Even though Jewish temple worship in Jerusalem is not the way Christians worship, the way they worship in their local synagogues week after week is similar," Timothy explains. "Since there was no synagogue in Troas or Philippi, I thought I'd show you the inside of the one here."

"Then let's go check it out right now," Luke says. "Besides, I need to stop and see the rabbi who lives next door on this side of the river and thank him for explaining some of the things Daniel said in his book. You know, the one I told you I rescued from the fire."

A few blocks down the street and across from the temple to Artemis, they turn left and cross a bridge over a deep ravine with a small but fast-flowing river below.

"You were right, friend. They rebuilt it. Nicer than the one they had before. Four columns in front now."

They go inside. They see a simple but large assembly room with smaller rooms on each side.

"The Jews read scriptures, sing a few psalms of David, then the rabbi or someone else sits in the speaker's chair up front, and talks about the scriptures and psalms."

"That's it?"

"But the priestesses in a lot of the temples whirl around and screech."

"That's them. Not us. Now, let's see if the rabbi is here."

They walk to the other end of the large assembly room, open the door, and look inside.

"No one here," Timothy says.

"Let's wait here in the *officium* a few moments. Maybe the rabbi will come."

"He seemed like a good man," Luke says.

"Who?"

"The rabbi."

"I'm looking forward to meeting him," Timothy says.

"Oh. Wait. I think I hear voices. Maybe that's him now."

The footsteps grow closer, and the door to the *officium* opens.

"Paul? Silas?"

"Where did you come from? How long have you been here?" all four ask each other.

"We just arrived from Thessalonica," Silas explains.

"You're walking bent over, Paul," Luke says.

"Well, we had our troubles in Philippi. We went to Thessalonica, and they created such a riot, we slipped out of town at night," Paul explains. "And here we are. What about you?"

"We have been in Troas, as you know," Luke says. "I found an academy of medicine there, and have brought the information back to my master to see if he would approve of me attending."

"I have been explaining the Jewish scriptures to Luke

to give him a good background in Christianity," Timothy says.

"And I told him what I knew about treating wounds and broken bones and anything else he said you might encounter among the enemies of Jesus," Luke adds, looking at Paul.

By now, the men have seated themselves on benches scattered around the *officium*.

"I have some great news for you," Timothy says. "We established the church in Troas. It is poor, but I think it is solid."

"I am very proud of you both," Paul replies with a wide grin. "I think I held you back when you were traveling with me before, Timothy, but I will not make that mistake again."

The door to the *officium* opens. Rabbi Natanel walks in.

"What have we here?" he says in his deep voice.

Luke introduces everyone. Timothy follows up. "Paul here was rabbi of the synagogue in Bethany near Jerusalem, and a member of the Sanhedrin in Jerusalem a while until he moved away."

Rabbi Natanel extends his hand to Timothy, Paul, and Silas, then addresses Paul. "We would be honored to have you speak to our congregation this Sabbath.

"By the way, Rabbi," Luke says. "Would it be possible for me to finish copying Daniel's writings? I could take it to Theophilus' house, or do the copying at the synagogue."

"Why don't you take it home with you? After all, you're the one who rescued it and kept it safe."

Two days later is the Sabbath.

"Well, would you like to witness worship the way the Jews do it?" Timothy asks Luke that morning.

"Yes, I would."

Upon their arrival and after seating themselves with the congregation, Silas is asked to read the scriptures. Then Paul is asked to sit in the speaker's chair and speak on whatever he chooses. His subject, as always, is Jesus fulfilling prophecies. The rabbi invites him to speak again the following week.

Having been so well received, Paul rents a shop and sets up his tent-making business in Berea. Timothy goes to Paul's shop every day to help him. Silas goes to work for a butcher who supplies hides for Paul. Luke spends each day copying out of the Jewish scriptures.

It does not take long for the curious Berean Jews to ask Paul if he can teach them more often. They go to his shop every day around noon, and he teaches as he works. Often Luke joins them.

"Master," he says every time he comes home from listening to Paul, "why don't you go with me? He is an brilliant teacher."

"I am sure he is, Luke. But I do not have time to go running after every new philosophy."

"But Paul is different."

"You are probably right, but I just do not have time right now."

During the second week, Luke finishes copying the prophet Daniel's writings.

"What would you suggest I copy next for my master's library," he asks Natanel.

"I would recommend the Psalms of David. He was our shepherd king. Since you brought Daniel back to us safe and sound, you make take the Psalms home with you."

"Thank you," Luke says. "My master thanks you also."

"He would be welcome to visit with me sometime."

"I know that, but he is stubborn. Won't believe anything until it has been proven."

The rabbi smiles broadly.

"So, okay. I'm the same way," Luke admits.

The following Sabbath, Luke, once again asks Theophilus to go with him.

"It's all too baffling right now. No one can ever show me the proof. Where's the proof?"

"But Christianity can be proven."

"You just keep copying their prophecies, and we shall see."

Every day, Paul teaches from his tent-making shop, where he must continue working to support himself.

Sometimes after one of Paul's afternoons of teaching, Luke walks one of the Jews home.

"Uh, Varius, what did you think of what Paul said this afternoon?"

"Wait up, Spurius. Wouldn't you say what Paul is explaining is true?"

"Well, Nicon. What do you think? Makes more sense than the oracles of those so-called gods. Nothing they predict ever happens."

It is now the third Sabbath since their arrival back to Berea. The synagogue is full.

This time Timothy rises and reads from the Law and the Prophets. Paul resumes his seat in the speaker's chair. He speaks for a while, then stops.

"Now, for your questions."

All is quiet. For once, there are no questions. Paul waits. He looks down on the main floor at Silas, Timothy, and Luke. The silence remains. He looks out over the congregation, and they say nothing.

Paul takes a deep breath, his fingers turn white, clutching the arms of the speaker's chair. He is aware that the scars on his back from the beating he endured just prior to escaping to Berea are burning. He takes another breath, this time a long one. He braces himself for the inevitable arrest that happens in nearly every city he goes to.

"Uh, Paul," Luke says, standing at his seat on the main floor. "They are ready."

Paul stares at Luke, then the outside door. Luke realizes what he is thinking.

"Oh, you think the Jews up in Thessalonica are after you? No, no, no." Luke smiles. "Paul, the congregation is ready." Luke turns toward the congregation. "Tell him."

One by one, men and women rise in place and say, "I am ready." Around the room, the same three words are heard.

"I am ready."

"Me too. I am ready."

"My wife and I are ready."

"I am ready."

Now, most of the congregation is standing.

Rabbi Natanel speaks for them. "We are ready to become Christians. We believe what you told us because everything was proven in the scriptures. We believe Jesus was the Son of God. We want to be baptized."

Paul looks around the room, and tears come to his rugged face with the crooked nose and one eye out. He looks down on the main floor at his friends. Silas is in tears. Timothy and Luke are grinning broadly.

"Everyone has brought extra clothes. Go with us down to the river, and we will be baptized there," the rabbi says.

The congregation sings a psalm, and most of them—though not all—adjourn to the river. They sing another psalm. Paul, Silas, and Timothy baptize the Jewish believers. Luke stands to the side, congratulating them all as they come up out of the water.

Later in the day, Paul tells Luke, "I must begin telling the good news to the worshippers at those temples in the city."

"I want you to start with my master," Luke replies. "He is a good man. A wise man. A fair man. He will listen to you."

"That is true," Timothy adds. "We have been staying with him for weeks, and his master is someone I admire."

That evening, Luke appeals once more to Theophilus.

"Please, Master, will you at least listen to what Paul has to say? If he comes here to you, will you make time to listen?"

Theophilus stares at his slave a few moments. "Well, okay. But he has to come tomorrow."

The following day late in the morning, there is a knock on Theophilus' gate. Before they can identify themselves, Luke opens it.

"Come in. Come in," he says to Paul and Silas, bowing with a flair, his blue eyes gleaming. Right behind Luke is Timothy.

"My master is waiting for you in his *officium*," Luke says.

"I have told him all about you," Timothy says. "Even

about your athletic days. He thinks you are an interesting man."

"He does not know half of it," Silas whispers under his breath.

Luke leads them to the *officium*. "Master, I would like for you to meet my friends, Paul and Silas of Tarsus. And this is my master, Theophilus."

"Welcome to my home," his husky voice says. "Luke speaks well of you. Come out to my courtyard. Sit. Sit. We will have some new wine shortly."

They settle on stone benches and look around at the columns surrounding the garden, and the mosaic tile on the floor between flower beds and a pond.

"Luke tells me you have met a new god."

"Oh, not a new god. He is God. He is the only God, the God who created the world and you and me," Paul says, diving into the conversation with his host. "You were a tribune in the Roman army, Luke tells us. You know that logic must be used at all times to outsmart the enemy. God has outsmarted his enemy, Satan. Satan kidnapped mankind because we all sin, and for eons held us hostage. But God sent his Son to buy our freedom. He bought it with his blood. That's what Satan always wants—death...."

The new wine is served, but Paul and Theophilus do not touch theirs. Instead, they go into the solarium and spar back and forth. Theophilus, with his challenge to Paul's last statement, and Paul's counter challenge to the fallacies Theophilus has been taught all his life.

 Challenge and counter challenge.
 Charge and counter charge.
 Attack and counter-attack.

The rest of the day, they talk. Into the night. Luke, Timothy, and Silas do not try to participate. The two old men go at each other so fast, none of them can keep up.

 Mental battle.
 Philosophical battle.
 Spiritual battle.
 Battle between the human and the divine.
 All night. Luke, Timothy, and Silas stay in the front

courtyard lying on cotton-filled pallets while their superiors spar with each other.

Morning comes. They waken to two coarse voices walking out of the solarium. Paul and Theophilus have their arms extended over each other's shoulders.

"Then, it is settled. I shall become a Christian. I believe Jesus was the Son of God. It shall be done now."

Without changing clothes, the two men climb into the reflecting pool in the outer courtyard, and Paul baptizes the old soldier.

When they come up out of the pool, Theophilus is grinning. "Tonight, I shall have all my friends come here and listen to Paul. Egidius, come here."

Egidius arrives from a nearby room.

"Egidius, you know who my friends are. You have served me for ten years since our army days. I want you to go to their homes and invite them all to my home tonight for an important announcement. I want you to start with Centurion Sopater."

The servant leaves and the four men return to the solarium.

Shortly there is a knock on the front gate. "Already?" Theophilus asks. "He just left."

Luke answers the gate. It is Rabbi Natanel.

"Paul, there is trouble. Jews from Thessalonica have arrived and are stirring up people in the city. You are in danger."

23 ~ THE CHALLENGE

"They're here?" Paul asks.

"Have you been expecting them?" Rabbi Natanel asks.

"They have followed me," Paul says. "The Jews there upset the whole city of Thessalonica lying about me, and have come here to do the same thing."

"The leader must be Rabbi Chagai," Natanel says. "I have known him for years. He is a real trouble maker."

"Where are they?" Theophilus asks.

"In front of the synagogue, but I heard them say something about our magistrates."

"Let's get over there," Paul says.

"No, you don't," Silas says. "Stay here with Luke and Theophilus. Timothy and I will go back with the rabbi."

"I do not run from a fight," Paul objects.

"You're not running. You are staying put," Silas says. "You're not the only strong man around here, you know."

Theophilus looks at Paul. "He is right. You have to choose your battles. Let the foot soldiers handle this one. Save yourself for the big one."

The three leave, and the others wait in silence. Theophilus goes to his *officium* and prays to the one and only God. Luke brings out the psalms he is copying, reads a little, and prays a little. Paul paces.

After a while, there is a knock on the gate. "It's us," Timothy calls out.

Paul opens the gate. "Well? What happened?"

Rabbi Chagai, who caused us so much trouble up in Thessalonica, declared he was going to close us down. Then

Rabbi Natanel demanded he leave town," Silas explains.

The next day at noon, Luke and Timothy prepare to go to their daily class with Paul.

"Well, since we moved his classes to the synagogue after the baptisms, we'll be safer there," Luke says.

When the two arrive at the synagogue, they see a crowd of militant Jews standing near the door with stones in their hands.

"How many do you think there are?" Timothy whispers.

"I'd say twenty or thirty," Luke says. "Each of them has a pile of rocks at his feet, ready to throw at us."

"Well," Timothy says, "let them do their best. We are not backing down."

"Let's do it," Luke says as he takes off running up the front steps.

The first rock hits Timothy in the head. He stumbles, and Luke grabs his arm. Both men catch several on arms, legs, and back before opening the door just enough for them to enter and close it behind them.

"Okay, we're the first ones," Timothy says while examining a bloody arm. "I'll man the door, you tend their wounds. Did you bring anything with you?"

"Yes," Luke says. "I was suspicious what they might be up to. I brought some swaddling bands and salve."

Shortly, they hear a thud on the door. Then another.

Timothy unlatches it, opens it just wide enough for a person to slip through, and lets two more men in. Sopater and his father, Pyrrus.

"They are not a very good aim," Sopater says.

"They got you good in the back," Luke says. "Let me look at it."

"No. I have been through worse. My back and I will survive."

Stones hit the door again. Timothy opens it, and Rabbi Natanel and his wife run in.

Over a period of an hour, the Christians arrive, rush through the barrage of stones, and escape inside the synagogue now turned into a church building.

With each arrival, Luke goes to them to see what injuries they have sustained.

"I am nearly out of bands to wrap on everyone's wounds," he finally says.

A few moments later, they hear a deep husky voice on the portico. They also hear the usual stones hitting the door and outside wall, but now hitting something metal.

Sopater quickly unlatches the door and lets the man in with the deep voice.

"Theophilus?"

"Yes, it is me."

"You took several hits, Master," Luke says.

"As you can see, I wore my battle armor. I sent one of my servants ahead to report to me what was going on and decided to wear this because I wanted to look my enemy in the eye. And I wanted them to face me."

"You didn't bring your sword, did you?" Timothy asks.

"Of course not. Paul told me Jesus is the Prince of Peace, so I left it at home."

For the next hour, the routine of letting bloodied people into the building continues. Finally, they hear no more.

Rabbi Natanel rises. "Paul will now bring us another lesson on the sayings of Jesus, our new king."

For three hours, they study together, asking questions, looking up answers in the scripture scrolls, and discussing them. They do not discuss their attack.

"Well, it is time for us to go home. How will we do it?" the rabbi finally asks.

"If I may make a suggestion," Tribune Theophilus says, "I think we should go on the offensive and all rush out at the same time, spreading across the portico in order to widen their attention requirements, then escape down the street."

"Then that is what we shall do," Rabbi Natanel says. "We shall put half the men in the front, then the women, then the other half of the men in the back."

After some shuffling, Tribune Theophilus calls out, "Charge!"

The front door is swung wide open, and all the Christians rush out. The stoning resumes but in confusion. Once they are out of reach, the Christians stop. They kneel—all but one who remains standing. Paul blesses their enemies.

"You are not fooling us," Rabbi Chagai calls after them.

For the rest of the week, the routine is repeated.

The first day after the Sabbath arrives, the day the Christians meet at the synagogue to worship Jesus.

"Where are all our enemies?" Luke asks as he and Timothy enter the building to take the Lord's Supper. "Do you think the Jews have given up?"

"I do not think so," Rabbi Natanel replies. "They are up to something. Whatever it is, may we remain strong and true."

The second day after the Sabbath, a loud noise is heard from the forum by people as far away as the market. Word spreads. People throughout the city head toward the forum.

"What's happening?"

"What's all the uproar about?"

"Has someone been assassinated?"

"Has an army invaded?"

"We had better hurry and find out."

When people arrive, they see a mob of bearded Jews with stones in their hands accompanied by unbearded sailors with daggers.

"Caesar, yes! Jesus, no!"

"Caesar, yes! Jesus, no!"

"Caesar, yes! Jesus, no!"

Tribune Theophilus shoulders and shoves his way toward the center, followed closely by Luke and Timothy until he can hear what the leader of the mob is saying.

"These men who have turned the world upside down have been inflicting their treasonous ways all the way across Anatolia and are now working their way across Macedonia. After Greece, it will be Rome. Then the takeover."

It is Rabbi Chagai. He is addressing Centurion

Menelaus.

"They have been declaring a man named Jesus is going to assassinate Caesar and take over as king. Their leader deserves death as a traitor. His followers too."

"Centurion Menelaus!"

The centurion turns at the sound of the familiar voice, straightens his back, clicks his heels together, and salutes. "Yes, sir, Tribune Theophilus."

"You will disburse this crowd and arrest anyone who refuses to leave."

"Yes, sir, Tribune Theophilus."

The centurion turns toward his four soldiers on duty. "Disburse the crowd. Arrest lingerers."

The soldiers draw their swords and march forward. Local Bereans, mere onlookers, are the first to flee. But that is all.

The bearded Jews from Thessalonica back up a little, but only a little. A standoff begins as they eye the soldiers and dare them to attack unarmed men, unarmed except for the stones still in their hands.

The sailors recruited from the docks of Thessalonica, frustrated at the lack of real action, plow forward, pushing the Jews out of the way, daggers aimed at the hearts and throats of those who dare challenge them

The Berean soldiers, shields up and swords extended, march forward toward the Thessalonican riff-raff as the Jews duck out of the way.

The cries of "Caesar," "Caesar" die away. Now it is soldier against savage. Man against man. Stubbornness against cowardice.

The Thessalonian sailors stop suddenly, drop their daggers, and run in the opposite direction.

Rabbi Chagai walks over from the sidelines and shakes his fist at Tribune Theophilus. "This is not over," he shouts. "I am not leaving until those Christians are arrested and disposed of. Especially their head. Especially Paul."

He stands nose to nose with the old soldier, saliva dripping down his gray beard. "You tell the coward, Paul, that I will hunt him down," he spits. "He cannot hide from me. No matter where he goes, I will go. You tell Paul he is a dead man."

With that, he turns and follows his hired thugs out of the forum.

Theophilus looks over the crowd and walks toward the Christians, all standing together. "Follow me to my house. You will be safe there."

At Theophilus' house, Paul stands at the gate as each one walks in, shaking their hands and forearms, and embracing them all.

"You are strong," he tells them as they seat themselves on benches, cushions, and the bare floor. "I am so proud of you. I wish I had gone to be with you. I am ashamed."

Silas steps in front of Paul. "Brothers and sisters, he is no coward. Do you have any idea how Paul lost his eye? He was stoned and left for dead for teaching about Jesus. Have you noticed he has one arm he does not use much? It was broken two different times while being beaten with rods by pagans. He has endured thirty-nine lashes twice—that's nearly eighty lashes—by jealous Jews, he has been shipwrecked, he has treaded water a night and a day, he has faced highwaymen, blizzards, hunger, and flooded rivers. He has...."

"Stop that right now," Paul demands, stepping back in front of Silas. "Stop that. Do you want to frighten them?"

"I am giving them courage, Paul. What you have endured for them is giving them courage."

Luke makes his way around the courtyard. "Are you okay? I have more medicine here. Are you in pain?"

Silas walks forward. "Everyone, we are all proud of whatever you have endured for being a Christian. You have a good-sized congregation here in Berea. It is time for us to move on. It will divert attention away from you if we go."

Theophilus stands. "They are right. Paul, you need to leave as soon as it is dark. I will let the guards at the south gate know you are coming, so they will let you out."

"But I do not run from fights," Paul protests.

"Our congregation will be safer with you gone," Theophilus says. "Centurion Sopater will travel with you, and Rabbi Natanel will. You, Silas, and Timothy, will be accompanied by these two men to the coast. Then you will decide where you will go until things die down. It is better that we not know where you are going."

"In that case, Silas and Timothy, I want you to stay here," Paul says. "I will go alone. I think I'll go to Athens.

"Timothy, you slip back up to Thessalonica and see how the congregation is doing. I can give you the names of a couple of converts there who will put you up. The Christians there live under constant threats. Strengthen them, Timothy, strengthen them."

He turns to Theophilus. "I look for great things from you. Also, from your slave, Luke."

"He is like a son to me. That is why he is leaving as soon as you do. He will go with Timothy as far as Thessalonica, then visit the church in Philippi, then sail back to Troas. I have agreed for him to go to a medical academy there so he can be my physician. He can strengthen the church in Troas while there also."

Paul walks over to Luke, still checking on people's wounds. "Timothy speaks highly of you. I wish I had someone like you to help me. Well, perhaps someday."

The next morning, Luke and Timothy head back north. Four days later, they arrive at Thessalonica.

They walk down to the docks where Luke finds a ship bound for Troas.

"Well, friend. I guess this is it," Luke says. "You have been a good friend to me. I guess you have answered all my questions about the scriptures. And I had a lot of them."

"And you, my friend," Timothy replies, "have shown me more ways I can take care of Paul. His life is not easy. I have been with him several years and have done my best to keep him alive so he can go to the next city and the next and the next to spread the word about Jesus. He will never back down until he is dead. It is my job to keep him alive."

They embrace, pound each other on the back, and walk in opposite directions.

"What do I do if I cannot answer someone's question?" Luke calls back to Timothy from halfway up the gangplank.

"Pray!" Timothy shouts.

Luke takes a few more steps. "Be careful until we are together again someday," Luke calls out, now on board the ship.

Sailors finish loading cargo onto the ship. Finally, Luke hears bells, the sound of anchors being pulled up, and shouts from the captain on the bridge.

Luke settles down on the ship next to a passenger who has brought a horse on board.

"What kind of horse do you have, sir?" he asks.

"Arabian."

"He seems very fine."

"Oh, he is. He's strong and can handle the heat."

"I had a horse once, but he died in the desert of Parthia."

"It's hard to lose an animal that has been loyal to you."

"Indeed, it is. The finest horse I have seen anywhere, however, is the big black Frisian. He is magnificent. Perhaps someday I will be able to own one."

But most of the time, Luke does not talk. Sometimes he walks around the deck, repeating the scriptures from Daniel and the Psalms that he had managed to memorize.

At other times, he sits off by himself and sings. The reassuring songs the Christians sing bring him courage and comfort and a knowing that the only real God is watching over him.

The winds and currents are contrary when they go near the Dardanelles, but finally, the ship docks at Troas.

Luke disembarks with his belongings and heads toward the home of *Medicus* Alekto.

"Luke! Luke!" he hears. He grins and turns in the direction of the voice.

"Luke, you're back," the sailor says.

"Hello, Oceanus. Didn't I tell you I would be?"

"You kept your word."

"How has the congregation been doing while I was gone?"

"We're still growing."

"Still meeting in your apartment?"

"Yes."

"Well, I am going to be here a couple years attending the medical academy of Alekto. So you will see a lot of me."

The men part and Luke continues on to Alekto's house. Arriving, he knocks on the gate. A servant lets him in.

"Do I hear Luke?" a growly voice says from a nearby room.

Medicus Alekto walks out onto the courtyard. He holds his arms wide and embraces Luke. He holds him at arm's length, and grinning, he says, "Welcome back, my boy. Welcome back."

"I'm not exactly your boy anymore," Luke retorts, laughing. I have been in my thirties a while."

"You will always be that boy who followed me around at the fortress bandaging my patients. By the way, I saved your room for you. Put your things away, and we will have something to eat."

"So, you are here to attend my school, I presume."

"Yes, indeed, I am.

The months go by. Luke memorizes the names of bones and muscles. He memorizes the functions of internal organs.

More months.

"Today, I am going to teach you how to treat burns..."

As always, Luke does not attend classes on the first day of the week.

"I do not approve of you missing my lectures like this," Alekto always says.

"I must put Jesus first," Luke always says, "because he put me first. Why don't you let me tell you about him?"

"Don't need another god. The one I have is fine."

"Would you go to our worship with me?"

"You just don't go around messing with the gods," Alekto says. "If I go with you and make my god jealous, he could hurl thunderbolts at me or worse. You just don't go around messing with the gods."

Still, each first day of the week, Luke meets with the church on the third floor of the insulae.

He teaches them some of the songs he had learned from Timothy. Sometimes one of them makes up a new song. They pray, they remember Jesus' death and resurrection. They share and encourage and grow.

Nearly two years go by. Alekto has just finished teaching the latest apothecary procedures and told his students they will spend their last year learning surgery. Some students like the idea of cutting into people, others do not. Luke is looking forward to it.

But he is also worried. He has about given up hearing from his master. Finally, a letter from home arrives. It is not from Theophilus.

FROM SOPATER OF BEREA TO LUKE OF TROAS. GREETINGS. I HAVE HESITATED TO WRITE YOU, BUT NOW FEEL COMPELLED TO. YOUR MASTER, THE TRIBUNE, HAS BEEN MISSING FOR SEVERAL WEEKS. IF HE IS WITH YOU, PLEASE REPLY AS SOON AS POSSIBLE.

AGAIN, I SAY, CONTACT ME AS SOON AS YOU RECEIVE THIS LETTER AND TELL ME WHETHER TRIBUNE THEOPHILUS IS WITH YOU.

"I have to leave," Luke tells Alekto.

"Not before your schooling is done," the physician tells him.

"I have no choice."

24 ~ GHOST FROM THE PAST

Luke grabs what he can carry in his largest leather pouch and rushes down to the harbor. He sees eleven ships tied up and goes to each one.

"Might you be going to the port near Berea?" he asks. "I know it is a small port, but I can't take time to go north to Neapolis or Thessalonica first."

"Sorry, we have no need to go there."

"Might you be going to the port near Berea?"

"Nope. Don't even know where Berea is."

One by one, Luke calls up to the guard at the top of the gangplank of each ship. Always the answer is no.

"Might you be going to the port near Berea?"

Out of the eleven ships, one says they have been there a few times, but aren't going in the near future. Luke returns to that one.

"Sir, could I speak with your captain?" Luke says.

"No, he's busy."

Luke takes out a silver coin and offers it to the first mate.

"As I said," the first mate says, "he is busy. However, he will give you a few moments. Go with this seaman."

Luke boards the ship, follows the seaman, and climbs up to the bridge. A door into the captain's cabin is opened, and Luke follows him in.

Captain Florian is of medium height, big-chested but slim in his arms and legs. His hair is windblown and dry.

"Sir, I have urgent business in the Olympic Mountains and need to get there as soon as possible."

The captain does not look up. "What's so important as to divert my ship and delay delivery of cargo and my pay?"

"Sir, Tribune Theophilus is…."

The captain's head jerks up. "Titus Pontus Theophilus?"

"Uh, yes, sir."

"I served with him at Fortress Capidava on the Black Sea," he says, looking up from the map. "Wasn't his first officer a centurion named Sosipater or Sosthenes or something like that?"

"Yes, Sopater, Centurion Sopater."

"Fine, man. Fine man. I respected him. Everyone did. He took me aside once right after I arrived and explained to me how to get along with the legate. He was one of the few who had figured out how," Captain Florian says, laughing and leaning back in his chair.

"He retired soon after I arrived, and then I transferred to ship service. Then I retired, and now I am a cargo ship captain. So, how do you know him? Were you one of his centurions?"

"No, sir. I was his slave."

"His slave?"

"Sir, I received this message from Centurion Sopater." Luke holds up the small scroll. "My master is missing. I need to look for him. I know his habits better than anyone. If he is injured somewhere, I can heal him. If he has been kidnapped, he gave me infantry training, and maybe I can figure out how to free him."

The captain leans forward, stares at his manifest, stands, looks at his map, then turns back to Luke.

"I would not do this for just anyone. But Theophilus is worth saving. I will divert my ship to the port near the Dion. Is that close enough to…"

"To Berea? Yes, sir. And thank you, sir," Luke replies, fighting back tears of relief, and pulling out his money pouch.

"No charge. Just settle in somewhere. We should be there in about a day and a half. And ask the seaman to give you some food."

The day and a half creep by. Luke often paces and recites parts of Daniel and the psalms, wishing he had learned more. Sometimes when he sits, he sings one of the psalms Timothy had taught him.

Now and then, he leans back and dreams. He does not like the dreams. In it, he is always running to Theophilus, who either keeps backing away from him or disappears.

"Land ho!" he finally hears. Luke is directed to a rowboat so the ship does not have to drop anchor in the silty harbor. He waves at the ship captain watching him from the bridge, then is rowed to shore. Once more, Luke turns, waves at the ship, then turns and walks with long and hurried strides toward Berea.

As he enters the city, he passes people on the street who greet him with, "Sorry to hear about your master," or "Glad you're back, but it's probably too late."

He arrives at the gate with the emblem of the Fifth Legion on it and knocks.

Egidius opens it. "Oh, Luke, it's you. I did not know if it was our master or someone from the fortress or what."

Luke walks in, stares a moment at the old man, and they clasp hands and forearms.

"You must be hungry. Master gave me the keys to his money box years ago, and I buy what is needed. It is running low, but we are okay for now."

Luke takes his leather traveling pouch to his room, then joins Egidius in the kitchen area. "So, what do you know? How long has he been gone? What time of day did you last see him?"

"He disappeared three months ago. He got in his chariot one morning and headed toward the fortress. I never saw him again."

"Three months?" Luke says. "I sent him many letters and never received any back from him. I wondered about it, but decided he had gone off to war in Parthia or Britannia and could not write to me."

"Luke," Egidius says, "he never received any letters from you. He decided you were too busy with your studies but kept writing you."

"I never received any letters from him. What could have happened?"

They hear a knock at the gate. Egidius looks at Luke. "Do you think you were followed?"

Luke climbs up onto the roof, looks down, then calls out, "It's okay. Let him in."

Pyrrus enters and asks for Luke. Luke arrives, and they clasp hands. The old man acts more feeble than he had two years earlier.

"One of my servants told me he saw you in town. I'm glad you're back. You know him better than anyone, I think."

"Yes, I have been with him nearly thirty years, so I guess I do. Come sit."

"Egidius says he last saw him when he left home in his chariot headed for the fortress," Luke recalls. "Did you see him after that?"

"Yes, I saw him mid-morning. I went to see him at the fortress about guards for a shipment of silver I was sending to the coast."

"In that case, I need to go to the fortress to see what I can learn there."

"I will give you a ride in my chariot," Pyrrus says.

At the fortress, Luke is escorted to the *officium* of Pyrrus' son, Centurion Sopater.

"You got my letter," he tells Luke. The centurion leaves his writing-table and moves to a marble bench, motioning for Luke to sit also.

"So far, I have traced him to the fortress his last day," Luke says. "Did you see him?"

"Yes. I shared some cheese and apple wedges with him midday."

"Did he look worried?"

"No. But, come to think of it, just as we were leaving, an aide arrived and gave him a message. He didn't say anything, and I didn't either. Let me see now. Who gave him that message? Come with me."

Luke follows Sopater into Theophilus' *officium*. "Help me look through these tiles. They are the daily rostrums of guards on duty when and where. Hopefully, they haven't been scraped and reused."

They look through the piles as fast and efficiently as they can.

"Here's the one I think we're looking for," Luke says.

Sopater looks at it. "Yes!" He goes out into the corridor and orders the guard on duty in front of his *officium* to bring Infantryman Labium to him.

They return to Sopatar's *officium* to wait. They sit sometimes and pace sometimes.

"A civilian came to the front gate and handed it to me," Labium says when he arrives.

"What did he look like?"

"I don't remember. Just a normal looking Italian."

"Did the tribune leave the fortress after that?"

"I saw him leave in mid-afternoon. Funny. He wasn't wearing his uniform, driving his chariot, or riding his horse. He walked out. Didn't even salute."

"Do you remember which way he went?"

"Out the west gate. That's all I know."

Sopater dismisses the guard.

"If he went out the west gate," Luke says, "and he was not in uniform, I do not think he was going to the Ionian side of Macedonia. He has no dealings over there."

"If he had been heading north, he would take the east gate out of the city and travel on the Via Ignatia," Sopater says. "That leaves south and the Bermian Mountain."

Luke stands and paces. "All I can think of is a retreat he has up there."

"But why would he go in the middle of the day?" Sopater asks.

"Didn't the guard say the messenger was Italian?" Luke says. "Most people in our city are either Greek or Thracian. The messenger must have been working for a foreigner."

"How could a foreign civilian get Theophilus to leave his post like that?"

"I am going to find out," Luke says.

"You're not going alone," Sopater objects.

"Yes, I am. If he went to his retreat out of urgency,

something is wrong up there. I know the trail and where to get off it so I can inspect the parameters."

"At least take some weapons with you."

"Well, I've always been good with the javelin. I'll take two of the shorter ones. And a dagger to get through some of the underbrush. That's all."

Within the hour, Luke is through the west gate and has turned south into the Bermian foothills. He walks for two hours. As he does, he realizes a noticeable path has been worn along the route that should not be there. *He never made a path because he never wanted anyone to know where his retreat was.*

Once he is within ten man-lengths of his master's retreat—a large leather military tent—Luke stays in the trees and walks around it, listening and watching. In the back of the tent, he lowers himself flat on the ground and creeps forward, dragging his javelins with each hand.

"You'll never get away with this, Centurion Blasius," he hears his master say.

"That's right. I am a centurion," Blasius bellows. "Not the infantryman you got me demoted to. A centurion. Do you hear? A centurion!"

Luke crawls closer.

"That was nearly twenty-five years ago, Blasius. We are old men now," Theophilus counters with a tired voice.

Luke is at the back edge of the tent.

"We are the same age. I should have been a tribune, not you. Oh, that's right. You captured the brother of a rebel leader down in North Africa. He was just his brother! He wasn't the leader!" Blasius shouts, his voice almost screeching. "But, no, they play favorites and make you tribune."

Luke lifts the bottom of the tent just enough he can see.

"Blasius, this has gone too far. My men are looking for me. You will be caught, arrested, and beheaded or crucified. Put a stop to this now and make your getaway. Save yourself."

Luke first sees the feet of Blasius. He is pacing.

"Do you have any idea how much I have hated you all these years? Hated, hated, hated. There wasn't a day go by that I did not hate you more."

Luke hears groaning. "Oh, your shoulder hurts, does it? Serves you right. Terrible mistake trying to escape. Terrible. Terrible. Your arm is swelling. Too bad. Too bad. I think I'll just wait around and let it kill you a little at a time."

Luke shifts over to the part of the tent where he had heard the groaning.

"Blasius, what do you want? I cannot change the past."

Luke lifts the edge of the tent slightly and sees his master on the ground, chained to the main tent pole. He is thin, and some of his gray hair has fallen out.

Oh, Master.

"Do you know what I was going to do with all my money?"

Luke puts the bottom of the tent back down and looks around.

"You mean money you stole from the army," Theophilus groans.

Luke picks up a long, thin stick, slides it under the tent edge a finger width at a time. He pokes his master's knee with it. Theophilus looks down, then back to Blasius.

"It was rightfully mine. It was back pay. I deserved it. Well, you didn't ask, but I will tell you anyway. I was planning to go to China. Surprises you, doesn't it? I was going to set up a silk business and export it back here."

Luke slowly edges the stick back out, ties a rope to the end, and slips it back in.

"Oh, here is my boy with some food from the market down there. Berea has some good cooks. Did you know that? Good cooks. Of course, you don't get any. You only get what you deserve."

Luke crouches on his knees and accidentally breaks a twig. He stays still in case it has been heard.

"Water, if you don't mind," Theophilus groans. "I could use a little water."

Luke eases around to the side of the tent and sees

Blasius' delivery man and guard sitting at the front flap of the tent.

"Well, since you need water to stay alive so you can die on my terms," Luke hears, "here is a sip," Blasius says.

There is a pause and shuffling inside. "How did you know about my retreat? Luke is the only one who ever knew about it."

Luke waits and watches Blasius' guard.

"So," Blasius says from within the tent, his voice garbled with food, "once I accidentally found out where you were living—and that's another story—I had you followed. When I learned Luke was still with you but left, I had your letters intercepted and learned he was going to be gone to Troas a long time. After that, I intercepted both your letters and his so I could find a way to trap you."

The guard at the front stands and looks around. Luke returns to the trees and circles around from beside him to be across from him.

"So that's when you decided to convince me that Luke never made it to Troas, but was being held captive up here by you."

As he talks, Theophilus continues to tie the rope around the tent pole behind him.

"Brilliant, wasn't it?"

Luke rushes from the trees, both javelins in his hands. The guard escapes into the bush, going farther up the mountain.

Blasius nears the entrance, as Luke knew he would when he heard the noise. The center tent pole collapses, and along with it, the tent. Luke throws his javelins, so they hold the tent down around Blasius. He slams his dagger into the front flap of the tent to hold it securely down.

Rushing around to the back of the tent, he raises the edge and looks Theophilus in the eyes. "Good thinking," Theophilus says. "That rope you slipped to me."

Luke crawls in and slides the chains from the tent pole.

"Can you run?" he asks Theophilus, shocked at his now thin body.

"I don't think so. I'm pretty weak."

"Climb on my back."

"What?"

"Climb on my back. I'm carrying you down."

The tribune obeys, and Luke takes off down the path from the retreat to safety. In half an hour, they are at a small clearing.

"Are you okay, Master?"

Theophilus does not speak. Luke continues on down the foothills. Half an hour later, he sees the fortress below.

"We're almost there, Master," he shouts. Theophilus does not answer. *Please still be alive, Master. Oh, Jesus, keep him alive.*

He rushes through the gate of the city and to the gate of the fortress.

"Let us in. It's the tribune."

A guard throws his cape down on the ground just inside the fortress, and Luke eases his master onto it.

"Please be alive," he whispers.

25 ~ NEW DIRECTIONS

"Luke," Theophilus says after having called his slave to the solarium.

"Sit down, Son." Luke beams whenever his master calls him that, though he knows he is not really his son.

"I would have died up there if it hadn't been for you. Not only did you rescue me, but you healed my shoulder and saved my arm. I do not know how you managed to do either one, but you did."

"Master, I..."

"No, do not interrupt me," he says, toying with a small scroll. "You have been with me some thirty years and have always been loyal. I have been trying to figure out how to reward you."

"Master, you don't..."

"You're interrupting again," Theophilus says, his voice still weak from his ordeal six months earlier. "I have decided how I am going to do it."

Theophilus hands the small parchment scroll to Luke, who unfolds and read it.

Luke stands, looks up at the sky, over at his master, then back at the scroll.

"My freedom, Master?"

"I am no longer your master. Now I am just your friend. You are welcome to stay on here and keep copying books for my library. I will pay you. However..."

"But, Mas...uh...sir."

"You're interrupting again, Luke. I think I want to send you to Athens. I heard there is a new Academy of Medicine there, and they specialize in surgery. Isn't that what you said you missed learning? Would you like to go there?"

"Well, yes. Of course. But what about you?"

"I will pay your tuition, then you can come back here to be my physician as we always planned. Of course, I will pay you."

Luke sits back on his bench. He stares at the scroll with Theophilus' signature and seal at the bottom, then at Theophilus. He says nothing.

"Then, it is settled. You will go down to Athens and enroll in the medical academy as soon as you finish copying the Jewish prophets.

"Now, there is one more thing. I need you to walk with me over to the neighborhood near the synagogue."

"Yes, uh, sir."

The two walk slowly down the street, across the bridge, and into a neighborhood with small houses.

"I wonder whatever happened to old Blasius," Luke says as they walk.

"Where ever he is, he knows not to come back around here if he does not want the entire fortress after him."

They pass a few of the houses and stop at one of them. "Knock on that gate."

Luke knocks and Egidius answers.

"What are you doing here?" Luke asks.

"Luke," Theophilus says. "This is your new home."

"Mine?" Luke enters and walks around the small courtyard. "It's mine?"

He opens the doors to the three empty rooms surrounding the courtyard and looks in.

How did all this happen? Jesus, you are so good to me. I just wish Rashah were here to share my house with me. And my father. I am not ungrateful, Jesus. Just thinking.

He returns to the courtyard where Theophilus and Egidius stand grinning.

"You deserve more than just a house for serving me most of your life. Egidius is here to help you get settled. Then, when you are through copying the last of the prophets, you will go to Athens to finish your medical education."

"I do not know what to say," Luke says, fighting unmanly tears.

Over the following seven months, Luke builds for himself a writing table, some benches, and a table with short legs on which to store blank parchments. On top of that table are two rows of cubicles large enough to slide a fair-sized scroll into.

At the market, he picks up a single serving bowl, a bowl to eat out of, and a plate to eat out of, then decides he should get two of each.

He develops a routine of living alone and going to Theophilus' house daily for his work.

Now Luke is on the Via Egnatia headed south. The sea breeze is on his face, and often he looks up and says aloud, "Thank you."

When he arrives in Athens, Luke asks the guards at the city gate if they know where the Academy of Medicine is.

"Not sure. But I would head toward the temples. Those physicians like to keep the gods happy."

Eventually, Luke finds the academy and is enrolled with money Theophilus has given him.

He settles in, then spends part of his time in class, but most of his time helping patients in their hospitium.

Late one afternoon, he hears someone calling out to him. "Luke," the aide says. "There is a hysterical man yelling for you down the hall. Don't you hear him? His name is Timothy, and he has a severely wounded man with..."

Luke grabs a vial of oil and honey and rushes down the hall. "Timothy? Timothy? Where are you?"

Timothy ducks out of the small patient room. "It's Paul," he shouts. "It's Paul."

Luke rushes into the room and sees what is left of Paul's bloodied back.

"Who did this to him?" Luke asks.

"Oh, Luke," Timothy says. "Don't let him die. Don't let him die."

Luke questions Timothy. "Does he have pain deadeners in him?"

"Yes, we gave him a spoon of opium just before we left

Corinth."

"You came all the way up from Corinth?"

"I will tell you about it later. Please make Paul live."

Luke applies the medicine in the vial to what is left of Paul's back, then stares at his soul saver. He stands and looks at Timothy. "I will personally check on him every hour through the night."

"Do you not ever sleep, Luke?" a grateful and exhausted. Timothy asks.

"Do you?" Luke retorts with a slight smile.

Luke returns periodically to pour medication over the exposed muscle tissue and give Paul a sip of opium for the pain.

About midnight, Luke lies down on a pallet in the corridor. Whenever he hears Paul groan, he goes to him and covers him in prayer. He does not sleep much.

"I do not know how he has survived so many beatings," Luke tells Timothy a few days later. "Every muscle in his back has been torn. I'm sure some of the ribs under them have been bruised or cracked."

"He has a strong will, Luke," Timothy replies in almost a whisper. "He is driven. It's as though he can never do enough."

"Why?" Luke stares at Timothy, trying to comprehend.

"When he was young, he hated Christians," Timothy explains in a low voice. "He put them in jail, he tortured them, and he killed them. I guess he is trying to make up for it."

"No man can do that."

Paul groans and they grow quiet.

"Well, I have other patients to see. I will be back as soon as I can."

Days pass. A week.

Dionysius, one of Athen's aristocratic high council magistrates who Paul had converted months earlier comes to see Paul sometimes. Demaris, too, widow of Athens' esteemed treasure comes every day. Others of Paul's converts in Athens come to see him sometimes. He is hardly aware. Some sit and weep. Some pray. Some softly sing him one of David's psalms.

Though Paul eventually is conscious again, Luke keeps the opium in him for the ever-present pain.

"He has been here five weeks," Luke tells Timothy one day. "He can go to someone's home now, and I will go there each day to see him. Is there someplace he can go nearby?"

"Dionysius has a secure estate, and his guards will stand duty day and night, but in disguise so as to not arouse suspicion," Timothy replies.

"I like Dionysius," Paul mutters.

"Then it is agreed."

Luke goes to Magistrate Dionysius' estate daily to minister to Paul.

"I don't see how you do it," Luke tells Paul. "Your pain level must be nearly unbearable. I never saw an injury like yours the whole time Theophilus and I were serving in the legions. You have my admiration."

Gradually Paul is able to lift himself up to his knees, gently swing his legs around, and sit up.

He sits on the side of his bed for a while, talking with Timothy or Dionysius or Luke, then goes back to sleep on his front. But each day he sits up a little longer.

During one of Luke's visits, Paul asks him to close the door to his room.

"Luke," Paul whispers. "I need you."

"Yes, I know you do."

"I mean, I really need you."

"I know what you mean, Paul."

"Will you go with me?"

"I have been thinking about it."

"I cannot stop, Luke. I have to keep doing it, no matter what they do to me. I have to keep snatching people from hell."

"I know that."

"They've battered my body pretty bad. But I've got to keep going. I cannot stop. I just can never do enough."

"Yes, I know."

"So, will you? I will write a letter to Theophilus and offer to repay him for your medical education. Will you go with me from now on?"

"The answer is yes. I will go with you and take care of you. And Theophilus will not take your money. He will understand."

Not long after, Paul sends Timothy and two others of Paul's assistants to visit congregations they had established along the coast of the Aegean, then to take a ship from Neapolis to Troas.

"Wait for me there," Paul instructs them. "By the time you visit all those congregations, I will be well enough to travel."

A few days later, while Luke gives him his treatment, Paul explains what he wants to do.

"The Passover is in a couple months. I would like to keep it in Philippi with Lydia. I always liked her. Also, that congregation has helped me more than any other."

"You have formed a pretty good scab," Luke tells him. "But your back was so full of scars before this, your new skin will not have much chance to be normal."

"Why don't we go on up to Berea?" Paul replies. "That way, we will be halfway to Philippi."

"You are not in any shape to leave here," Luke objects. He gently touches a spot on Paul's back. "Do you feel that?"

"Ouch. We can stay in your house while I get better."

"Lie still while I finish putting this medication on you. The other reason is that you cannot even walk yet."

"Okay. As soon as I can walk, I want to go to Berea. Then Philippi. Then Troas. Then Jerusalem. I have to get to Jerusalem."

Luke finishes his treatment and leaves. Paul shifts from his front onto his knees, eases his legs around, sits on the side of his bed, then slides his feet to the floor. He walks, bent over, the few paces to the door of his small room, and back to his bed.

After a week, Paul is able to walk around Dionysius' courtyard, though his back is still bent over. He refuses to acknowledge his pain.

"As soon as I can wear clothes, I will be able to leave, Dionysius. I cannot tell you how much I appreciate your hiding me in your estate, and putting up with me for so long."

"Paul, you saved us when we did not even know we were lost," Dionysius says. "This is the least I can do. By the way, as you know, the church has been meeting in the estate of Demaris. But now that you can get out of your room, the church would like to come here next Lord's Day, so you can worship with everyone."

Paul smiles. "I have missed them, not that I don't appreciate you sharing the Lord's Supper with me each week by ourselves. But it is not the same."

"Yes, I know."

"I have to figure out a way to put on a tunic. They do not want to look at my grotesque back."

"My maid keeps discarded clothing on hand to give to the poor. I will have her cut some up so pieces can be placed on your oiled back. Do you think you can handle it?"

"Let's give it a try next time Luke comes."

Later that day, Luke arrives, and Paul lies down for the treatment.

"Okay, I put extra olive oil, honey, and turmeric on your back. Now let's try a cloth over it. Are you ready?"

Paul braces himself. "Ready. Let's do it."

Luke starts at Paul's neck and shoulders.

Paul flinches. "Keep going. Don't stop."

Little by little, Luke lays the cloth on Paul's back. Paul clenches his fists and grits his teeth. The veins on his neck throb and he fights back hated tears.

Luke watches carefully, wanting to take the pain away from Paul. He reminds himself he must remain emotionally detached from his patient in order to do what needs to be done.

"Okay, it is on. Let it sit for a moment while your skin—what remains of it—calms down."

They wait in silence.

"Now, Paul, I am going to put another cloth on you to help absorb the oil so you can put on a tunic."

The process is slow, and Paul patiently endures, sending his mind to pleasant things. He hums, and the longer Luke takes, the harder he hums.

"Now, I need you to push yourself up by your arms so I can wrap this last cloth around your torso to hold the cloths on."

Paul complies, and when Luke has it in place, he moves to his knees, swings around, and sits on the side of his bed. "That was not so bad," he says with a forced smile. "Now for my tunic."

"No tunic yet. You cannot raise your arms. Here is a robe with extra ties in it to keep it closed."

"Okay," Paul says. "I will wear this around the house for the next couple days. If it works, come by early on the Lord's Day, and we will put a fresh one on."

Two days later, the small congregation at Athens arrives a few at a time lest an enemy of Paul is watching Dionysius' house. Within three hours, all have assembled.

Paul sits next to Luke on a bench. His back is to a wall, so the robe he is wearing backward can stay loose. He has a large pillow propped up on his lap that he rests his chin on.

"Paul, I am so glad you are better," a Brother says upon his arrival. *He looks so thin.*

"Paul, you are a brave soul. You have only survived by the grace of God." *But to live a life of pain from now on.*

"Paul, I admire you so much." *How does he keep going when people do this to him?*

They decide to ask Paul to say a few words before he becomes too tired.

"Brothers and sisters. We all must suffer in order to spread the good news about Jesus. Rulers of all religions will feel threatened and try to destroy you. They cannot. As Jesus said, 'They may destroy your body, but they cannot destroy your soul.' "

He stops, grunts softly, shifts in his seat a little, and notices Luke watching him. "I'm okay," he whispers.

"People do not know they are doomed to hell. You must do all you can to snatch them away from Satan. You cannot do it against their will, of course, but you must try. You must never stop trying."

He shifts in his seat again and leans heavier on the pillow under his chin. Everyone waits in silence.

"If one rejects Jesus, go to the next person and the next....This is your mission on earth....Though you have inner peace, you must discard that peace sometimes in order to take Jesus to people who do not know about him....Snatch them from the gates of hell....Give them heaven."

He stops and closes his eyes to once again get control of the pain. They wait.

"Let us now sing a psalm of David," Dionysius says.

As they sing, everyone continues to watch their beloved apostle. His eyes are still closed, but he is singing. Their Paul is singing.

They have the Lord's Supper. Paul sits up straighter and takes the bite of unleavened bread. He closes his eyes again, but they see tears flow down his cheeks.

After a time of personal meditation, the red wine is passed around. Paul looks up at the sky above the courtyard and whispers, "I am so sorry." Those sitting nearby hear and weep with him.

Another hymn. Paul—former boxer and all-around athlete—leans over on Luke's shoulder. As the others sing, Luke moves around to the front of Paul, helps him stand, and walks slowly with him to his room. In his bed now, he falls asleep to a sweet melody flowing to him from the church outside his door who loves him.

Days go by. Paul continues to practice walking in the courtyard.

"I think we are getting close to being able to travel," Luke announces on his next visit. "I am going to try something new today. I am taking the oil away. I have a paste of mud, aloes, and honey to put on you. It will help the scab harden so you can wear clothes without so much pain."

"Did you know I used to be a runner? I ran all the time. I loved running."

"No, I did not know that, Paul."

"Hey, that's cold! Poor Barnabas used to get so mad at me when I'd take off running and leave him behind out on the road between cities. But I wasn't completely heartless. I'd stop and wait for him at the next *mille* marker."

"Okay. Now we are not going to put anything over your back. We need your scab to harden. It should be good enough by the end of the week that you can wear a proper robe again. Maybe, by the time we get to Troas, you will be able to lift your arms enough, you can put on a tunic."

"That is good news. And Luke, thank you."

"Paul, it is my privilege. I think we may be able to leave for Berea in another week."

Indeed, they do. The Christians in Athens walk with Paul and Luke down to the docks and watch as they board a fishing boat to take them up the coast a little way. Will they ever see him again?

The stay in Berea is a good one.

Soon after settling in at Luke's little house, Theophilus comes over. Paul sends Luke to buy something for him in the market. When Luke returns, Theophilus tells Paul, "Then it is settled."

Theophilus stands and walks over to his former slave. "You have my blessing, Son. If I cannot have you as my personal physician, then I know of no other person I would rather have you serve than Paul."

"Thank you," Luke whispers.

The next first day of the week, a few of the Berean Christians crowd into Luke's house, so Paul does not have to worship alone.

"Where is Sopater?" Luke asks his father.

"He collected money for the poor in Jerusalem," Pyrrus says. "It was while you were still in Athens. He then went with Timothy and some others representing their congregations."

"That is who we are going to be meeting in Troas," Paul adds.

Four weeks later, Luke makes the announcement. "I think you are ready to travel, Paul."

He sends word to Theophilus, and the tribune comes. "I will make sure he writes to you," Paul assures Luke's former slave master.

"I will send you money periodically. I have more than one person needs." Just before he leaves, he slips a bag of silver coins into Luke's hands. "This should get you to Jerusalem."

The two men embrace and pound each other on the back. "I will miss you, Master."

"And I you."

The next day, a ship takes Luke and Paul to Neapolis. They spend Passover at Philippi, then board another ship to go on to Troas, border city between Macedonia, Greece, and Anatolia.

On the first day of the week, the congregation in Troas meets in Oceana's third-floor insulae apartment. By taking it slow and resting every few steps, Paul is able to climb the three flights of stairs.

"I'm afraid you are going to tear open some of your wounds," Luke says.

"Have more faith," Paul replies. "I can do this."

The following day before boarding another ship, Paul announces he wants to walk to Assos, where the ship will be docking to take on cargo.

"No, Paul," Luke says. "You are not strong enough."

"I will have Timothy with me. He has doctored me before. Maybe not as well as you, but as well as he could, and it got me through."

"No, Paul. Your back is still too fragile."

"Luke, I need to do this. Just one last time. I have walked a thousand miles. I may never be able to do it again. Timothy will take good care of me. Just one last time."

Luke gives Timothy instructions on how to care for Paul, then boards the ship. Once settled, he pulls out a piece of parchment.

FROM LUKE, PHYSICIAN TO THE APOSTLE PAUL AND ONBOARD A SHIP IN THE AEGEAN SEA, TO THE MOST EXCELLENT THEOPHILUS OF BEREA, GREECE. I COULD HARDLY WAIT TO TELL YOU WHAT PAUL DID LAST NIGHT WHILE WE WERE WITH THE CHURCH IN TROAS. A MAN FELL TO HIS DEATH FROM A THIRD-STORY WINDOW. PAUL, IN HIS WEAKENED CONDITION, WENT TO THE MAN AND BROUGHT HIM BACK TO LIFE USING JESUS' POWER. THAT IS CORRECT. THE MAN WAS DEAD, AND TODAY HE IS ALIVE. THEOPHILUS, CHRISTIANITY IS THE MOST AMAZING LIFE. I WISH YOU COULD HAVE BEEN

HERE TO SEE IT. I MUST CLOSE THIS LETTER NOW SO I CAN HAVE IT IN THE HANDS OF A COURIER WHEN WE REACH ASSOS IN A FEW HOURS. PROBABLY THE NEXT TIME YOU HEAR FROM ME, WE WILL BE IN CAESAREA OR JERUSALEM. UNTIL WE MEET AGAIN, I REMAIN FAITHFULLY YOURS. LUKE

The rest of his time on the ship, Luke walks around, watches the water, or sits, wondering. *What will a future will be like with an apostle?*

26 ~ JERUSALEM

*L*uke is relieved when Paul boards the ship, and he can resume his treatments. They move along the western coast of Anatolia, taking on cargo, then along the coast of Syria until they reach Caesarea.

Paul is accompanied by Luke, Timothy, and representatives of congregations in Corinth, Berea, Thessalonica, Derbe, and Ephesus, all carrying money to the poor Christians in Jerusalem.

They go to the large home of Philip, one of the first deacons of the church in Jerusalem at its beginning.

"I have a letter here from someone named Theophilus," Philip tells Paul. "Do you have someone in your group named Luke?"

"That is me," Luke says with a large grin.

Luke takes the small scroll, breaks the seal, excuses himself, and walks outside to read it. After catching Luke up on news of the church in Berea, Theophilus makes a large request.

....Remember all you went through to write a history of your Nordic people? If you would like to repay me for anything I have done for you, then write a greater history than that. Write a history of Jesus. You will soon be walking where he walked. Interview people who knew him. Check government documents to verify dates, places, and events. It will probably take you a few years to accomplish this because I want you to be thorough. Then your book will be the finest one in all my library. Greetings from the church here to you and all your companions. Your friend, and a friend of the only real God, Theophilus.

Later that evening, when everyone has settled in, Luke

approaches Philip.

"I understand you have been with the church since the beginning," he says.

"Yes. I was a young married man at the time. Now I have four grown daughters, all faithful prophetesses. I have been blessed."

"Would you tell me about it? And would you mind if I took notes?" he asks, pulling out a parchment, pen, and blackener from a pouch on his shoulder.

"Not at all. Let's sit in this room over here. It is small but private."

They are seated, and Philip leans his head against the wall behind him. He sighs. "I grew up in Cappadocia, a province in Anatolia where my father raised sheep. My parents were both Jewish.

"On one of our trips to Jerusalem for Passover, there was a riot. Being a young man, I followed the mob to see what was going on. They pushed through the street, out the gate of Jerusalem, and up execution hill.

"By then, I knew someone was going to be crucified. It's a horrible form of execution.

"Had you ever seen a crucifixion before?"

"Of course. I think nearly everyone has. But this one was different. One of them died after only six hours. Most take two or three days to die, but not him. I couldn't see it, but someone said he had been scourged almost to death ahead of time."

"Did you know who he was?"

"Not right away, but I overheard people call him Jesus from Nazareth. Anyway, the strangest thing happened about noon. The sun went dark, and it was almost like night until he died. Then there was an earthquake."

"Did you stay there to see the whole thing?" Luke asks.

"Well, after a couple hours, I went back into the city, found the hostel where my parents were staying, and told them where I would be."

Luke dips his pen in the blackener."

"Soon after he was nailed up there, he asked God to forgive those who were torturing him to death. I don't know what else he said while I was gone, but about the time I got back, he was talking to one of the thieves being executed with him, and promising him they would be in paradise together."

"Paradise?" Luke asks.

"Maybe Paul can explain it to you. Anyway, just before he died, he suddenly got a burst of energy, called God his Father, and said he was giving his spirit to him."

"That's how Christians die? They hand their spirit over to God?" Luke asks, setting his pen down a moment. "Is that the same thing as handing their soul to God?"

"Yes. Well, my parents and I were getting ready to go back to Cappadocia when we heard this wild rumor that he had come back to life."

They hear a knock on the door, and Philip answers it.

"Father, may I use the donkey to go to the market tomorrow morning? I've got quite the crowd to feed tomorrow."

"Yes, of course. Whatever you need."

Philip's daughter leaves, he sits back down and resumes.

"My parents had responsibilities at home, but I convinced them to let me stay until Pentecost. I was hoping to see this dead man who wasn't dead anymore."

"Did you get your wish?"

"No. We heard he had gone back to Galilee, where he lived. I had to wait around fifty days before anything exciting happened. But, in the meantime, I met this girl, and by the time Pentecost rolled around, we were negotiating a marriage contract. Since she was from Jerusalem, I decided to live there permanently. Are you married, Luke?"

"Luke takes a deep breath and is silent a moment. "We were betrothed, then she died."

"I'm sorry," Philip says. "At least I had nearly thirty good years with my wife. When she died, my daughters and I moved here to Caesarea.

"Well, moving along, when the Day of Pentecost arrived, I saw a mob again. Didn't know if there was going to be another crucifixion or what. When I got there, I saw Jesus' apostles standing on the rooftop of what seemed to be a large hostel at one time.

"I was amazed at what they said. They convinced us Jesus was not an ordinary man. Having come back to life, I knew he was the very predicted Son of God. There were three thousand of us baptized that day, and another five thousand a week or so later. Jesus said we were to take care of the poor, so they started a program to help widows."

"Yes, I've noticed that Christians are always helping less fortunate people," Luke says, dipping his pen in the blackener.

"I had some relatives in the city, including a couple of widowed aunts by marriage. They were Greek," Philip continues. "They came to me and said they could hardly get by. I went to Matthew, one of the apostles, and he was shocked. That's when the apostles decided to appoint deacons to make sure all the widows were taken care of. Then followed the good and the bad."

"How so?"

"The apostles gave us the power to perform miracles, but only if needed to prove our words were from God. One of the other deacons, Stephen, was arrested, and the Jews stoned him to death."

Luke drops his pen, stares at Philip, then the ceiling, he stands, goes out of the room to the courtyard which. It is now dark except for torches on a couple of walls. He puts his hands on his head and stands in place. "Why?" he calls out to the stars above.

Philip joins him and puts an arm over Luke's shoulder. "Satan was afraid of him, so went on the attack. Satan works through people just like God does."

"But they killed him. And they've been trying to kill Paul for years," Luke says. "This is a violent religion."

"No, it's not violent. Satan's ambassadors are violent. Peace is stronger than violence."

"Do all Christians die violently?"

"No, but a lot do. Here, let's pour ourselves some grape juice from that pitcher and stay out here. It looks like most of your companions have gone to bed."

Luke returns into the room, brings out the small table and parchment, and sets them next to a bench.

"Were you ever arrested?" Luke asks.

"No, but most of the Christians left Jerusalem because we were all in danger there. Since I knew what it was like to be an outcast, having been a Jew in pagan Anatolia, I decided to move to Samaria, capital city of the province of Samaria, just north of here. The Samaritans are half-Jews and hated by the pure Jews."

"I know what it is like to be an outsider," Luke says. "I have spent most of my life as one, as you can guess by my yellow hair."

"Yes, and you are big and muscular. You are Germanic, aren't you?"

"I am that."

"So, I taught the Samaritans about Jesus being the Son of God," Philip continues, "proving it by my performing miracles on them. They readily accepted and became Christians too.

"One of the men I baptized was a magician, and he caused a lot of trouble. But I'll let Peter tell you about it. Do you need a refill on your drink, Luke?"

"No, I'm fine," Luke replies.

"One of my daughters made some baklava. Would you like a piece?"

"Sticky fingers would not get along with my parchment. Maybe in the morning," Luke says.

"Well, one day, an angel appeared to me."

"An angel? Angels appear to Christians?"

"Not all, but he did me. He told me to walk in the direction of Gaza on the Great Sea. It's desert over there, so I stopped at an oasis. I noticed a royal chariot—all gold with inlaid mother of pearl.

"A man who looked almost like a king with his red silk robe was sitting in the chariot reading. He was tall, dark, and muscular. The Holy Spirit told me to strike up a conversation with him. I wasn't sure it was such a good idea; he looked dangerous. But I obeyed."

"So, was he dangerous?" Luke asks.

"Turns out he was the national treasurer for Candace, the queen of Ethiopia. I explained a lot of things about Jesus. He had a lot of good questions, so then…"

Philip looks over at Luke. His head is on the table, and he has dropped his pen to the floor. Philip smiles, scoots the table away from Luke, and puts Luke's arm over his own shoulder.

"Come on, big guy. Let's get you to bed."

The next day as everyone is having breakfast, they hear a knock on Philip's gate.

"Agabus, welcome," Philip says. "When did you get here from Jerusalem?"

"I arrived just now. I have been sent a warning by God."

Philip's smile disappears. "What is wrong?"

"I need to talk to Paul. He is here, isn't he?"

Paul and his eight traveling companions come to the courtyard.

"Which one of you is Paul?" he asks.

Paul steps forward, his back still bent. "I am."

Agabus reaches out his hands as though to greet Paul. Instead, he takes hold of the loose belt Paul has around his waist and wraps it around his own hands and feet.

"What are you doing?" Philip asks.

"I think I know," Paul says.

"You are going to be bound hand and foot when you get to Jerusalem. Do not go."

Silence.

"Timothy and I will get you on the next ship out of here," Luke says.

"No. I am going to Jerusalem. My mind is made up."

"Why?" Philip asks. "You are too valuable to be chained and imprisoned. The church needs you."

"Listen to him, Paul," Sopater says. "We are quite capable of delivering the benevolent money to the apostles."

"No, all of you," Paul says, raising his hands. "I am going to Jerusalem."

"But, Paul…"

"Don't you realize I know what is waiting for me there?

I have known for a long time. I must go anyway."

"Why?" Luke asks tears in his eyes.

"I am not only willing to be chained there, but I am willing to die there."

"But Paul," Luke says.

"Stop breaking my heart. I am going to Jerusalem."

Two days later, Paul walks out of the house of Philip and heads east toward Jerusalem. With him are his eight companions and several brothers from Caesarea.

Luke is the last one to leave. He stops a short distance down the street, and turns. Philip is still standing in the gateway.

"So, what did the Ethiopian treasurer do?" he calls out.

"He was baptized and became very happy!" Philip shouts.

Two days later, the nine men enter Jerusalem, some for the first time. Luke looks around and wonders if Jesus walked where he is walking.

The brothers from Caesarea tell Paul they have made arrangements for him and his friends to stay in the house of Mnason.

The next day, Paul takes everyone to meet Jesus' brother James, and the Jerusalem elders. James, who seems to be around fifty years old, explains that all Jesus' apostles have scattered and are telling his story elsewhere in the world. Luke is disappointed he could not have met them.

One by one, each man hands over the money he had collected from his Gentile congregation hundreds of miles from Jerusalem in the hub of the Roman Empire. Some say things like, "We hope this token of our respect will be accepted, even though we are not Jews."

Smiles all around.

All return to Mnason's home except for Luke.

"Sir," he says to James. "I know I am a stranger, but, since you lived with Jesus for three years, could you tell me about him? I want to write a book about his life. Just for an hour. I won't take up all your time."

James smiles and puts his arm around Luke's shoulder. "My friend, I am not one of the apostles. He did have an apostle named James, but he was beheaded about ten years ago for preaching so hard about Jesus and making people listen to him.

"Then who..."

"I did not know Jesus for just three years. I knew him my whole life. I am—or was—his half brother."

Luke stares at the man.

"Come, my friend. I have an apartment in this old hostel. Come with me, and I will talk to you for one hour. Do you have anything to write on?"

"Yes, I always carry blank parchments with me."

James escorts Luke to his apartment and gives him a table to write on. Then he puts his hands behind his head and closes his eyes.

"Where shall I start? My earliest memory of Jesus declaring who he was is when I was around ten years old. Jesus was two years older than me. We came to Jerusalem from up in Nazareth for the Passover.

"I keep hearing about the Passover. What is it?"

"Since you only get an hour, you should ask Paul, or maybe Timothy."

"So, there we were in Jerusalem, we had gone through all the ceremonies, and were on our way home in a caravan of friends from Nazareth. No one bothered to take a count of all the children. We were running around having too much fun to be counted anyway.

"But the next day, they decided to do the headcount, and one was missing. Guess who? My big brother, Jesus. We had to wait while my parents went back to Jerusalem. For three days, they looked for him, hoping he had not been kidnapped and turned into someone's slave. Believe me, you never want to be a slave."

Luke grins within himself and asks, "Was he being a disobedient child?"

"Not from his point of view. When my parents found him, he said he was taking care of his father's affairs.

"At the time, I did not understand who he was and

thought he was insulting my parents. But that's the way he always was—his thinking was always way ahead of everyone else's."

"But being the Son of God. When did you realize it?" Luke asks.

"Not for a long time. I was thirty-one years old when he was crucified. They claimed he came back to life, but I did not believe it. Then, one day while I was alone, he appeared to me out of thin air. Then I knew. Was I ever scared. I had been jealous of him all my life. But he assured me he understood, and I had a whole lifetime ahead of me to tell people who he really was.

"Hey, by the way, would you like to see the family genealogy? I have it all the way back to Adam and Eve."

Luke sets down his pen. "You do? How could I have been so lucky? Yes. And may I copy it? I have an extra parchment to put it on."

With his precious interview down in black and white, Luke rolls up his parchments and heads back to Mnason's house.

The next morning Paul announces he is going over to the temple to take care of a Jewish vow Luke never heard of.

"You shouldn't be going all over the city in your condition," Luke warns. "That last lashing you took in Corinth nearly killed you. You could get infected again. You could be bumped by a wagon on one of those over-crowded streets, and some of your old wounds broken open. Paul, it's just not safe for you."

"I will be fine," Paul says. "It will take a few days."

While they wait for Paul to do what he has to do at the temple, some go sightseeing. Luke goes out only long enough to see the temple, then the governor's mansion and Herod's palace. While at the palace, he asks to see the archives.

"I can show them to you, but only if I am present to guard them," the clerk says. "What do you want to look at?"

"Do you have the tax records going back to Augustus Caesar?"

"That was over sixty years ago."

Luke waits. Shortly the clerk returns. "You are in luck.

Here are the tax records during the time Publius Quirinius was governor over Syria, which at that time, also controlled Palestine because Herod had less status than the senator."

Luke looks through them and is grateful that he knows Latin. It does not take him long to find what he is looking for.

"Do you have records of government executions?" he asks next.

"What do you want all this for? You're not even Jewish. I can tell just by looking at you."

"I just do. If they are available to the public, may I please see them?"

"I'll need to know which governor ordered the execution you're looking for."

"I think one of his names was the same as my ma...a tribune I know. Was there a Governor Titus? No? Portius? No? Was there a Governor Pontus?"

"We had a Governor Pontus Pilate. Do you think that was him?"

"Perhaps. May I see his execution records?"

The records are brought to Luke.

NAME: JESUS
RESIDENCE: NAZARETH, PROVINCE OF GALILEE
CRIME: BEING KING
FORM OF EXECUTION: CRUCIFIXION.
TIME OF DEATH: 6TH HOUR

Luke sees that the last line has been crossed out and replaced with "He didn't."

Ole Pilate knew. He knew.

He also sees there were two thieves crucified the same day.

He takes a few notes, then leaves. He whistles as he walks down the street toward Mnason's house. *Pilate knew.*

27 ~ BACK TO THE BEGINNING

The next morning Luke stays at the house and looks over the notes he has taken so far.

"What are you doing?" Mnason asks Luke.

The old man has untamed gray hair and a white beard so long it nearly reaches his waist.

"I want to write an account of Jesus' life and thought this would be a good place to interview some people."

"Great idea, son," his host says. He turns to leave the courtyard, then turns back.

"You know, I think I could help you. Would you like me to take you to see old Lazarus?"

"Who is he?"

"He, my friend, is someone Jesus brought back from the dead. He and his two sisters are still over there in Bethany, where they have always lived. It is still early. Would you like to go this morning?"

Delighted, Luke and his host walk through the streets of Jerusalem and out through the Sheep Gate toward Bethany.

"Hello, there!" they hear. A middle-aged man comes running toward them, his shepherd's staff in his hand. "Mnason. Is that you?"

Mnason stops and looks in the direction of the voice. "Benjamin! Well, come over here. There is someone I would like you to meet."

The shepherd comes closer.

"Got your sheep all fattened up and delivered to the temple?"

"Yes, did it yesterday and just got paid."

"Benjamin, I would like you to meet my new friend, Luke. He is writing a book about Jesus' life. I believe your father was among the first people to meet Jesus. Why don't we sit over here by the road, and you tell Luke all about it."

Benjamin grins and walks beside the other two. "Yup. Not only that, but angels appeared to my father."

They squat on the ground facing each other.

"My father and his two friends were up in the hills between Jerusalem and Bethlehem with their sheep."

Benjamin's voice takes on an air of suspense. "Suddenly," he says slowly, "a light appeared alllll around them, even though it was midnight. They actually had to shade their eyes, the light was sooooo bright."

"Wait," Luke says. "I've got to write this down." He pulls out his parchment and blackener from his shoulder pouch, sets the pouch on his lap, and sets the parchment on it.

"They heard a voice out of the light," Benjamin continues. "The voice was booming." He flings his arms up to emphasize the boom. "The voice called out to them that the Savior of the world had just been born right there in Bethlehem."

"Then what?" Luke asks without looking up.

Benjamin stands. "It was like a star had burst. The whole sky lit up with angels everywhere." He sweeps his hand around his head. "And they all began declaring the Savior of the world had been born."

"Slow down," Luke says. "Okay. I'm with you."

Benjamin sits. "So, my father and his two friends put their herds in some nearby caves, blocked them with their tents and other supplies, and headed for Bethlehem. When they got there, it took them a couple hours to find him. When they finally did, he was in a barn."

Mnason rises and walks around, shifting his legs and feet around. Luke recognizes the common way to stop cramps.

"Joseph let them in," Benjamin continues, "and when my father and the other shepherds saw the baby," he pauses, "they knew." His eyes sparkle. "They fell down and worshipped him. Long before anyone else understood, they knew he was the Son of God."

"I cannot thank you enough for sharing this with me," Luke says. "This will definitely be in my book about Jesus' life. What a grand story it is."

Luke has his things put away in his shoulder pouch by now and rises. "Mnason, are we still on the road to Bethany?"

"My legs are beginning to give me some trouble. Is it all right with you if we go to Bethany tomorrow?"

"Yes, let's go back before your legs get worse. I can look at them if you like and see if I have something in my other shoulder pouch for you."

"You mean medicine?"

"Yes. I am a physician."

Back home, Luke looks at Mnason's legs and gives him a tea to drink. "This should help ease the pain," he says.

The next morning Mnason comes into the courtyard smiling.

"My legs haven't felt this good in a long time," he says to Luke. "Shall we try again to go see my friends in Bethany?"

The two men walk briskly and finally enter Bethany that afternoon. They walk through the market, past small houses, and up a hill where the finer houses are. They stop at a gate with an anchor on it, the top of which resembles a cross.

Mnason knocks. An elderly lady answers. She is tall, has a down-turned nose and small eyes that flitter.

"Martha, it is good to see you again."

Martha opens the gate wide and lets in the two men.

"Martha, I would like you to meet my new friend, Luke. He is going to write a book about the life of Jesus."

"Oh, how wonderful," she says, flapping her hands. "Mary! Come here, Mary."

Another lady comes into the courtyard. Mary has a pug nose, big eyes, and a small mouth. She walks toward the two men and seems to float.

"Welcome," she says, holding out a hand to each man.

"And who is this tall young man with you?"

"This is Luke. He wants to write a book about Jesus' life. Is Lazarus here?"

"He is, but he is confined to his room these days. The pain in his knees and hips makes it hard for him to get around. He even eats in there if we let him."

"Sister," Martha says, "we should take them up to see Lazarus, and we can all tell our stories together."

Luke and Mnason follow the two women up the stairs and to the first room at the top.

"Look who we have in our home today, Lazarus," Martha says.

"Well, good to see you again."

Mnason introduces Luke and explains their purpose for coming.

"Welcome to our home, gentlemen," Lazarus says. "Luke, why don't you sit over there by that table. Now, where do you want us to begin?"

"Is it true that you died and came back to life?"

"Indeed, it is true. On your way out of town, perhaps Mnason can take you to the cemetery where I was buried. And before you ask, no, I do not remember any of it. I just remember Jesus telling me to get up and come out of that burial cave. Was it ever hard walking in those bands they had wrapped around me."

"Did that convince everyone Jesus really was the Son of God?" Luke asks.

"Well, I kind of think it did. But those who were jealous of him and afraid they would lose their jobs when he became king, wanted to kill him and me both. To this day, I am a little suspicious around strangers. I mean no offense to you, however, Luke."

"Jesus came and stayed with us many times, whenever he was in Jerusalem," Mary adds. "We were kind of his Jerusalem home."

"Martha, why don't you tell Luke about that time you overdid it trying to impress him," Lazarus says with a sheepish grin.

"Lazarus, you are forever embarrassing me. Well,

perhaps I deserved it. One time when he was coming with his twelve apostles, for some reason I wanted everything to be extra special."

"So, was it?" Luke asks.

"Too special. I spent all day washing walls, making a new tunic for myself, buying new dishes, trying new recipes. I was run ragged by the time he arrived and didn't even have dinner started yet."

Luke is unsure whether to smile.

"But Jesus was kind to me. He said he didn't come to check me out. He just wanted to love me." She looks over at Mary and smiles.

"Is there anything else you would like to tell me?" Luke asks when he comes to a pause in his writing.

"Mary, go ahead and tell him," Lazarus urges. "Yes, Mary, tell him," Martha adds.

"Well, a few days before our Savior was killed, I wanted to do something special for him. I knew he was the Son of God. I knew he was the Savior of mankind. I knew he was King of the world. But I also knew he would not allow anyone to have the ceremony to make him king—the anointing ceremony.

"So I bought the most expensive anointing oil I could find, and when he came to our house the next time, I anointed him."

"You should have seen how mad his apostles got," Martha says. "She had just spent a year's wages on that fragrant oil."

"But that's what I wanted to do."

Mary grows quiet. No one says anything. She wipes away a tear.

"He called it his burial anointing. He knew what was going to happen. And it did a few days later."

"Well, if he had not died, he could not have come back to life," Lazarus says.

"Friends, Lazarus is growing tired," Mnason says.

"Thank all of you," Luke says, putting away his parchment and ink. "Your stories will be in my book."

It is mid-afternoon by the time Luke and Mnason

arrive back in Jerusalem and the house.

"Tomorrow, you shall meet John Mark," Mnason says. "He lived here in Jerusalem while Jesus was here."

The following day, John Mark arrives. Mnason meets him at the gate. He has a chunk of cheese in his hand.

"You don't mind if I eat while we talk, do you?" he asks Luke after being introduced.

"I have some baklava. Would you like a piece or two after your cheese?" Mnason asks.

"Would I ever!" John Mark says, rejoicing.

Luke walks over to a table with his parchment and blackener already out. Mark follows him and sits on a cushion on the floor.

"I cannot tell you anything more accurate about Jesus than his own apostles can. I was around him, but not as much as them. All I can tell you is what my cousin, Barnabas, and I did with Paul. But Barnabas is here in town. He will be here soon, and he can tell you himself."

Just as John Mark finishes his cheese and both pieces of baklava, Barnabas arrives. He is a big bulky man with a deep bass voice and reminds Luke of a bear.

Most of the rest of the day is spent with Barnabas talking about his adventures and misadventures with Paul.

"I was his mentor when we were in the temple school together, and after he became a Christian, I became his mentor again, and his protector. Everyone was afraid of him because he had imprisoned, tortured, and killed so many Christians.

"When he finally became a Christian himself, no one believed him or would go around him. So I stood at his side where ever he went and reassured everyone he was a new man in every way.

"But I didn't always protect him. There was that time up in Lystra where they tried to stone him to death...."

Barnabas talks most of the day. Luke, realizing what he has to say, is not about Jesus' life but is very important, puts his notes taken from Barnabas' memories on a separate parchment.

By the time Barnabas is done, it is mid-afternoon. "I

must go now," he says, wiping an unmanly tear from his brown eyes. Silently, as though in a dream of memories, Barnabas leaves without speaking more. Mark follows him out.

Luke uses the next day to organize his notes.

He hears pounding on the gate.

"Let us in!"

He recognizes Timothy's voice and opens the gate.

"Paul has been arrested! They beat him before the Romans could get to him.

"What?" Mnason says, coming out to the courtyard.

"Where is he now?" Luke asks, grabbing his shoulder bag with the medications in it.

Luke and Timothy run through the streets and leave Mnason to come at his own pace. They reach the Antonio Fortress and see a mob packed in the courtyard.

"Kill him!"

"Kill him!"

"Kill him!"

The crowd is suddenly hushed, and Luke looks up to see what they are staring at. It is Paul.

Surrounded by Roman legionnaires, Paul, trying to stand straight despite the opening of old wounds and infliction of new ones, raises his hands to quiet the mob. He tells the Jews about his conversion. Luke can hear the pain in his scratchy voice, see it in his eyes, watch it in his bearing. The mob remains quiet until he mentions asking non-Jews to become Christians.

The crowd shakes its collective fists and roars.

"Away with Gentiles. Kill Paul."

"Away with Gentiles. Kill Paul."

"Away with Gentiles. Kill Paul."

With that, Paul is pushed into the barracks by the legionnaires, and disappears.

"What will they do to him?" Luke asks Timothy.

"The Jewish Sanhedrin will make a pretense at a trial in order to cover up their plot to murder Paul, just like they did Jesus," he says.

"You need to go back to Mnason's house. As a Gentile,

you will be safe there—at least safer than out in the street," Timothy says. "If you see any of the other men who came with us on the ship, make sure they go back to the house too. Now run. I'm going to stay here and find out what is going on."

As Luke hurries through the street, he is baffled. *Why does Christianity make people so mad? Jesus is supposed to be the Prince of Peace. We're not fighting these people. Why are they fighting us?*

Within the next two hours, all of Paul's companions are back at the house. They exchange stories of what they had heard and seen. The rest of the evening, they pray.

Mnason's maid brings out food for them all. They cannot eat. All night they pray. By morning, Luke's eyes are red. So are the others'.

"Where is Timothy? Did they arrest him too?" Luke wonders aloud.

At noon, Timothy arrives. His red hair is scruffy, his eyes are swelled, his tunic is dirty.

"They had an illegal trial this morning. They had already decided to sentence him to death. When the Sanhedrin meeting turned into a riot, the tribune rescued him, and his centurions took him back to the barracks."

"Now, what?" Luke asks.

"I don't know. But the Sanhedrin is not going to give up."

"Will they let me into the barracks?" Luke asks. "That is where they took him, didn't they?"

"I think they will. Let's try."

"Isn't the fortress this way?" Luke says after they turn down a road Luke is not familiar with.

"Paul's sister, Bethania, lives here," Timothy explains. "She will want to go see him."

The two men, along with Bethania and her son, Daniel, head now toward the Fortress Antonio. When they arrive, Daniel knocks on the barracks door, and a Roman soldier answers it.

"I am Bethania, sister of your prisoner. This is my son, Daniel, and our close friend, Timothy. And this is Luke,

Paul's physician. May we come in for a moment? We have some food and medication for him."

The guard steps back, and Julius, a centurion, allows them in. They look around and see Paul sitting on his mat, his back bare and bleeding, his head down almost to his lap.

"Oh, Paul," Bethania groans. She wipes her eyes. "Why did you have to come here?"

Paul raises his head and forces a smile. "I guess I couldn't stop myself."

"Here, I brought some aloes and honey for your back," Luke says.

Paul lies down on his front for Luke's treatment.

"I am going to hang around in a tavern where I know a lot of your opponents go, to see if I can pick up on anything we need to know." It is Daniel.

"Here are some grapes and some cheese. Eat something. You need it," Bethania urges.

Paul sits up.

"Thank you, everyone, for coming," Paul says. "God's will shall be done."

With that he closes his eyes, leans his head down on his chest again, and his visitors leave.

28 ~ LIMBO

*T*he legionnaire kicks Daniel awake. He, Luke, and Timothy stir and jump up.

"We weren't doing any harm sleeping outside your gate," Timothy says.

"I don't care if you sleep here from now on," the legionnaire says. "Here is a note from Centurion Julius. Don't know why he wants you to know anything, but here it is."

Daniel takes the small scroll and reads it aloud by the light of torches around the fortress gate.

INNOCENT. DANGER. TRANSFERRING TO CAESAREA.

"You two go on with them," Daniel tells his companions. "I will go to Mnason's house and tell the others so they can catch up with you."

"Quick," Timothy tells Luke. "There is a stable nearby that provides horses for the cavalry. Do you have any money?"

"I think so," Luke says, keeping up with Timothy. They pound on the gate into the stable, the owner answers grumbling. They pay him and mount their horses barebacked. The two manage to catch up with the Roman legionnaires just as they arrive at the city gate. They leave Jerusalem with the military procession, heading toward Caesarea and the Roman governor, Felix.

During the night, Paul bellows a song. It echoes around the hills and back again. He sings about David. He sings about the only real God, creator of the universe. He sings about Jesus.

Luke and Timothy smile at each other. "He's trying to stay awake."

At noon the next day, they arrive at Caesarea. Centurion Julius delivers Paul and a letter from their tribune about Paul's innocence as a Roman citizen. Luke and Timothy are allowed to attend the brief hearing with Governor Felix, but not allowed to say anything.

"Keep him in the Praetorium until I figure this out," the governor says. "Let's see if the Jews send someone to press charges."

Luke and Timothy follow the guards to the government building housing both the Roman legionnaires and the courtroom. They are given one moment to tell Paul whatever they want to say.

"Paul, we'll be nearby and will visit you whenever we can," Luke says.

The two men leave and walk to the house of Philip.

"Back so soon?" he asks when his gatekeeper lets them in.

"What Agabus said came true," Luke says. He presses his lips together and looks down, then back to Philip. "He was arrested in Jerusalem during a riot, and brought here for trial." *If I had only pressed on him more to stay away from Jerusalem...*

"I want you to stay with me," Philip says. "I will call the church together so we can pray for him tonight."

Evening arrives, and they come.

"Jesus, free Paul. We need him."

"Oh Lord, Paul still has work to do."

"Jehovah, set Paul free so he can preach again."

"God, free Paul from his bondage."

Two hours before daylight, the congregation leaves Philip's house.

After a few hours of trying in vain to sleep, everyone wanders into Philip's courtyard.

"Luke, there are some people in our congregation that are willing to talk to you," he says. "You met them last night, but did not realize who they were."

"Thank you, sir," he says with an expression that is both pleased and confused.

"For your book, Luke. One is coming to see you this morning. He is about your age. When he was a boy, he almost died. What is most interesting is that Jesus was not even with him when... Well, I'm saying too much. Oh, I think that is him now," Philip says, watching his gatekeeper open the gate.

"Glad you could come, Claudius," Philip says, walking forward and clasping his guest's hand.

Claudius is middle-aged with an ample middle and curly brown hair. When he laughs, he snortles on the uptake.

Philip introduces the two men, then shows them to the same table Luke had sat at to interview two weeks earlier.

While Luke goes to his room to fetch his shoulder pouch with writing materials, Claudius is given a drink of apple juice.

"Just tell me what you remember," Luke says, picking up his pen and dipping it in the blackener.

"We were poor. My father was killed in a war up in Greece with some restless Thracians. I guess my father's centurion liked him because, when he was assigned to Tiberius, he sent for my mother here in Caesarea to come be his head maid."

"Where is Tiberius?" Luke asks.

"Tiberius is up in the province of Galilee. Herod's new palace is there. In fact, I used to play in the palace while they were building it. I had a friend named Asher who I played with."

"So, when did you get sick?" Luke prods.

"I was around ten years old. One night, in the alley room, my mother had rented, my legs started hurting. My mother tried putting cold water on them, then hot water, but nothing helped. They hurt all night, and by morning the pain had spread to my chest. I could hardly breathe."

Luke looks up at him. "I understand. Yes, it is very painful."

"Do you know what I had?"

"Yes, but continue. This is your story."

"My mother got a neighbor to watch me while she went back to work. The next thing I was aware of, she was back and crying, and the centurion's doctor was looking at me. He gave her some kind of oil for me to take."

"Yes, under ordinary circumstances, that would have helped you expel the poison. Go on," Luke urges.

"The next thing I knew, we were bumping around on the floor of a chariot. Then Centurion Demetrius was carrying me up some stairs and into a room. I think both he and my mother were in the room with me when I began to shake all over. Then I could not feel anything."

"And that's when your mother went to Jesus?" Luke asks.

"No. Centurion Demetrius told me later he had never heard of Jesus, but the man in charge of Herod's household told him Jesus could heal me. He was so desperate that, when he found out where Jesus was, he went to the local synagogue. He had built the synagogue for the Jews out of his own money, by the way. He asked them to ask Jesus to come heal me."

"Now let me get this straight. The centurion was not a Jew. Right?"

"You will never believe what happened. The centurion decided Jesus was God come down to earth and became afraid. And do you know what?"

"This foreigner decided Jesus was God walking on earth? Fascinating," Luke says, resuming his writing.

"He sent a message to Jesus that, if he wanted to heal me a long distance away, he could."

"Amazing," Luke responds. "But he was expecting too much to ask that of Jesus."

Claudius reaches up, folds his arms behind his head, and puts on a wide grin.

"He did it?" Luke asks.

"He did it. With just the centurion and my mother in my room, I suddenly could feel my arms and legs, sat up in bed, and asked if I could go outside and play."

"Definitely, this will go in my account of Jesus," Luke mumbles, scribbling on his parchment as fast as he can.

"Well, I have to get back to work," Claudius says. "I just want you to know everything I told you is the truth."

Luke stands and walks Claudius to the gate. "I believe you, Claudius. And I am overwhelmed."

That afternoon, Luke, Timothy, and Philip go to the Praetorium to visit Paul.

"No word yet," he says. "My guess is they're waiting for my accusers to show up from Jerusalem."

"You're probably right," Philip says.

"What can we do for you?" Luke asks.

"I'd like to dictate a letter to my sister, Batavia, in Jerusalem, to tell her I am okay. Could you write it for me, Timothy?"

"Of course."

Paul shifts his back several times. "Luke, I really need something for the pain. I won't admit it to my guards, of course."

Luke smiles, takes down his shoulder pouch, and looks through it. "I brought some medicated oil for your new injuries."

Paul lifts the back of his tunic and lies on his front. Luke applies what he recently had put together.

"Keep your tunic off," Luke says. "Give the oil a chance to help you."

"The church continues to pray for your release," Philip says.

"But not before I get a chance to tell the governor about Jesus and hopefully save his soul," Paul replies, lifting his head off his arms and looking up at his friends.

The next day, all the other six representatives of the Gentile congregations in the north arrive from Jerusalem. Philip, Timothy, and Luke take them to see Paul.

"We came as soon as we could," Sopater says. "Are they treating you right? Just let me know if they aren't, and I'll set them straight."

"They are treating me well, Sopater," Paul says, sitting up and holding a pillow under his chin. I need all of you to go home, now that you have delivered the benevolent funds from your congregations."

"You don't mean me," Timothy says. "We have been together for eight years."

"Timothy, I have been training you. You are ready to go out on your own. I need you to go back through the cities where you and I established congregations. That means Anatolia and Greece. Can you handle it?"

Timothy looks up at the ceiling, over at the wall, down at his feet that had walked so many *mille*s with the best friend he'd ever had. He remains silent.

"Please, Timothy. I need you to do this. You are a co-founder of those congregations. You are the best man for it."

Timothy stares at Paul. He swallows hard. "Yes, sir. But I will stay in touch with you. And when I am done with my tour, I am rejoining you."

"Fair enough," Paul says. He looks again at his other friends. "Aristarchus, I need you to stay with me."

The tall redhead beams and looks around at the others with a broad grin.

"Do not let it go to your head, Aristarchus. By staying with me, you will be risking your life. My enemies are always after me. Are you sure you can handle it?"

Timothy and the other six from Berea, Corinth, Thessalonica, Derbe, and Ephesus board the next ship heading north toward Anatolia and Greece.

"You look a lot like Timothy," Luke tells Aristarchus as they walk with Philip to Philip's home. "What kind of work do you do?"

"I sell silver chalices and other silver items for my employer. I am from Thessalonica."

"I hear the Jews there really hate Christians," Luke says.

"That is an understatement. They want to kill all Christians, and I am afraid that is exactly what is going to happen."

"They went after Paul and did almost kill him," Luke says. "I treated him in Athens, then at my home in Berea."

"You're a physician?"

"Yes, I guess I am. Plus a scribe, an apothecary, and most anything you need," Luke says with a grin.

"He is writing a book about Jesus' activities while walking among us," Philip says. "Well, we're here. Aristarchus, you can take Timothy's room."

As promised, the three men visit Paul every day. He has a trial before Governor Felix, then waits for the verdict. The Jewish lawyer grows tired of waiting and returns to Jerusalem. Felix gives indications he likes Paul, but still, he does not issue a verdict. They continue to wait.

Paul sends Aristarchus out every day to one of the many Caesarean temples to tell worshippers going in and out about the only real God in existence. Usually, he goes to the temple of Eros, then Aphrodite, then Isis, then Apollo.

"You are my hands, my feet, my mouth, Aristarchus," Paul always says. "Thank you."

When Luke is not visiting with Paul, he is out in the meadows and desert or walking along the seashore, looking for plants to add to his collection of medicinal herbs.

One day when he returns to Philip's house, two women are there he does not recognize.

"Luke, I would like you to meet the niece of Mary of Magdala, who was a good friend of Jesus. Also, this is someone Jesus brought back to life. They are traveling together and happened to stop by before boarding their ship.

"We do not have much time," Mary says. Not only does Mary have her aunt's name, but she also looks like her, eyes darting everywhere at once, pointed nose, and petite. Her hair is gray and fine.

"I understand you are wanting to write about Jesus while on earth. My aunt had seven demons in her at one time. From what I hear, the demons only attacked people who were trying to be godly. She tried to fight them, but they were too strong. Jesus made them leave her for good. After that, since she was wealthy, she helped support him as he traveled."

"Tell Luke about Jesus at his tomb," Philip prods.

"She spoke of that even on her death bed. An angel appeared to my aunt when she went to weep at his grave, and then Jesus appeared to her. She was the first Jesus appeared to after he came back alive. Then to hundreds of others. But she was the first."

"Ilana, before you ladies go, tell Luke about your experience with Jesus," Philip says.

"I do not remember much. All I know is that I died when I was about ten years old. My father, Jairus, was head of the local synagogue and went to get Jesus so he would heal me. Instead, I died while he was gone. So Jesus came, and I woke up. I just remember being sick, then being somewhere that was happy, then opening my eyes and seeing Jesus smiling at me. 'Welcome back,' he said."

"Amazing," Luke says, still writing.

"I was too young to truly understand and ran out to play. I wondered why my parents were crying."

"We do have to be going now," Mary tells Luke. "I hope we have been some kind of help to you."

"Ladies, the more I hear about Jesus, the more amazed I am. Thank you for talking to me. This is exactly what I need—eyewitnesses."

The two women leave, and Philip disappears, then comes back out to Luke carrying a large scroll.

"I secured a copy from the local synagogue about the beginning of the world and of Noah and Abraham, if you would like to read them," Philip says.

"Indeed, I would," Luke says, standing at his work table crushing leaves and berries. "And do you suppose I could copy them to send to my m... to my good friend, Theophilus for his library?"

"Well, first, you may not be here long enough. Second, these are not all."

"There are more?"

"Many more. There are books with the laws of Moses in them. Then there are histories of the Jews—though I do not think they are as urgent for you to read."

"Philip, thank you very much."

"Not done yet. Then there are five books of poetry that include many prophecies of Jesus."

"I am overwhelmed, Philip," Luke says, sitting down

and shaking his head with a smile. "I had no idea."

"They will help you understand some of Jesus' activities and words."

"I find it interesting that Jesus healed that paralyzed boy at the request of someone who was not even a Jew," Luke says, resuming his work with the herbs.

"Then you will find your interview with the family of Herod Antipas' headmaster interesting."

Luke puts his herbs away and walks out into the courtyard. The men sit facing each other.

"I thought Jesus just helped commoners," Luke says. "Well, I look forward to it. When can I see them?"

"They are members of our congregation in Caesarea but are traveling to see relatives in Egypt. They left right after you arrived and expect to be gone nearly a year."

Weeks go by. Months. Luke, Aristarchus, and Philip continue to visit Paul at the Praetorium every day. They talk. They pray. They write letters. They plan. But nothing happens.

"Right on time," Philip tells Luke one day.

"Felix is finally delivering his verdict?" Luke responds.

"I wish that were the case. But second best is that Chuza and his family are back from Egypt and have agreed for you to interview them in their home. Tomorrow."

The next day after visiting with Paul, Philip takes Luke to the home of Chuza.

"Everyone, this is Luke. He is from Berea in Macedonia, Greece. He is Paul's personal physician and is writing a book about everything Jesus said and did on earth. Well, there aren't enough books in the world to cover all that, but Luke wants to be as thorough as possible."

Chuza is tall and thin with sleek short gray hair on a small head. He smiles readily. "Welcome, Brother," he says, offering his hand to Luke.

"This is my wife, Joanna." Joanna, even at her age, is still graceful with freckles, a long straight nose, and lips that form a bow. She smiles and tips her head to Luke.

"And this big young man—who looks a little like both of us—is Asher. Thanks to Jesus, he did not die and grew up to be a fine young man."

"Thank you for doing this," Asher says, with black eyes sparkling. It will mean a lot to people to be able to read what Jesus actually said and did."

"Everyone, sit over here, and I will bring some refreshments to you shortly," Joanna says.

"Uh, Luke will need a table to put his parchment on if you have one available," Philip says.

They move to an area in the courtyard with a table.

"Well, we were up in Tiberius..."

"Where Herod's palace was being built?" Luke asks for clarification.

"Yes. You must have already talked to Claudius. He and Asher have remained friends all these years," Chuza says. "So one day, when they were playing, Asher became sick with a high fever."

"We didn't live in Tiberius, so I got Asher home to Capernaum as fast I could. Joanna tried all the treatments for fever she knew of."

"Such as silphium," Luke says.

"Among other things, yes," Chuza says. "We even took him to an old doctor who had trained Herod's personal physician. He thought it was just indigestion and tried several things, but none of them worked. As we sat there watching our son die, Joanna..."

"I told him about Jesus," Joanna says, entering the courtyard with apple juice and fig slices. "I had heard he had turned water into a wine at a feast not far from us. I asked around if anyone knew where Jesus was. Those who knew said he was probably in Jerusalem for our Passover."

"One of the yearly feasts Jews keep," Luke says, looking up briefly from his writing.

"Right," Chuza says, reaching for a fig, then holding it in his hand.

"I couldn't just sit there and watch my son die. It was dawn the next day by now, so I checked around the city, verified someone had seen him in Jerusalem, and counted the days, wondering if he had had time to get back to Capernaum. I decided he had not. Someone thought he might be in Cana, so I raced across the desert to Cana, praying Jesus would be there and that I could find him, never having even seen him before."

"In the meantime, I'm dying of fever," Asher chortles as though he knows the ending of the story, which he does.

"Yes, I found him and begged him to come heal Asher. He made no effort to leave Cana. Instead, he said, "Okay, your son is well now."

"That's it?" Luke asks, looking up from his parchment. "Just 'okay, your son is well now'?"

"That's it," Asher says. "I was outside, playing by the time my father got home. You should have seen the expression on his face."

"A year later, Centurion Demetrius' servant boy—Asher's friend, Claudius—nearly died. I told him about Jesus, and Jesus healed him without even being there, just like he did Asher."

"Oh, I interviewed him. So, what Jesus did for you came first, then what he did for Claudius came after that. I will have to make a note of it," Luke says, scribbling the margin.

"After that, we began supporting Jesus, and I even went along with some other women to help out in the crowds when he traveled and preached," Joanna adds.

"Will you stay and eat with us? We would be honored," Asher says.

Philip stands. "It is growing dark, and we have been gone all day. We need to get back home. Maybe another day."

More time passes. Luke now treats people in the city at Philip's house, so resumes looking for herbs to keep enough in stock. Aristarchus continues teaching at the temple steps every day, and Philip follows up with those interested in Jesus.

"What is keeping Governor Felix from rendering a verdict?" Luke asks Philip over and over. "A bribe?"

29 ~ SURVIVAL

*L*uke and Aristarchus walk behind Paul and three other government prisoners, all chained at ankles and wrists, led by Centurion Justice in the front and two other guards on each side.

"Two years! Two years it took the government to render a verdict," Aristarchus says. "My feet were almost stuck to the steps of those temples."

"If a bribe is what they were wanting, they didn't get it," Luke says.

They work their way down to the docks and over to one of the ships. Most of the congregation of Christians are assembled there waiting for them. They give Paul, Luke, and Aristarchus baskets of enough food to keep them through their voyage. While the centurion talks with an officer of the ship, they sing a hymn, pray, and say goodbye.

"Will we ever see you again, Paul?"

"I do not know."

They board a ship headed for the Adriatic and set sail.

Centurion Julius orders the chains be taken off the government prisoners. Out of formation now, Luke is close enough to hear the centurion converse with Paul.

"By the way, after hearing your defense in court, I am convinced you are innocent of all charges. I think you must be a good man, Paul of Tarsus."

Centurion Julius is exceptionally tall with black curly hair. His eyes are never still, always on the alert. His full upper lip twitches when things do not go according to plan. He gives the prisoners free access to the ship.

Paul smiles. He, Luke, and Aristarchus stow their belongings below in baskets, then return above board.

They walk over to the side rail and look back at Caesarea with its magnificent harbor, and can still see the great amphitheater. A little at a time, the city grows smaller and smaller until it finally disappears.

"Rome at last," Paul says. "Just think. In a couple of weeks, I will be able to stand before Nero Caesar himself and tell him how to save his soul from the gates of hell."

"Do you think they will let us in to watch the trial?" Aristarchus asks.

"Perhaps."

"How is your back, Paul?" Luke asks.

"What can I say? I can feel everything touching it a hundred times more than I did before all the scarring, and what I always feel is pain. Well, sometimes it itches, but only sometimes. I have learned to live with it."

"I brought a supply of brambles, aloes, honey, and oil for those scars," Luke says. "Keeping them soft alleviates some of the pain. I brought enough for three weeks. That should be plenty."

Sometimes they sit near the bridge and talk or pray or eat. Every day Paul stands in a stooped position and addresses the sailors while they work. If they don't pay attention to him, he bangs his sandal on the hull and whistles at them.

"I know the greatest navigator in the world," he bellows over the sound of the waves. "His name is Jesus. He walked on earth for a while. He even walked on water at least once. But now is back in heaven."

When he is through, he returns to his seat between Luke and Aristarchus, bows his head, and falls asleep. "I do not have any pain when I am asleep," he whispers to Luke.

Sometimes the other prisoners—Brictius, Galvius, and Ludo—sit with them. When they become embarrassed by Paul when he won't shut up about Jesus, they get up and walk away.

The winds are not favorable. It takes the ship ten days to arrive at the southern coast of Anatolia.

"Paul, I am sorry, but I need you to hold your hands out so I can rechain you." It is Julius. "The ship we are on is going to stay in this port until spring. I found a large corn ship sailing late in the season that we can go on the rest of the way to Rome."

Shortly, all four prisoners are chained and surrounded by Julius' four guards. They walk down the gangplank and step onshore. As before, Luke and Aristarchus follow behind.

"Are you sure this is a good idea, sir?" Paul asks. "Maybe we should stay here until spring."

"I am under orders to get you prisoners to Rome within two weeks. Nero is planning to vacation in Alexandria in a month and will not be able to hear your case the rest of the winter. Governor Festus wants your fate determined quickly."

The prisoners shuffle down the pier until they come to a large corn ship that dwarfs the one they had been on. It has red sails (the pride of Captain Milon). The stern has a gooseneck curling up and around, ornamented with brass and a large eye painted on both sides of the hull.

They take a ship-to-shore boat out to where it is moored. Julius hails the first mate and is given permission to board.

Once on deck, they see some passengers setting up colorful canopies with ornate lounging couches. Other passengers are setting up small leather tents on the spacious deck.

Around the outside of the main deck, they see small compartments which will sleep up to four people.

Some passengers, having settled in, stroll the deck wearing their finery, and others wearing plain tunics. All are smiles. The breeze wafts around them, and all is well.

However, upon seeing the prisoners shuffle on board with their chains, all but the sailors move back in fear. Parents with children grab them and hold them close.

"Stay away from the men in chains," they hear. "They are bad and dangerous."

The centurion finds the captain and salutes him.

Captain Milon is short with a bibulous nose, thick lips, small eyes, a receding hairline, and dark leathery skin.

"My prisoners will be no trouble to you," Julius reassures him. "By the way, how many passengers are you expecting on this voyage?"

"Two hundred seventy-six," Captain Milon responds. "Your prisoners must never be out in the open where the other passengers can see them. Is that clear?"

"Understood, sir," Julius responds. He salutes and returns to his charges.

"Everyone below," he announces.

A young man walks by. He is beardless with brown hair, a pointed chin, and a single dimple.

"Titus, is that you?"

The man turns with a smile which quickly disappears. "Paul? What are you doing here? And what are those chains?"

"I am determined to go to Rome, no matter what it takes. I will appear before Nero Caesar within the month. Jesus has promised me that," Paul says. "But what are you doing here?"

"I have been to Antioch in Syria. I saw Barnabas there. He asked about you."

"Okay, keep going," the centurion tells Paul.

"Dear, Dear Barnabas. The best friend I ever had," Paul replies. "But what are you doing on this ship bound for Italy?"

"I am on my way to Corinth. This was the only ship I could find this time of year even coming close. I will change to another ship in Crete."

"Get going, Paul."

Paul shuffles over to the hatch going below and calls back to Titus. "You are needed in Crete. When the ship stops there, go ashore and help the church there. Appoint elders too. Promise me!" He does not hear Titus' reply.

Paul and the other prisoners, along with their guards and Luke and Aristarchus descend below to the berth deck where passengers sleep on hammocks, and the poorest sleep under them.

"You are not allowed on this deck," one of the crew members says.

They continue on down to the orlop deck below the waterline. It is full of compartments holding corn, barrels of fresh water, preserved food, and larger belongings of some of the passengers, including horses and furniture. The smells are pleasant. There is no room for humans on the orlop deck.

Finally, they reach the dark bilge, the very belly of the ship where rigging and prisoners are stored, with just a hand span between them and the watery deep.

They smell putrification and hear rats.

The four guards carry torches. Even with that, it takes their eyes a while to get used to the darkness enough, they can find a place to settle in. Justus selects an upright beam. He chains Paul and the other prisoners to each side of the beam and gives each ten hand-spans of extra chain so they can sit, stand, or move around a little.

Nearby is another beam the guards take possession of. The centurion takes a third beam and invites Luke and Aristarchus to share it with him.

The guards find places on the bulkhead to secure their torches. Everyone sets his belongings down and settles in for the long voyage.

They hear the chains of the anchors being raised and the swooshing of water and know they are heading out to sea.

Now it is a matter of survival.

After an hour of silence, Paul bellows out a psalm of David so loudly, the others accuse him of scaring even the fish below them.

"Ha, ha. You should hear ole Barnabas singing. He could have made the entire hull of this ship quake and quiver."

But gradually, Paul's songs are cut short by the coughing that develops in his lungs, previously weakened from swallowing salt water while treading water so long years earlier, then being hit in his throat during one of his rod beatings.

They tell stories from recollections of long ago and not so long ago. They nap. They walk the ten-span length their chains allow. They do exercises, so their legs do not lose strength.

"Why did I have to draw prisoner duty?" one of the soldiers complains. "I get the same treatment as the prisoners. There had better be a good bonus in this for me."

"At least you get to go up on the main deck for a breather three times a day," prisoner Galvius says.

Paul's back becomes inflamed in the rancid air. His only relief is to sleep on his front with his nose and mouth on the deck where rats run.

"No, Paul. You are not going to lie on the stinking deck like that," Aristarchus objects. "I am spreading out my clothes so you can sleep on them, and you will lay your head on my lap."

"I cannot do that to you," Paul objects.

"Yes, you can, and you will. Otherwise, I am going to order Luke to stop treating you."

Paul smiles and peers over at Luke. Luke stares at the bulkhead whistling and trying not to snicker.

Regardless, the arrangement is settled on, and even Luke contributes his clothes for Paul to lie on. Still, most of the time, when Paul sleeps, he groans. They do not tell him.

Days run into eternal nights. They only suspect when the ship is on open sea. In the darkness, they do not know that the winds are against them, and, with difficulty, they finally reach the sheltered south side of Crete. They only know it has taken them over a week, then they are not sure because their only light is torches that keep going out.

More and more, the ship rolls and pitches.

"Julius, sir," Paul finally says after a bout of coughing. "We are in danger."

"There is going to be a lot of damage and loss of the cargo," Paul explains to the centurion. "Worse, our lives are in jeopardy. This ship must stop until spring. Go tell the captain. Please. He must be warned."

"Are you sure?"

"I am positive," Paul says with his strained voice.

Please tell the captain. I have a gift from God that tells me these things."

"I do not think you would make this up, Paul," Julius says. "I will go tell him what you said."

Weaker than ever, Paul falls asleep awaiting the centurion's return.

"Paul, wake up. Wake up." It is Julius. "I told Captain Milon exactly what you said. He told me we are in the Cretan harbor of Fair Havens, and it is not suitable to winter here. I waited while he conferred with his officers, and they all agreed the ship should be taken about fifty *mille*s farther west where Phoenix is. It is an excellent harbor. He will put in there for the winter.

"We will never make it," Paul says, trying to smother a cough.

The following day, one of the soldiers descends to the bilge after his breather. "A calm south wind came up, perfect for skirting Crete to the good harbor," he reports.

"I guess you were wrong, Paul," prisoner Ludo says with a grin.

Paul does not answer.

The soldiers celebrate by going up to the deck just above and helping themselves to some wine they had spotted in several barrels.

"I wonder what there is to do on Crete during the winter," Julius muses.

Late the next day, when they are close to the harbor of Phoenix, the ship is hit by a violent nor'easter. A shock wave takes hold, and the ship nearly rolls over onto its side.

Screams can be heard from the main deck all the way down in the bilge. Footsteps of running passengers and crew are so heavy, they too can be heard far below. Voices grow clearer, and gradually, the prisoners realize all the passengers have gone down to the berth deck for safety.

Paul and everyone else clings to whatever post they call home to keep from rolling with the ship.

On its side one way, then shifting and rolling on its other side.

Now they feel scraping below them.

"Have we hit rocks?" a soldier asks, wide-eyed with fear.

"Oh, no," Julius says. "I think we have hit the Libyian Syrtis Gulf. It is notorious for cross currents and sand bars many *mille*s across. Once stuck in them, you are there forever. Pray they get us out of here before it is too late."

Pitching back and forth, back and forth.

Prisoner Brictius holds his hand over his mouth. "Sir, I am going to vomit!"

Julius grabs his keys and unchains the man just in time for him to leap to a dark corner and unload his stomach.

He turns to the other three prisoners. "I am going to unchain all of you. Things are too dangerous right now. If we start to go down, perhaps you are a strong enough swimmer, you can escape."

The scraping sound disappears, but now the ship pitches and rolls even more.

They try to sleep. Most cannot. Paul does, though they are not sure if it is because of his weakened physical condition, or he simply believes he will live through it.

Hours later—probably the next day—they hear another scraping along the bottom.

"What's that?" Prisoner Ludo asks, jumping up, looking down at his feet and over on the bulkhead.

"The sound has moved from the bottom up the side of the bulkhead," Luke says. "I think they're pulling howsers around the ship to hold it together."

"How do they do that?" Aristarchus asks. "The storm is pitching us all over."

"Two of the sailors tie ropes around their waists, and each takes an end of the howser," one of the guards explains. "They jump into the water at the bow or stern, swim on opposite sides of the ship, then climb up the side—or get pulled up. Another of the crew grabs the end of the howser and wraps it around a capstan." My father was a sailor when he was young,"

"I hope that's what it is, and not the sand bars," Aristarchus says.

Paul stands, hangs on to the beam with both hands, and bursts out in song. Now nothing can be heard outside of the ship. No pounding of waves, no scraping of sand bars, or of howsers.

Everyone laughs, and some join in with him.

Eventually, he coughs so much he must stop, so everyone else does too.

Now silence again. Now the banging and badgering. Now the squeaking of beams and boards and planks. Paul slides his arms down the beam, sits, and falls asleep.

DAY TWO. Paul and the others hear men right above them in the orlop and in the hatch leading to the top deck. It is a bucket brigade. They start with the corn.

Throw it out. Lighten the ship. Save the people.

Someone descends to the bilge. They can hardly see him or anyone else, but the voice is unfamiliar.

"Here is a large supply of rope oakum," he tells the centurion. "If leaks break through, they will start down here."

He pulls two sacks down behind him. "Any time you see water seeping through, watch it. If it grows to the width of a nail, stuff this oakum in it. Send word up on deck if you ever need more. Let us pray to our gods you will not need more."

He leaves, and Julius reaches into the sacks and divides up the oakum between the eleven men in the bilge. They use it to soften where they sit, and hope it will not be needed to stop water from invading the bottom of the bilge.

They become quiet again. Paul coughs a little more.

DAY THREE. Sailors descend to the bilge.

Have they come to kill us and throw us overboard? Are we worth less than the wine they saved? Which one of us will they kill first?

The sailors go to the piles of chains and hand them up to someone on the ladder. They find an emergency sail and hand it up. They find oars and hand them up.

Paul and the others try to stay out of the way and out of their line of sight, hoping it will be forgotten that human bodies could lighten the ship significantly.

Paul coughs more.

DAY FOUR. They sit and stand and pace. They whistle, hum and sing. They talk sometimes and whisper sometimes and even snore at times.

They open their eyes, close them, and blink. They repeat stories they had told two weeks earlier. They dream of being home again. They pray to their gods.

The ship continues its wicked rolls, heeling to one side, then the other. Hull slamming into a wave trough, then up to the crest on the other side. Tossed like a stalk of wheat in a river's rapids.

DAY FIVE. Paul hears sailors right above them in the nearly empty orlop deck singing bawdy songs. Dancing with each other. Telling unseemly jokes. Roaring with laughter at nothing.

A stream of urine flows down the ladder and mingles with other putrid smells of sweat, dying rats, feces, vomit, and foul breath that stings the air.

Paul raises his arms. "Jesus, be our lighthouse. Be our watchtower. Be our anchor. Calm the waters as you once did on the Sea of Galilee long ago when you walked with us on earth." Then he coughs.

Aristarchus picks up the prayer, and he, too, raises his arms. "Oh, Lord Jesus, protect us. Help us find land soon. Give us life again. But whatever happens, your will shall be done."

Almost before Aristarchus is through, Luke stands. "God of heaven and earth. Guide us where we cannot see. Lead us where we should not be. Be our stalwart leader and give us sweet rest."

DAY SIX. It is a losing fight. The sea pounds and grinds and lambastes. The ship plows through waves and wind, daring them to stop its progress, though it is not progress at all. It is only survival.

In a maelstrom. The ship turns and twists and spins as the wind toys with it, and the waves dare to swallow it.

The surging billows roar, the crash of water pounds unendingly, leaving behind it an unrelenting hissing foam.

Paul hums, though the air he breathes stings and

burns his already irritated throat.

DAY SEVEN. The towering waves overhead and all around the ship claw at it like a giant monster.

The planks and fittings squeak and whine and screech like a death knell. The unrelenting waves pound. The men hang on to the nearest post to avoid being tossed up against the bulkhead and bones broken. Sometimes they are too weak and get thrown anyway.

Centurion Julius picks up pieces of rope missed by the sailors and hands them out. "Tie yourselves to a beam," he orders.

Paul tells stories from the ancients. He tells how Noah survived a torrent of rain that lasted forty days, all alone in his hand-made ship with his family and none others.

"What do you think it was like for Noah?" he asks, then coughs. Some pooh-pooh the story. Others try to identify with the old hero.

30 ~ DOOMED

DAY EIGHT. Still surviving. Still alive. Still enduring the impossible.

Paul wonders where they are after being tossed around by the sea like a mustard seed in the Great Salt Lake of Anatolia. Are they near the coast of Egypt? Are they near the coast of Palestine? The coast of Anatolia? Greece? Italy? Spain?

"Did I tell you about the time I was eight years old?" Paul says with the ship pitching to the right, "and went with my father to the port south of Tarsus?" The ship pitches to the left. "We saw men dressed in strange clothing and speaking strange languages. One of them was missing his leg." Paul stumbles down, having let go of his post. "I asked my father if it was bitten off by a shark. He said..."

A torch comes loose from the bulkhead and falls on Paul's shoulder. His clothing catches fire, and Aristarchus and the others grab whatever they can to smother it out.

"One less torch," prisoner Galvius says."

"Why do we need them anyway?" prisoner Ludo asks. "So, we can see what is stinking and eating away at us?"

Luke pulls the tunic off Paul and pours some of the cool putrid drinking water from a barrel provided for them in an effort to ease the fire pain, but knowing the bad water will also inflame the wound.

DAY NINE. The crashing waves continue to batter. The unearthly wind continues to pound. Hope continues to waver. The ship rocks onto its side and back again, onto the other side and back again. Battered. Bruised. Falling apart.

The course long ago abandoned. Sailing into the wind. Daring nature to capsize the ship and get rid of its misery.

Cracks appear in the bulkhead with water coming through. The prisoners and guards take turns stuffing rope oakum into them to keep out the water that has invaded their ship and wants to invade their bodies and their very being.

Paul continues to cough, and his burn continues to redden.

DAY TEN. Weaker now. No eating. Not much walking anymore. Crawling, but at least still moving. Keep moving. Keep talking. Sleep. No, don't sleep. What if you never wake up?

Thinking, not thinking. Dreaming, not dreaming. Hoping, but not sure where hope has hidden itself. Tired. Hungry. Weak.

Paul's delicate scarred back burns. He tells no one. Sometimes he pats Aristarchus on the hand.

"Is this what you were thinking of when you said you wanted to go with me?" he half speaks and half whispers.

"Well..."

"This is what my life has been like. Yet, I survived it all. Keep praying, son. Keep praying. God loves to answer prayer. Give him that chance."

"Paul, if this is what your life has been like, how have you been able to keep going?"

"When I am weak, I am strong," Paul says, coughing. "Do you understand?"

"I do," Luke says. "Whenever you are in a weakened condition, I see a strength in you I have not seen in any other."

"Well, it is not me, Luke. It is Jesus living in me. Do you understand it? I think you do."

Their talking done, they close their stinging eyes Once again, and hope to dream.

DAY ELEVEN. Aristarchus smiles. "Do you know what the first thing is I am going to do when we reach dry ground besides thank God?"

"No," Luke says, entering into a moment of fun.

"Eat. I am going to eat the biggest piece of cheese on the biggest piece of bread you have ever seen."

"Well, I am going to eat the biggest pomegranate anyone has ever seen," Luke declares.

Soon everyone is joining in. Laughter returns. Hope returns. But, at last, silence once again returns to engulf them.

The ship heels and twists and they wonder if and how long ago the captain has given up and joined the passengers.

They sit and stand, stoop and kneel. They stretch their muscles.

"Come, everyone," Paul says, between increased bouts of coughing. "A good athlete stays in shape. What if something happens and we have to swim for it? How far could you swim? Now get those arms out and swing them in place. Swing them forward ten times. Now swing them back ten times. Run. Run in place. Run like you are almost home."

The word home pierces their mind, their heart, their very being. To be home. Home with a cozy fire in the evening, a soft bed, breakfast in the morning. Home. Will it ever be again?

DAY TWELVE. Waves cresting as high as a mountain and with troughs that reach deep into the pits of the earth. Tossing. Turning. Foaming. Reaching high then dropping. Pounding, beating, destroying.

How much longer can the ship take the storm? When will it just give up, quiver, and sink to the bottom of the deep?

How much longer can the storm continue? Is there that much wind out there that it can go on indefinitely? Is it the end of the world? Is God mad? Who is God mad at? Or what? How to appease God. Think. Think of a solution so the wind will stop and go away.

Whining, groaning, roaring. Never letting up. Never easing. Never stopping. Wind, where do you come from? Wind, where are you going in such a hurry? Wind, what is so important that you will sacrifice us to get it?

Paul and the others sleep most of the time now. When

they do not, Paul makes them do their exercises, though he himself grows weaker.

"We must be ready. We cannot let our opportunity for survival pass us by when it comes. Raise those arms high. Raise those knees high. Bend. Jump. Stretch. One-two-three. One-two-three."

And sleep again.

DAY THIRTEEN. Becoming a part of the ocean. Becoming a part of the wind and the waves, the roaring, and the screaming. Merging with them. Going out of existence. The end is near. It has to be near. The end now has no choice.

Give up and die. Close your eyes and wait to die. Oh, death, where are you? Oh, death, why do you hover so far away?

Even the rats no longer scamper or scream. Even the slugs on the bulkheads have stopped their climbing. Even the water snakes have ceased slithering out of their dark corners.

Everything dying. Living, yes, but mostly dying.

"Lord, hear our prayer," Paul prays aloud with a raspy voice, his throat being eaten alive by the sickness in the stench. "If it is your will, Jesus, we will tell others how you saved us from the jaws of death. Go away, death. Come to us, Jesus, and make us live."

Once again, he sleeps. And dreams. Yet it is not a dream. It is THE VOICE. It is HIM. Do not be afraid. You are going to stand before Caesar and tell him about me. Listen. God has granted life to all who sail with you.

DAY FOURTEEN.

Paul wakens everyone. "God has spoken to me," he shouts over the sound of the wind. "Follow me." He climbs the ladder from the bilge to the orlop deck. Luke, Aristarchus, and Julius follow him. The guards and other prisoners do not.

At the orlop deck, he notices it is nearly empty except for sailors scattered around the floor half drunk, half asleep. The ship continues to sway, and he hangs on with steel will.

"Get up," he shouts at them, "and follow me."

Some of the sailors rouse themselves and crawl to the ladder, trying not to be slammed into the bulkhead by the rocking of the ship.

Paul climbs the ladder to the berth deck. It is filled with most of the two hundred seventy-six souls on board sleeping there. And whimpering, and whispering, and losing hope.

"Wake up, everyone," he says. "Wake up," he says louder. "I have something to tell you. Wake up."

He makes his way to the middle of the deck, where the people are huddled. He crawls part of the way until he finds a post to support him.

Once he stands, he realizes that even the captain and helmsmen are among them. All hopeless. All waiting to be thrown headlong into the raging sea and doomed. Doomed to their own hell.

Hanging on to the post with his one good arm, Paul shouts, "Okay. Face it," he shouts, trying to be louder than the wind pounding on the ship and the waves beating against it. "You should have listened to me and not set sail from Crete. You thought it was not safe there. What do you call this?"

"Shut up and crawl back in your hole," comes a groggy, come back.

"This ship is damaged beyond repair. Everything in it has been lost but us."

"So? We are next. So shut up," another calls back.

The ship heels the other direction, and Paul loses his grip. He, along with nearly everyone else, falls on other people. When the ship rights itself once more, he excuses himself to whoever he had fallen on, crawls back over to the post, coughs, and stands again.

"Listen to me. There is hope after all," he shouts. "God spoke to me last night. He is the God I belong to. The God I serve."

"I am telling you the truth. God stood right by me." God, help them all hear me. Return power to my voice.

"You're one of those criminals," someone shrieks. "Go back down in your hole and let us die in peace."

The ship lists and rolls over on its side.

"Yes, I am a royal prisoner. But I am guiltless. God told me last night I would live long enough to stand before Nero Caesar to defend myself and him."

"So what? We never heard of your God. He is nothing."

Paul coughs, then continues. "He has granted the lives of every one of you. You will live. You will all live. So, be brave."

"How is that supposed to happen when the ship is breaking up right under us?"

"God told me we would run aground on an island. Hope again, everyone. Hope again."

The ship heels the other way, throws people onto each other, and Paul himself goes tumbling with them. His back and shoulder scream along with the people.

Waiting again. Waiting to die. He cannot be right.

When will the final roll come when the ship does not right itself? When will the final struggle come? When will the final breath be breathed?

Sitting. Closing eyes. Trying to dream. Trying to escape reality.

Paul thinks he hears banging overhead that is not the wind or the waves. He turns to the guards and other prisoners who had finally come up from the bilge.

"I need to borrow everyone's safety rope," Paul says. "Something is going on up there."

"Forget it, Paul. It is nothing," one of the guards says. "Do you want to be thrown overboard before your time?"

Aristarchus and Luke untie the ropes around their waist and give them to Paul. Centurion Julius follows suit. The others do not budge. "Give him your rope!" Julius demands of both the soldiers and other prisoners.

Paul ties all the ends together and attaches them to the rope around his own waist. He loops the rest of it up in his hand for future use.

The ship lists, turns onto its side, and rights itself. Paul slides with the rest of them, then crawls over to the ladder and climbs to the main deck. He ties the end of his rope to an iron bar next to the hatch and climbs above board.

"What is he doing up there?" Luke wonders aloud to Aristarchus.

"Oh, no," Aristarchus shouts back over the sound of the storm. "Centuries ago, a prophet named Jonah saved a ship in a storm by allowing the crew to throw him overboard."

"I don't think Paul would do that," Luke responds. "He is determined to teach Nero. He wouldn't do that."

Aristarchus crawls over to Centurion Justus to warn him.

"Centurion Julius! Centurion Julius!" It is Paul's voice. He is on his knees, having half fallen down the ladder.

"Paul, let me help you up."

"Hurry. The main deck. Get your men. Hurry," Paul shouts. "If everyone does not stay on board the ship, it cannot be saved."

Immediately Paul starts back up the ladder while Julius calls his men. They are right behind. Shortly Paul returns down the ladder followed by the centurion and crewmen in chains and under arrest for preparing to jump ship.

The centurion tells Captain Milon what has just happened. "What now?" he asks.

By now, Paul has crawled over to the captain and centurion.

"May I have everyone's attention?" Paul asks the captain.

Immediately Captain Milon stands, hangs on to the post, and whistles. The centurion and his guards follow the example. Soon, all the passengers crowded together waiting to die look in their direction.

"Listen to Paul," the captain shouts over the sound of the wind, catching himself the best he can as the ship lists yet another time and pitches itself onto its side, then re-rights itself.

"Everyone," Paul calls out. "Today is the day. It is almost dawn. You have not eaten in fourteen days. You must eat now. You need your strength to save yourself."

The first sailor arrives with baskets of wheat. Paul

takes some of it and holds it above his head, Luke supporting him on one side and Aristarchus supporting him on the other side. They whistle yet again to get the passengers' attention.

"Oh, most holy God, creator of the universe, mankind, and this bread," Paul shouts over the sound of the screeching wind and pounding waves. "We thank you. Now preserve us this day until we reach land."

The food is distributed, everyone eats and dares to believe perhaps they can hope.

Afterward, the sailors throw out the remaining wheat, and everyone waits for dawn and their salvation.

The captain climbs the ladder to the main deck, works his way across by the ship's rail, and reaches the bridge. He climbs the ladder to the helm and straps himself to it. His helmsman goes with him. The centurion and his soldiers also.

Dawn arrives and, with it, a view of a strange island.

"Where are we?" the helmsman shouts to Captain Milon.

"It does not look familiar," he replies, turning and going through the hatch to his cabin. Shortly he comes back out. "I cannot find it on my charts. Head the ship into that harbor, and let us hope there are no rocks down there," he shouts.

Turning to the sailors who had followed him up from the berth deck, he calls down. "Cut the anchors loose, unbind the rudders, and hoist the foresail," he bellows.

He looks over at the centurion. "Bring all the passengers up on the main deck," he shouts.

"Hearing the orders, the guards look at their senior officer. "We will kill the prisoners as soon as everyone else has come up."

"No, you will not kill the prisoners. Do I make myself clear? Now go bring everyone up. And bring Paul to me. No chains."

Gradually the passengers work their way up the ladder to the main deck. They gasp when they see the condition of the ship atop. The compartments have mostly been demolished. The ornate canopies and elegant furniture are nowhere to be seen. Only one sail mast remains erect on the ship itself, the others having broken and crashed into the ocean.

Most passengers get on their knees to move out of the way of the hatch so others can come above board. They cling to each other, sometimes stranger to stranger.

The sea continues to roar. The wind screams on. Both relentless in their quest for human lives.

The captain watches the waters. "It's two seas. Two seas are meeting here. Full rudder ahead," he orders.

The ship fights what it cannot fight. It plunges to where it is not wanted. Still, the shore beckons. Come. Come.

The stubborn ship that has thus far refused to die plows ahead, a hand span at a time. Push. Thrust. Press on.

A thud. A crash. A terrible sound. The bow strikes a reef. It cannot work loose. Too late. Go back. It is doomed.

The stern fights for its life. It thrashes back and forth, back and forth. Then planks. Planks that strain and squeal, buckle, and burst. Planks fly everywhere.

With the stern fast disappearing into the deep, passengers scream, grab each other, and rush to the bow, now the highest part of the ship.

Paul stumbles toward the bridge, Luke and Aristarchus with him.

Screaming. Screaming everywhere.

"We're going to die."

"We're going to die."

Passengers pushing each other. Shoving each other to reach safety away from the stern now embedded in the relentless reef below.

His friends help Paul to the ladder going up to the bridge. Paul raises his hands. Luke and Aristarchus whistle. Others nearby whistle. Gradually they get everyone's attention.

"Swimmers!" Paul bellows. "Jump. Jump in. Swim. Swim for your life."

Passengers everywhere scream, "I can't swim. I can't

swim. What about me? I can't swim."

Paul continues. "Those of you who cannot swim, grab planks, and jump into the water. Hang tight to them."

He watches the passengers scramble, bumping into each other, facing the reality that the moment has arrived. They must save themselves or die.

Now in the water. Dropping one at a time into the cold swirling foam. Struggling. Fighting not to die. Elegant ladies. Prominent men. Children. Merchants. Craftsmen. Farmers. Sailors. Criminals. All as one now. All struggling to remain alive.

Keep the head above the water. Breathe. Claw. Kick. Breathe. Claw. Kick.

The wind shifts around so that it heads inland. The waves calm themselves. The roar dies slowly.

One by one, passengers struggle to the beach. Some alone. Some arm in arm with another. Some carrying someone else who is weaker.

Early survivors fall down onto the shore, then remember the others. They turn and wade back into the churning water, grabbing at the strugglers and pulling them closer to shore. Then back out again. Finding, pulling, saving.

Quiet.
Every passenger.
Every sailor.
Every officer.
All alive still.

People begin to stand and stumble around on the sand and rocks looking for loved ones. They call out.

"Marcus? Where are you?"
"Alexa? I can't find you."
"Basilius. I'm over here."

All now on the shore, they huddle together in the cold rain. United by an experience they can never forget, and new bonds they will never break.

With the last passenger ashore, Luke looks around for people with injuries. He rushes over to a man with a long sharp scratch up the side of his arm. Though Luke has made both his leather shoulder pouches as waterproof as possible, he finds all the herbs inside his medical pouch mixed with each other.

"Hug your waist with that arm so it will stay elevated," he advises.

He sees a woman with blood draining down into her face.

"May I look at your wound, Ma'am?" he asks. Having been given permission, he parts her hair and sees a small wound.

"Keep your head elevated. If you get dizzy, lie down, but put your head on someone's lap."

He looks around and sees a man with his foot turned the wrong way.

"Sir, it looks like you have broken your leg. I am a physician. I can put the joint back in place."

"The pain is so bad, it wouldn't be any worse."

Luke looks in his shoulder pouch and finds a vial with the lid intact. It has opium in it. He puts a few drops on the man's tongue and waits for it to take effect.

"Are you ready? If I touch your leg now, do you feel it?"

"I don't think I feel anything," he says.

With that, Luke puts the man in position, pulls on his leg, and puts the joint back in place.

Three months go by. The governor of the island of Malta entertains Paul, Luke, Aristarchus, and Centurion Julius. Paul heals the governor's father.

The centurion gives Paul full access to the island to do whatever he decides. For three months, Paul heals people, and he, Luke, and Aristarchus tell them about Jesus, the healer of their souls.

People ask Paul why he does not heal himself. "Healing is only to prove to non-believers my words are from God. I am already a believer. I will not abuse what God has given me."

Among those who become Christians that winter is Centurion Julius.

Spring comes. Another ship arrives. The passengers board the ship to go to their original destination, Italy. When they get off the ship, the passengers say farewell to each other, but know their bond will never break.

Centurion Julius personally escorts Paul to Rome along with Luke and Aristarchus. Paul is handed over to the Praetorium guard, who allows him to rent a house and receive visitors. His only restriction is the chains he must always wear. To his surprise, Centurion Julius is granted his request to be Paul's guard.

Soon after settling in, Luke comes out of the small room he has taken over to store his medications.

"I must say, all that saltwater did your back good, Paul. I have created a paste of fish oil, seawater, aloe vera, and mud to keep the tissue soft and keep pain at bay."

"Thank you," Paul says, looking up from a scroll he is writing notes on in his large hand. He sets the pen down, takes off his tunic, and allows Luke to treat his back.

"I wish I could have done something for your eye," Luke says as he begins the treatment. "True, your eye became basically dead. But still... How is your dizziness?"

"It comes and goes. Oh, that salve is cold."

"Be still. When did you start having those dizzy spells?"

"I don't remember for sure. Seems like it was after they beat me with a rod in Philippi. Wasn't that six or seven years ago?"

"I think so. That is about the time I met you."

"Sit up a little straighter. And your bad arm?"

"Well, I think I had it broken for me twice. Once just before I joined Barnabas and once with Silas."

31 ~ VISITORS

"I want to write about your travels. I bought a large scroll yesterday. Will you tell me about your conversion and then your travels? Others need to know what you did."

"There are other apostles who are doing as much or more than me," Paul objects.

"Yes, I realize that," Luke replies. "I would like to find them and interview them too. But, right now, I want you to tell me about you."

"Well, it would not be fair to tell you only what I accomplished. I need to tell you about my days when I hated Christians."

"Okay, we will start there."

It has been another four months. "I heard Governor Pilate's wife is here in Rome," Luke says. "I will be out for a while."

Luke works his way through the streets of Rome to the mansions. He sees a gold merchant to the wealthy who has a shop on one of the corners.

"I am looking for the home of Pontus Pilate. Well, I know he is dead now, but I heard his wife lives here as a widow. Do you happen to know where she lives?"

"You are in luck, sir," the merchant says. "Claudia Procula is her name. Just keep going the way you are, turn left at the next intersection and go down three blocks. Her house has an anchor on it, though I do not know why. Her husband was never a seaman. Funny looking anchor, though. It's crossed at the top."

Luke hurries on and finds the house. It is small. He

knocks, and a young woman answers the gate.

"My name is Luke from Greece. Does Claudia Procula live here?"

"Yes, but she is very old and frail."

"Could I just come in and speak with her a moment? I will not take long. I am also a physician and may be able to give her something to make her more comfortable."

The young lady opens the gate wider and lets Luke in. She leads him to a small room off the courtyard with a single bed in it.

"Is someone here, Atara," the woman says from her bed, raising an arm with the skin loose around it, and fingers gnarled.

"Ma'am," Luke says. "I am a physician. Is there anything I can do to ease any of your pain? Your arthritis, for example? I have a vial with crushed aloe vera and nettles mixed in a little olive oil. Will you let me put some on your fingers?"

"Well, I suppose so," she says with a voice resembling a child's.

While he applies the salve, he softly says, "Jesus. You tried to save him."

"Ohhh. Ohhh." Tears come to Claudia's eyes, and she rocks her head back and forth on her pillow.

Luke puts his hand on her cheek. "Shhh. It's okay," he whispers.

"I tried. My husband liked Jesus and regretted ordering his death the rest of his life. I always tried to ease his guilt by reassuring him Jesus had forgiven him. I am a Christian now, you know."

With that, Claudia closes her eyes and sleeps.

Another year passes. Aquila and Priscilla—now back in Rome--visit Paul often. So do Paul's sister and brothers who have all moved to Rome. Sometimes they send a letter to Nero Caesar, telling him how loyal a Roman Citizen their friend and brother has always been.

Another month passes. Both Luke and Paul hear Centurion Julius open the gate to let someone in. "Careful there," the soldier says.

"Timothy?" Paul asks, looking up from a brief nap.

Timothy appears carrying a man on his back.

"Who is he?" Luke asks.

"Epaphroditus. We came from Philippi, and he got sick right after we left."

Luke immediately motions for Timothy to follow him. The man is laid on a bed, and Luke kneels next to him. "Help me get his robe and tunic off."

"Oh, no," Luke says, looking at the rose spots in the man's lower chest. "How long has he been like this?"

"I haven't noticed the red spots before. He came down with a fever and nose bleeds the day after we left. I suggested we return to Philippi, but he said he needed to get the money to you."

"How long since then?"

"A little over a week. He got so he was too weak to walk."

"Epaphroditus, do you hear me? Does this hurt?" Luke presses on his patient's right side. The man gasps deep in his throat and squeezes his eyes.

"He has the nervous fever," Luke says. "He needs something strong. The only thing I can think of for something this serious is mithridatum. It has over fifty ingredients. It will take me a couple days to assemble them all."

Luke goes to his supply of medications and returns to the sick room. He hands a jar of borage leaves to Timothy. "Make some tea with this and give it to him as often as you can."

That evening, Luke returns to the house, twisting his mouth and clenching his fists. "I should have been able to find at least half the ingredients I need today. I'm going to have to go to another part of the city to see if I can do any better tomorrow."

For three more days, Luke goes from market to market in Rome. On the fourth day, he goes outside of the city and hunts the meadows for some of what he needs. Still lacking a few ingredients, he goes to the estates of some of the senators with personal physicians and is able to find the rest of what he needs for the medication he calls mithridatum.

Back at the house, Luke asks Timothy how the patient is doing.

"His fever has continued to rise, and he has delirium more often," Timothy explains.

Luke gives his patient a few drops of the rare mithridatum every hour.

"I do not know if it will work, but it is all I know to do," he says.

Epaphroditus has more and more trouble breathing. He rasps and gasps for air. He grabs at his bed clothing as though picking off stinging nettles. His nose continues to bleed at least once a day.

"The church in Philippi must be worried about you two," Paul tells Timothy. "I shall dictate a letter to them. Would you do the writing for me? You can take it back with you when Epaphroditus is well enough to travel.

A month later, Timothy returns to Philippi with Epaphroditus, then comes back to Rome to be near Paul.

More time goes by. Aristarchus, who has been going to the temple to Caesar every day, is arrested for insulting the emperor but is allowed to stay confined to Paul's house.

Timothy takes Aristarchus' place approaching worshippers at temples in Rome but stays away from the temple to Caesar.

John Mark, cousin of Barnabas, comes by. With tenderness, he explains Barnabas has been stoned to death on Cyprus. Paul weeps for his old friend for several days afterward. Luke and Timothy speak in whispers during that time.

Two months later, a visitor arrives and asks Centurion Julius' permission to enter. "I am an old friend of Paul's," he says. "We knew each other in Lydia."

"Rufus!" Paul calls out when he sees the younger man entering his house. "It's been so long. I knew you lived here in Rome and have been wondering what you were doing. Thank you for coming to see me."

Rufus is of average height, has a round face with thin beard, and is ample around his middle.

"Well, I partly came to see you, Paul, but I also came to see a man named Luke. I understand he is planning to write a book about Jesus' life here on earth."

"Of course, of course. Your father. He will definitely want to hear about that. Luke! Come out here. There is someone I want you to meet."

Luke comes out to the courtyard and smiles at the stranger.

"Luke, I would like you to meet Rufus. He wants to tell you about his father. Get out your parchment that you take notes on and write this down."

Luke shakes hands with Rufus and walks over to a writing table with his writing materials laid out.

"I cannot stay long, but I wanted to tell you about my father. His name was Simon, and at the time, we had just moved to Jerusalem from Cyrene in North Africanus."

Rufus watches Luke write a moment, then continues. "He was in town when they were taking Jesus up to execution hill. He was, of course, required to carry his own cross, but they had beaten him so relentlessly, he was almost dead before they could kill him, and he kept dropping it.

"My father was a big man and was there in the crowd trying to find out what all the commotion was about. The centurion recruited my father to carry Jesus' cross for him. He carried it all the way up execution hill and kept asking Jesus to forgive him.

"I was just a boy then, and remember every time he told anyone about it, he broke down and wept. And that's all I have to say."

"He ended up becoming Christian, as did everyone in your family," Paul adds. "Such a fine family you have."

"Well, I have to go now," Rufus says. "I just wanted to tell you this one thing."

Another couple months later, someone from Paul's distant past comes by. He is Onesimus, the physician slave of Philemon at Colossae in Anatolia southeast of Ephesus.

"I have run away, Paul. He respects you. What can I do?"

"I understand," Luke tells Onesimus.

"You can't possibly understand," Onesimus replies.

"Friend," Luke says, putting a hand on the slave's shoulder, "I was a slave until a few years ago."

Luke, Paul, and Timothy teach Onesimus about inner freedom. Luke spends most of the time with him.

"Even though my master is a Christian, I never understood before. He never explained Jesus to me," Onesimus finally says.

"Since you believe, Luke will go with you to a certain spot on the Tiber River we often use and baptize you. Then we will talk some more," Paul says.

Upon their return from the river, Paul tells Onesimus, "Now, you need to spend more time with Luke."

"We have already been exchanging experiences on treating wounds," Luke says. "He has given me some new remedies that should help you."

"I shall send a letter to Philemon, telling him to take you back and not to punish you because now you are brothers in Jesus," Paul says.

"And, I shall tell him to get a room ready. Centurion Julius tells me I will be appearing before Nero soon to defend myself. I am confident he will release me."

"That is wonderful news," Luke responds.

"At last," Timothy says.

Two days later, Centurion Julius is handed his orders. He is to present Paul in the court of Nero Caesar that afternoon.

"I will meet you there," Paul tells Luke and Timothy. Make sure my sister Bethania, and my brothers Andonicus and Junias get the word so they can testify for me also. If you think of anyone else, go notify them.

"Well, this is it. By this time tomorrow, I will either be food for lions or be free of these chains."

Late that afternoon, Paul returns to his rent house for the last time. He is no longer wearing chains.

"I am free," he tells his three companions. "Nero Caesar now knows that Jesus died to pay the price for his sins. I pray he will become a Christian."

He stares at them a moment, but says nothing more and begins gathering up his scrolls and clothes to pack.

Luke and Timothy follow him to his room. "We are ashamed we did not go with you, Paul," Timothy finally says.

"If we had been arrested, there would have been no one to take care of you," Luke says.

"God was with me," Paul replies quietly. "I was not alone."

"The first thing I want to do," Paul says, "is go to Colossae where Philemon has a room awaiting us."

"You still want us after we deserted you like we did?" Timothy asks.

"As I said, God was with me. We will speak no more of it."

Everyone packs.

Paul visits the church in Rome for the first and last time. They are still scattered in various homes, but he manages to see them all in one day. He encourages them. They sing. They pray. They weep.

After their worship together, an old man approaches Paul and Luke. He is big, but his back is bent now, and he walks with a cane.

Luke recognizes the cloak fastened at the shoulder worn only by centurions, though it is now worn and tattered.

"My name is Sergius," the old man says. Tears fast come to his eyes.

Paul, Luke, and Timothy wait.

Sergius clears his throat. "I, I crucified him."

They wait still.

His voice cracks. "I was in charge of his crucifixion. But deep down, I knew who he was. And after the daytime blackness and the earthquake, I had to say it."

The old soldier breaks into a sob, then controls it long enough to say what he needs to say. "I was convinced Jesus truly was the Son of God. Now I worship him."

By this time, Paul, Luke, and Timothy are all in tears themselves. But only briefly. Paul, his own back bent from the many beatings on it, reaches over and touches the man's hand resting on his cane.

"He forgave you," he whispers.

"I know, but..."

"He forgave you, just like he forgave me. I voted for his crucifixion. I was there and I heard what you said. It confused me. But he forgave both of us, didn't he?

A young woman comes over and takes hold of the old man's arm.

"Come along, Grandfather. It is time to go home and rest."

Paul and his companions go home with his sister and brothers, who have moved in together. They rejoice with him over his freedom, talk old times when they were children together, and say goodbye.

"Stay safe, dear brother."

Within a few days, Paul, along with Timothy and Luke, are on board a ship bound for Anatolia. They land at Ephesus and stay for a day before rushing on to Colossae. There, Luke is pleased to know Philemon has taken Onesimus back, and they have compromised by Onesimus only treating the general public once a week.

With his new-found freedom, Paul next takes Luke and Timothy north to Ephesus.

Timothy stays there. "You are needed here," Paul had said. "I will miss you, my friend. Oh, how I will miss you."

They embrace, weep, and part.

Luke boards a ship with Paul, and they cross the Aegean to Corinth. From there, they find a fishing vessel willing to take them north to Berea.

"What a grand surprise," Theophilus says when they enter his home. "Oh, it is so good to see you," he says to Luke.

"Are you taking care of yourself?" Luke asks. "Are you eating, right? Do you rest enough?"

"I am seventy-five years old, Luke. Not dead. Do I detect a little gray in that yellow hair of yours?" Theophilus teases.

"My research into the life of Jesus while he was here on earth has progressed. I have all my interviews so far written down, but it isn't ready to show you. I still have to find Jesus' apostles. They have scattered everywhere."

Four days later, Paul makes his announcement.

"We've got to go, Luke. I need to get to Nicopolis. Titus is supposed to meet me there."

"Perhaps you will be able to get the rest you need. You have been pushing yourself too much. You know that. I realize you cannot resist teaching. But perhaps the isolation for a couple months will be good for you. You can take as many naps during the day as you need."

"Luke, you are just like Barnabas, Silas, and Timothy. Always bossing me. But I have to admit, you guys were usually right. Not always, but usually."

"By the way," Luke says, turning to Theopholis, "what did you do with my house?"

"I've been renting it until you return."

"You need to sell it. Use the money as you see fit."

The following day, Luke embraces his mentor, his master, and his friend, and leaves with Paul.

As they sail farther north, Paul talks to Luke of his plans to go to Espanola next. He also dictates more of his travel experiences to Luke. "It's never enough, Luke. I can never do enough. I cannot make myself stop."

Luke rents them two rooms. It is next to the Synagogue.

"I'll have to preach to them when I get stronger and tell them their Messiah finally came," Paul says.

The routine they had had while Paul was under house arrest in Rome is resumed.

"I thought I was stronger than I really was. I need this time to gain more strength,"

"It will be quieter up here," Luke responds.

A few days later, Paul asks Luke to take dictation to a letter to Timothy.

"I left him in Ephesus pretty abruptly. I don't want him to think I just deserted him."

Paul signs the end of the letter with his large script. Luke seals it and takes it down to the docks to pay someone to deliver it to Corinth, then on to Ephesus."

"I have been writing down things about the beginning

of the church," Luke the next day. "But I do not think I have a good feel for what happened. It's going to be just the two of us now. You were there. You have told me some. But perhaps you can tell me a little more about it each day after you have rested."

Each morning when Paul rises, Luke gives him his first treatment of the day. Sometimes his back is more agitated than others

The winter passes.

"I can't wait for Titus any longer. Maybe he is at Troas. I told Timothy he could meet us there. I need to encourage the church there."

"I think the winter's rest has been good for you."

"Before I leave, I've got to preach to that synagogue next door. I think I can hold up under their insults if they turn on me. Don't you think so, Luke? I've been practicing walking without my pillow."

The following day is the Sabbath. Luke puts a drying agent on Paul's back so he can wear clothes. Though still bent over, Paul walks next door looking as dignified as he can. He tells the rabbi he is a former member of the Sanhedrin in Jerusalem. The rabbi consents to him speaking that morning.

Within an hour, there is shouting. "You are wrong, Paul. That Jesus did not take over the temple or the Roman government. And the Son of God would not have allowed himself to be crucified. Get out of here!"

Paul is now on the portico yelling back at them. "Your blood be on your own hands," he shouts.

About that time, Titus arrives in a cart. Stephanus is with him.

"You are just in time," Paul tells them. "Luke and I were preparing to leave tomorrow. Titus, I want you to go north of here to Dalmatia. They need the gospel. Take it to them, Titus. You can do it."

A week later, Paul and Luke arrive in Troas to encourage the church there. Paul has had time to rest from over-exerting himself at the synagogue in Nicopolis. It has been an uneasy one. The seas were restless.

They go immediately to see Oceanus.

"The church is doing well here," he says. "I am one of the elders. Carpus is another elder.

"Where is Eutychus?" Luke asks.

"He has married, and he and his little family now live in his former bedroom. I'm sure Carpus would like to put you up at his home."

A few days later, there is a rapid knock on Carpus' gate. It is Oceanus.

"I just came from the harbor," he tells Carpus, looking behind him, then slipping far enough in, they close the gate back.

"A ship from Rome just docked. The crew is saying Nero set fire to Rome and is blaming the Christians. He is ordering our leaders arrested. Paul is in danger."

Paul and Luke enter the courtyard just in time to hear the news. Oceanus turns to Paul.

"You must leave and go somewhere else where they cannot find you."

"I would have to go completely out of the Roman Empire to do that," Paul says.

"Then do it. Go to Persia, to India, to China."

"We do not have money to go that far," Paul says.

"I will give you the money," Carpus says. "You must leave now."

"The church is meeting again tomorrow morning," Paul objects. "I must meet with them. Then I will leave."

"When you do, do not tell us where you are going in case they question us."

Oceanus leaves, and Paul and Luke begin gathering up their clothes so they can leave immediately after they meet with the church the next morning.

"Carpus, I cannot travel in a hurry with everything," Paul says. "Could I leave my scrolls here with you? Perhaps I can send for them later. Also, it is getting warm; I do not need my robe."

"Leave here whatever you need to. I will keep them safe."

That evening Paul and Luke decide to go see Oceanus

and Eutychus for one last private time together. As they walk, they think they hear someone behind them. Moments later, they know they do. They turn just in time for six Roman legionnaires to grab hold of the two men and chain both their hands and feet.

"You are under arrest for inciting the Christians in Rome to burn the city."

32 ~ GOODBYE

"I tried to get you both released," Centurion Julius says.

"I know you did," Luke replies. "I almost feel guilty for being given my freedom, while Paul is down in that dungeon. The smell is almost unbearable."

"Yes, I know. Remember when we were in the bilge of that ship?"

"True. They aren't much different."

"What are you going to do now, Luke?"

"Have you found the man I told you about?" Luke asks.

"Not yet. But why would you want to go see him at all?"

"I just do. Keep looking. By the way, Julius, thank you for letting me stay with you."

"Being close to retirement age, they let me rent an apartment in this insulae. I have been used to living in a barracks with a hundred men around me. I needed the company."

"Well, it is time for me to go see Paul."

Luke walks the short distance from the insulae to the government buildings. He walks but does not want to. He walks but wants to run the other way. He walks to see the condemned.

"Sign here," the guard says. "If you cannot write, make a mark, and I'll watch you do it."

Luke picks up the pen, dips it in blackener, and writes "Luke of Berea" in his fine hand.

"Now I have to search you."

Luke takes off his robe, hands it to the guard, and holds out his arms.

Satisfied, another guard ties a handkerchief over his nose and mouth and unlocks the inner door with his large key. He takes a torch off one wall, tells Luke to do the same, and enters the dark corridor.

The smell hits Luke hard, but he tries to think of his youth when he was in hospital tents helping to bandage wounded soldiers. The smell from the wounds themselves sometimes had made him wretch. But he always had managed to wait until he was outside to do so.

Shadows on the walls. Dark shadows that toy with the imagination and create demons like the undead he used to have nightmares about by the Nordic Sea. Shadows that make the unreal real. Shadows that jump out at you, and go inside you, and swirl around in horror in your inner being.

The deeper they go, the more slippery the floor. Slippery with vomit and dung and liquid excrement. Slippery with dead dreams, dead hope, and dead flesh floating away into slimy nothingness.

The guard stops and hands the torch to Luke. His keys rattle, the hinges groan and scrape, and he nudges the metal and rotting wood-door open wide enough to let Luke in.

Luke sees Paul on the floor, shielding his eyes from the bright light of the torch.

He looks so old. So much older than he did only last week in Troas.

Luke looks around and finds a place on the wall to set his lantern. Paul leans forward, makes it to his knees, then stands.

Though it burns his mouth to even open it, Paul speaks, and Luke detects a smile. "I would give you my hands in greeting, but I believe I would be giving you some..."

Luke steps forward and embraces Paul, careful to touch the back of his head and not his back. After a few moments, Paul begins to draw away, but Luke is stronger and unwilling. *I cannot let him see my tears.*

"I am so sorry, Paul. I tried to get you out," Luke

groans. "They wouldn't listen to me. Oh, Paul."

Luke shakes a moment, sniffs, the old man draws away again, and this time succeeds. They stand at arm's length, Luke now clinging to Paul's hands.

"Centurion Julius even tried," Luke continues, "and they threatened to transfer him back to Caesarea. The Christians here are too afraid to speak on your behalf. In fact, half of them have already fled. Nero is..."

Luke looks down at Paul and weeps anew.

"What is it, Luke?"

"Nero is capturing Christians, chaining them to poles and setting fire to them. He says they burn a lot longer than torches and illuminate his courtyard magnificently. Nero is going mad."

"Their pain will only be for a few moments. Then they will be with our Lord. Even as we speak about it, they are already there, walking the streets of gold and beholding the very face of God."

"They say he has been threatening suicide. I wish he..."

"Don't say it, Luke," Paul interrupts, his voice scratchy from the putrid air. "God will deal with Nero. I wish I could have persuaded him at my trials. I tried."

Luke lets go of Paul's hands and steps back to wipe the embarrassing tears from his cheeks.

"What about my family?" Paul asks.

"I haven't seen them."

"Go to them—my sister Bethania, and brothers Andonicus and Junias. Tell them to leave immediately. Nero knows who they are and will arrest them as co-conspirators. Promise me you will go to them and convince them to leave. Tell them I will be okay and will find them after I am released."

"But, Paul, how do you know..."

"You need to go now. And Luke, thank you for coming, even though the news of what is going on out there is not good. Tell the Christians to be strong and keep fighting the good fight. Never stop."

"I will, Paul. But, before I go, lift up your tunic. I have

some paste to put on your back. It should help protect it down here."

Paul turns around, and in the dark shadows, Luke applies the thick medication.

They face each other. "I will be back tomorrow," Luke says. "I promise."

They look deep into each other's eyes. Luke calls to the guard outside the door, takes the torch off the wall, and leaves.

The tall Norseman lags behind the guard. He walks slower and slower until he is barely moving. He puts his contaminated hands up to his eyes, and sobs again, his shoulders shaking.

"Better come on if you don't want me to lock you in here with them," the guard growls.

Luke catches up, steps in the outer *officium*, throws the torch onto the floor, and rushes out to the street. He runs but does not know in which direction. He leans against the wall of someone's home along the street, slides down, sits, and gives in to the blackness of the world around him.

It is dark when he opens his eyes again.

"God!" he cries out at the empty sky. "Why is Christianity so hard? Why do they hate us so?"

Somehow he finds his way back to the insulae and up to Julius' second-floor apartment. He enters. Julius is there.

"You've been to see him, haven't you?" Julius asks. "You've got to get control of yourself, if for no other reason than for Paul's sake. My guess is that he is being more brave than you. Am I right?"

Luke sits on a wooden bench and lowers his head to his hands.

"You cannot do this, Luke. You must control yourself."

"I cannot."

"He will be able to tell."

Luke takes a deep breath, fights back the tears that nearly reappear, and looks up at Julius.

"How have you handled all the wars and hatred all these years?

"I think about the ultimate purpose. You must do the

same. And think of something you can do when your spirit is this far down."

Luke smiles slightly. When I was a boy, I used to run just as hard as I could when I was upset."

"Good. Then that is what you shall do now."

"Now?"

Julius smiles.

Paul's personal physician leaves and comes back an hour later, perspiration on his forehead.

"I'm okay now."

Luke continues to visit Paul. A few days later, he asks Julius the same question he has asked him for a week.

"Did you get the information I am looking for?"

"Yes. But I do not know why you would want to find him."

"I just do. I need to talk to him. I need to know if what I heard is true."

"Well, he is in the same dungeon as Paul, but in a different part where they keep men until they die on their own."

"Is there such a thing?" Luke asks. "I thought Rome executed rebels."

"Most they do, but there are a few exceptions where, by law, they cannot execute someone who deserves it," the centurion explains. "So they put them in a deep dungeon where they spend the rest of their life wishing they were dead."

"And he is one of the exceptions?" Luke asks.

"Yes. He was sentenced to death for leading a deadly insurrection against Rome. But some political manipulations happened, making it impossible to execute him, so they sentenced him to the dungeon the rest of his life."

"So, all I need to do is go to the dungeon and ask for Barabbas."

"That's right."

Luke rushes out the door and returns to the dungeon.

"You were here just this morning to visit that Paul. Back already?"

"No, I came to see someone else this time."

"You don't hang around very good people, sir. Who are you here to see now?"

"Barabbas."

"What for? He has been in here for thirty-five years, and I don't think anyone has ever visited him."

"Thirty-five years?" Luke asks, putting a fist up to his forehead. "How could anyone have such a strong will to live?"

"Don't know. He's an odd case," the jailor says. "Sentenced to be executed for treason, his sentence was waived, then they rearrested him for the same thing but sentenced him to this place the rest of his life. Do you know what he did that made them so mad?"

"I'm pretty sure I do. The problem is the one who took his place to be executed."

Seeing that Luke is through discussing it, another jailer goes through the usual routine of covering his nose and mouth with a handkerchief, unlocking the inside door, handing Luke a torch, and taking one for himself.

This time, once they get a few steps down the corridor, the guard turns left instead of right. They walk through the same nightmare and finally stop.

"He's dangerous. Are you sure you want to do this?"

"I do," Luke replies.

The guard unlocks the door but cannot force it open. Luke helps him, they hear rust crackle and grumble and scrape. The door opens.

"I'll be right out here. I have my sword drawn in case there is trouble."

Luke enters, and the door clangs shut behind him. He stares at the skeletal man and takes a step toward him.

The skeleton moves a hand up to its eyes to protect them. The skeleton sits up, stares a moment longer, stands, and lunges at Luke.

Luke puts the torch on the wall with one hand, and grabs hold of the skeleton's other hand now around his neck.

"I hate you," the skeleton growls.

"Well, I love you," Luke replies, easily untangling the

skeleton's hands from around his neck. "Now, Barabbas, sit down, and let's talk."

"Why?"

"I want to talk about Jesus."

Barabbas backs away, raises both arms, grabs what is left of his thin gray hair, and pulls on it.

"Stop that," Luke says, grabbing the man's hands and squeezing them hard enough they loosen.

"If you do not want to sit, then we will stand," he continues. "I just want to know if it is true that Jesus took your place on the cross."

"That name," he shrieks. "That name." The shriek turns into a whimper."

Barabbas kneels and weeps.

Luke kneels with him. "Then, it is true."

"Yes, it is true. I wish I had died with him. I have died thousands of times since then."

"You know, he forgave you. While still hanging there in your place, he forgave you."

Barabbas looks up. "You know, I used to be tall and bulky and muscular, and everyone was afraid of me. Not anymore."

"I know," Luke says. "Here, I brought you some cheese and grapes. Eat them slowly, so they do not shock your system."

"Will you come back?" Barabbas asks.

Luke does not answer. He tells the guard he is ready to leave, and soon he is back on the street and headed for home again. That night he prays for Barabbas.

Luke's continues his daily visits with Paul.

"Hello, Paul," Luke says after the door is through clanging. "I brought you some decent food and good water in this urn. It has a lid on it to keep worms and bugs out."

Paul steps toward Luke and holds out his arms. As usual, Luke embraces the bent old warrior, and for a while, they cling to each other.

Paul pulls back. "Did you say food? Thank you, my friend. It is much appreciated. From now on, I will let the rats have the rations my guards bring me."

"I put your food in a pot with a lid. I knew a basket would not last in here with the... Well, would not last in here."

"What is going on out there, Luke?"

"It is not good. Panic actually. Your sister and brothers are gone. Most of the church is gone. I suppose you and I are about the only church left in Rome now. And Centurion Julius."

"That is enough for now. We shall be content."

"Yes, sir. Of course, you are right," Luke replies.

"This bread is good. And the fresh grapes. Oh, my, Luke. You do spoil me."

"Is there anything else I can do for you?"

"Yes. The next time you come, try to convince the guards to let you bring in a table, stool, and writing supplies. If you can, I need to send a letter to Timothy over in Ephesus, where I left him. There are some things I need to tell him while I am still...well, while I am still here."

Luke sits with Paul on the slimy floor with Paul's back to him. This time he applies oil and aloes. "We need to keep those scars soft to avoid more pain."

They sit in silence a while. And think. And remember.

"Well, I guess it is time for me to go. I will try to return tomorrow with a table and one of your blank scrolls."

Luke returns to the insulae and writes about his interview with Barabbas.

Julius returns, and Luke has some fresh cheese for him."

"I have some interesting news for you," Julius says.

"Oh?"

"Barabbas died this afternoon."

Luke does not reply.

The following morning, Luke gathers up a parchment and rolls it up to put in his shoulder pouch along with blackener and pen. He picks up a tall table, carries it by one leg, and returns to the dungeon.

They arrive, embrace, and pull back from each other. Paul notices what Luke has brought with him.

"Thank you, Luke. I knew if anyone could do it, it would be you," Paul says. "Let me see now what I want to tell Timothy."

Luke perches his pen above the scroll.

"To Timothy, my beloved son. I recall your tears when we saw each other the last time, and long to see you...I am imprisoned like a criminal. But the Word of God is not imprisoned....I know the time of my leaving earth is near....

"Try to come before I give up my life. Everyone has deserted me, but Luke...Bring Mark with you if you can, and also the robe and scrolls I left with Carpus in Troas..."

Luke rolls up the scroll. "I will hire someone to deliver this to Timothy in Ephesus. Let us hope and pray he receives it before.... Well, that he receives it."

"I am sure you will do all you can to get it to him. God bless you, Luke. You have been a good and loyal friend. You have kept me going when no one else could."

Luke gives Paul's back a treatment. "You have defied death more than any man I have ever known," Luke always says.

They clasp hands and forearms, Luke calls for the guard to come, and he leaves with the scroll, table, and torch.

Luke comes daily when he can. Paul tells him more of his tours with Barnabas, Silas, and Timothy.

Hours. Days. More hours. More days. A week perhaps. Perhaps two. Perhaps three.

"When did you get here?" Luke asks, answering the door.

"We came as fast as we could," Timothy says.

"Well, are you going to let us in?" John Mark asks.

"I am so glad to see you," Luke says. "Well, sorry. Come in. Come in."

"When can we see him?"

"First thing in the morning," Luke says.

"And how has he been doing?"

"Surprisingly positive," Luke says. "His back is not doing very well in the filth, but I try to keep it protected with oils and salves."

"It will be good to see him again."

"Don't be shocked when you see him. He has lost a lot of weight, is stooped, and has aged a lot."

The next morning, the three old friends of Paul walk quickly through the street of Rome to the door into the dungeon *officium*. Luke explains the routine on their way.

With four sets of footsteps in the dark corridor, Luke knows Paul is suspicious that his end is near, and by now is boldly standing by his door. He also hears sniffing from his two friends and understands.

"Look who I brought with me," Luke calls out as they near Paul's door, and it is unlocked.

"Oh, Timothy, you came," Paul says. "And Mark. Oh, my hearts."

The three men draw close to each other and embrace—always careful of the remains of Paul's shredded back—and sob. No words. What can they say?

Luke watches.

They step back from each other.

Timothy finally breaks the silence. He forces a smile. "Here, I brought your robe. Would you like it on your back?"

"Yes, thank you. It is cold down here, and that makes my back pain worse."

Timothy gently lays the robe on Paul, and their eyes smile.

"I remember the times you carried me on your back to get us out of danger and to help," Paul says with a grin. "I still do not know how you did it."

"As I look back, I do not know how I did it either. We had some times together, didn't we?"

More silence.

"Uh, I brought the scrolls for you," Mark says.

"Good. I can use them. I often dictate letters to Luke," Paul says. "Did you start writing about your experiences with Jesus in Jerusalem yet?"

"Yes," Mark says, "and Peter is helping me with what Jesus said and did when I was not around."

"I would invite you to sit, but I do not think you want to share your seat with the rats. They have gotten used to me, but they could bare their teeth at you or worse."

They sit anyway.

In a circle.

The four remembering.

Together again.

Mostly in silence, but sometimes recalling earlier times.

"By the way, John just arrived in Ephesus," Timothy says almost in a whisper.

"Dear beloved John," Paul says softly. "Is Mary still alive? Is she with him?"

"Yes. She is nearly ninety years old and in poor health," Timothy replies.

"I must go see her," Luke says. "I have so many questions for her."

"Yes, you need to do that, Luke," Paul replies.

Once more, silence.

And thinking.

And remembering.

And wondering.

Finally, they stand. "We will be back every day until..."

With tears, they each draw Paul—the once tall, robust former athlete—to their chest, kiss the top of his head, and wonder how much longer they will have with their apostle.

They whisper, "Goodbye for a while," and Paul smiles.

The three men walk out of the dungeon and toward the insulae in silence. They arrive but do not go in.

"Let's walk over to the river instead. He loved rivers." Luke's voice is soft.

"Yes," John Mark says. "He did."

"Such a strong man," Timothy says with a sigh.

"The strongest."

They arrive and sit on the Tiber Riverbank. They watch the waters drift in and ebb away. They watch the ripples emerge and disappear. They watch the river as it passes them by and flows on eternally.

They know.

They all know.

The next morning they do not return to the dungeon.

Their Paul is dead.

33 ~ NEW BEGINNING

Mark boards a ship headed toward the Black Sea. Luke and Timothy board a ship to Greece and then to Anatolia.

"I hope John Mark is able to find Peter and tell him," Timothy says.

"Yes," Luke responds. "There will never be another like our Paul."

"The world will be much quieter now," Timothy says with a sad smile."

"That it will."

Timothy walks around the ship a while, then returns to Luke, still standing at the railing.

"I hope you do not mind us stopping in Berea on our way to Ephesus," Luke says.

"That was some trip to Athens we took half-dead Paul on so you could save his life," Timothy says, remembering just a few years earlier.

"How many times did you save his life over the years, Timothy?"

"I guess I lost count."

"Yes. We'll have to get a fishing vessel from Athens to the river delta closest to Berea. Big ships do not like to go into the Thermaic Gulf. Too much silt."

Small talk helps as they quietly mourn.

Two days later, the fishing vessel stops at Dion and lets Luke and Timothy off. The two tall men have no trouble walking the twenty-five *milles* to Berea and arriving by nightfall.

"It is so good to see you again, Luke," Theophilus says when they arrive. "And I see you brought Timothy with you. Where is Paul?"

Silence.

"Oh. We all knew it was bound to happen, didn't we? In Rome?"

"Yes," Luke says, unmanly tears returning to his swollen eyes.

"So, what now? Come sit out here in the solarium and tell me your plans. Do you have any?"

"I am going to fulfill my promise to you, Master," Luke says. "I am going to finish a thorough account of Jesus' life."

"I thought you took care of that in Jerusalem."

"I did meet a fair number of people who talked to or were healed by him. Even some raised back to life. But I did not get a chance to talk to any of his apostles. They were all gone from Jerusalem twenty years after Jesus died. I was about ten years too late."

"Do you even know where they are?"

"Several people told me where they thought they went. I think I have a good enough idea I can find them, or at least most of them."

"For example?"

"Well, I heard Thaddeus and Nathaniel are in Armenia around Mount Ararat, Andrew is in Scythia somewhere, Thomas is either in India or Kushan Afgan-Archostan. Let me see, uh, Matthew is in old Persia I think, Little James is possibly in Syria. Timothy, do you remember where the rest are?"

"I heard Philip is over in Gaul, and Simon is in Britannia."

"Son, it will take you years to find them all."

"What else is there to do? I will just work my way through those places and support myself as a scribe or a physician or both."

Theophilus stands. "In that case, come with me. I think it is time to give you something that has always been very dear to me and which you have always admired."

"I do not want your money," Luke objects.

"No, no. It is not money. It is better," he says, laughing.

Theophilus leads Luke out to the stable, Timothy tags along. They walk past his chariot, past his chariot horses, and to the back. He opens the stall and stands beside a big black horse.

"He is yours," Theophilus announces.

"Your Frisian?"

"Of course not. I got that first Frisian when I got you forty years ago."

"Are you that old?" Timothy teases, elbowing Luke in a rib.

"Forty-eight isn't so old. You're no better than me," Luke fires back.

"Now, boys. Behave," Theophilus says, laughing. "So back to your Frisian, this horse is the grandson of the one I got in Frisia."

"How did you find a female Frisian?"

"Just before I retired at Fort Capidava while you were in Parthia, I mated Thor. They had twins, so I took one of the foals with me back here to Berea.

"Then, while you were traveling all those years with Paul, I visited Fort Amphipolis up north and happened to see another Frisian, a female. So I was able to mate Thor Jr., and the owner was agreeable to me paying for the foal. I brought the foal home with me, and now he is grown, broken, and ready for you."

"Thor the Third," Luke says, stroking the big horse on the nose.

"Why don't you take him for a ride while Timothy and I go back to the house and tell tales about you? Here is the tack. He loves going up in the mountains south of town."

Two hours later, Luke is back.

"He is magnificent. How can I thank you, Master? You have already done too much for me."

"Oh, you are going to repay me by writing down everything you discover about Jesus' life and teachings. You are going to need Thor the Third if you hope to make it through those mountains in Scythia, Persia, and India. He has inherited Nordic ways and will love the snow. Yes, you will repay me many times."

"Well, we are heading out tomorrow for Ephesus, my first stop," Luke announces.

"So soon? Which apostle is there?" Theophilus asks.

"John. I heard he was Jesus' closest friend, even growing up. And I heard Mary is still living."

"Mary, Jesus' mother? That would be something."

"Yes. I really hope she is still alive and not too frail to talk to me."

"It is too bad you were unable to write the history of your people as your father had wished. Perhaps this will make up for it. More than make up for it."

"Jesus' people are my people now," Luke responds.

A week later, Luke, Timothy, and Thor board a shark boat going down the coast to Athens.

"It's a good thing the captain was willing to take my master's bribe," Luke says.

"I'm not sure Thor is too happy about being stalled with all those dead sharks," Timothy chuckles.

"Well, it was either that or the tackle. He'll survive. As soon as we get to Athens, we can switch to a larger vessel. We'll find one with stalls for animals on the deck."

"Will they let you exercise Thor?"

"Yes."

"How do you know so much about this?"

"I had another horse a long time ago. He died of heat exposure in the Parthian desert."

"If Frisians like snow, how do you know Thor will survive the desert?"

"Frisians are very adaptable. Plus, I know a little more now about how to take care of horses."

The shark boat docks at Athens. It does not take Luke long to find a ship headed across the Aegean to Ephesus, and capable of taking on horses.

Well, on their way, Luke and Timothy sit on the deck across from Thor in his stall.

"Did you ever think about getting married?" Timothy asks.

"I was married once. Well, I was betrothed, which was the same thing there. She was Rashah from Parthia. She had spirit in her and loved to ride."

"What happened?"

"She died."

"Oh."

"About the same time that my father died," he adds. "And you?"

"I'm not too old to marry, yet I don't think. Forty-eight isn't bad. I am thinking of going back to Lystra where I was born," Timothy says. "Maybe I will find a nice widow there and settle down."

Two days later, the ship weighs anchor in Ephesus.

"I still have a rented house here," Timothy says. "We will go there first. I do not have a stable, but there is one down the street near me."

"It is mid-morning," Luke says. "Could we go see John and Mary today?"

"Well, I don't blame you."

"John must be around seventy-five now, the same age as Theophilus," Luke says. "Mary had Jesus pretty young, so she must be around ninety."

"And healthy when I saw her last."

The two men rid themselves of their traveling packs and the horse. Luke picks up his writing supplies in his leather shoulder pouch for one side, and another leather shoulder pouch with medical supplies in it for his other side.

"I'm ready."

They walk down three blocks, then turn and go another block until they arrive at the house. The gate is simple wood, unadorned, but sturdy. They knock on it. John answers it himself.

"Yes, who is it?" he asks as he opens it. "Oh, it's you, Timothy. Did you have a good trip to see Paul?"

Timothy is silent.

"Oh. I see. Another one gone. One by one. Well, we shall all be together again someday. Come on in. Let us not talk out in the street. And who is your friend? Let me guess. You are Luke? I heard the two of you looked almost like twins. Other than red-haired with green eyes, and yellow-haired with blue eyes, you do look remarkably alike."

"Who do we have here?"

A little lady walks into the courtyard. Her gray hair is wispy and thin, her checks are almost hollow, and she walks with a slight gait. She has a twinkle in her eye and a smile on her lips.

Mary holds out her thin hand with gnarly fingers, and Timothy holds out his open palm so she can lay her hand in it without pain.

"Mary, I would like you to meet my friend, Luke?" John says. "He was a companion to Paul and took care of him after all those years of being beaten on."

"Took care of Paul, you say? But not anymore," she says, looking up into Luke's sad eyes. "Oh, I am sorry."

"Mother, I have a nice cushion for you on this bench by the wall," John says. "You can just lean back and tell Luke whatever he wants to know for his book."

"Yes, I understand you are going to write a book about my son. I am glad you are talking with eyewitnesses. There are too many stories going around about him already that just are not true. He never talked when he was a baby or performed miracles as a child. Such nonsense," she says, flipping her hand at the wrist for emphasis.

Timothy walks Mary over to the wide bench and sits next to her.

Luke pulls out his writing supplies and sets them on a table just right for him.

"I need you to start at the beginning, ma'am."

Mary leans back and closes her eyes. "It started with the angel. Did you ever see an angel? I never had. My, I was frightened. But he was patient and explained that I was going to bear the Son of God miraculously.

"He told me I should go see my elderly cousin Elizabeth who was also miraculously pregnant with John who you probably know of as John the Baptist. My parents gave me permission to go see her.

"She lived in a little country village out from Jerusalem where her husband, Zechariah, served as a priest. They were such fine people."

Mary opens her eyes and raises six thin fingers.

"She was six months along when I arrived. I stayed three months, long enough to see her miracle baby born. Then I went home. In a way, I dreaded it because I was so afraid I would lose my Joseph."

Mary closes her eyes again and leans back.

"But God sent an angel to explain to him that I was pregnant miraculously. So, we had a hurry-up wedding. About the time Jesus was due to be born, everyone was ordered to go to their ancestral home for a census. Both of us having descended from David, we had to go to the other end of the country."

Mary opens her eyes and looks at Timothy. "We almost didn't make it. I thought I was going to have my baby on the road. But we did make it, and I ended up," Mary giggles, "having him in a barn. Well, that was all right with me. No gawking people in that overcrowded town."

"So, how long did you keep your baby a secret?" Luke asks.

"Not long," Mary says in a sing-song voice. "In the middle of the night, here they came."

"Who?"

"Why the shepherds, of course. The angel who appeared to me came down and brought his friends, and they all announced the birth of my baby to the shepherds out in the field. The men couldn't wait to see him, so arrived in the middle of the night.

"Well, it turns out they asked at all the taverns in town and no one knew of a baby born that night. I guess if they had, we would have had a barn full of ale drinkers," she says with a grin.

"What about the priests at the temple?" Luke asks. "Didn't Zechariah tell them about it? He was one of their priests."

"He did, but they didn't believe him. Or perhaps they did not want to believe him. However, not all disbelieved. Eight days later, we went to the temple to dedicate Jesus to God as the first-born.

"While we were there, an old man who worked at the temple but wasn't a priest found us. His name was Simeon. He told us God had informed him he wouldn't die before my baby was born. He took baby Jesus into his frail arms and blessed him, but warned me that he would bring both love and heartache to me. How right he was...."

Mary's voice ebbs, and she becomes quiet. The men wait.

"Luke," Timothy says, "Mary and Joseph took their baby to the temple in order to fulfill one of the Laws of Moses for our people."

"Okay. Now I understand."

"Well," Mary continues, her eyes sparkling again, there was also a very old lady at the temple. At least to me she was, I being only about fifteen years old and she being about the same age that I am now. Her name was Anna. I will never forget her. I heard she passed on not long after our visit to the temple."

"Mary, let's stop for a while," John says, re-entering the courtyard. "Here is a cup of milk. Would you like to take a few sips?"

"Oh, John, you spoil me, just like you spoiled my sister." She turns to Luke. "My sister, Salome, was three years younger than me. She passed on about five years ago. I do miss her."

"So, she was John's mother," Luke says.

"That's right." She takes another sip of milk. "Oh, my. We are so rude. John, come give a glass of milk to our guests."

"I'm not sure..."

"By all means," Luke says, interrupting Timothy. "Milk is good for everyone. Thank you."

Luke takes a sip of milk. "So, what happened after you took care of your ceremony at the temple?"

"Well, some other things happened that I do not want to talk about right now," she says, her voice drifting off again.

"So, anyway," she says, brightening, "we ended up back in Nazareth where Jesus grew up. He was such a fine boy. He grew so fast, he was taller than some of the other boys in the synagogue school. And smart? Yes, smart. And do you know what? I always suspected he could read people's minds. He always seemed to be answering questions before they were asked."

Mary claps her hands together and smiles. "It seems funny now, but it wasn't so funny then."

"What's that?" Luke asks with a smile.

"We went to the temple every year for the Passover. Timothy, does Luke understand the Passover?"

"Yes, I explained it to him."

"Good. So, anyway, Joseph and I went to the Passover in Jerusalem every year, but never took our children. We thought King Herod was dangerous. But after he died and Archelaus was waiting for Caesar to confirm his kingship, he turned meaner than his father. When Jesus was eleven, Archelaus ordered thousands killed right there in the temple. What if Jesus had been there?

"Well, that is the sad part. But the happy part is that Caesar exiled Archelaus and sent a Roman to rule us. I hate to say it, but things calmed down after that, and we finally took our children to Jerusalem for Passover when Jesus was twelve.

"How exciting it was to have our whole family together. Plus, that is the first time Jesus and his cousin, John, met. They became inseparable. Elizabeth and I were so happy about that," Mary says, clapping her hands again.

"When the feast was over, we headed home in a caravan of other families from Nazareth. Jesus had always been so responsible, we assumed he was with some of the neighbors. It wasn't until we stopped for the night we realized we had left Jesus behind."

"I was rather independent like that at his age," Timothy says with a large grin. "I got in trouble more than once. I assume you found Jesus. Did he get in trouble?"

"It was so strange," Mary says. "It wasn't until the third day of searching for him that we thought to look in the temple. And there he was. Do you know what he told us? It really jarred me."

"What did Jesus tell you?" Luke asks, laying down his pen and touching Mary's hand.

"He told me he was taking care of things for his father. He knew. By the time he was twelve, he knew who he was." Mary's voice drifts off again.

"I'm a little tired," Mary says. "I shall go rest for a while now."

The men rise in respect as Mary shuffles to her room.

"Would you like me to fill you in on the beginnings?" John asks, seating himself where his aunt had been. "You know—John the Baptist as they called him? I am John's cousin, you know, and even named after him."

"Certainly," Luke says, bringing out a new parchment from his leather shoulder pouch.

"My aunt already told you about John's miraculous birth."

"I heard he dressed like a wild man and lived in the desert."

"Not at first. His father, Zechariah, was a priest, so he inherited the office."

"Uh, and when was that exactly?" Luke asks. "I mean, who was ruling then?"

"Tiberius was Caesar, and Pontius Pilate was governor of Judea, the province where Jerusalem is. Herod Antipas was governor of Galilee, the province where we all lived. Let me see now. Oh, Herod Philip was governor of Iturea and Trachonitis, Lysanias was governor of Abilene, and Annas and Caiaphas shared the high priesthood of the Jews. Does that cover them all, or do you need more? I just don't think I can remember any more of them."

"That's fine. Good," Luke says. "Now, you were saying..."

"The reason John began dressing as he did is that it was common in the old days for prophets to dress in animal skins. Elijah was the first prophet to dress like that, and in fact, a lot of people called John Elijah. Oh, you don't know who Elijah was, do you? Timothy. Can you tell him later?"

"No problem," Timothy says. "But, since I've heard all this before, I'm going to leave now. Give my love to your aunt when she rises from her nap." Timothy leaves.

"So, anyway, John the Baptist kept telling people to change their ways because the Kingdom of God was about to begin, and they needed to be on the good side of God when it happened."

"Did very many people believe him?"

"A lot did and were baptized as a form of cleansing themselves. Then Jesus came to him to be baptized. An amazing thing happened then. God's Spirit descended on Jesus' shoulder like a dove, and God actually spoke out of heaven, announcing who Jesus was: 'You are my beloved Son,' he said."

"God actually spoke?"

"It has seldom happened in the history of the world, but he spoke this time. I was there, and I heard it.

"So now, it was time for Jesus to begin the Kingdom of God. He went out into the desert to be alone and plan. Satan tempted him with all kinds of evil ways to introduce his kingdom to the world. Jesus rejected them all, worked out his own plan, and returned to civilization."

"One thing I forgot to tell you about John. He was outspoken and condemned Herod Antipas for marrying his brother, Herod Philip's wife. That was his undoing. He was beheaded over it."

John waits a few moments as Luke catches up with him, his pen flying.

"Okay, I'm ready now."

John rises and walks toward a doorway. "Did you have a good nap, Aunt Mary?"

"Oh, how wonderful," Mary says to Luke. "You are still here. There are some things I forgot to tell you if you are interested."

"Indeed, I am. Just whatever you want to tell me."

"When Jesus was a boy in Nazareth," she begins, her hands folded primly in her lap, leaning forward, and looking off into the distance, "most people liked him. But, he was so smart, some of the children were jealous of him. So, when he got grown and tried to preach in Nazareth, the jealous ones were also grown, and they tried to kill him."

Mary looks at Luke, and he puts down his pen. "Luke, why are people like that?"

He does not answer. He looks in Mary's eyes, and it is enough.

"Oh, would you like to see his genealogy?" she says, perking up and with the gleam back in her eye.

"Your son, James, gave it to me in Jerusalem."

"Good. I wish he'd come see me sometimes. Jude, Simon, and Joseph Junior too. They're all scattered."

"Yes, ma'am."

"Oh, well then, I guess the only thing left to tell you about is..." She hugs herself, leans forward, and rocks. "Well, you know."

"Yes," Luke whispers. "Tell me about it, as only a mother can."

"Even as a boy, he always knew—about the end, you know. He knew about the cross and everything else. I used to hear him cry at night sometimes, even up in his twenties, asking God to not make him go through it. I refused to believe it until it really happened.

"Most of the people loved Jesus, and he loved them back," she says with a brief smile. "Sometimes he said what the people were thinking and were too afraid to say out loud—how hypocritical their leaders were—and the commoners loved him for that too. Of course, it cost him his life.

"The Sanhedrin hated him because they were afraid of him. But I think Pilate liked him—admired his audaciousness, you know. Herod Antipas had mixed feelings about him. But the bad ones finally won.

"They beat him, you know. I was outside the barracks and heard his cries and their laughter. All I could do is pray that God would give him some of my strength and give me some of his pain."

She weeps. Luke waits. John kneels in front of her and takes her feeble hands in his own.

Mary dabs her eyes with a handkerchief and takes a deep breath. "Did you know, Luke, on the way to his execution, he saw me and the other women who had helped him, and stopped to encourage us. He never asked us to feel sorry for him. Not once.

"When they put the nails in him, I wished his hands were mine. I wished his pain was mine. I just wished …

"They made fun of him, you know. They said the same thing Satan was always telling to him—IF you are the Son of God… But he forgave them. He was so forgiving." She takes a breath and sighs.

"Then, he was gone. I couldn't eat. Couldn't sleep. Could hardly breathe…

"Three days later, Mary from Magdala came running to me at the home of the third Mary, John Mark's mother, and told me he was back." She looks over at Luke. She laughs an old woman's faltering laugh. "He was back, and no one could ever take him from me again."

"Yes, ma'am."

"My daughters had understood who he was early on, not my jealous sons. But he appeared to them, and together we convinced them their half-brother was God walking on earth in that body…

"He went back to heaven, you know. And I shall see my son again after all these sixty years. And do you know what? I shall worship him."

Silence. Luke looks over at John, who has by now moved to sit on the bench with Mary.

John smiles at Luke. "Sometimes people around here in Ephesus want to worship her, and you should see her pounce on them!" he says, laughing. "Don't you, Aunt Mary?"

"They'd better not worship me, or I will hit them over the head with…with something."

"Well, I guess I need to be going now," Luke says, putting his writing equipment away in his shoulder bag. "Is there anything I can do for you, Mary? I'm a physician too."

"No, no. Don't you go bothering with me. I'm as healthy as they come. I have no complaints. No complaints."

"May I?" Luke asks.

Mary smiles. "Yes, you may." She stands.

Luke steps forward and embraces the mother of his

Lord. She comes halfway up his chest. She snuggles in. He puts one hand on the back of her head with the wispy gray hair, and kisses it."

34 ~ AND BEYOND

*L*uke is astride Thor and headed east on the broad Roman road. He passes Magnesia, Laodicea, Colossae, and Apamea. It has been a long day. He stops at a *mille* marker and puts up the leather tent made for him by Aquila and Priscilla back in Ephesus.

That night Luke, before going to sleep, remembers back. Back to Paul and Timothy. Back to Theophilus. Back to his boyhood so long ago. All worlds he has now left. He remembers his father's song and needs, once again, to sing it.

> *Tho I vander long avay*
> *Over all da mounts und seas*
> *To da end uv da verld,*
> *I vill alvays tink uv home*
> *Und keep you in my heart*
> *Til I hold you once again.*

The following day he rides on to Antioch in the province of Pisidia, where he spends his second night. Titus is no longer there. He goes to a market and looks around for weavers and tailors. He finds what he is looking for.

"Are you Thracian?"

"Yes, sir."

"I would like two of your capes," Luke says.

"Two of them? You must be heading for the mountains."

"Oh, and I want that leather tunic, a pair of those high

leather boots. And that leather hat."

The next morning, Luke continues east but stays slightly north to avoid the Taurus Mountains as long as he can. That night he camps near Tomissa near the northern watershed of the Euphrates River in the province of Cappadocia.

He rises the following morning, ready to enter Armenia, a kingdom he knows has been fought over by the Parthians and Romans for centuries. *So ole Nero has finally given in and agreed for Tiridates to be king. Tiridates has already been king thirteen years. Ha. Ha.*

Luke can no longer avoid the mountains. He enters the far eastern side of the Taurus Range. The wind picks up. He pulls his robe tighter around him and raises the hood. It is not enough. He stops and pulls out his leather tunic and one of the Thracian capes he had purchased in Antioch, and puts on the long leather boots and leather hat.

He recognizes the forested mountains all around him now and knows he is near the Royal Road he had taken thirty years earlier from the Black Sea to spy out Parthia.

"Oh, Rashah, how I miss you," he whispers as Thor works his way up the foothills of the range. *And father, why did you have to die too? Both of you taken from me forever right after I found you. It isn't fair.*

He grits his teeth and raises his eyes. "Oh, God, why did you let it happen?" he shouts, his voice echoing between heaven and earth.

He sees along the road a *mille* marker. Tigranocerta is a few *milles* farther and near the headwaters of the Tigris River. He enters the city's western gate, dismounts from Thor, and stops at the market.

"Do you happen to know a couple of dark-haired men named Thaddeus and Nathaniel?"

"Sorry, never heard of them."

Luke works his way through the market. He goes to the forum and asks government officials.

"Do you happen to have heard of a couple of dark-haired men named Thaddeus and Nathaniel?"

"Sorry. I don't recall either name."

Luke works his way around the city for three hours.

"Why don't you try Bitlis over on the Salt Lake, or the Dead Lake as some people call it?" the guard at the east gate says. "Maybe your friends are there."

Remounting, Luke heads higher up into the Ararat Mountain Range. The wind steadily picks up and grows colder. With steady foot, Thor moves on. Toward the end of the day, Luke nears Bitlis. Far below the city, he sees the Great Salt Lake.

Luke stops and puts up his leather tent. His body heat keeps it warm inside. But when he comes out the next morning, snow is on the ground.

He and Thor go on into the city and to the market.

"Do you know two dark-haired men named Thaddeus and Nathaniel?"

"No, I don't. Maybe someone else knows."

"Have you heard about two dark-haired men named Thaddeus and Nathaniel?"

"Never heard of them. Try someone else."

Luke works his way through the city market, the forum, and some of the houses.

"Maybe they're up in Erzurum," someone says. "It's a day's ride and cold up there. I see you're wearing leather. Good. Better buy some bands to wrap your fingers in. You'll need them too."

"Doesn't look like the apostles are here either," Luke tells Thor.

It is noon when Luke rides out through the north gate. The mountains rise higher and steeper. The wind and snow blow in his face, and he keeps his head lowered. They climb higher.

"Steady there, Thor," he says. "Let me know when it gets to be too much for you." *That's a foolish thing to say. Thor was bred for the mountains, whether they be around the Nordic Sea, the Black Sea, or this Salt Sea.* He smiles to himself.

The road becomes slippery as it rises higher into the mountains. The wind whistles and howls through the forests around him. Thor stops.

Luke looks around. The snow comes down in larger flakes so close together, and with such wind force, he strains to distinguish the green trees alongside the road from the ground cover of snow now growing deeper. He dismounts and leads Thor by his reins, watching closely for turns in the road as it winds its way up even higher.

He realizes he does not know where he is. He cannot tell one side of him from the other side. He cannot tell up from down. Surrounded by nothing but white, Luke stops dead.

"Thor, you and I are going to have to lie down right where we are and take it like men." Luke puts an arm over Thor's strong neck and tugs at the reins in the other hand. "Come on, Thor, you can do it. Down. Down Thor. Bend your knees."

Luke continues to lean on his horse and tell him what to do, though he wonders if the horse hears anything other than the wind howling around them. He reaches down and taps on the horse's knees, still pulling down with the reins. "Come on big fellow. Down, Thor. Down."

Thor kneels. "That's right. Down the rest of the way. You can do it." Luke leans on the horse's back and neck.

The horse is down. Luke lowers himself on the side of Thor with the least amount of wind, though it is not always so with the wind constantly shifting. He scoots down next to the animal, puts an arm over his big neck, and lets the wind sing him to sleep.

Luke opens his eyes. The sky is a deep blue, and the snow has both man and beast nearly buried in it. Thor neighs, shakes his head, and stands, shaking the snow off the rest of his coal-black body.

"We made it, friend," Luke says. He looks around again. "But do you see the road anywhere? And where are the drop-offs? Now what? Well, I suppose we can eat while we think. I sure hope the last of the cheese did not freeze."

Luke opens the flap of the bag on Thor, feels around, and brings his hand out with the cheese.

"Here is some for you and some for me. I am nearly out of barley, but here is a hand full. Maybe I can buy some for you in Erzurum, where ever that is."

Luke takes Thor's reins and goes one step along what he believes to be the road. Then another step. One at a time. Testing first with the toes. A little at a time.

Luke stops. He listens. Men's voices. Laughter.

"Over here!" Luke shouts. "Over here!"

Two men approach. "Shhh. We don't want to start an avalanche, do we?" one of them says in a loud whisper and coming into view.

"Just follow us now. You'll be fine."

Luke smiles and walks forward, still one hesitant step at a time. He reaches the strangers who then turn and follow their own footsteps to a small hut beside the road.

"You'll have to bring the horse in for a while. We don't have a stable. The wind is still strong. Probably be a good idea."

Luke follows the men inside and leads Thor with him. There is a fire on the floor to one side. Luke leads Thor to the other side, takes some barley out of a small bundle on his horse's back, and feeds it to him. One of the strangers brings a pail of water for him.

"Come sit and warm yourself, friend," the other stranger says. "This is Thaddeus. I am Nathaniel."

"Who?" Luke asks, stopping in his tracks, his eyes wide.

"This is Thaddeus, and I am Nathaniel."

"Thank you, Lord Jesus," Luke shouts, raising his arms in the air.

"Who did you say?"

"I said thank you, Lord Jesus. I am Luke," he says, his eyes glistening and a broad grin on his face, "a friend of the apostle Paul. I have been looking for you."

"Well, have a seat by the fire," Nathaniel says, "and tell us what you are doing up here."

Nathaniel is short, with large eyes and big ears. His hair has receded significantly, leaving only whitish-gray around the fringes.

"I'll bet you're hungry," Thaddeus says. "Here's something hot to drink first. How are your fingers? We can put them in cool water to unfreeze them."

Thaddeus is of medium height with long legs and black hair that is well oiled.

Luke unwraps his fingers and sees they have turned blue. "Well, at least they aren't black yet. Yes, cool water would be fine."

"Wait, we need to check your toes, too," Nathaniel says. "Let me get these long boots off you."

"Here is some water in a couple bowls for your feet," Thaddeus says. "You've got such big feet, only your toes will fit. But that is good enough."

Nathaniel sits across from Luke. "So why in the world are you looking for us?"

"I promised someone I would write a book about the life of our Lord Jesus on earth. I went to Jerusalem, where I interviewed a few people, including James, his brother, and a few others. Then to Rome, where I interviewed some more."

"You do not look Jewish. Not with that yellow hair. What were you doing in Jerusalem?"

"Paul took several people from Greece and Anatolia with him to donate money for the poor Christians in Jerusalem."

"Did you say, Paul?"

"Yes, I served as his physician the last few years."

"Last?"

"Yes, he is gone from us now. It happened in a dungeon in Rome about a month ago."

Nathaniel and Thaddeus shake their heads. "We're sorry. First, it was James, then Stephen, and now Paul. Are there any others gone now?"

"Maybe you heard of Barnabas."

"Of course."

"He was stoned to death."

Silence for a moment.

"I went to Ephesus and interviewed Mary and John. And now, I am here to interview you. As soon as my hands are sufficiently thawed, I need you to tell me what you remember about Jesus' activities and speeches so I can write them down. Can you do that for me?"

"You came all this way to find and interview us?"

"You're just the first. I plan to find all Jesus' apostles."

"We would be delighted. We tell the story of Jesus every chance we get anyway."

Luke takes his hands and toes out of the water. "If you have some heated water, I believe I could handle it now. Oh, and if you would look in the bag on Thor..."

"Oh, we forgot to take the load off your horse," Thaddeus says, laughing. He puts a hand full of dried corn up to Thor's mouth, and it is happily consumed. "This should make up for it," he says. "Now, in this bag?"

"Yes. Pour everything out. But be careful. I have some vials that could spill. They have oil in them. The small pouches have herbs in them. They are labeled. Open the one with mandrake in it. Then, would you be so kind as to make some tea for me? The pain of thawing is rather challenging to me right now."

"Perhaps one of us could do the writing for you. We have all day to talk and for you to thaw your hands."

"Thank you," Luke says.

"I was always fascinated by his stories," Nathaniel says. "Thaddeus, can you write while I talk?

"For example, Jesus said, a man is wise if he builds his house on a rock, but foolish if he builds it on sand. Then, when the rain comes, the house on the rock will still stand, while the house on the sand will fall. He was talking about what we build our lives on."

"Yes, yes, I see it," Luke says, taking his hands out of the water long enough to hold a mug between his two palms, and take a sip. "Of course. Good. Good."

"Uh, here's another one. Jesus said a man went out to plant seed. He apparently did not have much land, so planted it everywhere he could. Some he planted on a path. Some he planted among rocks. Some he planted among thorns. Some he planted on good soil. Now, guess what he meant by that. Let me give you a hint: The seeds are the word of God planted in hearts. Now, you take it from there."

Luke grins. "Uh, well, the seed he planted on the path would just be trampled on and never given a chance to grow.

It would just sit there and wait for birds to come along and eat it."

"Yes, and the birds taking the seed away are like Satan taking it out of our heart if he let him.," Nathaniel says. "Now, what are rocky hearts?"

"Well, uh, the seed might grow in it briefly, but it could never take root."

"Right again. What do you think the thorny hearts are?"

Luke wrinkles his brow. "Well, thorns choke the good seed. I suppose such hearts would be daily activities choking out the Word of God, so a person isn't interested very long."

"And the last one? The good soil?"

"'That's easy. It's the good and honest heart that, after testing what he is told, believes it and lives it. That's it, isn't it?" Luke says happily.

"Okay, my turn," Thaddeus says. "You do the writing now, Nathaniel." The men switch seats.

"It must have been fun being around Jesus," Luke says.

"Well, sometimes it wasn't, but other times it was. Now this story is about a lamp."

"Okay. What did the lamp do?" Luke asks with a large grin.

"The lamp was put inside a jar."

"It would go out. How irrational."

"What if the lamp was put under a bed?"

"Of course. It would go out too," Luke says with mocking chagrin.

"So, guess what you think Jesus really meant," Thaddeus says.

"Hmmm. If the lamp represents our hearts, our love would go out if we didn't show it. And if it represents our actions," Luke says, tipping his head back and forth, "the good we do would no longer be seen by mankind. Is that what he meant?"

"You have it, Luke.

"Okay now, one time, Jesus was trying to recruit enough men to cover all the places he had preached so they could reinforce his teachings, and he could follow up. He asked one man to go with him, who said he needed bury his father. Jesus replied that the dead should bury their own dead. What did he mean?"

Luke puts his chin in his hand. "Well, if his father had already died, he wouldn't be out listening to speeches, he'd be at the funeral. So, I guess the father hadn't died yet. It sounds like the man was using his father as an excuse. So Jesus was saying some people are dead spiritually, and can bury others who are dead spiritually while those alive spiritually are out helping others be alive spiritually. Am I not right? Brilliant. Just brilliant."

"And don't forget what Jesus said about plowing," Nathaniel says, looking up from his writing.

"Yes. Yes. Another man Jesus was trying to recruit said he wanted to go back and say good-bye to his family," Thaddeus continues. "Jesus said he had already put his hand to the plow, so why go back. What did he mean?"

"Wellll," Luke begins, his eyes rolling toward the ceiling, "I think he meant the man had already committed himself to helping Jesus before he left home, so why would he want to go back and make the commitment a second time."

"Good. Now, one more and we need to eat. How are your fingers and toes doing, Luke?"

"A little at a time, they are thawing. I'm pretty sure there won't be any permanent damage. Now tell me your next—what did you call it—parable. This is marvelous."

"There was a man traveling on a mountain road. Some robbers attacked him, stripped him, took everything he had, and left him for dead. A priest happened along, saw him, but passed on the other side of the road and kept going. Later, a temple aide saw him and did the same thing. Finally, a half breed that everyone hated saw him. The half breed stopped and treated his wounds, took him to an inn, and paid the innkeeper extra money to take care of him. Which one was being neighborly?"

"That's easy," Luke says. "The half breed."

"Let's eat," Nathaniel says. "I have had this pot of stew

over the fire all morning. Can you hold a spoon, Luke? Of course, you can't. I'll put yours in a mug so you can drink it."

Nathaniel moves the parchment out of the way and sets two bowls and a mug on the table. Luke sees the two men close their eyes, so he does too.

"Thank you, Lord Jesus, for keeping Luke alive during this early winter storm. Keep him safe to write about your life on earth. And thank you for this stew, and this little hut that keeps us warm, and for Luke's mighty horse. Amen."

"What kind of horse do you have?" Thaddeus asks. "He is a magnificent animal."

"He is a Nordic Frisian. The people in my homeland of Frisia breed them."

"I don't think I have ever seen one like it before. No wonder he adjusted so well to our snow."

"Uh, I hate to rush you, but I am anxious to hear more of Jesus' stories."

"Of course, you are," Nathaniel says. "We have spoken of them many times and have forgotten how exciting they can be hearing them the first time."

The table is cleared off, and Luke's parchment is spread out on it again.

"One time, Jesus said there was a shepherd with one hundred sheep, but one wandered away," Nathaniel says. "He left the ninety-nine and went after the one lost sheep. He came home with the sheep and told all his neighbors, 'Rejoice with me. I have found my sheep that was lost.' Then Jesus told the meaning: There will be more rejoicing in heaven over one sinner who repents, than all the self-righteous ones who think they are saved."

"Fascinating," Luke says, taking another sip of his stew. "Absolutely fascinating."

"Here is another one with the same meaning. He said a woman had ten silver coins, but lost one of them. She lit a lamp and swept the house, searching in every corner and under everything. Finally, she found it, and told her neighbors, 'Rejoice with me. I have found my coin that was lost.' Again he explained the rejoicing in heaven over a single sinner who repents."

Thaddeus interrupts.

"Your horse is used to cold weather. He has thawed out, and I'll bet he would be happier out in the sunshine. Let me tie him up outside. Then when I come back in, I'll tell the next story, and Nathaniel will write them as I talk. Isn't that right, Nathaniel?" Thaddeus says with a wink.

As he opens the door and guides the horse outside, they hear a neigh, and they laugh. "He's happy now," Luke says.

Thaddeus comes back in with a pail of snow, sets it by the fire, and sits back down across from Luke. "This next parable is very touching.

"A man had two sons. The older one who was going to inherit the house and farm always helped their father. But the younger son told their father he wanted his smaller portion of the inheritance right then so he could go out and enjoy it.

"He went far away and spent his money on prostitutes and wild living. But a famine hit the country he was in, and eventually, there was no more money. He got a job feeding pigs.

"One day he woke up and said to himself, 'My father's servants eat better than I do.' So he went home, and he was so embarrassed and sorry over what he had done, he told their father to just make him a servant because he was no longer worthy to be his son. So, what do you suppose the father did?"

"Forgave him, of course," Luke says.

"More than that."

"More?"

"He had a feast for him and told him to invite all his friends. The father kept saying, 'My son was lost and is found. My son was dead and is alive.'"

"He sounds like a good father," Luke says.

"But there's more. His older brother got mad because he never forsook their father and did all those bad things, but their father never rewarded him with a feast.' He was jealous that their father still loved his sinful younger brother."

"That is an amazing story. Yes, I can understand what he was saying," Luke says. "I have seen men go off to war and all come back but one. When the one straggled in later, there was more celebrating over the one than all the others who returned on time. The other soldiers did not get mad because of it. And you say that even the angels in heaven rejoice with us? Amazing. Christianity is so refreshingly good."

"Here is another one.," Thaddeus says. "There was a judge who did not like or respect God or anyone else. A widow begged him to intervene for her, but he didn't care what happened to her. So she started following him around, begging for his help. Finally, he helped her just to get her to quit bothering him."

"It doesn't make sense for the judge to represent God," Luke says, his eyes squinting.

"That's the point. If unloving people will do something for others sometimes, can you imagine how much a loving God will do for us?"

"I like it," Luke declares. "That is so true. The one real God is not like those fake gods who either tolerate us or throw thunderbolts down on us, so to speak."

"Now, try this one. There was a really religious man who always prayed, 'Thank you that I am able to be so good.' There was also a man who cheated people, and he prayed, 'Forgive me, I am a sinner.' What do you think this story means, Luke?"

"Well, I guess it means God forgives even the worst sinner but doesn't forgive someone who refuses to admit any of his sins. Very interesting," Luke says. "I never thought of it that way. Very interesting, indeed."

"Tell Luke the parable of the vine-growers," Nathaniel says, laying his pen down.

"You tell it. I'll take over writing again. I write better than you anyway," Thaddeus says, punching his friend in the shoulder as they pass each other.

Luke laughs. "Are you sure you two are apostles?"

"Of course we are," Nathaniel says. "We'll just give you

a chance to watch us at work teaching the pagans around here when you are thawed out. But, in the meantime, you are our project."

"Here's the next one. Jesus loved telling stories. There was a vineyard owner who sent his slave to his vineyard to get the grapes. The vine keepers beat the slave and sent him away with nothing. The owner sent another slave, and they did the same thing. And a third slave. Finally, the vineyard owner sent his own son, thinking they would listen to him. But they killed the only heir in the hopes they would inherit the vineyard. What do you think the owner of the vineyard did?"

"That's terrible. The owner of the vineyard either reported them to the authorities or took vengeance on them himself." Luke pauses. "Was Jesus saying something about people killing the Son of God?"

"Sadly, yes," Nathaniel says.

"Mary said he knew all along they would kill him."

"Yes, he knew all along."

35 ~ MORE MOUNTAINS

"Good morning, Luke. Did you sleep well?" Nathaniel asks.

"A lot better than that night out in the snow."

"Well, today, we plan to take you on into the city and show you our work," Thaddeus says. "We have a fine new congregation in Erzurum. We started another congregation in Babert, a little farther north of there.

"Friends, I need to move on," Luke says. "I feel something driving me. Perhaps I was around Paul too long. That's the way he was. Always looking forward to the next place. I just need to go."

"Where to now?" Nathaniel asks.

"Scythia. I heard Andrew is there."

"You know you are going to have to go into more mountains, then the other side of the Caspian Sea and desert."

"Yes, I know. I'm surrounded by mountains."

"And that means you are going to have to go to Erzurum after all," Thaddeus says with a gleam in his eye. "We want you to meet some of our Christians. It will encourage them to meet you since you, too, stopped worshipping idols to worship Jesus."

"Okay, you win," Luke says, smiling.

Since the two apostles do not have horses, Luke leads his as they walk into the city of Erzurum. They take Luke to a merchant who specializes in dried meats and is also a Christian.

"You are going to need enough to last you two weeks,"

the merchant says. "Crossing the Caucasus Mountain Ranges, a sea, and into a desert—well, you will have to be prepared. May our Jesus keep you protected."

Thaddeus and Nathaniel take Luke to several other merchants and craftsmen who are Christians.

"This is fascinating," Luke says. "They do not know me, but all say they will pray or me. Fascinating."

Last, they take him to a stable where Luke buys enough barley to keep Thor happy and healthy. He presses it down, binds it tight, and ties it to Thor's rump.

"Now, when you leave here, you will head across the Ararat Range to Artashat, then Yerevan," Nathaniel explains. "Then be ready to descend fast on the other side. Your port on the Caspian is very low. Don't be shocked. You will go from cold to hot fast."

With that, the men kneel by the side of the road and pray for Luke's safety.

Luke mounts Thor and resumes his journey to find Jesus' apostles and learn more from the all-important eyewitnesses. "Next is Andrew somewhere in Scythia. That's a big place," he says.

As he works his way up farther into the Ararat Mountains, he notices two peaks ahead, completely covered in snow. *They said the ship Noah and his family were in landed in these mountains. Must have been that tallest peak, the one that would have stuck out of the water first.*

He and Thor continue east.

Did Noah and his family come down out of the mountain to where I am right now, or the other side where the Caspian Sea is?

What was it like for them? Being the only ones left in the world? Were they lonely? With the whole world to choose from for their land, how did they choose? Was it as exciting for them to have the best land with no one to compare with?

Now and then, Luke stops and lets Thor rest, giving him a bite of barley and a drink from one of the many springs they cross on their way across the range. He is surprised he has seen so few people on the road with him. *Where is everyone?*

By the end of the first day, the peaks are to the north of where he sets up camp. "Sure hope it doesn't snow this time," he tells Thor.

At dawn, Luke gets an early start. With the sun straight ahead of him, he shades his eyes with one hand. He arranges his hood so he cannot see except down, and lets the horse finds his own way.

Luke finds himself looking around and behind him. "What was that?" he finally says aloud. *Oh, nothing.*

Once again, Luke locks his knees, puts his chin on his chest, and nods off to sleep.

Thor shakes his head back and forth and wakes his rider. Luke pats the side of Thor's neck. "Calm down, ole boy. We're up here alone. Don't let the bears and wolves get to you. You're fine."

They reach the summit, then begin their descent. With the sun higher in the sky now, Luke relaxes and looks at his surroundings. Just more mountains.

Thor perks up his ears and points them one way and then another.

"What do you hear, ole boy? There's nothing out there to concern yourself with," Luke says. *I shall sing you a song. It always soothed me.*

Tho I vander long avay
Over all da mounts und seas
To da end uv da verld,
I vill alvays tink uv home
Und keep you in my heart
Til I hold you once again.

His father's song echoes from peak to peak and finally dies.

Silence. Everything around him silence. "Oh, my, Thor. Why am I singing this now? My father is dead and gone. Just like my Rashah. Dead and gone."

Thor neighs and shakes his head.

Luke laughs. "Well, it's true, friend. But I shall survive. Survive, if for no other reason, than to tell the story.

Oh, Jesus, how I wish I had met you in person."

Thor stomps his front legs and turns his head back and forth.

"Thor, what is wrong with you? Calm down. There is no one around but the two of us."

Thor stops, then starts again.

"Well, I guess you need a little rest."

Luke slips down off his horse, still holding the reins, and looks around.

"See. I told you there was nothing there. Nothing and no one. Well, I may as well walk a while and get some exercise."

An arrow finds its way into the ground beside Luke. Shocked, he looks in the direction from whence the arrow had come. Another one whizzes by.

He runs to the side of the road and ducks behind some high boulders. Another arrow. Then nothing.

Luke raises his head and calls out. "Hey, what are you doing? We're harmless."

Another arrow, but not aimed directly at him.

"What do you want?" he calls out.

No answer. Only another arrow.

How fast can you run, Thor? That's a dumb question. No one can outrun an arrow. Maybe they'll run out if we wait long enough.

Luke picks up a rock and tosses it over to one side. An arrow plunges into the ground next to it. He picks up another rock and throws it to the other side of him. Another arrow next to it.

"What do you want? Money?" he shouts.

An arrow flies over his head.

"Hey, I've got a couple of capes you can have. They're real warm, and, as long as the snow stays away, I doubt I will be needing them."

Staying stooped, he goes to a bag tied to Thor, looks inside, and pulls out the capes. He looks around the ground and sees a long stick. He attaches the capes to the stick and waves the stick above his head. Another arrow.

"Okay, then. Do you want food? Is that what you are

wanting?"

Luke pulls out half the dried meat and sets it on top of the boulder he is hiding behind. He leads Thor over to another boulder in which to hide behind.

"Come and get it," he shouts.

Another arrow. Luke glances at it. *What is there about that arrow?*

Luke decides to test the situation. As simultaneously as possible, he throws two rocks, one toward his left and one toward high right. When he does, a single arrow lands. He stares at it a moment. *No, it couldn't be.*

"So, there is just one of you," he shouts back. "Well, I only have two things left to offer to you—my horse, which you are not going to get, and money."

Luke pours out half his silver coins from his pouch and lays them on top of the boulder he is hiding behind.

"If that's what you want, then come get it."

Nothing this time. No arrows. *He is either out of arrows, or I have offered him what he wants.*

By now, the sun is low in the west. Luke stays behind the boulder until dark. Slowly, he walks Thor out from behind the boulder, and walks beside the road in the dirt rather than be heard on the cobblestones of the highway.

Thor is calm. *Whoever it was is either asleep or satisfied.* Luke slides back up onto Thor and breaks him into a lope. Once satisfied he has left danger behind, he slows Thor to a walk. He does not stop until daylight.

When the sun is full up, he looks down at the valley below. It is green and inviting. He sees beyond a sea larger than the Black Sea. He pulls over beside the road and sleeps only a while.

"Hey, mister," he hears. "Are you just inviting the robbers to take everything you own?" the stranger asks.

Luke looks up and sees a man on an Arabian headed the same direction he is.

"Huh?"

"If I were you, I would get out of these mountains as soon as possible. There are some desperate people living up here." The stranger resumes his own trip down the mountain.

By the end of the third day, Luke has guided sure-footed Thor down the steep side of the mountain. That night beside the Kura River, he sleeps in the plain. *We should be able to make it to Baku by mid-morning.*

Luke's prediction is correct. He looks around the harbor of Baku for a ship willing to take a horse. Finding one, he pays the fare and boards with Thor. Standing at the rail and looking back west, he sees the two peaks of the Ararat Mountains. *Goodbye, Noah,* he whispers.

It takes three more days for the ship to cross to the other side of the Caspian Sea. As they progress, the winds grow hotter. Realizing he will probably not need the leather tunic, hat or boots, he takes them out of his bag and walks around among the sailors.

"If you expect to be going through the mountains when your ship returns, I have a real deal for you. These will keep you warm in the fiercest wind and deepest snow."

With no takers, he waits, then tries again.

"I'll take them just to get you to shut up," one of the sailors says. "But, you only get half what you're asking."

When Luke returns to his horse, he adjusts the packs on his back. When he does, he notices some feathers on the broken end of an arrow. He looks at it. "Those feathers look familiar. Where have I seen them before?"

On the last day before landing on the other side of the Caspian, Luke counts his money. *I hope I don't run out before I can find Andrew.*

The ship lands at the oasis of a desert port. All Luke sees are camel caravans. No cities or even villages nearby.

"Well, Thor, I guess I'd better fill up my largest leather pouch with water for you. No telling where the next oasis will be. So, shall we go north or south, east or west?"

He stops a camel driver. "Which way should I go to find the nearest city?" he asks.

"North just grows lower, dryer and hotter. Go south. You will go higher, and it will be a little cooler. Not much, but a little cooler."

Luke gives the man a copper coin and thanks him. He

watches caravans move to the southeast and decides to follow one of them. The caravan is slow, so he walks beside Thor.

At dawn on the second day, Luke confirms where the first city will be, mounts Thor, and heads in that direction. As the sun is about to go down, he sees a city on a hill. He has reached Farava.

The following morning, he goes into the city and to the bazaar.

"I am looking for a dark-haired man named Andrew. Have you met him?"

"Not that I know of."

He goes to the next booth. "I am looking for a dark-haired man named Andrew. Have you seen him?"

"Not me."

He works his way through the bazaar. No one knows of anyone by the name of Andrew.

Luke buys a fresh supply of dried meat, dried fruit, and barley for Thor. He refills his and Thor's waterskins, and heads to the next city.

Maybe we can make it there before dark. He arrives just before the gates are closed, and goes inside.

"What city am I in?" he asks the guard.

"You are in Nisa."

Luke begins to work his way through the bazaar, always found near the city gates.

"I am looking for a man named Andrew. The name is probably foreign to you, so you might remember it. Do you?"

"Yes, it is odd sounding. But no, I have not heard it before."

"I am looking for a man named Andrew. Might you..."

"Never heard of him."

I've got to keep trying. But maybe I went in the wrong direction, Scythia is so large. Maybe I should have gone back to the Black Sea and north of there. What am I going to do? Keep trying. That's all I can do.

"Have you run into a man named Andrew?"

"Not here."

Luke wanders through the city, searching and trying

to reassure himself he is doing the right thing. Still, he searches. The answer is always the same—no.

The next morning, Luke goes to the south gate and asks where the next city is.

"If you turn left, you will run into Marv. If you go straight, you will run into Tejon."

'Well, Thor, which one shall we try next?"

Luke lets go of the reins, and Thor chooses.

"Then south it is," Luke says with a smile.

At the end of the day, they see an oasis in a valley. He approaches and sees there is a little settlement there. Nearly dark, he stops for the night.

The next morning at dawn, he finds a small bazaar and begins his usual inquiries.

"Have you met a man named Andrew?"

"Do you know a man named Andrew?"

"How about a Christian? Do you know any Christians?"

A man at a weaver's shop hears the word, Christian. "Are you a Christian?" the man asks Luke.

Luke grins broadly. "Yes, I am. Are you a Christian?"

"No. But there is a man on the other side of the caravan over there saying that word a lot."

Luke gives the man a copper coin and hurries in that direction. As he draws closer, he hears it—the word Christian.

A small crowd has gathered around the man. He uses the words, Jesus and Christian, several times, and Luke's hopes soar.

At the end of the speech, Luke walks up to the man. "Uh, sir. I am looking for a man named Andrew."

"Well, you have found him, friend. And you are?"

Andrew is short and slim. His hair has receded significantly, and there is a black patch around the lower part of his scalp.

Luke reaches out his hand, and Andrew takes it. "I am Luke, companion of the late apostle Paul.

"How long ago?" Luke asks.

"About a month ago. Well, a little longer than that

now."

"I am truly sorry. What a complicated man he was. Well, come to my camp with me. My wife and I are traveling around the country, telling people about Jesus. We were planning to go east in the morning, then head back north. So, what are you doing out here in the desert looking for me?"

As they walk, Luke explains his mission. They arrive at the camp, and Andrew introduces his wife to Luke. "Her name is Esther. It means star."

"That is a beautiful name," Luke says with his easy smile."

After they eat, they sit around a fire to stay warm as the cool night air moves in.

"What would you like to know about Jesus?" Andrew asks.

"Just anything you want to tell me," Luke says, his parchment on a small board on his lap.

"Well, my brother, Peter, and I had known Jesus a long time before he declared to people who he was and began working miracles.

"My best friend was Philip. We had a list of prophecies about the coming divine king and decided to see if we could find someone who might be fulfilling them.

"He and I had heard about John the Baptist preaching down near Jerusalem and decided to go down there to hear him. So I got permission from my father, Jonas, to be gone for a while, and Philip got permission from his father. We walked several days to get there.

When we arrived, John announced God's Lamb was there. We were overjoyed we had finally found him. We looked to see who it was and realized it was Jesus. That was confusing, to say the least, because I had known Jesus since we were boys. He was always a little different from the rest of us—smarter, you know.

"Philip and I talked a long time with Jesus and realized he was actually the one who had been predicted for so many thousands of years.

"The following day, when I went into town and was

over by the fish market, I actually saw my brother, Peter. 'What are you doing down here so far from home?' I asked him. He told me, and I told him he had to come with me to meet Jesus for himself. He did, and that was how it all started, at least for us. We went back north with him and stopped at a family wedding in Cana, and Jesus actually performed a miracle. Then we knew for sure Jesus was the predicted one.

"When we got back to Capernaum where Peter and I lived, Peter's mother-in-law was sick, and Jesus healed her. Then the whole neighborhood came, and he spent most of the night healing people."

"So, were you apostles at that time?" Luke asks.

"Not yet. But a little while later, Jesus rented a house in Capernaum, then contacted the twelve of us. He told us he wanted to train us to tell the world about him so they could be saved from hall. He didn't want anyone to go to hell."

"Is that when you agreed to go with him?" Luke asks.

"Yes. We agreed. Then he gave us the power to perform miracles so we could prove our words were God's words."

"That must have been the most amazing thing that ever happened to you."

"Yes, it was. But he warned us that it would come at a price. He told us we would be persecuted everywhere we went."

"And are you?"

"Yes. Every place I go, people are worshipping made-up gods. When I convince them there is only one real God, their priests come after me. I've been beaten more than once."

"So, Paul wasn't the only one."

"No. And I am convinced it is the way I will die."

Luke stays with Andrew and Esther for three days. Andrew tells his stories, and Luke writes them down.

"Some people say Jesus' apostles are ignorant, but you do not seem ignorant," Luke says on the third day.

"That was just their way of getting people to not pay attention to us. But we all do our preaching and healing and letter writing to make sure the congregations we begin stay true."

"You write them letters like Paul did?"

"I don't know about him, but yes, I do."

That evening, Luke puts away his writing supplies, double checks his medical supplies, and washes out his other tunic so he can wear it the next day.

"Are you going back to Berea now? You did say that is where you are from."

"No, I am going next to find Thomas. He is south of here, possibly in India or Parthia. I hear there have been some wars since I was there as a young man and things have changed.

"That's a big place to look," Andrew says.

"I found you, didn't I?"

"There are some wicked mountains and deserts down there."

"Yes, I know. I was in them twenty-five years ago."

36 ~ A RETURNING

*L*uke and Thor head south. "I think it is going to take us longer to find Thomas than any of the others," he tells his horse. "If we ever do find him. Where does India start, anyway? Too many border wars."

Back in his routine. One step at a time. Closer to what?

What if Theophilus has been killed by your enemies, Lord? Is he in danger? Am I in danger? Lord, keep me going. I must do this.

Luke works his way south just out of reach of the Torkastan Mountains, though he cannot avoid the foothills. After two days, he arrives at the Citadel of Herat on the Hari River.

At the bazaar, he asks around. The city having been founded and populated by Alexander the Great and his men, Luke speaks Greek.

"Have you seen a man named Thomas?"

"Not me."

"Do you know a man named Thomas?"

"Never heard of him."

"Have you heard a man talk about Jesus or Christians?"

"Who are they?"

Luke and Thor work their way out the south gate of the city. After another day of travel, they come to the Ferah River and the citadel by the same name.

To conserve what money he has left, Luke camps in his tent outside the gates. The nights are cold.

The next morning, he is inside the city and at the bazaar.

"I am looking for a man named Thomas. By any chance..."

"Sorry. Don't know anyone by that name."

"Have you heard anyone going around making speeches about someone named Jesus."

"No."

"Do you know anyone named Thomas?"

"No."

Out the south gate. Another day of travel.

At least I have Thor. It would take me forever to travel to all these cities on foot.

On and on he goes. "Lord, make it be the next town. Make Thomas be there. I need to talk to Thomas."

He comes to the Helmand River and knows there will be a city somewhere along its banks. He works his way up the shore until he sees it—Lashkar Gah.

I'm almost out of money. I may have to get a job if I don't find Thomas here.

After a night in his tent outside the city, he enters and begins his search. He goes to the bazaar, the forum, residential areas. No luck. Nothing. Thomas just is not here.

Discouraged now, he wanders through the streets, leading Thor by the reins. He watches all the people around him, talking to each other and laughing and yelling and crying and laughing again. He sees people greeting each other or doing business with each other or working together.

Since Paul has gone, I am lost. Don't feel that way. You are on a mission. But I have no one to really talk to. No one who really understands. If I only had my father. If I only had my Rashah. Oh, how I miss you, my love.

Luke goes back to the forum and asks around for anyone needing a good scribe, but finds no one. He goes back to the bazaar and approaches a man making and selling parchment.

"Sir, I am a very good scribe. Do you know anyone who would like to hire me, even temporarily?"

"There is another city not far from here that has a king

in it," he says. "Lots of government dealings. Maybe you can find work there."

"What king?" Luke asks.

"King Vima. He has been king now for five years. The city is Kandahar."

Luke's head reels. *How can I go there and torture myself? The place where my father died and my wife died. The place where I had everything, then lost everything. The place that was my heaven and then my hell. Not Kandahar.*

Luke leaves Lashkar Gah and sleeps that night on the other side of the river. Morning comes, and he finds himself on a road with more and more busy people. Important ones in gilded chariots. Frightening ones marching side by side in columns. Fine ladies behind curtains of floating litters.

Could one of them be my Rashah? Stop thinking that way. She died long ago.

He rides closer to the city. The city he does not want to be in. But the city he is drawn to. Like pressing on a wound to see if it still hurts.

He sees the bazaar just inside the gates. He looks around and realizes he does not remember where anything is. *Where is the palace? No, don't go to the palace. Stop torturing yourself. Remember your mission. Look for Thomas. Look for Thomas.*

"Sir, could you tell me if there is a man in your city named Thomas."

"Well, of course, I can. He is very respected."

"You can? He is?"

"Yes. He is directing the building of an addition to King Kadphises' palace."

"King Vima Kadphises?"

"Yes. Do you know him?"

"Who? Thomas? Not really. Well, I know of him. I have been looking for him."

"Is it bad news? I don't think the king wants him to be distracted. He has developed a temper since becoming king."

"No, it isn't bad news," Luke reassures the man. "Which way is the palace?"

"Just keep going up this street. You'll come to a statue

of his father..."

"Oh, yes. I remember... Uh, that is, thank you, sir."

As Luke walks up the street and sees the statue ahead of him, his heart races. *Stop that. They are not here. No father. No wife. Thomas. Remember your mission. It is Thomas you are looking for.*

He turns left at the statue and sees ahead of him the palace. As he draws closer to the front gate, he realizes there are many more guards than when he had been here twenty-five years earlier.

He walks over to the side of the street, facing the gates and squats as he had done a lifetime ago.

He watches people come and go, closes his eyes, lowers his chin to his chest, and tries to dream. He cannot. *It has been too long ago. I cannot even remember what she looks like.*

Luke watches but is not sure what he is watching for. Then he sees it. A wagon of bricks pulled by two oxen. He approaches it before the driver reaches the palace gate.

"Uh, sir. I am looking for Thomas. Do you know him?"

"Of course. He is the one who designed the palace addition. He is in charge."

"Do you think there is any chance I could speak with him?"

"I don't know. He is very important and very busy."

"Could you wait just a moment?" Luke asks, reaching into his shoulder pouch. He pulls out a small clay tablet and quickly etches on it.

COME TO GATE. JESUS' FRIEND.

"Okay," the brickmaker says. "But I do not know if I will be seeing him."

"That is fair," Luke says. He returns to his place across from the gate, squats, and watches for the brickmaker to be admitted to the palace grounds.

As he watches, he finds himself looking for a guard with long yellow hair. *Stop that. If he were alive, he would have gray hair by now. But he is not alive. Just stop that.*

Night approaches. Luke leads Thor outside of the city where he sets up his tent on the banks of the Arghanadab River.

"I'm out of money and out of food. Sorry, Thor. At least it is winter, and there is water. I do not know how I survived that summer here."

Every day Luke packs up his tent, leads Thor back into the city, resumes his position across the street from the palace gate, and waits.

Days go by. Scarce clouds roll in.

"It actually rains here?" Luke says to Thor. He watches as people on the street run for cover. The wind comes in, then the unexpected rain.

The soldiers do not move. Neither does Luke.

The water collects in ruts in the street. The soldiers and Luke do not move.

Then, as suddenly, the rain stops. As it does, he notices a man walking out of the palace and staring at him. The man is well dressed and looks angry. *Well, I am about to be sent on my way or arrested as a spy.*

"Do you know Jesus?" The man asks. He has a big head, large mouth, wide eyes, and a flat nose.

"What?" Luke asks, rising.

"Do you know Jesus?"

Luke squints as though it will help him hear and see better. "Thomas? Are you Thomas?"

"Yes, I am. And any friend of Jesus is a friend of mine. How long have you been waiting for me?"

"About two weeks," Luke says.

"I am so sorry," Thomas says with a frown. "My men were adding bricks to the wall and noticed your message just before the rain melted your words away.

"Come into the palace with me. I have an *officium* there where we can talk. By the way, I do not know your name."

"I am Luke, a companion of the apostle Paul."

"Oh, I remember Paul. How is he?"

"Nero executed him about two months ago."

"I am sorry, but it is not a surprise to me. This man is with me," he tells the guards who then open the gate for them.

"Your horse will be fine in this visitor's stall," he says, once inside.

Luke watches the guards that are on duty, remembering their barracks was next to the gate. He looks for long yellow hair. He sees maids come and go, and looks for an especially beautiful one with black hair. *Stop that. They wouldn't look like that now, even if they were still alive, which they are not.*

They walk down a corridor with dust and workmen everywhere. Thomas opens a door, and they go into a room that is tastefully furnished, though not opulent.

"Sit here," Thomas says. He sits on a marble bench opposite Luke.

"So, what is going on? Why are you looking for me? Has something bad happened in Jerusalem?"

"Well, the Jews are making the Romans madder all the time. When I left Rome, there was talk of sending several more legions down there and just destroying the whole city. But that was just talk."

"What about the other apostles? Have you seen any of the others? I admit I am hungry for news of them."

"I saw Jesus' brother, James, while in Jerusalem with Paul a few years ago. That's when they arrested him. Oh, and I saw John. He is in Ephesus now."

"Is Mary still alive?" Thomas asks.

"Yes. I interviewed her. She is old and frail, but childlike in her enthusiasm for life."

Thomas smiles. "Yes, she was always like that. You say you interviewed her?

"Yes, I promised a friend I would write an accurate account of Jesus' life. So I am traveling around trying to find all the apostles. That is why I was looking for you."

"What a grand thing you are doing, Luke."

"And I found Thaddeus and Nathaniel in Armenia, and Andrew up in Scythia near the Caspian Sea. I am really lucky I found you. All I heard is that you were somewhere in India."

"Well, I plan to go farther down into India when I'm

one evangelizing here. I want to go somewhere on the west coast. I was a sailor in my youth. I miss the ocean. I have converted many in the palace among the slaves and servants over the past five years.

"But desert living sometimes gets to me. Technically, the king here only rules over the Kushans. But he is aggressive and has led several raids in northern India. He will conquer much of it, I am sure."

"Uh, sir, I want to talk about Jesus. I brought my writing supplies in with me."

"Of course. The unusual rain has caused a little bit of a problem. So while my men get things back under control, I will be happy to tell you about him."

Luke waits.

"He was the actual Son of God," Thomas says, becoming serious. "And I walked with him."

"You knew he was, partly because of his miracles. Can you tell me about some of them?" Luke asks.

Thomas puts his hands behind his head and stares at the wall behind Luke. "Oh, my. There were so many. He constantly amazed me. Amazed all of us.

"Let me see. I remember he was traveling around Galilee—that is one of the provinces in our country. A leper actually came into the city, even though he was required by law to stay away from people. He was ragged, of course, unable to buy new clothes and forced to live in a cave with other lepers. Anyway, he came into the city and asked if Jesus might want to heal him.

"You know what Jesus did? He actually touched the man. Touched the leprosy. As soon as he did, the leprosy was gone, and he was a normal man again. He wasn't bad looking either, I must say. Looked rather dignified, other than his rags.

"We went to another city then. Jesus was always traveling so he could preach to everyone. In that city, he was preaching in someone's house. It was packed with people inside and out in the street."

Thomas stops, laughs, and slaps his knee. "Right in the middle of his sermon, we heard noise overhead. The next thing we knew, there was a big hole in the roof. Jesus just watched, sat down, and waited for them with a smile. They lowered a paralyzed man on a mat. Jesus was so pleased with their faith, he made the man able to walk again."

Thomas leans forward and lowers his voice. "Then he did something I never imagined. He gave us the power. All twelve of us. He gave us the power to perform miracles so we could help him teach. But he warned us that we would pay a price for it. The enemies of the one real God would go after us and try to kill us."

"Has anyone tried to kill you, Thomas?" Luke asks.

"Yes, several times," he replies, leaning back again and putting his hands on his knees. He shakes his head. "He told us to just leave there and preach somewhere else, and not think our words were unheeded. People trying to kill us was an indication of how afraid of us they were.

"Let me see," he says. "By the way, you do not have to write on your lap, Luke. Come over here and put your things on the writing-table."

Luke picks up the blackener he had set on the floor by his foot, puts a lid on it, then takes it and his parchment over to the writing-table.

"Did you know Jesus was so powerful, he raised a boy back to life?"

Luke lays his pen down. "I had heard that. Did you actually see it happen?"

"It happened just as the funeral procession was nearing the cemetery. Everyone was wailing. The next thing we knew, the dead boy was sitting up and enjoying himself talking to everyone."

Thomas smiles. "How could anyone not believe Jesus was the Son of God? It is beyond understanding. But Satan has hold of some people, and they defend their own beliefs, even if they are wrong."

A knock on the door. "Come in," Thomas calls out.

"Sir, we are out of bricks again. Some of the bricklayers are threatening to quit."

"Tell them I will pay them for the work they do not do if they will stay on until another load arrives. There should be another one tomorrow."

"Yes, sir." The door closes.

"It is late. Why don't you go home with me? My wife will be happy to meet you. Besides, she is a very good cook."

Luke puts his writing materials into his leather shoulder pouch and leaves with Thomas. They stop by the guest stable to get Thor on their way out.

As they walk through the streets, Luke stops and looks around.

"That song."

"What song?"

"*Though I vander long avay.* It almost has the accent right."

"Oh, that song," Thomas says. "Everyone sings it—the maids, the guards, people in town. It has been popular for a long time. Do you know it?"

Luke stares at Thomas, tears in his eyes.

"It is my father's song. He died long ago. I helped him escape from here."

"He was here?" a confused Thomas asks.

"Yes, but it was long before you were here. You were probably still living in Jerusalem at the time."

Luke leads Thor to the side of the road and sits on his heels. Thomas joins him. "I am so sorry. What happened to your father?"

"I helped him escape. He was a slave. They caught up with us right after we boarded the ship to freedom, and took him back to be executed."

"Are you sure about all that?"

"Yes, I am sure."

Silence for a while.

"Well, are you okay now?" Thomas asks.

Luke stands and takes a deep breath. "Yes."

That evening after the first meal Luke has had in three days, Luke brings his parchment back out, and Thomas tells his stories.

"Would you believe he could also control the weather? We were on our boat on the Sea of Galilee, and the storm came up. We were about to go down when Jesus just told the wind to stop acting up, and it obeyed. You have no idea what it was like to be in his presence.

"The very next day, when we were ashore, he made a legion of demons leave a man. Satan is stronger than we know. But no one can conquer Jesus."

"Yes, I am learning that," Luke says. "What else do you remember? Anything?"

"He raised a twelve-year-old girl from the dead. He fed five thousand followers with a hand full of bread and fish. He made a stooped woman able to stand straight again. He made a man full of edema well again. He healed ten lepers all at the same time. I could go on and on. But his greatest miracle is when he made himself came back to life."

Luke hurries to write everything Thomas has just told him.

"It is late," Thomas says. "Why don't you spend the night and we will talk again tomorrow as long as you like."

37 ~ THE SACRIFICE

The sun is barely on the horizon. "I could not stay in that city any longer where I lost them both," he tells Thor. "I hope Thomas was not offended by me leaving him a note and slipping out before he got up."

I will never know everything about Jesus anyway. Thomas told me enough of Jesus' miracles, I just wonder how anyone could have not believed.

The big black horse walks slowly. Luke lets him go at his own pace.

"Thor, I want to go home. I want to go back to Frisia. As soon as I am through with this book, I want to go home."

Luke heads toward the coast where the Indian Ocean meets the Persian Gulf. *Perhaps I can find work there and earn passage up to Parthia, then head across to Syria.*

"At least it is still winter, Thor. You wouldn't believe the heat down here during the summer. No wonder there are so few towns."

As Luke rides, he allows himself to remember.

> *Tho I vander long avay*
> *Over all da mounts und seas*
> *To da end uv da verld,*
> *I vill alvays tink uv home*
> *Und keep you in my heart*
> *Til I hold you once again.*

"Thor, would you like to go home? You have never

been there, but I know you would like it. Your ancestors lived there, just like mine did."

Luke hears a squawk and looks up in the sky. He sees seagulls and knows he is going in the right direction to get to the coast.

I am so lonely. Thaddeus and Nathaniel had each other. Andrew has his wife. Thomas has his wife. I have no one. Stop thinking like that.

Luke rides on. Closer to the shore. Closer to home. Closer to returning to life as it is rather than as it should have been.

I wonder what Theophilus is doing. I hope he is still alive. He was three months ago. Looked healthy. Nothing is going to happen to him.

He has been so good to me. I didn't deserve it. No slave in the world was ever treated as good as he treated me.

The seagulls are more numerous now, and they're squawking louder. Luke hears bells. The road now descends sharply. He looks over to the side of the road and sees the harbor below.

"Thor, we are going on board a ship again. You did well before. Just stay calm, and you will do fine. Too bad you're so big, though. Some ship captains are hesitant to take horses like you on board."

Luke arrives at the docks and calls up, asking where each ship is headed.

"Anyone going to old Babylon?" he asks. "Or Persia or Parthia or whatever you call it?"

No, no, and no. All headed out to the open sea. Luke notices a small vessel and comes close to it. It is a riverboat just for passengers.

"Sir," he says, leading his horse to someone who looks to be in charge. "Are you the captain of this vessel?" he asks.

"Yes, I am," comes the reply.

"Are you going north?"

"Yes, do you need a ride?"

"Indeed, I do. But I do not have any money. Might there be anyone on board needing a scribe?"

"What for? We never go that far. You need to find one

of the ocean-going ships. Now, what we need is a physician. The owner of this boat is onboard sick and refuses to let us progress until he feels better."

"Oh, well, I am a physician, also."

"I do not believe you."

"It is true," Luke says. He reaches over to the leather shoulder pouch he stores his medical supplies in. "See, I have all these pouches for different herbs. Here is a tool I use to pull arrows out of people. Here is…"

"Okay, I believe you. If you can get the owner well, I am sure he will give you free passage and maybe even a little money on top of that."

"Lead me to him," Luke says.

"Not with that horse. He will throw the whole boat off balance and sink it."

"He may be big, but he is gentle. I do not go without my horse."

"You had better be right," the captain says.

A second gangplank is placed next to the one already there, and Luke carefully guides Thor up onto the deck, so the boat does not tip one way or the other.

"Tie him up here. The owner is in the cabin off the bridge."

"Do you have a little barley? He is hungry."

"We have barley for ourselves," the captain says. "Oh, all right. I'll have the cook bring up some barley for him to eat while you are with the owner."

Luke walks up the ladder leading to the bridge and opens the door into the cabin. He ducks his head and enters. Standing by the door, he introduces himself.

"Have you come to heal me?" Farnaspa groans from his berth.

Luke walks over to him and kneels. He feels the man's face. It is hot.

"You have a fever. Have you been around anyone else with a fever?"

"No. But my legs are getting numb."

Luke pulls down the man's cover and notices one leg is swelled. "Is it both legs or just one?"

"I guess it is just one."

Luke feels around the leg.

The man screams. "Stop! Don't touch it!" Luke notices a scar in the man's thigh. "Have you ever been injured there in the past?"

"Well, a long time ago. I served in the Parthian army for thirty years. Got an arrow shot into me there."

"Did you pull it all the way out?"

"I got out what I could. It finally healed, and I have been fine."

"You're not fine now. I think part of the arrow's tip is still in there. I can open it up and take it out."

"Oh, no, you don't."

"I have some opium I can give you. It will be over before you know it."

"Promise?"

"Promise. But I need to get someone to watch my horse while I tend to you."

"Horse? No horses."

"If he goes, I go."

"Oh, all right. But you had better make sure he stays under control. Open the door and call for my captain. He's probably nearby. Tell him to put someone in charge of your horse until this thing with my leg is done.

Thor taken care of, Luke returns to Farnaspa's berth.

"Okay, give me the opium, and let's get this fixed."

Farnaspa sleeps the rest of the day and that night. Luke is still with him the next morning when he awakens.

"Your fever is almost gone. I pulled half of the arrow tip out of you. You should be able to walk with a cane now."

Luke helps the owner swing his legs around and sit on the side of his berth. He sits a moment, then stands and tests his leg.

"I think you have taken care of my problem, sir," Farnaspa says with a grin. "By the way, what is your name?"

"My name is Luke."

"What can I do to pay for this?"

"I need passage up to the mouth of the Euphrates and Tigris Rivers for both me and my horse."

"I forgot about your horse."

"He is gentle and has not caused any problems so far."

"Okay. But I need to give you more than that." The captain feels around in his mattress and pulls out a pouch. He reaches in and hands Luke some of the contents. "Here are two pieces of silver."

"Thank you very much," Luke says. He walks toward the cabin door. "If you need me, I will be right outside."

The following day the boat lands on the north shore of the Persian Gulf. Luke leads his horse ashore and walks to the open bazaar. He buys cheese, dried fruit, and bread for himself and barley for Thor, all of which are packed tightly on the horse's rump. He fills a large water skin for Thor and a smaller one for himself.

He mounts Thor and heads north, following the river. When it comes to a split, he follows the west river, which he knows to be the Euphrates.

For two days, Luke works his way north through western Parthia. He is alone now. Not many people along here, even with the river nearby. Between the Euphrates and what he knows to be the Tigris to the east are marshes. To the west is desert.

"Too bad I never found Matthew," Luke tells Thor. I know he is in Parthia somewhere—or at least I heard that. Parthia is just too expansive. There is no way I could find him."

Thor's ears perk up and turn in different directions.

"What's wrong, Thor?" Luke says, patting one side of his horse's neck. Thor stops.

Luke listens, then looks around. He looks at the floor of the desert for a snake. There is none. He looks for wolves or foxes and sees none.

He listens again. A scream over to his left. Dust. Someone running toward him. He turns Thor's head and hurries in the direction of the runner.

He climbs off his horse and approaches the runner. It is a woman. She is still screaming. Her arms are outstretched.

"Help! Help me! Please. Help."

"What is wrong?" Luke asks, speaking in his rusty Parthian.

"My son. They're going to kill my little son."

"Who?"

"The priests. Hurry. They're going to kill my son."

Luke helps the woman onto Thor and mounts in front of her. He heads in the direction the woman had just come from, urges Thor into a gallop, and hangs on to the woman's arm seated behind him.

He sees up ahead large dunes. He goes around them, then spots it.

"Tammuz! Tammuz!" the woman shouts.

Luke tries to think back. *Tammuz...*

He sees a great fire on the floor of the desert. On the edge of the fire is a throne with a larger-than-life statue sitting on it. The statue's arms are outstretched.

Above the fire on a tall dune, people are standing. He hears flutes and harps. Then the drums.

He heads his horse up the dune. As he does, he sees tall men walking in front of and behind short men. The short men are veiled.

"My son! My son! Tammuz! Tammuz!"

Horrified, Luke realizes the short men are children. He pauses long enough to lean down and grab a long staff out of the hand of a priest. The woman slides off Thor as he does.

The music and drums stop. He urges Thor forward. He draws close to the end of the procession and slams the long staff into the backs of two of the priests using a sweeping motion.

By now, the other two priests in the back and the two in front have turned around. Luke uses the same sweeping motion to knock the final priests at the end off their feet. The children run in circles, their hands being bound, and no way to lift their veils.

Children screaming. Women screaming. Men shouting.

Luke slides off Thor, who turns to go back down the dune. Still, with the staff, Luke charges toward the priests who had been leading the procession of children. Holding the staff in both hands, he pushes it into the chests of the priests and pins them to the ground.

He turns and sees the other four priests back on their feet and running toward him. As he does, one of the men grabs his fellow priest from behind, wrestles him to the ground, and sits on him. The other two priests run down the dune.

Luke turns his attention back to the priests who had led the procession. He grabs both of them by the back of their neck, holds tightly, and forces them to walk forward, their feet barely off the ground. He pushes them to the ground, and women who had been screaming rush forward and sit on the priests.

By now, those who are apparently mothers have reached their children, lifted their veils, kissed them, and unbound their hands.

Luke notices the priest sitting on another priest is looking up at him and grinning. Standing, the grinning priest puts one foot on his victim's back, and greets Luke.

"Hello, friend. You are just in time. My name is Matthew."

Luke's eyes grow wide. "Matthew? Jesus' apostle? That Matthew?" he asks in Greek.

"Yes, that Matthew. And who might you be?"

"I am Paul's, Luke."

"The Paul who became an apostle after Jesus left us?"

"Yes, that Paul."

"Do you carry any rope on that big black horse of yours?" Matthew asks.

"Some. Why don't we tie the priests hands with the rope they used on the children? I'll use mine to string them together. Then what shall we do with them?"

"We need to take them back to Najaf. The sheik there outlawed this religion because of child sacrifices."

"Well, let's get started tying," Luke says in agreement.

"But first," Matthew says, "we need to convert them."

"What?"

"We need to convert them. The fire down there will burn itself out. Line them up. And put two parents or musicians behind each priest to hold them down. We shall convert them all.

"What language do they speak?" Luke asks.

"Well, Aramaic and Parthian. I have the gift of tongues and can understand whatever language they speak in."

"Would you mind doing me a favor?" Luke asks. "I have been traveling around interviewing Jesus' apostles and other witnesses to Jesus' life and teachings so I can put everything together in a book. I used to know Aramaic, but not much. I know Parthian more. If you wouldn't mind speaking in Parthian, I could take notes."

"Agreed," Matthew says, smiling.

For the first time, Luke notices Matthew is has a big, bulky torso, small head, big mouth, small eyes, and a bulbous turned-down nose."

"I'll be right back," Luke says, whistling for Thor. Thor comes galloping back up the dune and to Luke. He takes out writing materials from his large leather pouch along with a small board to write on.

By now, Matthew has everyone arranged in rows. Luke sits where he can watch both them and Matthew. "If I hold up my hand," Luke says, "It means you are talking too fast and need to slow down for me."

"Agreed."

Matthew turns to the villagers. "Everyone. Attention, everyone. You may not have ever heard of Jesus, so I am going to tell you about him. Jesus was the Son of God, and he walked on earth thirty-three years teaching love.

"Jesus called himself the light of the world. You and your priests claim Tammuz controls the fires of the sun. So, when the days get short, they claim he will bring long, warm days back to you if you will sacrifice your children to him.

"Not so! You and your priests are wrong. As the light of the world, Jesus said to bring the children to him so he can hug them. He loves little children. He said that whoever is kind to a child is being kind to him.

"He also loves you. He said you would be blessed if you hunger for him. He said you would be blessed if you weep for him."

One of the priests tries to wriggle free, and one of the fathers pins him down to the ground by the shoulders.

"If the pagans around here mistreat you because you want to follow the very Son of God," Matthew continues, "rejoice. Love your enemies. Do good to people who hate you. Bless those who curse you. Pray for those who mistreat you. If someone hits you on the cheek, turn your other cheek to him. If someone grabs your coat from you, offer him your tunic also."

Luke holds up his hand. Matthew notices, smiles, and walks among the crowd, pointing. "He loves you, and you, and you." Luke indicates he has caught up, and Matthew returns to the front to resume his sermon.

"Do to others the way you want others to treat you. Do not be judgmental. The way you judge others is the way they will judge you. Don't go around trying to take sawdust out of someone's eye while you have a shepherd's staff in your own eye."

Matthew pauses and points to one of the priests. "Do you want proof? I notice you have a patch over your eye," he says to the priest. "Well, you do not need it any longer. By the power of Jesus Christ, Son of God, your eye is whole again." He reaches over, takes the patch off the man's eye, the man looks around and shouts, "I can see! I can see."

Matthew walks over to a man who is missing a foot. My words are God's words. Do you need more proof? "By the power of Jesus Christ, Son of God, you now have your foot back."

Before the eyes of the people, the man's foot grows back. His eyes grow wide, he shows a mouth full of teeth in a broad grin, and all the villagers gasp.

"What will you gain if you gain all the riches and power in the world and lose your soul in hell?" Matthew asks. "All of you are sinners. I am a sinner. Luke over here is a sinner. Everyone sins. Satan has held mankind hostage because what we earn by sinning is death and separation from God, who is sinless.

"Jesus paid the ransom and set us free. How do I know? Because he died, then he came back to life, overcoming death for us. I touched him and saw him die with my own eyes. I touched him and saw him alive again with my own eyes.

"Jesus is the one who makes people's bodies whole again. He can make your souls whole again too. If you believe Jesus did all these things for you as the Son of God, come imitate what he did for you. Die to your sinful nature, the part of you that sins and doesn't care. Be buried as Jesus was buried. Then rise up out of your grave as Jesus did."

"But how?" someone asks. We would die if we were buried out here."

Matthew raises his arms and laughs. "You can do it with water," he announces. "Where is your drinking water? What pond or well or cistern do you use? You can do it with your own water. Or you can do it when we get into the city. It is your choice.

"But how will we make a living?" a priest asks.

"God knows who you are. He will take care of you just like he takes care of the sparrows. He has numbered every hair on your head. You are much more valuable to him than the sparrows.

"Do not worry about what you will eat. Think about the lilies of the field. They do not work, but God takes care of them and keeps them beautiful. Enter God's kingdom and spread the word about it just like you used to spread the word about Tammuz, and God will take care of you."

Another priest raises both of his hands, which are tied together. "I believe. What do you call people who believe?"

"Christians. You can all become Christians."

Matthew looks over at Luke. Then he smiles, and announces to Luke and all the parents, "Untie everyone."

Luke stares at Matthew and shrugs.

"Don't worry, Luke. I know where their cisterns are," Matthew says, speaking Greek again. "I infiltrated these people over a month ago and have been living with them. They can all be baptized there. Would you like to help?"

"I wouldn't miss this for anything," Luke replies, grinning.

Luke takes the reins of Thor and walks beside

Matthew as they make their way to the nomadic village of the strange people of Parthia.

One by one, tall Luke with the long arms lowers the believers into the cistern and back out as Matthew says the words over each one, "I baptize you in the name of God the Father, God the Son, and God the Holy Spirit for the forgiveness of your sins and so you will receive the Holy Spirit."

It is nearly sunset when they are done.

I'll be happy to share my tent with you tonight," Luke tells Matthew. "I am going to have to leave in the morning."

"I have my own accommodations with the villagers, but let's talk." Matthew builds a bonfire and the two men sit cross-legged across from each other.

Luke spends the rest of the evening catching Matthew up on news of other apostles and other eyewitnesses of Jesus he has met.

"Have you been to see my brother, Little James, yet?" Matthew asks.

"No. I thought I'd try to find him if he is still in Syria."

"Yes, he is. But don't let the name fool you," he warns. "My father and I are big men, but Little James is bigger than both of us. Only difference is that he is skinny like our mother, Mary, and I am big-boned like our father, Alphaeus."

38 ~ RESCUES

When morning comes, Luke embraces Matthew, wishes him luck with the local priests, and mounts Thor.

He heads toward Syria. *I'll guess I'll start in the southern cities and work my way north. Bosra first, then Damascus.*

"That was one of the most refreshing things I have ever lived through," he tells Thor. "Matthew sure didn't look or act like a tax collector. I heard all tax collectors were mad all the time and never gave anyone a break. If he used to be that way, he isn't now. What a man. I wonder if his brother is anything like him."

Luke pulls out a piece of dried fruit given to him by one of the grateful mothers and eats it. "Oh, I forgot about you, Thor." He pulls out some barley from a large stack he has tied together and attached to Thor's rump. He reaches around, Thor takes it in his mouth and chews as he walks.

Not much out here but sand and boulders. I cannot imagine why anyone would want to live here. The mountains around Berea are beautiful. And those around my homeland are even more beautiful. Only strange people live in deserts.

Luke comes to an oasis. "May as well spend the night here. We should be at the first city in another couple days."

He pulls out his tent and sets it up, then notices someone else at the oasis. After eating an evening meal, he walks over to the stranger.

"Hello there, I am Luke from Berea in Greece. Greetings."

The other man stands. "I am Masista of Babylon.

Greetings."

"Are you traveling east or west?" Luke asks.

"I am traveling west. And you?"

"I am traveling east. Have you ever heard of Jesus of Nazareth?"

"The name sounds familiar, but I do not believe so."

"I can tell you about him if you would like company for a while," Luke says.

"Certainly. Have a seat by my fire."

"Well," Luke begins, "Jesus was the Son of God who walked on earth for a while. We know it is true because prophecies of his coming were made for hundreds of years before his birth. Even the town he would be born in was prophesied—Bethlehem."

"Bethlehem, you say?" Masista asks, his eyes wide.

"Yes. Many foreigners believed in him. People from Rome and Greece, Lebanon, and..."

"What about Babylon? Seems like I have heard of this happening."

"You have? All the way in Babylon? I heard some magi from Babylon, Persia and India saw his star the night he was born, then went to see him in Bethlehem," Luke says. "Of course, figuring out the meaning of the star and taking a caravan across the desert took time. But eventually, they got there and worshipped him."

"Oh, yes. I remember now. My father was one of the magi who went to see him."

"Your father? How providential is that? Oh, you must tell me all about it. I am searching for eyewitnesses so I can write an accurate book about Jesus' life and teachings. Wait here while I get my writing supplies. On second thought, it is getting too dark. Maybe you can tell me, and I will write it down in the morning."

"Well, where shall I start?"

"Start with how they figured out the meaning of the star," Luke urges.

"My father was the chief of the magi. All the other magi paid attention to whatever he said. He had studied the stars much longer than anyone else. He knew that the appearance of a new star meant a new god had been born."

"Your father must have been very smart. But how did he know where Jesus was born from a thousand *milles* away?"

"He had maps. Maps of the heavens, of course, but also maps of important places on earth. He knew that the Greek empire would thrive a while, then be replaced by the Roman empire. He also knew that this new god-king, Jesus, would take over as the next emperor of the world."

"Well, I guess you could call Jesus emperor of the world," Luke says. "Go on. How did he know Jesus would be born in Bethlehem?"

"My father knew that Bethlehem meant house of heaven."

"But Bethlehem means house of bread," Luke says.

"I was getting to that. The new god-king lived on the bread of heaven. All other babies drink milk when they are born. But Jesus began eating the bread of heaven right away."

"I see," Luke says. "And did your father come see Jesus?"

"Oh, yes. My father convinced the king of my country to let him come see Jesus."

"How did he get here?"

"My father was a student of Zoroaster. Zoroaster gave him special powers so that, as soon as he wished it, he appeared in the very room where baby Jesus lay. His bed was gold, and his pillow was a cloud."

Luke stands. "I am sorry, friend. I do not believe your story is going to be in my book."

As Luke walks over to his tent, he shakes his head and chuckles.

"Thor, if he tries to bother you during the night, you have my permission to bite him. Well, to nibble on him a little."

The next morning at dawn, Luke leaves the oasis and heads farther west toward Bosra. That night he arrives. By now, having been used to living in his tent instead of a hostel, he spreads his tent out and spends the night by the city gate.

"I am looking for a big man named Little James," he explains to the first merchant he sees the next morning at the bazaar. "He tells people about Jesus."

"Don't know any big men named Little. Sorry."

"Excuse me, sir. I am looking for a big man, taller than me, who people call Little James and who talks about Jesus of Nazareth a lot."

"Never heard of him."

Luke works his way around the bazaar leading Thor behind him, goes to the forum, and stops a few people in a neighborhood with small houses.

"Well, Thor," he says, remounting his big Frisian outside the city gate, "looks like we'll be going to Damascus next."

It is mid-morning when Luke heads out. He and Thor arrive outside of Damascus just before sunset. "This should be interesting," Luke tells his horse.

The next morning, Luke goes into Damascus and to the bazaar. "Are there any Christians in this city?" he asks the first merchant.

"Yes. There are many of them. They meet in an old synagogue two streets over."

Luke smiles, gives the man a copper coin, and leads Thor to the old synagogue. When he arrives, he tries the door and finds it unlocked. He walks in and calls out, "Any Christians here? Any Christians here?"

A man walks into the large room and calls back, "All we have here are Christians. Are you a Christian? Have we met before? My name is Ananias."

Luke holds out his hand to the old man. "I am Luke. I believe Paul told me about you."

"Oh, you know Paul?"

"I knew him. I was his personal physician the last few years of his life."

"He is gone?" Ananias says. "I am not surprised. A stubborn young man he was. He should have outlived me. I am eighty-six years old. Yes, he should have outlived me."

"Sir, did you ever meet Jesus?"

"No I never did, I am sorry to say. But I can tell you a lot about Paul."

"I would like that. Then I need to talk to people who personally met Jesus. I am writing a book about his life and activities and am interviewing eyewitnesses."

"What about Joseph? He was a member of the ruling council, the Sanhedrin. He buried Jesus in his garden tomb. He is older than me and is confined to his bed. But I am sure he will be thrilled to speak with you. I can take you to see him now."

"I would be honored to meet him," Luke says. He waits on the front portico while Ananias locks the front door of the old synagogue.

"While we're going there, let me tell you about Paul. I baptized him, you know."

"Yes, I knew that. Tell me about it."

When they arrive at Joseph's house, they see a bench on the street across from his gate, and Ananias finishes telling his story.

"Now, I shall introduce you to Joseph."

They knock on the old man's gate, and a young man answers it.

"Oh, it's you, Ananias. My grandfather will be pleased to see you."

"Medad, this is my new friend, Luke. He is writing a book about everything Jesus said and did and is interviewing eyewitnesses, people who actually saw and talked to him."

Joseph is reclining on a couch with a sheet over him. He sighs. "Have a seat," he says, and sighs again.

Other than seeing a lot of messy gray hair on his head to match his beard and noticing his small eyes, Luke cannot tell much about the man.

"I am afraid I let Jesus down," Joseph says with a weak growl. "I heard him speak all over the temple complex and even made a special trip to Bethany to hear him speak at the synagogue there. His wisdom was far beyond his age. He had become very powerful by the time I met him, but you would never know it being around him. Did you ever meet him, Luke? Did you say your name is Luke?"

"Yes, sir, but I never met or heard him personally. However, I spent several years with Paul, the apostle, who told me about him."

"Oh, yes, Shaul, as we Jews called him," Joseph continues. "He thought he could outsmart Jesus, but the opposite happened. I never saw a man make such a turnaround as Shaul did."

"But about Jesus." Luke urges.

"Oh, yes. I heard him several times. So did my friend, Nicodemus. We both decided he was who he claimed to be, but we let him down. Nicodemus and I were both members of the Jewish ruling council, but we did not speak up and defend him as we should have."

"What about at the end?"

"The high priest held an emergency session in the middle of the night and did not notify any Jesus sympathizers," Joseph continues. "So, the vote was unanimous to kill him.

"The least Nicodemus and I could do was give him a decent burial. Of course, it cost me my seat in the ruling council, but I no longer desired to be one of them.

"I have spent the rest of my life defending Jesus, but it does not make up for my failures."

"I understand. Have you met Little James?" Luke asks.

"Yes. He was here a couple days ago, and I believe has gone up into the hills to tell people up there about Jesus."

"He is not going until tomorrow, Grandfather," the younger man says.

"Oh, he is still here?"

"Yes, and I believe he is preparing to confront the priests of Elagabalus, the sun god. He is going to Emesa tomorrow, where most of the priests live. Would you like me to take you to James?" the young man asks Luke.

"Indeed, I would. How fortunate."

"Ananias, would you stay here with Grandfather while I take Luke to James?"

Half an hour later, they are at the home of the apostle

and have given him the reason for Luke's visit.

"James, you are as big as your brother said you were," Luke says. "I'm not used to looking up at other men, but you are the exception."

"Welcome and have a seat," James says in his base voice. "So, you are writing a book about the life and teachings of Jesus? I'm sure my brother was a big help. How is he, anyway? Staying out of trouble?"

"Actually, I think he is running the priests in Parthia in circles."

"That sounds like him. Ha. Ha. So, what do you want me to tell you?"

"Tell me how you know Jesus was the Son of God."

James looks at Luke, then at the wall behind him. "He fulfilled all those prophecies in his life. And he performed amazing miracles. But it was more than that."

"Would you mind if I take notes?" Luke asks as he opens his leather shoulder pouch and brings out a parchment. "In what other ways did he convince you?"

"He knew what people were thinking. well, he was a mind reader. For example, some men brought a friend to Jesus, who had been paralyzed. He told the paralyzed man his sins were forgiven. Jesus' enemies always followed him around, trying to make him look foolish and be reduced in the eyes of the people."

"Yes, everyone tells me that," Luke says.

"As always, his enemies were there that day and grumbled to each other about him blaspheming because only God can forgive sins. They didn't even have to say it out loud. Jesus knew what they were thinking and said it was just as easy for him to make the man whole again as it was to forgive his sins. Then he did both.

"Another time, we were in a synagogue, and a man was in the audience with a withered hand. I don't know if Jesus' enemies planted the man there or not. They wanted to see if Jesus would fall for their trap and heal someone on the holy day."

"I don't understand," Luke says.

"That's right. You're not a Jew. You wouldn't

understand. The Jewish Law of Moses says it is a sin to work on the holy day, the Sabbath."

"Healing someone is work?" Luke asks.

"Of course not. But his enemies tried to turn the smallest thing into sin, so declared helping a sick person was a sin. Jesus knew what his enemies were doing. So he stared them down, had the disfigured man come forward, and asked his enemies if it was a sin to do good on the holy day."

"Without waiting for an answer, he glared at them, healed the man, then glared at them again. Were they ever mad."

"So Jesus never backed down for anyone?"

"Exactly. Everyone had to be careful around him. He even knew the thoughts of us apostles, and we were his friends," James says with a grin.

"Amazing," Luke says, returning the grin.

"One time, we were in another room arguing over which one of us was most important to Jesus and his cause. Do you know what he did? He called us to the room he was sitting in. Then told us the least important and most childlike of us was the most important to him."

"I can imagine how difficult it must have been being with a man who could read my thoughts."

"But that's the point. Even today, he knows our thoughts. What is the difference whether he does it from earth or heaven? He knows."

Luke shakes his head and smiles. "I never thought of it that way. What else did he say or do to convince you he was God walking on earth?"

"What is that noise out on the street?" James asks, heading toward the outer gate.

Both he and Luke go out and see the street full of people talking and crying.

"What has happened?" James asks a stranger passing by, wailing.

"Haven't you heard? Jerusalem has been destroyed—the city, the temple, everything. All gone."

James looks at Luke. Both are stunned.

They go back inside and close the gate, sit, and stare. They are silent, though they can still hear the din in the street.

"And he knew the future," James whispers. "He knew this day would come."

"What do you mean?"

"He said Jerusalem would be surrounded by armies, and they would destroy it completely. He warned that, once the armies arrived, people had better flee immediately. They were not to go back into their houses to get anything. They were to flee as fast as they could. He said Jerusalem would be trampled underfoot by the Gentiles."

James stares at Luke. "The day has come, just as he predicted more than thirty-five years ago."

Silence.

"He even repeated it on his way to the cross. Even after being beaten nearly to death, he warned the women following him."

Silence again.

"And the last reason I believe he was the Son of God: I saw him rise up from the ground, float up to the clouds, and disappear. I saw him rise."

Luke finishes writing and puts down his pen. "I wish I could have seen and heard him."

"Through the words of your book, people centuries from now will see and hear him. And they, like you, will believe."

39 ~ NEAR

"Well, Thor," Luke says, mounting his horse the next morning, "I guess we will not be able to go back to Jerusalem after all. It is gone. All gone.

"We shall go where we can. I would like to see the city where he was born, but it is too close to what is left of Jerusalem. It might be dangerous to go to Bethlehem.

"Ummm, we could go to the city where he grew up—uh, Nazareth—and the city he lived in by the Sea of Galilee—Capernaum, I think. After that, we could go down to the province of Samaria, then go over to Caesarea.

Then I guess I will be done. We can get a ship from there and go home."

Traveling on. Now on the roads Jesus traveled. *As close to Jesus as I will ever be.*

Wondering. Imagining. Trying to recapture the past of now long ago.

Luke arrives at a fishing village on the Sea of Galilee. He asks the first person he sees if he knows where Capernaum is and is told this is it. He wanders through the streets, wondering which house Jesus lived in. He works his way down to the lake and squats on the shore. After a while, a fisherman walks nearby, and Luke calls out to him.

"Uh, sir. Sir. Have you lived here very long?"

"All my life," the man says.

"Did you ever meet Jesus? Or maybe his friends James? John? Andrew? Peter?" He pauses between each name.

"That was before my time, but my uncle saw them. He

worked for Zebedee after his sons, James and John, left. All dead now, I guess." The man walks on.

Luke stays and dreams a little longer. He tries to imagine Jesus walking along that same shore, perhaps stopping and preaching on the very spot Luke is on. He sighs and heads back the way he had come. Once more, he stops a stranger. "Can you tell me how to get to Nazareth?"

"Just stay on the Roman road and veer to the west at the fork."

It is noon when Luke arrives. He is surprised. Nazareth is just a small village on a hill. He walks Thor along the streets, wondering which house Jesus grew up in. He sees a synagogue and imagines Jesus going to school there as a boy and worshipping with his parents there.

On his way out of the village, he wanders through the market, wondering if Jesus ever sold any of his woodwork at any of the booths. Finally, he asks a merchant whether Nain or Gadara is closest.

"Nain is southeast of here, but not very far. Then you can go straight east, cross the Roman road to Gadara."

Luke thanks the guard and travels on to a little back road to Nain. When he arrives, he enters through the gates and goes to the market place.

"Sir, did you ever hear of a boy being brought back to life here? It would have happened thirty-five or forty years ago."

"Yes, I have heard it, but don't believe it."

"Sir, did you ever hear of a boy coming back to life here about thirty-five or forty years ago?"

"Yes, but I don't know for sure if it is true."

"Sir, did you ever hear of a boy being brought back to life by Jesus from Nazareth?"

When Luke steps over to the adjoining booth, the merchant is already standing, his hands on the counter in front of him.

"You know about it?" the merchant asks Luke. "I overheard you."

"I have only been told about it," Luke says. "I'm trying to find someone who witnessed it."

"It did happen," the merchant says. "I was a witness. Actually, I was that boy."

Luke's eyes widen.

"My mother and a lot of the people who were at the funeral have died. But I know what happened—all of it. By the way, my name is Jonathan."

Jonathan has brown hair and black eyes, one of which twitches. He has an easy smile.

"My name is Luke, and I am overjoyed to meet you."

Luke takes his leather shoulder pouch off Thor, then steps inside the booth. "May I take notes to what you say, Jonathan? I am investigating all the things I have heard about Jesus and talking to eyewitnesses to verify everything. Whatever I verify will go into a book about Jesus' life and teachings."

"I am very glad you are doing this," Jonathan says. "I will be happy to answer any of your questions."

Luke remains standing and sets the parchment on the countertop. "You just tell me what you want," he says with his pen dipped in blackener and ready.

"About a year after my father died, I got the same disease. It was harder and harder for me to breathe. My mother pounded me on the back a lot to ease my breathing. She also did all the other things she had done for my father. But, just like him, nothing worked."

"How old were you?"

"I was a teenager. I had to quit my after-school job, then I had to quit school. I really felt sorry for my mother."

"When you died, were you aware of anything?"

"Yes, I remember being able to breathe and being happy. But then a voice asked me if I would like to go back. I think it was Jesus' voice. I remembered my mother and how sad she was. So, I accepted the voice's invitation to come back."

Luke dips his pen in the blackener and writes as fast as he can. "Yes. Yes. Then what?"

"The next thing I knew, I woke up on a bier, and we were at the edge of the cemetery."

Jonathan grins and shakes his head. "You should

have seen everyone when I sat up and said hello to Jesus and my mother. They backed up; I don't know what they thought I was going to do to them." He shakes his head again, still grinning.

"I think the rabbi was mad because he had organized the funeral, and this was not in his plans."

Luke smiles.

"My relatives were there. My school friends too. And some hired mourners, though my mother could not afford many of them."

"So, it actually happened. You came back to life."

"It actually happened."

"Do you still follow Jesus?"

"Of course, I do. There is a congregation in our town, and I am one of the elders, having a wife and believing children of my own now. Would you like to come home with me and spend the night? It is nearly time to close up."

"If you have children, you may not have room for me. I can go on my way," Luke says.

"No problem at all. Please stay. It has been a long time since I have had anyone new to tell my story to."

Luke consents. After the evening meal, Luke lets Jonathan's older children take turns riding big Thor. That night, Jonathan retells his story to his family as though he had never told it before.

The next day, after receiving directions from Jonathan, Luke heads straight east for Gadara. When the Sea of Galilee appears on his left and a cemetery on his right, he knows he has arrived.

He guides Thor carefully around the tombs and stops. He looks around and tries to imagine Jesus standing there, confronting the thousands of demons—him against all of them. *What a frightening sight it must have been.* He takes out his parchment, writes a few notes, and tucks it away again.

He turns east and follows the road to the city itself. He goes to the market as always, but this time does not say anything to anyone. He just leads Thor slowly up and down the streets.

Finally, he is away from the market and sees it. A building that resembles a synagogue. Luke ties Thor up at a post in front and knocks on the door. Someone answers.

"Sir, do Christians meet in you building?"

"Yes. Many of us do. We have been here for thirty-five years. Are you a Christian?"

"Yes, sir," Luke replies. "But not nearly as long as you."

"Is there anything you need? Food? A place to stay? You are traveling, aren't you?

"Well, uh, sir, I do have a strange question to ask you. Please do not think me crazy. All I know is that I heard it was true. I just don't know."

Pinchas smiles and lets Luke in. "It is true."

"You know what I want to ask you?"

"You want to know about the man who had a legion of demons in him, and Jesus made them leave him alone."

"You heard of it happening?"

"I was one of the swine herders. I was so mad at Jesus for making my herd panic and run over the cliff, I literally wanted to kill him. He had ruined my source of income to support myself and my family."

"Did Jesus try to make friends with you?"

"No, he left. But Minoan, now free of the demons, came back home. Minoan was my brother. The family had tried everything to keep him under control while he tried to fight the demons in him.

"When he appeared at our gate that afternoon cleaned up, wearing a fresh tunic, and his hair out of his eyes... And then when he started talking like a sane man again..."

"You knew."

"Yes, after seeing Minoan like that, I knew. The whole family knew."

"What about your income?"

"Since we both needed a way to make a living again, we went together as partners and became sheepherders. It took us a while, but... Would you like to meet him?"

"Minoan? Yes, indeed."

"He has the flocks just south of the city. I will take you

to him. We're both getting too old to go chasing after stray lambs, but we're still at it."

Luke leads Thor out of the city, walking beside Pinchas. He spends the rest of the afternoon with Minoan, writing down the account of what happened.

"I cannot begin to describe it. I constantly fought the demons. I never had any rest. It would have been easier for me to just accept them. But I could not.

"There were just a few. Then, just when I thought I'd gotten rid of them, more came. It was never-ending. Relentless."

He looks over at his brother. "Did you know I prayed mightily while I was out there in the cemetery fighting for my soul?"

"We had no idea, Minoan," Pinchas says in a quiet voice. "We did not understand."

Late in the afternoon, Luke bids goodbye to Minoan and Pinchas. He returns to the Roman road and heads south again.

He arrives at Salem just before sundown, sets up his tent, looks over his notes, and falls asleep.

During the night, Luke awakens to the sound of Thor stomping and neighing. He crawls out of his tent but does not see Thor.

"Stop! Thief!" Luke shouts as he runs in the direction of the neighing. He detects several hoof beats, but he is too late to see anything through the darkness.

He whistles, and hears neighing off in the distance. Then the sound fades away.

"Lord, what am I going to do?" Luke prays, walking in circles around his tent with his hands on his head.

He walks away from his tent until he can hardly see it. He returns to his tent, then walks the same distance from it in another direction, searching. He sees no one else camping nearby. He sits, unable now to sleep, and waits for daylight.

As he waits, he remembers back to when he lost another book. That time, it had been in a cyclone.

Luke's head leans forward, and he nods off to sleep.

He starts, his neck jerks, and he sees now that it is daylight.

He goes into the tent to gather up what is inside and sees the parchment he had written on earlier the previous day.

Maybe I got all my parchments out of my pouch. His muscles tighten, he clenches his teeth and digs through his blanket and clothes.

Nothing. He pulls everything out of his tent and looks through them again. Still nothing. He only has the one parchment. The rest of his notes are gone.

He takes a deep breath, gathers up what he has, sets them on his now-flattened tent, and rolls them up together. He is not far from the city gate and walks over to the guard.

"It seems my horse and several important items in my luggage were stolen during the night."

"Them again," the guard says. "Go to the forum and report the thefts to the magistrates. They will probably help you search for them."

A clerk takes the information and reassures Luke they will send someone out to all known haunts of horse thieves up in the hills.

Luke goes to the market and looks around for shops carrying parchments and books. No one has purchased his.

He goes back to the forum. No one has been sent out to look for Thor yet, but they will soon. He goes over to one of the walls, slides down, sits, and waits. All day he waits.

"Well, they didn't get to it today," the clerk tells Luke, "but I am sure they will search tomorrow. Did you have a nice horse? Too bad."

For the next three days, Luke goes every day to the forum and is told one of the city guards is out looking for his horse and horses of other victims. For the next three days, Luke goes every day to the market to make inquiries. No new books showing up. No new horses. No anything.

I could walk from now on. I'm still strong. No, I cannot. I cannot leave behind my book about Jesus. Oh, Jesus! Not again!

He looks around the city for a synagogue and finds one. No one, however, has recently purchased any new books there either.

He goes to the richer part of town and knocks on gates.

"Sir, do you have a tutor for your children? Might he have purchased a book about Jesus lately?"

"Sir, I seem to have lost a book I have been writing. Has anyone in your home purchased a new book in the last day or two?"

He goes over to hostels and stables. "Have you seen any unusually large black horses?"

Have you heard of anyone obtaining a large black horse?

Illusive.

Gone.

Luke now knows what he must do. He has no other choice. He walks out through the gate of Salem and south on the Roman road, all his work forever lost.

That evening, he arrives at a well outside of Sychar. He spreads out his tent and tries to sleep. During the night, he overhears a man say the word, Jesus. By instinct, he crawls out of his tent.

"Did you say Jesus? Was he Jesus from Nazareth?"

"Yes, one of the men replies. Did you know him?"

"No, I never met him. Did you?" Luke asks.

"Today is the thirty-eighth anniversary of him healing us of our leprosy. My name is Nachum. This is Eitan. We come here every year to remember."

"I cannot sleep anyway," Luke says. "Would you tell me about it?"

The rest of the night, Luke hears their story. He repeats it back to them twice.

Morning comes. Luke sees a road toward the Great Sea, takes down his tent, wraps his belongings in it, puts it all on his back, and heads west.

That afternoon, he arrives, but the city does not look familiar. He stops someone coming out of the city.

"Is this Caesarea?"

"No, it isn't. This is Joppa. I am headed that way," the old man says. "Would you like to travel to Caesarea with me?"

"Thank you," Luke says. "My luck has been very bad the last few days. I suppose all my good luck in the past is just being evened out."

"It is going to take us the rest of the day plus tomorrow to get there," the stranger says. "Well, you could probably make it in one day. It will probably take these old legs two days. Anyway, I will listen as long as you want to talk."

Luke is silent. *Why burden him with my problems?*

"Young man, you are very quiet. Your burdens must be very heavy."

"Did you ever think everything in your life was working together toward you doing something great?"

"Indeed, I have. I started out my life, wanting to make great things happen, but my life stayed ordinary. I was at work one day and not accomplishing anything I wanted to.

"A man came along who seemed to know everything. I invited him to my work, and he made me an overnight success. My partners and I all shared in that success. Then this man told us to break away from our business and partner with him instead.

"Well, we decided that, if he was good at everything he did, we should join him."

"So, did you?"

"Indeed, we did. He traveled everywhere, and everything he did turned out the way he said it would. His competitors tried to stop him, but they were powerless next to him."

"You were very lucky," Luke says.

"Just when we thought he was going to take over the country, I did something stupid. His enemies became stronger, and I became afraid of them. I didn't want to go down with him, so I told them I didn't even know him. I cried for weeks after that. So, you see, it can happen to anyone."

"By the way, my name is Luke."

"Mine is Peter."

Luke stops in the road. "Simon Peter, son of Jonas and brother of Andrew?"

"How did you know?"

"I have been looking for you." Luke pauses. "But it is

too late."

"Too late for what?" Peter asks.

"The man you were talking about who helped you with your business was Jesus, wasn't he?"

"Yes. I watched as he became more and more popular with the people, I was there when he appeared shiny like a star. Then, after all that, I denied even knowing him."

Luke walks to the side of the road and squats. Peter follows him.

"Peter, I have spent the past year traveling all over the world tracking down the stories I have heard about Jesus to make sure they were true. I interviewed eyewitnesses and have made a special effort to find his apostles. I had only you, Philip in Frankish Gaul, and Simon in Britannia. Then I was going to write my book."

"You can't now? What is stopping you?"

"My horse was stolen, and my manuscript was with him. I thought I was too tired to relieve him of my supplies for the night and left them on him."

"So, all your notes are gone?"

"All gone. I am on my way to Caesarea to board a ship and return to my homeland."

"You cannot give up, Luke. What you are doing is important."

"You mean what I was doing."

"I have not yet told you how I salvaged what was left of my mission with Jesus. Yes, they killed him, but he came back to life and forgave me. Jesus can bring your manuscript back to life. Give him a chance."

"How? It is impossible. I am going home."

"Luke, you go on ahead. I am just slowing you down. Go to Caesarea. Go down to the docks. Line up a ship, and you will see a resurrection. Trust me. Go now."

Peter embraces Luke, prays for him, slips a small pouch of coins into Luke's belt, and sends him on his way. Luke walks the rest of the day. The sun disappears as he approaches the gate of Caesarea. The gate is still open.

"May I come in? It is past dark," Luke says to a guard.

"We're expecting someone important, but you are

welcome to come on in while we wait. You look harmless."

Luke walks through the gate, listens for ship bells at the harbor, and walks down to the water. Though it is night, activity does not stop. He hears, shouting.

"No, you are not taking both of you on board my ship."

"I told you I am. I have the money to pay passage for both of us."

"No. Absolutely not. Never. He will just get on board and cause problems."

"I promise you he will not."

"In that case, neither of you can board my ship."

"But I have to get to Egypt."

"You may go to Egypt, your friend may not."

Now realizing this ship is not going north to the strait through to the Black Sea and on to Germanicus, Luke decides to go on down the dock to continue looking for a ship that is.

"Sir."

He hears the voice of the man who had been arguing. He is not interested in getting involved and does not reply.

"Sir," he says again. "Could you use a good strong horse? I'll let him go cheap.

40 ~ RENEWAL

*H*aving secured Thor to a stall built onto the sides of the ship headed across the Great Sea, Luke takes his leather shoulder pouch, holding his parchments off the animal and sets it in his lap.

How did Peter know? And when did he slip this money in my belt? I will have to pay him back. But he did not tell me where he was shipping off to.

Luke puts the pouch in his arms and holds on to it as though keeping it from disappearing.

"Sir, you are going to have to exercise your horse twice a day. Maybe three times," the first mate says. "We do not want him becoming restless and destabilizing the ship."

Being one of the largest corn ships on the sea and with no need to skirt the coast, the *Anona* sails to Cyprus. Luke goes ashore and asks around for anyone who remembers Barnabas or John Mark. The ship does not stay in port long, so he reboards without success.

The ship goes on to Crete, then Malta, stopping at both places to take on fresh food for the crew and passengers.

At Malta, Luke remembers the winter he and Paul had spent there. He goes ashore, walks around, takes notes to what he remembers, learns there is a different governor now that would not remember him, and reboards the ship.

The *Anona* arrives at Sicily. Luke goes ashore and buys more parchments. "I have two more important interviews, and then I will be ready," he tells Thor.

It has been a week, and they are halfway to Frankish Gaul.

"We have been lucky with no storms," he tells one of the crewmen. "I remember one storm I was in..."

"We've all been through storms," the sailor interrupts, walking away.

Luke continues to exercise Thor three times a day. He spends much time looking through his parchments and putting them in what he thinks is chronological order. Sometimes he sings. Always when lonely, he sings.

> *Tho I vander long avay*
> *Over all da mounts und seas*
> *To da end uv da verld,*
> *I vill alvays tink uv home*
> *Und keep you in my heart*
> *Til I hold you once again.*

A sailor slips on the deck twists his foot, and it swells so large, he can no longer walk on it.

"Let me look at his foot," he tells the captain after the man has been taken below board. "I am a physician."

After that, other crew members and some of the passengers go to Luke with their physical problems.

"That's Sardenia ahead," the captain tells Luke while going for his afternoon walk around the deck. "We have had a very good trip. No incidents at all. In a few days, you will be at your destination."

Luke prays, sometimes aloud. "Help me find Philip and then Simon. And anyone else you want to send my way. And thank you again for Thor. I just don't know how Peter knew he would be returned to me. Yes, I do know. Thank you, Lord. Then help me go home."

At night, Luke lies the tent he has set up on the deck, lets the waves rock him to sleep, and dreams he is eight years old and sitting on his father's lap. Or sometimes he is all grown up, and Rashah is sitting on his lap.

It is morning again. The sun is in his eyes looking toward the stern, so he puts his back to it.

"Offf!

Luke is thrown off his feet. Thor struggles to maintain

his balance. Equipment breaks loose and goes sliding across the deck.

The ship tips to one side then rights itself.

"Pirates!"

Sailors come stumbling up onto deck carrying daggers, swords, bows with a supply of arrows, and slingshots.

The captain is on the bridge, his sword drawn.

Sailors continue to come stumbling up onto deck.

"Look out!"

Luke looks up just in time to move out of the way of the broken mizzenmast. He grabs the two-man-length pole, holding it broadside in both hands. He sees the pirates boarding the corn ship and runs toward them with his makeshift javelin, pushing them either back onto their ship or into the water.

Hand-to-hand fighting now among those who have managed to come on board. The fighting pirates protect their partners who have formed a relay to take bags of corn on board their own ship.

Amidst the chaos, Luke grabs at every pirate he can and throws him overboard.

Apparently satisfied, the captain of the pirate ship slowly backs off, showing its bronze bow and the gash in the *Anona*.

Luke dives into the water, grabs floating boards, and takes them to the gaping hole in the side of the corn ship. Crewmen of the *Anona* dive after him and follow suit. Other crewmen fight their way through water, now filling up the lower deck. With hammers, they struggle to secure the rescued boards onto the edges of the damaged hull.

On the upper deck, sailors armed with bows and a few arrows shoot at the pirate ship. The pirate ship continues to back away, leaving the *Anona* crippled and sinking.

Ropes are thrown off the uninjured side of the *Anona*, and the crewmen in the water climb back on board.

The captain heads his crippled ship away from Frankish Gaul.

"Corsica," he shouts.

The pirate ship now gone, the first mate sounds a bugle. Over and over, he sounds it. Then another bugle is heard in the distance. When they see the other ship, they cheer. It is a rescue ship.

When close enough, the rescue ship throws cables over to the *Anona,* where the sailors secure them. Boards, too, are stretched from one vessel to the other, and the sailors escape to the rescue ship.

Luke stays behind and comforts Thor. Some of the other passengers and sailors stay behind for their own reasons. On the bridge, the captain of the *Anona* stays at the helm.

With the *Anona* now lightened, the rescue ship pulls the *Anona* eastward until both ships reach the island of Corsica midway between Italia and Frankish Gaul.

Luke puts his hands and face on Thor and whispers to it. Thor remains calm. When they dock, a wide gangplank is made available, Luke leads Thor onto the shore.

"Sir!" he hears. "Are you Luke?"

Luke turns and sees the captain of the *Anona* following him.

"Here, take your fare back. I saw what you did to help save my ship. Thanks to you, I believe we can salvage it and put it back out to sea."

Luke refuses the refund. The following day, he boards the rescue ship, which takes all passengers of the *Anona* to the mainland of Frankish Gaul.

He asks around and learns he has landed at Marseilles, and it is near the Rhone River. He sees a stable and buys barley for Thor and some cheese for himself. When he pays for them, he remembers he has some of the money left Peter had stuck in his belt.

"Peter. You knew about everything, didn't you?" He asks around for a tentmaker and has just enough extra silver left to buy a two-man leather tent.

"You need a rest, friend," he tells Thor. The two walk south toward the river, then beside it as they work their way inland. They spend the night near the river bank.

"Well, Philip, I sure hope you are here."

Luke mounts Thor, and they work their way toward the fountainhead on the Roman road. Luke holds the reins only a little to let Thor regain his self-confidence. They stop for something to drink as often as Thor wants.

As they progress, Luke is impressed with the civility of the country. Whereas he had expected the country to be overrun with uncouth natives, he finds most wear the usual Roman tunics, and even some wear togas of the elite. He sees villas scattered along the countryside and a young growth of spring crops.

"You know, Thor, I was so anxious to get safely on shore, I forget to ask if any of the Gauls on the ship knew Philip. I sure hope I do not pass him and waste our time. I'm not going back."

Not having reached any cities by sundown, Luke dismounts, takes the tent rolled up on Thor's rump, and sets it up for his first good night's sleep in a month. *I hope.*

Safely inside the tent is his leather pouch with the manuscript in it. It serves as his pillow.

The next day, they continue to follow the Rhone River. In mid-afternoon, they arrive at an old city named Lyonsium.

Luke goes through the gate and finds the market. He notices most people are speaking in Latin and switches to the language he had first used to communicate with Theophilus.

"Do you happen to know a man named Philip?"

"No. So don't ask me."

"Might you have ever met a man named Philip?"

"Maybe yes. Maybe no. But probably no."

"Have you ever heard of a man named Philip?"

"Get out of here and leave me alone. I'm busy."

"How about Christians?"

"What's that? Get out of here."

After asking around enough places in the city that Luke is satisfied, he walks Thor to the east gate, mounts him, and continues on west to the next city.

Not as many elegant ladies and gentlemen inland, but there still are some. Luke continues to be impressed.

The farther west he goes, the fewer cities. More people

dressing as the natives apparently do. The top half of their tunic they call a shirt, and the separate bottom half is held up with a string around the waist and up the middle.

He notices people walking up to each other from opposite sides of the road, shouting, arguing, jabbing each other with their fingers or whatever is in their hand, then going back to whichever side of the road from whence they had come.

"Don't these people get along with each other?" Luke asks Thor.

Philip, I need you to be at the next city. I do not want to write the story of Jesus without you telling me what you remember.

It takes two more days to reach the next city. It is Parisia.

Luke dismounts and walks with Thor to the market.

"Excuse me, sir, but do you know a man named Philip?"

"Excuse me. I am looking for a man named Philip."

"Sir, I am a friend of a man named Philip. Might you know where he is?"

"What type of work does he do?" a merchant finally asks.

"I am not sure," Luke answers, wishing he had asked Peter.

Luke sees some stables. He walks Thor toward them. A man stops him in the street on the way.

"What a fine horse," the man says.

"I am looking for a stable with a stall large enough for him," Luke says.

"Well, come to my stable. I am prepared for anything."

Luke follows the stranger to his stable. It is clean, the animals appear well-groomed. Each has its own supply of fresh hay on the ground, and fresh oats and water.

"I am impressed," Luke tells the stranger.

"I was raised around horses. My father was a breeder down in Palestine."

"Palestine? You are a long way from home."

"This is my home now. I've been here for the past

fifteen years. Since you are new in the city, I would like to invite you to meet with a group that likes to encourage people to be good to each other."

"From what I've seen, these people could use a little of that."

"The group meets first thing in the morning once a week in the field just as you go out the west gate of the city."

Well, I may as well make some friends while I'm here. One of them may know Philip.

Luke finds a hostel near the stable so he can clean up after fifteen days onboard ship and four more days on the road.

The next morning, Luke walks to the location the stable owner had described. He sees people sitting on the ground in the meadow and joins them over to one side and in the back.

The man from the stable rises and stands before the group. He has chestnut hair, is tall, ample around his waist, and snorts when he gets excited.

"The kingdom of the one real God will never end. Jesus sent me to you so you will know about his never-ending kingdom."

Luke stares at the speaker. *That's Philip?*

"God does not dwell in lakes and streams, and mountains like you have been told. He made them. God is not his own creation.

"To prove to you that I represent the one and only God of the universe, he gave me the power to heal you. Only those approved of by God have this power. So now, if you have anything wrong with you, come forward. I can help you with the power of Jesus Christ."

No one comes forward.

Philip walks among the people. "You have trouble seeing. Now you can see perfectly because Jesus loves you." He walks more. "I notice you have a cane to help you walk. Stand up, my friend, and throw away your cane. You can now walk without pain."

Someone shouts from the other side of the crowd. "I'll bet you can't help my father. He doesn't even have an eye. It was put out in a war with another clan."

Philip walks over to the speaker and sees a man next to her with a cloth strip angled over one eye. "You have two eyes now and can see perfectly." He helps the man remove the cloth.

"I have both eyes back! He is right! He is from God."

Philip walks back to the front. By now, Luke, who has his pouch of writing supplies on one shoulder and medical supplies on the other shoulder, has pulled out a sheet of parchment. His vial of blackener is on the ground, and he is writing as fast as he can.

"Your druid priests will try to keep you out of the kingdom of God. They want you to follow them, not the only real God. They drown you in rules to keep you under their control. Jesus did not come to bring you rules, but to bring you peace and help you go to heaven when you die.

"Jesus is putting on a spiritual feast for you. A feast for your souls. Come to Jesus. Just as his power made your body well, he wants to make your soul well."

Philip sees a child in the crowd. He walks up to the child, smiles at the mother, then picks up the child. The child smiles. Come into the kingdom of God like a little child, trusting Jesus every step of the way the rest of your life.

"There are people in the world who hated Jesus and killed him."

Luke hears a collective gasp from the crowd.

"Do not worry, my friends. Jesus is so powerful, he came back to life. That is because Jesus was the Son of God.

"You have seen my miracles. Jesus gave me the power. If you believe in Jesus, come. Get rid of your household idols that are only statues. Come.

"Stop worshipping the water you drink, the mountains you climb, the air you breathe. God created them. Worship the creator. Come.

"Those things in nature you worship—rocks, trees, the sun—do not love you. Jesus loves you. He wants to show you how to live with him forever in heaven. Come."

It is now early evening. The crowd has disbursed. Luke walks back to the stable with Philip.

"I knew you had to be Philip. You are, aren't you?"

"Yes. And who are you, Luke? I mean, besides your name, who are you?"

"I was a physician for Paul the apostle the last few years of his life."

"Paul is gone?"

"Yes. So is James, but you knew that."

"Have you seen any more of us?"

"All but Simon. I have been everywhere trying to find you."

"You have an insatiable curiosity about Jesus and the kingdom," Philip says.

"It is more than that. I promised someone I would investigate Jesus' life and talk to eyewitnesses, then write everything about Jesus I can verify in a book."

Philip stops and looks at Luke. "Thank you. We are so busy teaching, we do not have time for books. We write letters to congregations we establish, but that is all we have time for. Thank you for doing this."

Philip puts a hand on Luke's shoulder, and they arrive back at the stable.

"So, I take it you are going over to Britannia to see Simon," he continues. "You know we called him Simon the Revolutionary. Be very careful over there. Those druids are dangerous.

"Well, I guess that's why Simon went there," Luke replies. "From what the other apostles have told me, he never backs down from a fight."

"If you come back this way, I may be gone. I want to go down to Egypt where my grandparents were born. I need to tell them about..."

Luke does not hear. As he saddles Thor, his mind is already on Britannia. Then home.

41 ~ OVERCOMING

The next day, Luke and Thor are at Portus Ittus on the far western shore of Frankish Gaul, the closest point to Britannia.

"I would like passage over to Britannia," he tells the first mate of several ships lined up at the dock.

"Are you sure you want to go there?" the first mate asks.

"Yes. Why?"

"I heard they give the governor a hard time over there. Stubborn people those Brits."

"From what I understand, the governor is Quintus Petillius Cerialis, and he has recently brought the tribes in the northeast part of the country under control. There is not much left of Britannia to conquer," Luke says.

"Suit yourself," the first mate says. "I'm glad to take your money. We will set sail in a few hours. Are you coming on board now?

"No, I thought Thor and I would walk around a while."

"You haven't paid for that horse yet."

"I was told fare for both of us was what I just gave you."

"Whoever told you that was wrong. Now hand over the rest of the fare."

Luke hands him the money and turns toward the dock.

"Listen for the bells. When you hear them, come on board. If we leave without you, no refunds."

Two hours later, Luke and Thor are settled on the

ship, Thor is in his assigned stall on the port side, and Luke is leaning on a pile of sails used as replacements after a storm.

"Well, Thor, this is it. Our last stop. Then home. You will like it there. Lots of cool weather and streams and green grass. Even though you were not born there, you will recognize your homeland when you arrive."

Thor neighs and Luke smiles.

The wind between the two countries is balmy. Luke falls asleep. When he awakens, it is dark. He falls asleep again, then the sun comes up behind him.

Luke stands and sees land before him. The small ship docks, a large and heavy gangplank is put out. Luke and Thor disembark.

"By the way," the first mate calls down to them from the deck, "you are in Chichester."

Luke waves at the man and heads into the city. He immediately begins his search. *If I can find Simon right off, we can go right home.*

"Have you run into a man named Simon?" he says, continuing to speak in Latin.

"Nope."

"Do you know anyone named Simon?"

"Why do you want to know?"

"I'm his friend."

"Then, you should know where he is."

"I am looking for man named Simon. Do you know him?"

"No. What's he look like?"

"I heard he's tall with bushy black hair."

"Lots of people around here look like that."

"Have you met anyone named Simon?"

Luke works his way out of the city. *Well, I guess he isn't here.*

He mounts Thor, rides away from the city on the Roman road going north and into the forests.

"Let's see what this country is like. At least it isn't desert. Didn't you get tired of all that sand and heat? I did. At least we didn't go through a lot of it in the summer. That's the mistake I made the first time. That's when my chestnut horse... Well, never mind."

At mid-afternoon, Luke arrives at a city on the Thames river named Londonium. The buildings look fairly new and very Roman. Most of the people seem to be elitists, wearing long tunics, and some wearing the togas of aristocrats.

He sees fine horses, chariots, and litters. He sees baths and parks and a forum. Londonium is walled on all sides except the one lined by the River Thames. He works his way around the outside of the wall and counts seven gates. He enters through Moorsgate and dismounts.

"Do you happen to know a man named Simon?"

"No. Sorry."

"I have a friend named Simon. I am looking for. Have you seen him?"

"Never heard of him."

"Have you heard of a man named Simon?"

"No. Why?"

"Are there any Christians in your city?"

"What are Christians?"

"Do you know of any Christians here?"

"Yes, but I don't know who they are."

Luke leads his horse out the same gate he had used to enter the city.

"Well, Thor. We go to the next city. Just follow the Roman road. It should lead to something."

In a few hours, Luke is in the town of St. Albans. Its buildings are not as large and people not as refined as at Londonium. Still, it is very Roman. He continues to hear Latin spoken all around him.

He goes to the market and asks for Simon or Christians. He finds neither. He stops at a stable and buys oats for Thor, and cheese and bread for himself.

Back on the Roman road, he continues north through the forests. Luke pulls over to the side of the road to put up his tent. A man stops.

"Hey, you with the big black horse. I wouldn't spend the night in this forest if I were you."

"Thank you, my friend. But I have traveled the world

and have not had any problems yet. *Well, not many.*

"I warned you."

The next morning arrives without incident. Luke learns he is on the outskirts of a city named Leicester. As always, he enters, makes his way to the market, and asks around for Simon. It is foggy, but Thor knows his way, even in the mist.

As is always the case, no one has ever heard of Simon or Jesus or Christians. Back on the road. He heads for Lincoln. The forest is denser.

"Whoa!"

Thor rears up on his hind legs and neighs. Luke is punched in the side with a long branch and falls off. Men from both sides of the road rush at him and tie both his hands and feet together. They slip a heavy wooden rod under the ropes and lift him by the rod as though he were being led to a festive fire to be roasted and eaten.

His captors sing. Those not carrying him dance around him. Now they are off the road and running through the forest. Sometimes a low-hanging branch hits him in the face. Sometimes they drop him on his back, laugh, and pick him up again.

They come to a clearing where there is a wide, fat hill surrounded by round shacks with thatched roofs. They take Luke up the hill.

At the apex stands a tall man. Luke wonders if he is standing on stilts. What he knows for sure is that the man is tattooed all over his body.

The men carrying him drop him on his back onto the ground, still attached to the rod by his hands and feet. Luke squirms, and the men laugh. They rip his clothes off—all but a loincloth.

Gradually, men, women, and children come out of their roundhouses and walk up the wide hill. The women take turns poking Luke in his torso and limbs. The children come. They most delight in poking Luke in his face—nose, ears, eyes, cheeks, neck.

The sound of a horn and flute, accompanied with steady drums fills the air in the forest.

The tall man raises his arms, and everyone stops making noise. They kneel.

He opens his mouth, and out comes noises that Luke does not believe is a language. He grows louder. Luke hears a baby among the crowd.

A hot iron, still red from the fire, is brought up the hill and handed to the tall man who Luke has decided is their druid priest and possibly also their king.

Luke watches the hot iron as long as he can, hoping in vain he can will the iron to turn cold. The priest raises it above his head, then throws it into a tree.

The women return with vials of something. They take turns emptying the vials onto Luke. It is honey.

Now it is dark. One by one, the people on the hill retreat until Luke is there alone, still naked and still bound to the pole.

Now alone, Luke twists his body until he is on his side and can move a little in the dirt. He stops and listens. He thinks he hears Thor. He whistles for Thor and waits. He waits in vain.

He twists himself around so that he is in a position to half scoot and half roll down the hill. He manages to get himself halfway down. He cannot go farther. His arms, legs, hands, feet, back, chest, shoulders, and face are scratched. He knows the blood will attract as many insects as the honey.

He begins to itch and knows the insects have found him. He clenches his eyes and mouth closed. He presses his fingers and toes together. He balls up his fists. He rolls over on his back and tries in vain to raise up his knees. He arches his back for as long as he can before he grows too tired to do it any longer.

Still, the insects and whatever else crawling along on the ground come to him. He tries to sleep but cannot. After an eternity, he senses a slight grayness in the sky and wills it to be morning. He has survived. So far.

Luke hears children. They are laughing, they are running toward him. They have picked up sticks and are poking him all over.

Luke sings. He sings as loudly as he can. He sings some of the psalms of David he had memorized while still in Berea with dear old Theophilus. Does he dare? He cannot help it. He sings his father's song.

> *Tho I vander long avay*
> *Over all da mounts und seas*
> *To da end uv da verld,*
> *I vill alvays tink uv home*
> *Und keep you in my heart*
> *Til I hold you once again.*

Over and over, he bellows it. Now all is quiet except for his song. The children are gone. Everyone is gone. *Where are they?*

Then the screaming. The screaming and chanting and yodeling and shouting and roaring. Up the hill, they come. The entire village. As many as can get to Luke pick up the pole, he is still tied to, fighting each other to see who is the strongest and will carrying him back up the hill.

He shouts to them as his back scrapes the ground. "Jesus! I come to you with the love of Jesus! Jesus made you and loves you! Jesus smiles on you!"

They get him to the top of the hill. The druid priest is there. He has a broad sword. One in each hand.

Those carrying Luke push the pole he is tied to upright, so he is now in a stooped standing position. *Are they going to let me loose? Will I be able to make a run for it?*

He slides slightly down the pole, then the thud. They have planted it into the ground. The tall priest raises the swords above his head and swings them around. Luke presses his eyes tight.

Someone appears in front of him now. He has a torch. He holds the torch close to Luke.

Fire or blade? Which way will I die? Jesus, make it quick.

More noises. Coming from the edge of the forest. Now at the bottom of the hill. Shrill. And hoof beats. Luke opens his eyes and sees Thor rush by. At the top of the hill, Thor rears up on his hind legs and paws the air.

He sees a rider on Thor. The rider has black bushy hair. The rider slides off Thor and points at the priest who is taller than the rider. The priest backs up.

Still, the rider points his long arm at the priest. The priest no longer backs up. The priest is frozen in place. The priest does not move. He is a statue.

The rider stands with both legs far apart and his arms above his head. His voice booms.

"In the name of Jesus, fire turn to ice."

The man holding the torch shrieks. Not only is the torch ice, but his arm is too.

The rider turns around and faces Luke.

"In the name of Jesus, come forth."

The ropes around Luke dissolve. He stays where he is.

"In the name of Jesus, I say come forth."

Luke takes a step forward.

The rider's back is to everyone. The rider winks at Luke and smiles. "In the name of Jesus, leap for joy."

Luke, never very good at leaping, turns in circles and waves his arms.

"Give me the rope," the rider declares to Luke, who gathers it up off the ground. The rider takes hold of the rope, turns to face the crowd on the hill below him, holds it over his head spanned between both hands, and shouts, "Behold. The rope for the false priest."

The women rush forward, grab the rope, and wind it around the priest who is still frozen in place.

"Now," the rider booms, "sit."

Everyone sits, and the rider smiles. "Good morning, everyone. Has your druidic priest been giving you a hard time again? Now today's lesson is about miracles."

Luke stares at the rider, then at Thor still standing where the rider had slid off of him.

With the crowd now seated, the rider begins a psalm of David, and they join in. As they sing, he goes over to Luke.

"Greetings, brother. My name is Simon. They used to call me Simon the Zealot or Simon, the Revolutionary, and I guess I still am. They didn't bother you too much during the night, did they? They love the old honey-and-ant trick."

"Oh, I brought you a clean tunic. Sorry, it is made out of leather, not the fine linen or cotton you must be used to. And here is a skin of water and a rag to wash that honey off."

"How?" Luke stares at Simon as he smiles and occasionally turns to his congregation to get them to sing the next verse.

"How?" Luke repeats.

"How did I know? Your horse told me. I saw it eating grass beside the road. I looked in the leather pouches on it and saw your manuscript. You are Luke. Right? And you are writing a book about our Lord. Am I right?"

Luke shakes his head and manages a smile. "Would they have set me on fire?"

"They're still afraid of that druid priest they kicked out of their village. Whenever he comes back, he puts them under his spell. So I have to keep pretty close watch over them.

"Why don't you go over and reassure your horse, clean up a bit, then come sit down with the others. It is the first day of the week. I shall preach about Jesus' miracles in order to prove he was the Son of God, then I will remind them of his death, burial, and resurrection. Following that, we will have the Lord's Supper with some bread and new wine. Then I'll preach again, and I have no idea how long that will last. If you fall asleep during my sermon, I will remind myself you had a rough night."

"Behold!" Simon bellows to the villagers. "I bring you, Jesus. By his words, the world was created. By his words, he still controls the world around us.

"Jesus can control the wind and water. During a storm, he commanded them to stop churning, they listened to him and obeyed. I saw it myself.

"Jesus can control your crops. He can wait until you have made bread with your grain, then multiply it enough to feed a whole city. I saw it myself.

"Jesus can control the fish of the rivers and lakes and seas. If he wants them to all swim to you, they will all swim to you. I saw it myself.

"Come now. Let us eat the Lord's Supper. Jesus voluntarily took your place by taking the punishment for your sins. Now he says come. Come to Jesus and live forever in heaven."

Luke does not fall asleep. He has taken his writing materials out of his leather shoulder pouch and written as fast as he could everything Simon has said.

The sun is just past the pinnacle of the sky. Simon leads his congregation in a final song and prayer.

"I need to take you home with me now," Simon says after dismissing the congregation. "I live in a nearby valley where I can keep close tabs on this congregation."

Luke puts his writing materials away, takes Thor's reins, and walks with Simon to his round, thatch-roofed home.

"Did you get everything you wanted to know?" he asks Luke. "Do you have more of us to go see?"

"More of Jesus' apostles? No, you are the last one. I was planning to take all my notes and write my book in Jerusalem, but it is no longer possible."

"Why? What's wrong in Jerusalem?"

"It is no longer there. The temple either. They insisted on their own way one too many times. Rome marched on Jerusalem. Now it is gone.

Simon shakes his head. "Jesus predicted it would happen. We thought it was impossible. It wasn't. So, where are you going to write your book about Jesus' life?"

"My home. I left it when I was eight years old, newly made a slave. I have longed to return to my village in Frisia. It has been over forty years. It is time for me to go home."

42 ~ HOME

Luke stands next to a stall aboard the ship on the Nordic Sea between Britannia and Frisia. He smiles, pats Thor on his cheek, and looks toward the other shore of the Nordic Sea. A shore he cannot see.

"Two days, Thor, and we will be home."

Home. Without warning, the word swirls around in his head, plunges, soars, struggles, flies free, then dives.

Home. What is home? Where I am? Where I will be? Where I was?

With the reality looming after forty long years of wishing and hoping, Luke's heart leaps, his eyes strain, his breathing races, and he looks into the broad stretches of the sea before him. Never before has he questioned the word home. Never before has he doubted home would always be what it always was. Never before has that word entered into a realm of mist and fog and wondering. Luke panics.

Home? Home without family? Will it really be home? Father and mother forever gone. Betrothed forever lost. No children. No aunts or uncles. No bloodline.

"Are you okay?" the first mate asks. "Your fingers are going to break through that railing. Have you spotted something out there we need to know about?"

Luke returns to reality, clears his throat, takes a deep breath, and smiles. "Oh, I guess I was daydreaming. The day is beautiful, isn't it? And I love the sea breeze. I guess I have always loved it."

"Well, by your yellow hair, my guess is you are originally from that peninsula over there surrounded by the

Nordic, a gulf, a river, and peat bogs. I can see why sea air would remind you of home."

There it is again. That word. Home. Try not to imagine what it may be. Remember what it once was.

"It's a good thing your friend provided you with a rowboat. There is no way our ship is going to get anywhere close to shore."

"Yes, I was very fortunate. I had forgotten about it, actually. You can wade way out into the ocean there. Well, that's what I heard the grownups say."

"Forty years is a long time. Do you remember anything about your home?"

"I remember my house was very long. My family lived in the front part, and our cow, some goats, a hog, and some chickens lived in the back part. Maybe we had a horse too. Or a donkey. I'm not sure now. But, I do know we had animals back there. The winters were too cold to go out and feed them, and of course, the streams they drank out of always froze."

Luke is grateful for the man's questions.

"Seems like our fireplace was on the floor. And we had a few wooden benches to sit on, and beds that were really shelves. That's all we had. It was all we needed.

"Didn't you have tables?"

"Yes, I guess we did. For eating, not for writing. My father could not read or write. Our Frisian language did not even have an alphabet for each of the sounds. He made me promise."

"Promise?"

"Yes, that I would learn to read and write the language of the soldiers around us, then write the history of our people."

"So, did you?"

"I did learn to read and write Latin. Yes. When I got good enough, I started writing the history. But a few years later it was destroyed in a cyclone. I had been away too long by then to remember enough to rewrite it. So it was lost forever."

"Didn't your father help you?"

Luke turns away from the first mate, strokes Thor on his back, and looks up at the clouds.

The first mate walks away.

Will I even be able to find it? The old people used to talk about the seashore changing with every tide. What if I can't find it? Will it even be there anymore?

The day continues. Luke alternates between standing, sitting, and pacing. Sometimes he takes Thor for a walk around the deck, whispering to him to keep the big animal calm. Sometimes he daydreams, sometimes he reads, sometimes naps. His song comes back. Softly, he says, "Vather, dhis is vor you."

> *Tho I vander long avay*
> *Over all da mounts und seas*
> *To da end uv da verld,*
> *I vill alvays tink uv home*
> *Und keep you in my heart*
> *Til I hold you once again.*

Day two. Luke thinks back over the way Theophilus had found him and how patient the tribune always was whenever he spoke of his father. He remembers back over all the fortresses they had lived and served in. He recalls meeting Timothy, John Mark, Paul. Jesus, in a way too. And his quest to find witnesses to Jesus' life and teachings.

"Baduhenna? Is that where you said you wanted to go?" It is the first mate again.

"Yes. That is all I remember. We worshipped Baduhenna, the goddess of war. She was a mother goddess, so maybe she was a goddess of springtime too. I do not know for sure.

"I vaguely remember her being honored in a grove of trees on a hill. Hills and trees is what kept us safe from the waves of the Nordic Sea."

Luke looks down at the seawater. "It seems we had a river. Vessel or Gessel or Yssel. Yes. That's what it was—the Yssel River. It didn't look like much of a river to me. To me, it just looked like another marsh. But, I guess the grownups saw water moving through it, so maybe it was a river after all.

"There were Roman legionnaires around sometimes. They would come to our village and demand animal pelts as our tax. Sometimes they built good roads for us. Well, I guess the roads were for them, but I thought in my child's mind they were just being nice to us."

If only I had asked Theophilus how to find exactly where I lived. He could have helped me. Until now, it has not occurred to me I could have asked him.

"I wonder if it is at all the same as when the Roman military was there forty years ago. Are the roads even there anymore? Maybe the sea washed them away."

The first mate does not answer.

"Sometimes, I wonder about my name. Who was I named after? I kind of remember a village named Luuk, Luukville, or Luukemborg. Did I come from a famous family? If we were famous, maybe I will run into someone who remembers us."

Even if I do not run into anyone who remembers me... Well, if I had my father with me and my betrothed, we could start over. I am still strong. I could build us a nice longhouse that will withstand the long winters here. I could dig dikes to protect our land from the waves of the sea and plant crops. Oh. I forgot to bring any seeds.

The next morning when Luke awakens, he looks east as always. This time he sees it. Land. In the distance, but still, land. His land. His homeland. Home.

Through the morning, he watches. He strains to see animals—perhaps seals—along the shore. And people. And houses. Are there any to see?

Closer the ship draws to the shore.

"Well, sir," the captain says, approaching Luke, "this is as close as we get. One of the sailors will help you lower your boat into the water. We can lower a gangplank for you. I suspect you are going to have to jump in the water with your horse, so he isn't surprised at what he is going to have to do. It'll be a pretty cold boat ride for you. But you look robust enough. You will survive."

"Yes, I think you are right," Luke answers.

"Is your horse Nordic?"

"Yes. He was not born here, but his breed is from here. By the way, he is sniffing the air and swishing his tail, I think he knows."

The captain holds out his hand. Luke takes it and thanks the captain for going out of his way for him.

A wooden panel is removed from a part of the ship's side, and a gangplank lowered to the water held at an angle by two heavy chains.

"Make it quick," the sailor says. "Don't know how long our chains will hold your big horse."

A few moments later, Luke and his belongings, including his leather tent, his medical pouch, his writing pouch, and a few clothes are safe aboard his boat, and Thor is happily swimming behind it, though he sometimes comes beside it.

"Hey there," Luke says. "You really like this water. Anxious to get home? Me too."

It does not take Thor long to touch the floor of the sea and wade the rest of the way to shore. Luke follows close by, pulls the boat all the way onto the beach, then sits in the sand to wait for the sun to dry him out.

While the sea breeze wafts through his hair, Luke watches the birds as they land and play and fly away. The seals eye him with curiosity.

"Thor, we are almost out of food. You stay here by the boat while I see what I can find. There should be some good berries for both of us. If not, maybe I can make a spear and grab a couple of fish. Hope I remember how to make fire with my bow drill."

Luke walks inland until he sees bushes offering him something for a mid-day meal. *Hmmm. The tide must be just going out. Too marshy already. And deeper than I expected. I wonder if I could manipulate the boat through here.*

Luke goes back to shore, tells Thor to stay put until he returns, leaves his leather tent and two leather shoulder pouches on the animal's back for comfort and safety, and pulls the rowboat to the marsh.

He climbs in and pushes his way deeper with an oar until he is floating. Cranes fly away upon his approach, and he laughs. He finds he cannot row at all, so keeps pushing his way through.

"There you are," he says, grinning at the low bushes bearing crunchy red berries. "So you think it is already autumn here," he says. "Good for you. And good for me."

Luke reaches over as far as he can to pick some of the berries until all on the outer parts are harvested. He pushes his boat in closer to the center of the low bushes but still cannot reach them.

Well, I got wet before, and it didn't kill me. He climbs out of the boat and wades up to his thighs in the water. He picks a few more berries and turns to toss them into the boat. He finds it hard to turn. Then he cannot turn at all. He struggles, and his body becomes heavier.

Quicksand! I've got to get out of here. The more he turns, the more his feet sink into the clay below. He rocks back and forth, but nothing happens. He reaches over to get a rope on the boat and tries to work his way hand over hand to it. Only the boat moves.

It is late afternoon. Shadows move in. Luke grows colder. His legs grow numb. He tries to flex the muscles in his legs, partly to get the muscles active again, partly to keep them warm, and partly to keep himself conscious.

I cannot whistle for Thor. He will get stuck in here too. "Help! Help!" *Please, Thor, do not come.* "Help! Help, someone!"

Luke calls out until his voice is hoarse. *Is this why I came home? To die? What am I doing here? What is so great about Frisia anyway?*

He hears noise on the other side of the bushes. "Help! Over here! Help!"

A beaver jumps into the water, eyes Luke, then swims away.

"Help! Help!"

The sun is nearly down.

I've got to rest. He pulls the boat closer and leans over on it, resting his head on the edge. *What if I fall asleep and my head slips under? I've got to rest. Sleep. I am so tired.*

He awakens with a start. He thinks he hears neighing. *No, Thor. Don't come in here.* "Lord, help me escape this. And do not let it be Thor who gets me out. Would you mind sending me an angel?"

The wind picks up. *Cold. I'm so cold.*

"Help! Help, someone!" Luke shouts again. "Anyone. Is anyone out there? Help!"

Quiet again. Luke sleeps. With a start, he opens his eyes. *Don't close your eyes. Don't fall asleep. Stay awake. Stay alive.*

He looks up through the thicket and can see the stars. *Oh, Vather, I need you. Help me, Vather.*

He sings. In the darkness, he sings.

> *Tho I vander long avay*
> *Over all da mounts und seas*
> *To da end uv da verld,*
> *I vill alvays tink uv home*
> *Und keep you in my heart*
> *Til I hold you once again.*

His voice grows weaker. It is quiet again.

Jesus, is my work here on earth done? Have you brought me home to die? Is that how it will happen? I will join my father in the sky? And my beloved Rashah? Is home the portal to heaven?

Luke's hands are numb. He rubs them together. He holds them under his arms.

My legs. I cannot feel my legs. Jesus, show me how to die. Help me die with courage.

"Help," he calls out with hardly any voice left. "Help..."

God, I made it. I guess this is all I ever wanted—to step onto the soil of my homeland.

Luke smiles, and tears come to his eyes. *Stop that! You're a man. You're not eight years old anymore. Be a man.*

He begins to sway. He knows he will sink deeper if he sways.

Tired. I am so tired. Rock me to sleep, Jesus. Rock me

until I awake in your home. Bring me home, Jesus. I am ready, bring me home.

The sky is light gray now. A few ducks awaken, fly in circles, and land again.

Luke raises his head off the edge of the boat. He struggles a little more. *May as well get it over with. May as well go under now than later. Jesus, I am coming home.*

"Jesus! Do you hear me?" he cries aloud. "I am coming home!"

Quiet. Then, "Hellooo."

It is not Luke.

Huh? Is that you, Jesus? Or an angel?

"Hellooo."

"Hello," Luke whispers, his head still leaning on the edge of the boat.

"Shake some bushes if you're there," the voice says.

Luke shakes what bushes he can. But each time he does, his feet sink a little lower in the mud below.

Something now heads in his direction. He sees the bow of a rowboat.

"Over here," he mutters.

A man, who Luke considers to be about his same age, rows his boat to the opposite side of Luke and his boat. A younger man climbs into Luke's. They both have long-handled shovels.

"This sometimes happens around here when people come and do not know what they're doing," the rescuer says. "What we are going to do is dig the clay loose around your feet. Once we get enough water under them, they will float up on their own. Ready?"

"How long will it take?" Luke immediately wishes he hadn't asked. "I have been here all night. Take your time."

"Well, we have other things to do today. We will get you out as soon as possible."

Nothing more is said. The middle-aged man and the younger man, whom Luke assumes are father and son, dig around his feet steadily. Gradually, as water flows under his feet, he begins to feel buoyancy in them.

"Stay still. Let the water lift you up. If you have ever

carried a pail of water, you know how heavy it is. Let it lift you up."

Luke watches the man. What is it? His mannerisms? The way he phrases his words? The way he tips his head?

After another half hour of digging, the water lifts Luke. He leans over on his boat, trying not to struggle and start the whole process of being stuck happen again. A little at a time, his feet and legs float to the top of the water.

The middle-aged man pulls on Luke until he is completely in the boat.

Luke turns around, sits, and stares. "Thank you," he says with an exhausted smile.

"Where did you come from? The beach?" his rescuer asks.

"Yes," Luke says, his voice still scratchy. "A ship from Britannia dropped me off, and I rowed the rest of the way to shore. I was looking for food. My horse is still there, along with my supplies."

"Your horse must be a good swimmer," the rescuer says.

"He is good at everything he does."

Luke smiles. "By the way, my name is Luke. When I used to live here a long time ago..."

"Lukvert?" the other man asks, his eyes questioning, but his grin broad.

"Uh, well, yes. I am Lukvert." Luke stares at the other man. "Do I know you?"

"Do you know me?" the man says, laying both oars in the bottom of the boat. "Do you know me? Of course, you know me. We were best friends. I am Logmarr. And I can still out-throw you with the javelin."

Luke stares a moment longer. "Logmarr? Is that you?"

The two men lunge at each other, stop, and laugh. "We'd better save this until we get on solid ground. Where do you say your horse and supplies are?"

"Just over that way somewhere on the shore."

Logmarr takes the boat closer to the beach until it scrapes bottom. He hops out, and Luke does too. Together they pull the boat onto solid ground.

Luke whistles. Thor comes galloping up the beach.

"Thor, meet Logmarr," Luke says with his still scratchy voice. "Logmarr, meet Thor."

"We can walk up the beach until we come to the path to my home," Logmarr says. "The boat will keep."

"So, old friend, how have you been?" Luke asks. "I notice you are not speaking our Frisian language."

"Some do still. But most of us began speaking the language of the Romans, so we can trade with them."

"You're not enemies anymore?"

"That was a long time ago."

The two big yellow-haired men take long strides up the beach. Luke and Thor follow Logmarr up the path until they come to a clearing. Luke sees ahead of them a hill with a longhouse on it.

"Your house is exactly the way I remember it," Luke says, slapping his old pal on the back.

"No, my friend. That is not my house. My house is on a hill farther back."

"Oh, well, then let's get to your house. No detours."

Logmarr stops. He sits on the edge of the clearing and grows solemn. "Luke, sit a moment."

Luke's smile wanes. "What's wrong? Logmarr, whatever it is, I will stand by you. We were best friends once, and we will be best friends forever. It will always be you and me."

"Sit, Luke."

Luke kneels on one knee.

"Luke, your father..."

Luke sits all the way down and twists his mouth. "Was your father killed in the battle?"

"He survived," Logmarr says. "How about yours?"

"He was taken prisoner and ended up as a slave in Espanola. He was there ten years, then was sold to a prince in Parthia. That is where I ran into him. I helped him escape, but we were caught, and he was taken back for execution."

Logmarr puts his hands up to his face, covers his mouth, and clears his throat. "Uh, did you ever marry?" he asks.

"Can't we talk about this on our way to your house?" Luke asks. "I'm a little tired, old friend."

"You're right. So, did you ever marry?" Logmarr puts his hand back up to his mouth and wipes across it as they resume their walk.

"I was betrothed, which in that society was the same thing as being married. Just before I took her into my house, she died."

"That must have been hard, losing both your father and your bride."

"You have no idea."

"Oh, by the way," Logmarr says, "I need to stop in this house and pick up something. Do you want to go in with me or wait out here?"

"If I stay out here, you won't talk to your friends so long, and we can get to your house sooner. I will stay out here."

"Suit yourself."

Luke leans against a tree near the front door. Logmarr disappears in the house.

Luke waits. He hears voices.

"Come on, Logmarr," he calls in. "I'm getting tired."

The door opens. A momentary silence.

"Son?"

"Huh?"

"Oh, my son."

Luke stares at the big gray-haired figure in the doorway.

"Father?"

Luke takes two long steps, stares into the eyes of the old man, and envelops him in his arms. They weep, step inside the house, and weep more..

Logmarr waits.

He then clears his throat.

"Uh, Luke, can the two of you break apart a moment?"

"Logmarr, you do not understand. I thought he was dead."

"Stop, Luke. Stop and look at me."

Luke pulls away from his father, twists his mouth, and

looks at his childhood friend. Logmarr steps aside.

A petite woman stands in the middle of the room. She has long black hair with some gray around the temples. Her eyes sparkle, her face blushes, she smiles. Luke stares a moment, then opens his arms wide, and she steps into his embrace.

"Oh, Rashah. Oh, my Rashah."

Logmarr stands over to one side, a shoulder leaning against the wall, his big arms crossed over each other, and with a large grin. He watches as the three embrace and weep.

Finally, they hold each other at arm's length so they can look into their eyes and absorb the impossible that has become possible.

"But how?" Luke continues to ask.

"Come, sit my son," Sigmundrr says.

Logmarr pulls up two long benches. He and the old man sit together on one. Luke and Rashah sit together on the other.

"After my capture, all they did was brand me. Then, when I reached seventy, I was too old to be an effective guard, and they set me free. Personally, I think it is because the king didn't want to feed me anymore. Anyway, I..."

"He came to me and asked if I wanted to go back to Frisia with him," Rashah continues, "so we could wait for you. I did so want to. I have never stopped loving you."

"And I you," Luke says, squeezing her hand and absorbing her with his eyes.

"I worked out the whole thing," Sigmundrr said. "One day, when Rashah was supposed to go to the market, I met her, and we just kept going. Once we were out away from the city, every time someone saw us, I hit her with my stick, claiming I was taking the king's slave back to the palace."

"We worked our way through Parthia, then up into Scythia past the Caspian Sea and over to here," Rashah says. "Depending on where we were, either I was the king's runaway slave, and he beat on me, or he was my runaway slave, and I beat on him. Well, we didn't beat hard enough to hurt, but we made it sound like we did."

Luke sits and stares at the two. "You both are

amazing."

"Do you remember one time when you were in Scythia just a couple years ago that someone was shooting arrows at you out in the desert?" Rashah asks.

"That was you?" Luke says with a confused look on his face but mixed with a slight grin.

"I thought you would recognize my arrows," she says. "We needed to make sure it was you."

"I did notice them, but could not remember where I had seen them in the past."

"Well, before we could get you to quit running from us, you slipped away in the night, and disappeared."

"Those capes you left behind sure helped when we crossed the mountains," Sigmundrr says.

"I was headed south while you were headed north," Luke says. "We came that close to being together then?"

"Son, we have been here since then, waiting for you. We knew you would come home someday. Thomas said that is what you would do. He had never met you, but said you would be like me."

"Thomas?"

"Yes. The apostle Thomas. He helped us plan our escape."

"Did you, by any chance..."

"Yes, we did. We became Christians."

A week goes by. During that time, Luke builds a large table.

"I have a promise to keep," Luke tells his wife and father, "to a man who kept me hoping for forty long years."

Sitting at the table, Luke pulls out his priceless collection of parchments, sorts through them, puts them in order, and begins to write.

"MANY, WHO FROM THE BEGINNING WERE EYEWITNESSES AND SERVANTS OF THE GOSPEL OF JESUS CHRIST, HAVE TAKEN IT UPON THEMSELVES TO COMPILE AND HAND DOWN TO US AN ACCOUNT OF THE MIRACULOUS THINGS ACCOMPLISHED FROM THE BEGINNING.

"IT SEEMED FITTING FOR ME ALSO, MOST EXCELLENT THEOPHILUS, HAVING INVESTIGATED EVERYTHING CAREFULLY, TO WRITE IT DOWN FOR YOU IN CONSECUTIVE ORDER SO YOU MAY KNOW THE EXACT TRUTH ABOUT THE THINGS YOU HAVE BEEN TOLD

ABOUT OUR LORD.
"IN THE DAYS OF HEROD, KING OF JUDEA..."

Sometimes as Luke writes, his father hums.

Tho I vander long avay
Over all da mounts und seas
To da end uv da verld,
I vill alvays tink uv home
Und keep you in my heart
Til I hold you once again.

THANK YOU

Thanks for reading my book! I'm so honored that you chose to spend your precious time with my characters. You are appreciated. I'm an independent author who relies on my readers to help spread the word about stories you enjoy.

Would you take a few minutes to let your friends know on Facebook, Pinterest...wherever you hang out online? Also, each honest review at online retailers means a lot to me and helps other readers know if this is a book they might enjoy.

I welcome contact from readers. At my website (below), you can do so. You can also sign up for my monthly newsletter (below) for half-price paper and 99c ebooks for the whole family - novels, non-fiction, storybooks and first peek at my newest release.

GET ALL 8 BOOKS IN THE HISTORICAL SERIES
INTREPID MEN OF GOD

Novel 1 ~ Lazarus: The Samaritan
Novel 2 ~ Paul: The Unstoppable
Novel 3 ~ Luke: Slave & Physician
Novel 4 ~ Mefiboset: Crippled Prince
Novel 5 ~ Joseph: The Other Father
Novel 6 ~ Michel: The Fourth Wise Man
Novel 7 ~ Stephen: Unlikely Martyr
Novel 8 ~ Titus: The Aristocrat

HISTORICAL BACKGROUND

The 'doctors' in ancient Rome were not nearly as highly regarded. The profession itself, outside of the legions, was considered a low social position, fit for slaves, freedmen and non-Latin citizens....The bulk of doctors, at least early on, were self-taught or apprenticed practitioners....With the introduction of a medical school in the 1st century AD, the health care of ancient world become more uniform and practical.

Slaves in Rome might include prisoners of war, sailors captured and sold by pirates, or slaves bought outside Roman territory.

The Battle of Baduhenna Wood was a battle fought near Heiloo, Netherlands in 28 AD between the Frisii and Roman legion, Legio V, led by Roman General Lucius Apronius. Tacitus wrote of it in his book 4, chapter 73 of *Tacitus's Annals*. (Future movements by Theophilus and Luke are based on the movements of this legion).

"Most Excellent" Strong's Concordance ~ **kratistos: strongest, noblest. Original Word:** κράτιστος, η, ον. **Definition:** Most excellent, an official epithet, used in addressing a Roman of high rank, and in the second century one of equestrian (as distinguished from senatorial) rank.

The equestrian class was originally composed of the Roman cavalry. By the time of Claudius, after serving in the army as an officer, a potential equestrian might become a procurator – an agent of the emperor. He could then become a prefect. Equestrians could rise to the rank of senator. Equestrians did not have to be Roman or Italian by birth.

Tribunes commanded portions of the Roman army, subordinate only to the higher magistrates, such as consults, praetors, and legates.

Frisia was mostly in today's Holland on the North Sea and considered by the Romans to be part of Lower Germanicus. Baduhenna Wood was within their borders.

Friesian horses originating in Friesland, in the Netherlands. They resemble giant draught horses but are graceful and nimble for their size. They are usually sleek black.

Cruptorix: "Soon afterward it was ascertained from deserters that nine hundred Romans had been cut to pieces in a wood called Baduhenna, after prolonging the fight to the next day, and that another body of four hundred, which had taken possession of the house of one Cruptorix, once a soldier in our pay, fearing betrayal, had perished by mutual slaughter." (Tacitus Annals 73)

- Publius Cornelius Cethegus was a Roman senator who governed Germanicus, and was noted for his "bad life."

- Lucius Apronius. In AD 28, he was Legate of Lower Germany. He led the combined forces from Upper Germany in raising the siege of a Roman fort by the Frisii, only to be defeated by them soon after in a pitched battle at Baduhenna Wood.

- Olennus, Governor of Frisia, demanded a tax of a certain size and quality. The Frisians could not keep up. According to Tacitus, therefore, their cattle were first taken, then their fields and eventually their women and children were slaughtered as slaves. In the year AD28, Roman tax collectors were hung up by the Frisians and afterward the Frisians drew up against the Roman governor. Olennius, however, managed to escape. When the Frisians learned the Romans sent reinforcements, they retreated into the Baduhenna forest. Here it struck 900 Romans and killed another 400 people.

- Fort Nova-Esium was located near Neuss, Germany.

- Fort Bonna was located near Bonn, Germany.

- Fort Amphipolis was near today's Rodovolis,

Greece.

Fort Capidava was near today's Dobruja, Romania

Vardanes I of Parthia was a Prince of Iranian and Greek ancestry. He ruled the Parthian Empire as King AD 40-45.

Akhal-Teke is a rare and ancient **horse** breed with a metallic-like coat that **shimmers** as if every silky hair was a strand of fine **gold**. Many consider it among the most beautiful in the world!

The Dasht-e Margo Desert ranges from Parthia (today's Iran) down to India, and across the middle Kushan Empire (today's SW Afghanistan) with hardly an oasis anywhere. The name is Persian for Desert of Death.

Ecbatana was located near today's Hamedan, Iran. It was built in the 5th century BC by the Medes. Queen Esther of the Bible lived there.

Nordic Voorde horses are small and sure-footed in mountains with mild temperament. They are usually light brown ~ dun ~ in color.

Kandahar was founded in 330 BC by Alexander the Great, and was part of the Kushan Empire. It still exists today.

Kushan Empire had its capital city in Bamyam, Afghanistan. It ranged to the northern half of

India in the south up to today's Russia. Also from Persia (Iran) to the west and China to the east.

Vima Takto was a prince in Kandahar and later king. His empire covered northwestern Gandhara (part of which included Afghanistan) and greater Bactria toward China, where Kushan presence has been asserted in the Tarim Basin.

Kujula Kadphises was a Kushan prince who united the Yuezhi confederation during the 1st century, and became the first Kushan emperor.

Zoroastrianism was an ancient monotheistic religion founded around 1500 BC in the area of Persia and India.

Ascilipius was a hero and a god of medicine, healing, and doctors. His symbol is a staff - called the Caduceus wand- with a serpent wrapping it around, which is still used today as the symbol of pharmacies. The word "pharmacy" also comes from Greek, meaning medicine.

Pyrrus Epirus was a Greek general and statesman of the Hellenistic period. He was king of the Greek tribe of Molossians, of the royal Aeacid house, and later he became king of Epirus. He was one of the strongest opponents of early Rome.

Homer was a historical poet who lived in the 6th century BC. Many of his epic poems were about the Greek gods, and it is from him that a majority of Greeks got the names and backgrounds of their gods.

Mount Olympus is in Greece north of Athens and south of the biblical Berea. Homer claimed the gods lived there.

Sergius Paulus, governor of Malta, was the brother of Seneca, Nero;s tutor.

More on Paul and Luke is in book 2 in this series, PAUL; THE UNSTOPPABLE.

The Romans built highways everywhere in their kingdom. Every mile, they set up a post along with a bench and well. At about every other ten-mile marker they built an inn for Roman citizens to rest in.

The apostles' locations in this book were based on research of the various places tradition says they preached (not where they died). Much came from Eusebius.

BUY YOUR NEXT BOOK NOW
Check out what they are about and a buy link.

HISTORICAL NOVELS FOR ADULTS

THEY MET JESUS Series of 8
http://bit.ly/TheyMetJesus

INTREPID MEN OF GOD Series of 8
http://bit.ly/IntrepidMen

HISTORICAL STORYBOOKS FOR CHILDREN

A CHILD'S LIFE OF CHRIST Series of 8
(Parallels Adult *They Met Jesus*)
http://bit.ly/ChildsLifeOfChristSet

A CHILD'S BIBLE HEROES Series of 10
http://bit.ly/Bible-Heroes

A CHILD'S BIBLE KIDS Series of 8
http://bit.ly/bible-kids

A CHILD'S BIBLE LADIES Series of 10
http://bit.ly/BibleLadies

DISCUSSION QUESTIONS

CHAPTER 1:
* Are you in a living or working situation where you have lost control of what happens to you? Or do you know someone who is? How can you cope?

CHAPTER 2:
*Think about the children you know. Are any of them without a father or more? What can you do to make them feel special?

CHAPTER 3:
*What is it like to have many people in charge of you, some with different standards? How can you handle it?

CHAPTER 4:
*In what ways can we defend someone our acquaintances are falsely accusing?

CHAPTER 5:
*Losing precious possessions in a storm can be devastating. What are some ways old family photos could be replaced?

CHAPTER 6:

*How many times have you moved? What are some things you can do to feel a part of a new community?

CHAPTER 7:
*Have you been assigned to a job that was too much for you? How did you handle it?

CHAPTER 8:
*Early on, Luke had been a failure at trying to heal people. Have you tried a special project and it failed, so gave up? What would it take for you to try again?

CHAPTER 9:
*Even though Luke was a slave, he showed a positive attitude. Nelson Mandela served 27 years in prison for fighting for freedom. He kept a positive attitude, even among the guards. Are you in a bad situation that is unfair to you? How can showing a positive attitude help?

CHAPTER 10:
*What is the best way to handle someone who is jealous of you? What should you do if you cannot appease that person?

CHAPTER 11:
*How does Luke's situation as a slave in a mine remind you of Joseph in the Bible who was enslaved

by jealous brothers? If you are put in a bad situation you cannot get out of, how can helping others in the same situation help you?"

CHAPTER 12:
*What is it like to lose a loved one? Describe the helplessness and loneliness.

CHAPTER 13:
*Oh, happy reunion! Think about a time when you recovered something or someone you thought was lost forever. How did it make you feel about the way you had mourned when it was first lost?

CHAPTER 14:
*What are different ways people mourn? Is there a right and wrong way? How can you help a person in deep mourning?

CHAPTER 15:
*What are different ways people mourn? Is there a right and wrong way? How can you help a person in deep mourning?

CHAPTER 16:
*Do you think a young person experiencing deep misfortune handles it differently than an old person? Which do you think is better?

CHAPTER 17:
*Do you recall a time when someone asked forgiveness and you do not recall anything they did that was bad? How is it an expression of love?

CHAPTER 18:
*In what way can you challenge your religious beliefs to see if they are really true?

CHAPTER 19:
*To find out whether what you believe is true or not, use a concordance which lists every word in the Bible. It is in book form or on the internet. Pick a word and see what you can find out about it.

CHAPTER 20:
*Recall a time when you accidentally ran into a friend from many years ago. How did you feel?

CHAPTER 21:
*Do you think it is wise to put a new Christian to work? If so, in what ways?

CHAPTER 22:
*Is it good or bad to challenge a religious belief? Why?

CHAPTER 23:

*Do you or have you missed something important in your community because it happened during a worship time or Bible study time?

CHAPTER 24:
*What kinds of things can we rescue people from, whether physical, emotional, or spiritual?

CHAPTER 25:
*Is there or was there someone in your life who was faithful to you through good and bad times and never left you? Do you need to reward that person? In what ways can you?

CHAPTER 26:
*Luke verified dates and places he was going to be writing about. How can we verify dates and places in the Bible to prove whether they existed?

CHAPTER 27:
*Have you ever visited someone in prison? When was the last time? What kinds of things did they tell you about? How did it make you feel afterward?

CHAPTER 28:
*Do you have a relative who knows things about your family that will be left unknown when that relative dies? Go see or write that person, asking them to share. Do you know things about your

family others may not? Write them down for future generations.

CHAPTER 29:
*Sometimes someone know is enduring a storm in their own life that they cannot be rescued from. What are some ways you can wait the storm out with that person?

CHAPTER 30:
*Do you know of someone who has been a Christian a long time and accomplished a lot as a teacher, missionary, or etc.? Try to go see that person and ask them to recall some of those highlights in their life. If you do not know someone nearby, how can you "visit" them in some other way? In what ways would it encourage both you and them?

CHAPTER 31:
*Have you ever gotten yourself out of a difficult situation, then something unexpected happened to get you back into it? How did you handle it?

CHAPTER 32:
*Have you lost a loved one and did not get a chance to say goodbye to them? If you did get such a chance, what did you say to each other?

CHAPTER 33:

*What are some things a single person is able to do for the Lord that a person with a family does not have time to do?

CHAPTER 34:
*Some people say Luke wrote his life of Christ while with Paul at the prison. But he would not have been able to interview all the apostles. They had all left Jerusalem less than twenty years after Jesus' death. Have you ever taken on an ambitious project that was harder than you originally thought it would be?

CHAPTER 35:
*After Jesus had preached just one year, the religious leaders began trying to figure out how to have him killed.. How did that train his apostles to be treated the same way someday?

CHAPTER 36:
*Returning to a place where you experienced deep feelings and return those feelings to you. Is it all bad?

CHAPTER 37:
*When Jesus and his apostles performed a miracle, it was a true miracle. They made people's missing arms and legs come back, they raised the dead. If the purpose of miracles was to prove God is

powerful, why didn't they just go through hospitals and heal everyone?

CHAPTER 38:
*How can you prove to yourself whether what a person says about Christianity is true or not?

CHAPTER 39:
*Luke went through a lot to make sure what he wrote about Jesus was true. What kinds of things can you do to make sure what other people tell you about Christianity is true?

CHAPTER 40:
*Have you ever tried to study the Bible with a religious leader in order to lead him/her to the truth? How would it be different for a leader to leave his/her religion than an ordinary member?

CHAPTER 41:
*What would it be like for a missionary to live among people whose religion was much different? What kinds of things could s/he do to build their trust?

CHAPTER 42:
*Coming home is almost always a sweet thought. Why is that? Can a person truly come home, even after things have changed?

ABOUT THE AUTHOR

Katheryn Maddox Haddad spends an average of 300 hours researching before writing a historical novel—ancient historians such as Josephus, archaeological digs so she can know the layout of cities, their language, culture, and politics.

She grew up in the northern United States and now lives in Arizona where she doesn't have to shovel sunshine. She basks in 100-degree weather, palm trees, cacti, and a computer with most of the letters worn off.

She is author of 77 books, both non-fiction and fiction. Her newspaper column appeared for several years in newspapers in Texas and North Carolina ~ *Little Known Facts About the Bible* ~ and she has written for numerous Christian publications. For over twenty years, she has been sending out every morning a daily scripture and short inspirational thought to some 30,000 people around the world.

She spends half her day writing, and the other half teaching English over the internet worldwide using the Bible as textbook. She has taught some 7000 Muslims through World English Institute. Students she has converted to Christianity are in hiding in Afghanistan, Iran, Iraq, Yemen, Uzbekistan, Somalia, Jordan, Tajikistan, Sierra Leone, Pakistan, Indonesia, and Palestine. "They are my heroes," she declares.

With a bachelor's degree in English, Bible and social science from Harding University and part of a master's degree in Bible, including Greek, from the Harding Graduate School of Theology, she also has a master's degree in management and human relations from Abilene University. She is a member of American Christian Fiction Writers, Historical Novel Society, International Screen Writers Association.

CONNECT WITH
KATHERYN MADDOX HADDAD

Website: **https://inspirationsbykatheryn.com**

Facebook: **bit.ly/FacebooksKatherynMaddoxHaddad**

Linkedin: **http://bit.ly/KatherynLinkedin**

Twitter: **https://twitter.com/KatherynHaddad**

Pinterest: **https://www.pinterest.com/haddad1940/**

Goodreads: **https://www.goodreads.com/katherynmaddoxhaddad**

GET A FREE BOOK
Sign up for Katheryn's monthly newsletter with half-price books for the whole family and insider tips on what's coming next.
http://bit.ly/katheryn

JOIN MY DREAM TEAM
Members get the first peek at my newest book and have fun offering me advice sometimes. I have a point system of rewards for helping me get the word out. Check it out here: **http://bit.ly/KatherynsDreamTeam**

www.ingramcontent.com/pod-product-compliance
Lightning Source LLC
Chambersburg PA
CBHW021427080526
44588CB00009B/446